HOW TO TEACH PSYCHOLOGY

AN EVIDENCE-INFORMED APPROACH

PAUL CLINE & MIKE HOBBISS

Together we unlock every learner's unique potential

At Hachette Learning (formerly Hodder Education), there's one thing we're certain about. No two students learn the same way. That's why our approach to teaching begins by recognising the needs of individuals first.

Our mission is to allow every learner to fulfil their unique potential by empowering those who teach them. From our expert teaching and learning resources to our digital educational tools that make learning easier and more accessible for all, we provide solutions designed to maximise the impact of learning for every teacher, parent and student.

Aligned to our parent company, Hachette Livre, founded in 1826, we pride ourselves on being a learning solutions provider with a global footprint.

www.hachettelearning.com

Although every effort has been made to ensure that website addresses are correct at time of going to press, Hachette Learning cannot be held responsible for the content of any website mentioned in this book. It is sometimes possible to find a relocated web page by typing in the address of the home page for a website in the URL window of your browser.

Hachette UK's policy is to use papers that are natural, renewable and recyclable products and made from wood grown in well-managed forests and other controlled sources. The logging and manufacturing processes are expected to conform to the environmental regulations of the country of origin.

To order, please visit www.HachetteLearning.com or contact Customer Service at education@hachette.co.uk / +44 (0)1235 827827.

ISBN: 978 1 9152 6195 3

© Paul Cline and Mike Hobbiss 2025

First published in 2025 by
Hachette Learning,
An Hachette UK Company
Carmelite House
50 Victoria Embankment
London EC4Y 0DZ
www.HachetteLearning.com

The authorised representative in the EEA is Hachette Ireland, 8 Castlecourt Centre, Dublin 15, D15 XTP3, Ireland (email: info@hbgi.ie)

Impression number   10 9 8 7 6 5 4 3 2 1
Year   2029 2028 2027 2026 2025

All rights reserved. Apart from any use permitted under UK copyright law, no part of this publication may be reproduced or transmitted in any form or by any means, electronic or mechanical, including photocopying and recording, or held within any information storage and retrieval system, without permission in writing from the publisher or under licence from the Copyright Licensing Agency Limited. Further details of such licences (for reprographic reproduction) may be obtained from the Copyright Licensing Agency Limited, www.cla.co.uk

Illustrations by DC Graphic Design Limited, Hextable, Kent.

Typeset in the UK.

Printed in the UK.

A catalogue record for this title is available from the British Library.

Contents

About the authors iv
Praise for *How to Teach Psychology* v
Introduction 1
Section 1:   The teaching framework 21
    Section 1A: Learning fundamentals 25
    Section 1B: Disciplinary fundamentals 51
    Section 1C: Pedagogical implications 61
Section 2:   Curriculum 133
    Section 2A: Macro-decisions around curriculum 137
    Section 2B: Micro-decisions around curriculum 157
    Section 2C: Psychology in the 21st century 183
Section 3:   Teaching core content 199
    Section 3A: Teaching assessment objectives 213
    Section 3B: Teaching core content 237
    Section 3C: Teaching evaluative writing 337
Section 4:   Assessment and feedback 363
    Section 4A: Principles of assessment 365
    Section 4B: Assessment in psychology 371
    Section 4C: Feedback that can feedforward 379
    Section 4D: Interpreting test and exam results 405
Section 5:   An evidence-informed psychology department 423
    Section 5A: Managing a psychology department 427
    Section 5B: Developing a subject culture 441
Conclusion 457

About the authors

Since completing both a BSc and MPhil in psychology, Paul has spent nearly 20 years teaching in, and leading, psychology departments in a range of schools across both the state and independent sectors. He is currently director of teaching and learning at an independent school in Suffolk and leads on all teacher professional development, including delivering CPD and teacher coaching. He blogs about all things pedagogical at apsychologyteacherwrites.wordpress.com, regularly speaks at education conferences such as researchED, and delivers online CPD for psychology teachers. He lives with his wife and two young daughters in Suffolk, where he enjoys trail and road running. By the time you read this he will (hopefully!) have completed his first ultra-marathon.

Mike spent eight years teaching psychology, both in the UK and abroad, before taking time out of the classroom to complete a PhD investigating attention and distraction in everyday environments, focusing especially on classrooms and other educational settings. He has published research on attention, distraction, memory and mood in educational settings, as well on teacher habit formation. Back in the classroom since 2020, he is currently head of psychology at a school in Lincolnshire, where he lives with his family. He blogs at hobbolog.wordpress.com and enjoys providing CPD to support teachers and schools in implementing evidence-informed changes which are appropriate for their settings. When not thinking about education, he tries (and fails) to play cricket as well as he remembers doing years ago.

Paul Cline

Mike Hobbiss

Praise for *How to Teach Psychology*

I wish this book had been around when I first started teaching A-level psychology! Psychology explores memory, cognition, learning and various social or environmental factors affecting human behaviour. Yet, there is a dearth of systematic, subject specific, practical application of these insights to teaching, designing courses and supporting effective study habits and routines in psychology.

How to Teach Psychology is an essential resource for trainee psychology teachers and a valuable tool for experienced teachers looking to refine their practice. As someone who trained in a different discipline, I know firsthand how useful it will be for teachers in the same position. Exploring the ideas here, over an academic year perhaps, will help develop the expertise of Psychology teachers and departments.

Paul Cline and Mike Hobbiss' practical expertise as current teachers is combined with their subject and pedagogical knowledge to great effect in *How to Teach Psychology*. The multiple worked examples are immediately useful in lessons and helped me think about how the underlying principles could be applied in my own context.

Ben White
Psychology teacher, assistant head teacher,
education author and consultant

A really useful book for both new psychology teachers and more experienced ones. Lots of practical advice and ideas to make your teaching even better and support your students to reach their full potential in psychology.

Deb Gajic
CPsychol, AFBPsS

Given the number of education books published in recent years, when a new one reaches us, it is always reasonable to ask, 'What does this one add?'

In Cline and Hobbiss' case, the answer is undoubtedly 'a great deal'. It is genuinely rare to find a book this well-researched, clearly sequenced and comprehensive. Opening with a general discussion of learning, Cline and Hobbiss outline concepts that may recur in other works but do so with an uncommon level of analysis and detail. This characteristic continues through the main body of the book, which delves into the practical teaching of psychology in a way that is fascinating, nuanced, and genuinely groundbreaking. As a profession, we now have a decent idea of the 'theory' of good teaching. What we don't have enough of an idea of is how we actually implement that theory in different classrooms and in different subjects. Until now, nobody had done this critical work for the teaching of psychology, and it's hard to imagine how anybody could have done it better than Cline and Hobbiss. If you teach psychology, this book should become your bible.

Adam Boxer
Science teacher and director of education at Carousel Learning

This book is worth a read for all teachers, not only teachers of psychology, as it lays the fundamentals for good teaching independent of the subject. It can also provide psychology teachers with new content to expand the curriculum on how we learn.

Paul A. Kirschner
Emeritus professor of educational psychology

By writing *How to Teach Psychology* Paul and Mike have managed distil years of research with their own excellent classroom experience. This book contains within it such an excellent overview of how learning happens, and what teachers can do to support it, that it would benefit teachers of all subjects. As a psychology teacher I really found the concrete examples and scenarios helped me fully understand how to put the theory into practice and it left me with tangible strategies I could try in my class the very next day. I would strongly encourage all psychology teachers to buy this book for effective and sustainable improvements to their lessons.

Adam Robbins
Science and psychology teacher, managing editor at CogSciSci

What Paul and Mike have written here is brilliant! Combining both the key learning fundamentals with the disciplinary fundamentals of psychology means this book is a brilliant resource for psychology teachers. And I have no doubt this book will be valuable to all teachers regardless of what they teach. The WHAT mindset they describe is a great framework and offers incredible food for thought.

Bradley Busch
Author and psychologist at Inner Drive

What an immense book! As a psychology teacher of 13 years, I can honestly say there is no other book that accomplishes so well what Cline and Hobbiss have done with *How to Teach Psychology*. It is so thorough, practical, and applicable for any and all teachers of psychology. And it is equally valuable for both new teachers of psychology and those who've been at it for years. I will frequently be revisiting this book to better my classroom and my teaching.

Blake Harvard
Psychology teacher and author

Psychology proves to be one of the most popular subjects in the country. Happily, the subject now has a book on how to teach it that should match that popularity! If you want to know how young people learn best - and how to apply it to every psychology classroom - this is the perfect book for you. It is packed with practical examples, student vignettes, and research evidence communicated clearly and usefully. It is rare to find a 'How to teach...' book this comprehensive and this good – so buy it!

Alex Quigley
Author, consultant and head of content and engagement at the Education Endowment Foundation

I found *How to Teach Psychology* by Paul Cline and Mike Hobbiss to be a multifaceted and fascinating read. Not only is the book evidence-informed, but the experience and expertise of the authors shines through every page. They have developed deep and meaningful insight that only someone that has spent significant time in the classroom, specifically the psychology classroom, can possess. The potential challenges and problems that arise in the psychology classroom are addressed with practical solutions, guidance and advice. I can confidently and highly recommend this book, a book that teachers will absorb and no doubt return to again and again to support and enhance their practice.

Kate Jones
Senior associate for teaching and learning at
Evidence Based Education

Introduction

The unique appeal, and challenge, of psychology

Since the introduction of the first A-level in 1971, psychology in secondary schools has been a huge success story. In 2024, 76,130 students were entered for A-level psychology, making it comfortably the second most popular A-level nationally, behind mathematics. At GCSE, although the overall numbers remain significantly smaller, they are rising sharply. 18,095 students sat GCSE psychology in 2023, up nearly 30% on the number for 2021. And it's not just in the UK; across Europe, the US and the rest of the world the numbers of school-age students studying psychology is growing. There is an enormous appetite for psychology within schools, and with that comes a great demand for psychology teachers.

So, what are the reasons for this rise in popularity? And what are the challenges that arise from trying to teach psychology in schools?

Students choose psychology for all sorts of reasons

In an interesting recent study, Sokolová (2023) found that UK students were less likely to report that their motivation to study psychology was driven by beliefs about the difficulty of the subject. They reported lower levels of agreement with statements such as 'I believe that other subjects are more difficult than psychology' and 'Psychology is easy to study'. The optimistic interpretation of this finding may be that the old stereotype of psychology as a 'soft' subject in which it is easier to achieve good grades may be on the wane, at least according to student perceptions in the UK. (If this is true, then we now just need to get the message out to some universities!) Students also strongly agreed with statements relating to understanding themselves and the behaviour of others, such as 'I want to understand how the mind works' and 'Studying psychology will help me to understand myself'.

These findings support what Jarvis (2011) has called the 'sexy subject' hypothesis – the idea that students study psychology simply because it is interesting and something they are intrinsically motivated to find out more about. Psychology provides a unique opportunity for students to find out about themselves and the behaviour of those around them. Studying it in school, during adolescence, provides the opportunity to learn about these things at a time in their lives when puzzling out the complexities of human social interactions – and our place in them – is of utmost importance.

Supporting students on a journey of self-discovery can, of course, bring its own difficulties. We are teachers rather than clinicians, and so we must be alert to those students who seek to study psychology for insight into, or help with, their own challenges. A clear line needs to be drawn with respect to the level of support we can offer as classroom teachers, and what needs to be referred to pastoral teams. An associated concern is that students learning about different types of conditions or disorders often have a tendency to self-diagnose somewhat and identify all kinds of symptoms in themselves. Indeed, right at the inception of A-level psychology in 1971, this was raised as a potential problem:

> There were misgivings in University Psychology departments and other places on the grounds that the subject demands a level of maturity beyond what could be expected of the average 16-year-old, and worse, it might lead to morbid introspection perhaps actually increasing the incidence of some disorders. (Cocker, 2020, p. 2)[1]

A particular challenge of psychology teaching therefore arises when discussing any kind of atypical behaviour. Psychology teachers need to be able to confidently explain that in most cases we should think of

---

1 This concern presages contemporary discussions about the 'prevalence inflation hypothesis' (Foulkes and Andrews, 2023, see Section 2, 'Choosing which disorders to teach', page 171).

identifiable syndromes, conditions and disorders as representing the extreme end of a particular spectrum, rather than a binary position, and that many 'symptoms' are perfectly common within the general population, all without conflating the everyday and the pathological.

Psychology is a complex discipline

So what? Well, the very features of psychology that make it fascinating can also make it challenging, both to learn and to teach. The mind-blowing complexity of the human brain, and the social systems we have created around it, can be just that... mind-blowing! Fundamentally, psychology is trying to answer the question, why do people do what they do? The answer to that question is phenomenally complicated and has a number of consequences that are not always present in other scientific disciplines.

For starters, it means that often in psychology there are very few categorically 'right' answers, but rather multiple competing or overlapping explanations for behaviour that vary by context (situation, culture, time period and so on). This makes psychology challenging to teach, partly because of the different ways that students may respond to it. Some people are appalled – how can a discipline claim to be scientific when it doesn't produce any concrete 'truths'? Others are delighted – if there are no correct answers then anything goes, right? Both types of students are tricky to deal with because neither have (yet) really grasped the nuance of psychology.

This challenge is compounded by the lack of a coherent single paradigm in the subject, meaning that we can't even agree on the right questions to ask or how to ask them let alone on what conclusions to draw. Many students, even very successful ones, therefore develop the impression of psychology as essentially a disparate collection of sub-disciplines rather than a single subject. This is not an entirely inaccurate depiction, but neither is it the whole truth. There are meaningful connections to be drawn between seemingly independent and competing explanations of human behaviour. It is also possible (we would argue important) for students to develop the understanding that apparently competing explanations do not have to be mutually exclusive, but instead can be describing the same thing from different levels of explanation. It is perfectly possible, for example, to analyse a behaviour from biological, cognitive and psychodynamic perspectives and find some use in all of these.

The same thing goes for methodology. Students may struggle to accept that no methodology is perfect, and that it would be impossible to study behaviour in a completely scientific manner – if that were even considered desirable! They may find it hard to accept that in psychology we are often trying to investigate things that are essentially hidden from view and therefore can only be assessed via various imperfect proxies.

All of this creates a subject-specific challenge for psychology students... and their teachers!

Psychology teachers face the difficult task of narrowing down such a complex field clearly enough to allow students to make sense of psychology as a discipline, without leading to the sorts of oversimplifications that, as we saw previously, were already worrying universities in 1971 at the very beginning of the A-level. In the classroom, we will often be aware that there is more nuance to add to any consideration of a particular behaviour, and we have to actively weigh up the trade-offs between exposing that nuance versus reducing the content to a simple enough level for novices.

Psychology cohorts typically vary a lot

In addition, psychology teachers must also grapple with the variety of their cohorts. If you wander into an A-level physics class you'll often encounter a pretty familiar group of students. They've mostly got pretty decent prior attainment, a string of 7+ grades at GCSE and will likely be taking at least one of mathematics, chemistry or biology too (and quite possibly all of them). We don't want to overgeneralise, but in most cases physics teachers probably have a reasonably good idea of who they're going to get.

In contrast, a typical psychology class may include those taking a range of science courses, humanities courses and alternative qualifications such as BTEC diplomas. Some may be confident mathematicians, while others prefer essay writing; some will favour exams, and others coursework. Some will have chosen psychology because of a clear interest in the subject (whatever they perceive it to be!) while for others it may have been simply something to fill up their timetable.

Of course, every subject has variety, but accommodating such a range of different students with different academic profiles is a common and specific challenge for psychology teachers. Knowing how best to cater for such a mix is a tricky challenge. This is made even more difficult by the inherent variety in students' interests. Quite often it's the more applied topics like clinical or criminal psychology that appeal to prospective students, but these cannot be easily accessed without firm foundations in the fundamentals. This means that for any given topic it's possible to have students in a class who absolutely love it alongside those who find it utterly boring, which can lead some to give up on the subject before they even get to the bits that they signed up for in the first place. A further challenge, then, for psychology teachers is to ensure all topics are delivered with the same passion and enthusiasm (regardless of their own potential biases and knowledge base), with a clear sense of how each topic contributes to the bigger picture.

Not all psychology teachers are psychology specialists

A related issue is that sometimes the popularity of the subject can overwhelm schools' abilities to provide psychology specialists as teachers. Although exact government initial teacher training (ITT) data does not contain explicit figures for psychology (it is grouped into the delightful category of 'other', along with media and communication studies and social studies), in 2022 this category trained only 426 teachers, which was just 19% of the target of 2240 (DfE, 2023). In 2021, only 25% of the target were trained. This isn't helped by the fact that there are relatively few postgraduate teacher training places available; for example, at the time of publication there are only seven university PGCEs in psychology in England, with a smattering of other school-centred routes and apprenticeships making up a pretty unsatisfactory picture for the second most popular A-level in the country.

As a result of all this, an unusually large number of psychology teachers have either their main degree or their teacher training qualification in a different subject.[2] Conversely, many psychology teachers find themselves also delivering other subjects to fill up their timetable. Such non-specialism does not necessarily have to be a weakness – far from it – but it does create challenges, especially early on in a teacher's psychology teaching career. Research suggests that different teaching and learning activities may be relatively more important for success in different subjects (Burgess et al., 2022; Langbroek et al., 2024). This is why throughout this book we always try to ask the question, what does this mean for psychology? We look at how we can best interpret evidence given the specific characteristics of our subject. In doing so, we hopefully provide a grounding for all psychology teachers regardless of their background.

Psychology students are relatively senior

Another challenge to consider is that psychology students are relatively senior members of the school community, even from the first moment they set foot in your classroom. As a result, we naturally don't want to treat them exactly as we might treat a class of embryonic Year 7s. However, our experience is that starting the course with an intention to 'treat them like adults' is an approach fraught with perils. For one thing, these are still young people, only a summer break removed from being in Year 11 (or Year 9 for those studying GCSE). For another, the things we are trying to do in classrooms are *also hard for adults*. As a result, there is no contradiction between respecting our students as adults and also explicitly and repeatedly emphasising the systems, rules and expectations of your classroom.

Of course, this is not a problem confined to psychology lessons alone, but is perhaps potentially more significant in psychology for a few reasons:

- The discursive nature of the subject, along with the lack of 'right' answers, may appear to lend itself to a type of lesson that needs less rigidity.

---

2 This is also true for both of us. One of us was advised that an ITT course in science would make them 'more employable'.

- The heavy content load of psychology specifications, which places a greater demand on student independent learning and revision.
- The idea that students have chosen to study psychology suggests they are more intrinsically motivated (see Section 1A: Learning fundamentals).
- The varied intake of psychology cohorts that often includes those who have struggled to succeed academically so far, some of whom may present more behavioural problems.
- Psychology teachers working in post-16 or sixth-form settings may find their centres have more relaxed systems and fewer centralised policies for behaviour than may be the case in secondary schools.

Academic learning is really hard!

A final, more general problem that psychology teachers face is a general one: the problem of learning. Our remarkable brains are dazzlingly good at learning... some things! Academic learning, however, is often effortful, slow and inefficient. Our brains are also dazzlingly good at forgetting things that are not deemed meaningful or useful enough, or that are not practised enough. The sort of knowledge we are teaching in school is going to be a prime candidate for this process. Students can sometimes get very frustrated at this apparent paradox – the 'amazing' brain that we spend our time in class celebrating also seems to let us down surprisingly often! This creates myriad challenges for every teacher to try to navigate in terms of motivation, pedagogy and content choices.

Put all these challenges together and we don't think it's an exaggeration to say that psychology is a uniquely challenging subject to teach. Of course, all subjects have their own distinct nuances, and this isn't to pretend that psychology is harder or more special than geography, economics or physics – although clearly we think it's better! It's to say that the particular nuances of academic psychology, the context of the subject within many schools and colleges and the difficulty of effective learning all create a blend of challenges that deserve bespoke approaches. These bespoke approaches are what we will present in this book.

An evidence-informed approach to teaching psychology in schools

We strongly believe that the best way to face these myriad challenges is through taking an **evidence-informed approach**. In the words of Stephen Chew and colleagues, we need to 'practice what we teach' (Chew et al., 2018). They write that:

> Psychology educators should not only employ scientifically validated principles of learning and evidence-based pedagogies but should use the methods of psychological science to test the effectiveness of their teaching practices empirically. [We urge] more psychology educators to become leaders in innovative and effective teaching by leveraging our disciplinary understanding of the fundamentals of teaching and learning.

We heartily agree with this sentiment. Taking an evidence-informed approach to psychology teaching involves designing learning experiences that take into account what we know about how we learn in general and also what we know about how we learn in psychology. We start with two fundamental questions:

1. What do we know about how people learn in general?
2. What are the specific features of psychology as a discipline that impact how we learn it?

These help us answer a third question, the one which is in fact the most important: what should I actually do in my classroom?

Putting all of this together, our model of psychology teaching looks like the below. We call this the 'psychology teaching framework'.

The psychology teaching framework

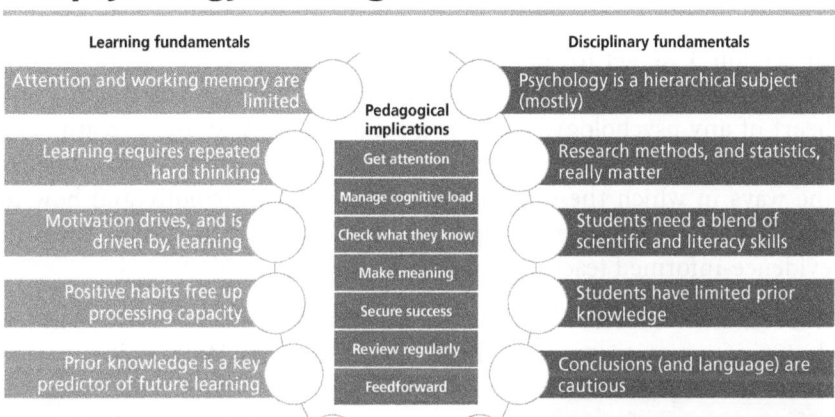

The teaching framework underpins all of the thinking around which the rest of the book is structured. Section 1 looks at six 'learning fundamentals', which are crucial principles of learning that have important implications for how we teach. However, lessons from research can only be successful if careful thought has been given to the context into which they will be applied. As a result, we then set out our 'disciplinary fundamentals', which are six essential features of psychology (or at least of psychology courses at secondary school level) that also impinge on how students learn and how we teach. Finally, putting both of these strands together, we identify and describe seven key pedagogical implications for psychology teaching.

In Section 2 we will examine the psychology curriculum. In an exam-based subject like psychology, an awful lot is driven by the exam specification, and it can seem like curriculum discussions are somewhat limited. However, we will explore the ways in which teachers do have some choice in their curriculum, from the macro decisions such as which specification or option topics to teach, to the micro decisions around topic sequencing or choosing appropriate research evidence to include. We'll examine how the teaching framework can assist us in making informed decisions about our curricula. We'll also consider some of the big challenges facing psychology in the 21st century, such as diversity in the curriculum and the need to balance a sound, historical perspective with up-to-date research.

In Section 3 we get to the core content. Here, the teaching framework will be put into practice. No matter which specification you teach, at the heart of any psychology course is a set of theories, studies, treatments, methods, approaches, perspectives, issues and debates. We'll consider the ways in which these need to be considered differently and how to ensure students gain a meaningful understanding of all of them through evidence-informed teaching.

In Section 4 we look at how the teaching framework can assist us in the design of assessment and feedback for psychology. With such a varied mode of assessment (students may be assessed via a wide range of different types of questions in an exam) and such a range of demands on students, figuring out how best to assess their learning is key. At the same time, balancing the need for useful data, formative feedback and managing workload is crucial.

In Section 5 we will consider some of the broader issues around teaching in, or leading, a successful evidence-informed psychology department. We'll look at ways to try to recruit the right students, providing rich co-curricular opportunities, supporting students in applying to study psychology further and considering the professional development of you and your team.

Putting it into practice - example teaching segments

The aim of this book is to provide a picture, in as clear a manner as possible, of what we do in the classroom and why. In order to do this, we have interspersed 'example teaching segments' throughout.[3] These segments show the teaching framework in action and provide a concrete demonstration of how the pedagogical implications can be applied. The teachers and students described in the segments (and other scenarios) are fictional; the experiences – both the triumphs and the disasters – are all based on our own.

---

3   Burns and Anderson, 1987, define a 'segment' in the classroom as 'a block of time with a particular focus or intention'.

The teaching segments therefore provide the best window we can offer into what our 'evidence-informed' classrooms actually look and feel like. Importantly, however, this book is *not* written to suggest that your classroom needs to look or feel exactly the same.

What it means to be 'evidence-informed', and what it doesn't

Being evidence-informed in teaching means simply that we attempt to use findings from research to inform the choices we make in the classroom. It means we think we can use knowledge from psychology, cognitive science, neuroscience, education and other fields to identify the best starting points for a professional journey, which is then continued through reflection and refinement.

However, being evidence-informed does not mean we think the research tells us exactly how to teach. This is partly because although we increasingly know a lot about the general mechanisms of how we learn, we still know relatively little about how students learn best *in schools*; in other words, how we can harness these general mechanisms most efficiently in our classrooms and school systems (Perry et al., 2021). It is also because all pupils, classrooms and school are different, and even the same class in the same school may behave differently from one day to the next. Mary Kennedy (2016a) writes that:

> Each new student, each new group of students, and each new topic to be taught requires teachers to think anew about how they will portray curriculum content in this new situation, how they will foster engagement in this new situation, how they will expose their students' thinking in this new situation, and how they will contain student behaviour in this new situation.

This diversity is a large part of what makes teaching such a stimulating but also challenging career. As a result, it would be naive and wrong to suggest that we can use research to cut a single path for everyone to follow blindly. What we can do, however, is to let the research take us as far as it can, and then make the rest of the journey ourselves in an informed and critical manner. Evidence-informed teaching is an approach and a mindset more than it is a recipe. Two evidence-informed teachers may use different pedagogical approaches in their classrooms; the similarities they share will be in the thought processes they have worked through. The aim of this book, then, is to demonstrate best *process* rather than best practice.

The WHAT mindset

What is good evidence-informed teaching? That's the answer, as well as the question! We think you can tell an evidence-informed teacher, whenever they are considering something new in their classrooms, because of what they do. We call this the '**WHAT mindset**':

W – (know) Why
H – Humble beginnings
A – Assess
T – Tweak

(Know) Why

For any classroom strategy that we may devise (or have recommended to us), a crucial consideration is whether we can see *why* it may be likely to work. The mechanism that leads from the strategy to more effective learning should be explicable. Knowing why, rather than just how, is the ingredient that allows us to reflect and adjust later on. If we don't know what the mechanism is, then it's very hard to know what to do in the event of our new system not quite working as we had hoped. Such overly simplistic (or overly prescriptive) interpretations of the messages of research findings have been termed 'lethal mutations' and may in some places cause more problems than they solve. Knowing why leaves us better placed to avoid these.

Humble beginnings

As we will see in more detail later on, it is very difficult to change classroom behaviour. This becomes even more true the more sizable the changes that we aim to make. In addition to making it more difficult to create meaningful lasting change to our practice, choosing goals that are too large and too ambitious also increases the chance that other useful features of our lessons are forced out in order to make space for the shiny new thing. As a result of this, no matter how impressive the evidence findings may seem it is always a sensible policy to start with the simplest and easiest possible strategy that you can derive from them, and ideally something you can stack onto something you already do.

Assess

As teachers we are told to 'reflect' on our teaching after each lesson. This process of reflection will be much more powerful if we know the 'why' of any strategy. Being reflective also involves treating any new strategy like a pilot study rather than a finished product. Pilot studies (as we know well as psychology teachers) are designed to reveal what the unexpected issues created by the implementation are. They are not meant to provide a definitive statement about whether the intervention is completely effective, although inevitably we will notice whether or not the intervention seems to be working.

Tweak

Just as with any pilot study, when we find that improvements can be made to our original design, the intervention needs to be adapted and re-piloted. However, just as we need to start small, we should adjust small, or 'tweak'. Changes need to be manageable and easily adoptable in our current working routines. Improvements in our teaching do not come from single foolproof ideas that can be dropped into our practice, but instead from small improvements that are slowly accrued over multiple iterations.

The **WHAT mindset** is designed to be applicable to teachers at any stage of their careers, rather than just those early in their career. Indeed, there is evidence that teachers may be better placed to use evidence to solve teaching problems as their careers progress (Greisel et al., 2023). This should not be surprising; our mental models for what goes on in the classroom will be far more complex and detailed after a few years of service. Therefore, with each passing year we may actually be *more* prepared to usefully incorporate evidence-informed changes successfully into our practice.

How to take an evidence-informed approach to teaching, and to this book

We believe that no amount of research evidence is a guarantee of success in the classroom, and that evidence therefore represents the starting point in a developmental process rather than the end of the conversation. This book represents the present outcome of this developmental process for the two of us – at the time of publication at least, as the process of reflection and development never stops! We will explain the evidence base and the thought processes involved in turning this base into concrete strategies in the psychology classroom.

As we do so, it is important to stress that other people may have taken different paths from the same evidence base as they adapted it to fit their own settings and styles. As a result, it is important to also treat this book as the start of the conversation rather than the end of it. It is not a record of the single best and most effective way to teach psychology in secondary schools, because no such way exists. Just like the evidence base on which it is founded, this book will give you a series of reasoned, well-founded starting points for your classroom practice to be moulded, adjusted or discarded as your professional judgement sees fit.

As we have established, knowing *why* you are doing something in the classroom is essential. In this book, the learning and disciplinary fundamentals provide the 'why' for what we do in our classrooms (the pedagogical implications), and also for how we more broadly structure and think about our curricula. But there are more 'whys' to consider. Why might one pedagogical approach be more (or less) likely to work in one school compared to another, with one class compared to another, or even with one student compared to another? Why might the features of your school make it easier to implement one approach in your classroom compared to another?

Schools are hugely complicated places, full of people who are even more complicated! Your knowledge of these contextual details and your expertise in knowing how best to approach the specific challenges of your own unique setting is valuable. It is entirely your prerogative to read this book and to decide not to implement a single idea from it. Provided you continue your professional development journey with a **WHAT mindset**, then you are just as 'evidence-informed' as anyone else.

Introduction

Know thy specification

Before we dive in, a caveat. At the time of publication, we are both teaching the AQA and Edexcel A-level specifications (although we also have experience of teaching others). Necessarily, we will draw on our knowledge of these specifications to illustrate the various ideas and themes throughout the book. We present examples of teaching sequences and discussions of things like curriculum design and how to approach areas of core content based around our in-depth knowledge of the specifications with which we are most familiar. We think the principles we set out and the ideas we share should apply to any context in which you are teaching psychology, but there will inevitably be specific examples that may not quite fit for you. In our attempt to be as inclusive as we can and consider examples from across specifications, we may have missed certain nuances that you only come to understand from delivering a particular specification through multiple cohorts. As noted above, your knowledge of these contextual details is important and should act as a lens through which to view what we consider here.

The wider benefits of an evidence-informed approach

Of course, the main reason to use the **WHAT mindset** and take an evidence-informed approach to teaching is that it can help us to shape effective learning experiences for our students. But this is not the only reason.

One important secondary benefit is that of motivation for further professional learning. Having a coherent and empirically grounded framework for our teaching has allowed us to analyse our practice in more depth, and with greater specificity, than we ever had previously. We have been able to identify our (many!) weaknesses with greater accuracy, and also to address these in a systematic way. As a result, our motivation for further professional learning has been sharpened.

When we look at student motivation in Section 1 (see '**Motivation drives, and is driven by, learning**'), we will examine how motivation can be increased by feelings of autonomy, relatedness and competence. An evidence-informed approach can increase our own autonomy (by giving us ownership over our professional development), competence (by making us feel that we are getting better at our craft) and relatedness (by opening us up to new communities of colleagues who are experimenting with their practice in similar ways). Motivation in our jobs not only makes it more likely that we will do them well, but motivated teachers are less likely to suffer burnout (Mašková et al., 2022). Related to this, first year teachers who are using evidence-informed pedagogical strategies have been found to report higher levels of school-based wellbeing (Mennes et al., 2023).

A further benefit of the **WHAT mindset** is that becoming evidence-informed can also benefit our colleagues. Given some of the challenges we've outlined already (and which we will examine in greater detail in Section 1), collaboration between teachers is important in ensuring we are giving students the best possible chance of success in our subject. However, sharing good practice can easily fall foul of simply passing on 'what I do' without any meaningful decomposition or, at times, even consideration of what it is that makes something work well and why.

An evidence-informed approach therefore gives us a means by which to break down the principles behind our practices, to identify the 'why' (the active ingredients that facilitate learning) and develop a shared understanding and language of what could make for effective teaching. This is especially important if we are in a position in which we need to support colleagues' development, either with more novice teachers or trainees, or those finding themselves facing specific challenges with particular groups or areas of their practice. The curse of expert knowledge can be a challenge here (see Section 1, page 48) as we may not be consciously aware of exactly what it is we're doing, which makes us less able to share our practice with others. Therefore, a commitment to an evidence-informed approach – not only as an individual but at a departmental level – is of benefit to all.

A final benefit for us as teachers is confidence. If, following the **WHAT mindset**, we know exactly *why* we are making a particular change, and what we expect the benefits to be, then we can approach our classroom activities and our professional development much more effectively. Once we begin to see the benefits of the approach, the confidence boost is further increased.⁴ Confidence is an essential feature of effective teaching, as is the trust that it can generate from students. Teaching psychology in school inevitably means teaching students who are rapidly approaching the largest and most important test of their academic lives thus far, and possibly ever. The trust that students place in us is, when you stop to think about it, quite remarkable and humbling, if not also a little terrifying! It is also something we want to encourage, as students' trust in their teachers is related to their own academic self-confidence and motivation (Al Nasseri et al., 2014).

---

4   We need to be patient, of course, as sometimes the benefits may not appear immediately. Iqbal and Mahmood (2010) found that teachers implementing strategies often experienced an initial drop in confidence before it picked up as the strategy embedded. We will discuss this further in Section 1 when we look at habit formation.

References

1. Al Nasseri, Y. S., Renganathan, L., Al Nasseri, F., & Al Balushi, A. (2014). Impact of students–teacher relationship on student's learning: A review of literature. *International Journal of Nursing Education*, 6(1), 167.
2. Burgess, S., Rawal, S., & Taylor, E. S. (2022). Characterising effective teaching. *Nuffield Foundation*.
3. Burns, R. B., & Anderson, L. W. (1987). The activity structure of lesson segments. *Curriculum Inquiry*, 17(1), 31-53.
4. Chew, S. L., Halonen, J. S., McCarthy, M. A., Gurung, R. A., Beers, M. J., McEntarffer, R., & Landrum, R. E. (2018). Practice what we teach: Improving teaching and learning in Psychology. *Teaching of Psychology*, 45(3), 239-245.
5. Cocker, J. (2020). *ATP 50 years of A level Psychology*. Association for the Teaching of Psychology. https://www.theatp.uk/uploads/ATP%20History/ATP_book_paged_A5_mono_2.pdf
6. Foulkes, L., & Andrews, J. L. (2023). Are mental health awareness efforts contributing to the rise in reported mental health problems? A call to test the prevalence inflation hypothesis. *New Ideas in Psychology*, 69, 101010.
7. Greisel, M., Wekerle, C., Wilkes, T., Stark, R., & Kollar, I. (2022). Pre-service teachers' evidence-informed reasoning: Do attitudes, subjective norms, and self-efficacy facilitate the use of scientific theories to analyze teaching problems?. *Psychology Learning & Teaching*, 22(1), 20-38.
8. Iqbal, Z., & Mahmood, N. (2010). Unraveling the changing pattern of prospective teachers' self-confidence: Transition from theory of teaching to practice. *Journal of Behavioural Sciences*, 20(2), 15-35.
9. ITT new entrants, recruitment targets and trainee characteristics by subject' from "Initial Teacher Training Census", Permanent data table. (2023). Explore-Education-Statistics.service.gov.uk. Retrieved February 17, 2024, from https://explore-education-statistics.service.gov.uk/data-tables/permalink/39e69f67-4e43-4009-8bd9-08dbe514ee42
10. Jarvis, M. (2011). Defending the honour of psychology A-level. *The Psychologist*, 24 (9), 674-675.
11. Kennedy, M. (2016a). Parsing the practice of teaching. *Journal of Teacher education*, 67(1), 6-17.
12. Langbroek, S., Brinke, J. T., Duchatelet, D., & Camp, G. (2024). Enhancing teachers' instruction on how to study: An exploration of the effectiveness of learning strategies for particular secondary school subjects. *Frontiers in Education*, 9, 1340120.
13. Mašková, I., Mägdefrau, J., & Nohavová, A. (2022). Work-related coping behaviour and experience patterns, career choice motivation, and motivational regulation of first-year teacher education students – Evidence from Germany and the Czech Republic. *Teaching and Teacher Education*, 109, 103560.
14. Mennes, H., von der Embse, N., Kim, E., Sundar, P., Hines, D., & Welliver, M. (2023). Are "well" teachers "better" teachers? A look into the relationship between

first-year teacher emotion and use of evidence-based instructional strategies. *School Psychology.* Advance online publication. https://doi.org/10.1037/spq0000593

15. Perry, T., Lea, R., Jørgensen, C. R., Cordingley, P., Shapiro, K., & Youdell, D. (2021). Cognitive science in the classroom. *London: Education Endowment Foundation (EEF).*
16. Scutt, C. (2019). Is engaging with and in research a worthwhile investment for teachers? In Carden, C. (ed.), *Primary Teaching* (pp. 595-610). London: SAGE Publishing.
17. Sokolová, L. (2023). Motivation toward choosing psychology as a secondary school subject: A cross-cultural comparison. *Teaching of Psychology, 50*(1), 41-46.

Section 1: The teaching framework

Lauren

Lauren is teaching schizophrenia to Year 13. She knows that students are really interested in the topic and have been engaged in learning about the common misconceptions and myths around the disorder. They enjoyed looking at case studies and identifying symptoms like hallucinations and delusions. Lauren is due to teach biological explanations and treatments next and is starting to do some planning.

Lauren is a bit worried about this aspect of the topic. She knows that the students found biological psychology challenging in Year 12, with many of them struggling to learn the material effectively and performing poorly on biological questions in their end of year exam. Some of them seemed capable of learning the key terms correctly but weren't able to write about the concepts in a meaningful way.

Lauren knows it's quite a complex topic with lots of technical detail that the students have to get to grips with, such as the actions of antipsychotic drugs. She knows they'll need to work hard both during and outside of lessons in order to feel confident with the content, but that they don't have the best study habits. She's concerned they won't find the topic as interesting and will lose motivation, and she's worried that when they get things wrong, she won't know what to do to get them back on track.

What are the specific teaching and learning challenges that Lauren is facing? What areas of theory and research could help her to tackle them?

- Understanding more about **attention** will help Lauren think about ways to ensure her students are fully engaged in lesson.
- Understanding more about **memory**, and **cognitive load theory** (CLT), will help Lauren think about how to deliver the information in a way that increases the likelihood that students will learn it.
- Understanding more about the importance of **prior knowledge** will help Lauren think about how to plan her students' learning to build on what they already know – or don't know – and how to help her students **make meaning** of the new information by connecting it to what they've learned before.
- Understanding more about **habit formation** will help Lauren think about how to embed effective study skills in her students, both in and out of the classroom.
- Understanding more about **motivation** will help Lauren think about ways to ensure students persevere when they have to grapple with a difficult topic.

In this section we will set out a teaching framework that will help to understand:

- The **learning fundamentals** that Lauren needs to be aware of. What are the factors that influence how students learn?
- The **disciplinary fundamentals** of psychology. What does Lauren need to be aware of that is specific to being a psychology teacher?
- The **pedagogical implications** for the classroom. How can knowledge of how students learn, and the disciplinary nature of psychology, inform the approaches Lauren might take in her teaching?

Section 1: The teaching framework

Learning fundamentals

- Attention and working memory are limited
- Learning requires repeated hard thinking
- Motivation drives, and is driven by, learning
- Positive habits free up processing capacity
- Prior knowledge is a key predictor of future learning
- Feedback must change the learner for the better

Pedagogical implications

- Get attention
- Manage cognitive load
- Check what they know
- Make meaning
- Secure success
- Review regularly
- Feedforward

Disciplinary fundamentals

- Psychology is a hierarchical subject (mostly)
- Research methods, and statistics, really matter
- Students need a blend of scientific and literacy skills
- Students have limited prior knowledge
- Conclusions (and language) are cautious
- There's so much we still don't know

Section 1A: Learning fundamentals

The aim of this section is to provide a broad theoretical underpinning of some key ideas around teaching and learning. Back when the authors trained as teachers, the psychology was largely limited to the work of Skinner, Piaget and Vygotsky. While all have their place, it was somewhat surprising that no-one thought teachers needed to learn much more about how learning actually happens. Given what we know about the impact of limited working memory in the classroom, for example, it seems remiss that this was not introduced into the initial teacher training (ITT) core content framework until 2019[5] (even more so since Baddeley and Hitch first proposed the 'Working Memory Model' back in 1974).

Of course, being psychology teachers may seem to put us at something of an advantage here, but it should be noted that our psychology specifications, even within seemingly relevant topics such as memory, often don't overlap with the science of learning. This means that our specification-specific subject knowledge may not always be helpful in telling us how to structure learning in our classrooms. Certainly, in both of the authors' experiences the 'pedagogical content knowledge' of how to design learning experiences that utilise the science of learning has developed almost entirely separately from our content knowledge.

Indeed, there is some evidence that knowledge about how students learn may be an even more important factor in boosting student achievement than content knowledge (Kramer et al., 2024). What follows is a discussion of six learning fundamentals, which for us constitute the most important foundations to effective learning. While not intended as a comprehensive review of all research in each area, being evidence-informed means *knowing enough* about the key principles underlying what research has found about learning in order to be able to make

---

5   The ITT Core Content Framework can be accessed at https://assets.publishing.service.gov.uk/government/uploads/system/uploads/attachment_data/file/974307/ITT_core_content_framework_.pdf

intelligent decisions about why we are doing something and how best to apply this to our teaching using the **WHAT mindset**.[6]

Attention and working memory are limited

Attention

One of the most crucial things that we as teachers need to know about selective attention is just how limited it is. Attention forms the 'gateway to cognition' – it is the process on which all more complex and higher order processing relies. But it is a narrow gateway. Many psychology teachers will be familiar with the 'Multi-Store Model of Memory' (Atkinson and Shiffrin, 1968), which, although a little outdated, still provides a useful visual illustration of this attentional bottleneck into our memory systems.

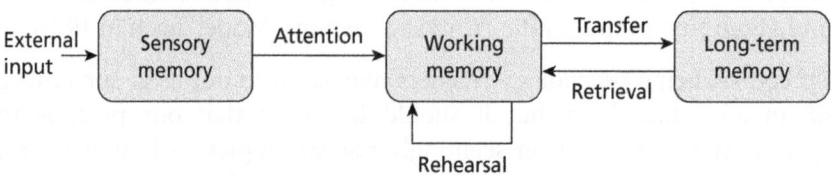

Source: Kelleher & Dobnik (2019)

What the model doesn't tell us is just how tight this bottleneck is. In experiments, finding a target (such as the letter 'X') from a display of six letters can be enough to seemingly exhaust our attentional capacity (Forster and Lavie, 2008; 2011). Having a very limited attention capacity creates a number of problems for students and their teachers. The first is that a 'limited capacity system' can only cope with a certain amount of information at a time, so if there's more task-relevant information than we can process (for example, asking students to watch a video and annotate a diagram with terms listed on a different page) then it is easy to become overwhelmed, even when we are entirely focused on the task in hand. We simply don't have the bandwidth for all of what we want to take in.

---

6 And to be able to **share the rationale** with our students, for why we are doing things the way that we are.

A second problem occurs when there is already some task-irrelevant information being attended to. In this scenario, our processing of any other information will be severely reduced as some of our very limited capacity is already being used for other things, leaving even less capacity for task-relevant processing. This is a major challenge. Often task-irrelevant information in schools is far more salient (i.e. 'attention capturing') than the task-relevant information we are asking students to focus on. We think back to our first years of teaching, when our default assumption was that if we spoke loudly and clearly enough and maybe said it a few times then even if students weren't entirely focused, *it would probably sink in*. We now know that is highly unlikely to have been the case. In fact, it's more likely that they were unaware of our very existence!

Students are distracted a lot... by a lot!

Students self-report experiencing a range of different sources of distraction in the classroom for up to 50% of their lesson time on average (Hobbiss, 2019), including:

- Other people
- Background noise
- Mind wandering
- Electronic devices
- Displays in the room

Students who struggle the most with attention control are most distracted in classrooms (Hobbiss and Lavie, 2024). In other words, students report being distracted a lot of the time, by a lot of different things.

Attention really matters to educational outcomes

School discussions on attention are sometimes seen as more of the preserve of the SENCO, who focuses on students with clinically diagnosed attention problems such as ADHD. In fact, there is good evidence that attention skills (or lack of them) strongly predict academic attainment for all students, not just those with a diagnosis. Merrell et al. (2017), for example, found a linear relationship between inattention scores at age five and Key Stage 2 performance in mathematics and English. In other words, even relatively minor decreases in attention skills have a measurable impact on school attainment across the whole distribution of grades. The same linear relationship has also been found for GCSE scores (Sayal et al., 2015); here, teacher ratings of inattention at age seven had a linear relationship with GCSE points scores nine years later! As the authors conclude: 'Across the full range of scores at a population level, each 1-point increase in inattention at age seven years is associated with worse academic outcomes at age 16.'

Attention really matters.

Working memory

Once we have allocated attention to a particular piece of information, that information is able to proceed further down the processing stream. Now we enter a second limited capacity environment: working memory. The capacity of working memory varies depending on the information that is being processed; it has been found to be between six and seven for digits, and less for more complicated 'chunks' (Cowan, 2001).[7] These chunks can vary considerably in size depending on how much relevant information we already have stored in long-term memory. The more information we already have stored, the more we can fit into a single chunk. This is one reason why prior learning is a key predictor of future learning (see page 48).

Working memory is also crucial for keeping track of our current goals and prioritising the processing of the task-relevant chunks. This means that overloading working memory with too much information or too complex a task can make people more susceptible to distraction, and therefore poor task performance. Either incoming information will not be processed, or an 'in-process item' will be dropped for a new one.

Filling working memory with the right things

Attention and working memory clearly work together to ensure we are processing task-relevant information in an effective way. If we can **get attention** (see page 62), we are more likely to get the right things from the environment into working memory. However, other things also compete for processing space in working memory:

---

7   This capacity may of course vary according to which sub-systems of working memory are being used by a particular task, as we may teach our students when discussing the working memory model. For the time being, however, we will consider working memory in general terms.

- Ongoing goals and priorities, which is why having clear targets and a positive mindset can be beneficial (see Section 1, 'Priming attention, page 62).
- Worries and anxieties, which is why we try to establish a positive culture around assessment and feedback (see Section 4, page 365).

Summary

- Both attention and working memory have serious capacity limitations, which can severely hinder learning if they are not filled with useful task-relevant information.

Learning requires repeated hard thinking

While there may not be consensus in education over the exact definition of the word 'learning', we can all probably agree that, for our students to feel confident as they enter their exams, they will need to have large amounts of information committed to memory in the form of detailed and interconnected schemas.[8] We look at how such representations can be created in this section.

What sort of memories are we trying to create?

We all naturally want to make our lessons memorable. However, there is an important difference between the sorts of memories that we are trying to form through our teaching and those that make life events such as weddings or birthdays memorable.[9] These latter kinds are examples of *episodic memories*, which are memories of specific experiences, with a time and place attached to them. In education, we are aiming primarily to create detailed *semantic memories*, which are not restricted to a particular episodic context and can therefore be more successfully transferred to new situations and challenges.

The problem with episodic memories is *cue-dependency*. If not enough cues (i.e. pieces of contextual information that match those which

---

8   Schemas, of course, are often a key element for our students to understand as well. We look at how we can teach this key piece of conceptual understanding at the example teaching segment at the end of this section on page 114.
9   This distinction will, of course, already be familiar to most psychology teachers depending on your specification.

were present during learning) are present, then we struggle to retrieve the information successfully. This is a major problem for students who will be assessed in what are usually very different environmental contexts and physical states (anxious in an exam hall) than the ones that they were in during initial learning (relaxed in their classroom). Semantic memories, which are formed from multiple overlapping episodic representations, allow us to move beyond reliance on specific cues or environmental contexts.

A classic example of this distinction in the classroom is the experience of a memorable lesson that is remembered for the lesson activity, but not for the psychological information. Examples that stick in our minds from years gone by have been lessons that used a random electric shock generator (taken from a party drinking game) to try to 'liven up' the teaching of ethical principles, getting students to throw ping pong balls around to model synaptic transmission, and making neurons out of plasticine and jelly sweets. In all of these cases, the lessons were fondly recalled by students for many months afterwards, but when they were pressed on the finer psychological details, recall was disappointingly vague. In each case, we had not done the follow-up work to convert the single episodic memory into a more secure – and transferable – semantic one. This is not to say that there is no value in such 'showpiece' lessons that create episodic memories, but to stress that at the end of this process we have (sometimes time-consumingly) produced but a single partial representation of the key information, which is likely to be highly susceptible to cue dependency. Converting this into a more secure and generalisable semantic memory will require careful follow-up and retrieval (or relearning) of the key material.

How are strong (semantic) memories formed?

Psychologists and neuroscientists generally divide memory into three key processes:

- Encoding – the initial formation of a representation of new information from the environment.
- Consolidation – the stabilisation of this memory trace in our neural circuits for storage.
- Retrieval – the process of bringing stored information to mind for use.

Encoding

When we perceive new information, our immediate interpretation of it is shaped by our prior knowledge (van Kesteren et al., 2012). So right from the outset, we aren't 'seeing' the world objectively, but rather through the lens of our schemas. The process of encoding is an active one, driven by the content of our schemas. Therefore, a student's failure to recall some information correctly might not be a failure of retrieval, but rather because it was never encoded 'correctly' (i.e. as the teacher intended) in the first place.

One way in which we can start to form effective memory traces is through semantic (or elaborative) encoding. This involves attempting to relate new information to existing knowledge as much and as meaningfully as possible. Doing this creates a stronger initial memory trace as it links the newly formed memory with as many existing traces as possible (Staresina et al., 2009). It also helps form semantic rather than episodic memories, as the more links a memory has with other traces the less it is likely to be restricted to the particular episodic context.

Another feature of encoding that has been shown to be beneficial for subsequent memory is distinctiveness, which is the degree to which the information stands out from its context (van Kesteren and Meeter, 2020). This includes methods that cue attention to the most important pieces of information to be encoded, such as highlighting or bolding keywords. For this reason, when we **get attention** from students we need to think very carefully about exactly what we want them to attend to.

Thinking ratio and participation ratio

If **learning requires repeated hard thinking**, then we want to use classroom approaches that will allow as many students as possible to achieve this. In his book, *Teach Like a Champion*, Doug Lemov uses the term thinking ratio to denote how hard the class is thinking about the material being studied, and the term participation ratio to denote the proportion of the class actively taking part in the lesson. Below are examples about what this looks like in practice.

	Low-participation ratio	High-participation ratio
Low-thinking ratio	Asking just one or two students some simple, factual recall questions.	Asking the whole class to put their hands up to say if they agree or disagree with something.
High-thinking ratio	Engaging in extended, probing questioning with one student.	Using mini-whiteboards to get all students to complete a complex problem independently.

Consolidation

Consolidation is more than just storage of encoded information. It involves the incorporation of encoded information into existing knowledge, as the information is combined with whatever helpful existing knowledge is called to mind from long-term memory. The memory is 'reactivated' (replayed) in tandem with activation of the relevant pre-existing schemas (Deuker et al., 2013). A lot of this happens when we are 'offline' (when we are asleep, for example) and is a continuous process, occurring not just in the immediate hours and days for initial learning but for months afterwards. This is one reason why, when we **review regularly**, we often do it spaced out in time, as this allows for adequate consolidation of a memory before we strengthen and deepen it further through retrieval.

Retrieval

Retrieval is another form of reactivation. The process of retrieving information from memory (re)activates the memory trace, leading to a stronger and more stable consolidation of the memory. Retrieval is also not subject to the same time constraints as consolidation, so in effect it is a mechanism that allows for faster consolidation (Antony et al., 2017; Cottingham, 2022a and 2022b). Reactivation of overlapping memory traces – called co-activation – also allows for similarities and differences to be more clearly identified, and so can lead to reduced interference between similar memories (Ritvo et al., 2019) and a shift from cue-dependent episodic memories to more flexible and generalisable semantic ones.

However, the benefits of retrieval are not simply in strengthening the existing memory trace. Reactivating a memory also provides the chance for reencoding and reconsolidation. In other words, retrieval seems to take memories back into a state of fresh plasticity, where they can be adjusted and combined with new material or feedback given by the teacher (which is one reason why post-retrieval feedback is so important), and the whole cycle of consolidation can then begin afresh with a new, more complex schema.

Reconstruction

Bartlett (1932) proposed that when we recall information, we aren't simply reproducing information from memory; we are actively reconstructing it. Bartlett famously showed this in his 'War of the Ghosts' study, where participants changed the details of stories they had heard to make them make sense relative to their own prior knowledge. The act of reconstruction happens every time you recall that set of information, and memories retrieved after consolidation may have a different neural architecture to when they were encoded (Dudai et al., 2015). Furthermore, post-event information – information received after the original encoding of the event – may become combined and integrated with the original information, making the two impossible to distinguish.

Now consider this in a learning context. A student attends a class, takes some notes and learns some new pieces of information. A few days later, they are looking at a popular psychology revision website on the same topic that includes some additional information that wasn't mentioned in the lesson, along with some statements that seem to contradict what their teacher said in class. The student may integrate the two sources of information together and perceive them as one coherent chunk, all learned together. Now imagine the teacher is asking some questions to check what the class remembers from the previous lesson. When our student is called upon to answer, they give a response that is from the website, not the lesson. 'Not quite,' says the teacher, 'if you remember, we said that…' The student in this situation may experience confusion and frustration because they believe they gave a correct answer that the teacher taught them!

… and repeat all over again!

All this explains why retrieval practice has been found to be so effective at promoting long-term learning in educational settings (Kornell and

Vaughn, 2016; Roediger and Karpicke, 2018; Yang et al., 2020). Retrieval practice is the name for the simple idea that the more times you are required to get some information out of your memory (by retrieving it), the more secure it will be in your memory. It is absolutely clear from these studies, however, that *multiple* reactivation opportunities are required for a memory to be effectively learned. This is why we **review regularly** in our lessons.

In his book, *The Hidden Lives of Learners*, Graham Nuthall wrote that, from his experience of conducting detailed observations of classrooms, students needed to encounter information three or four times to learn it. This ties in remarkably well with the neuroscientific evidence, which suggests that multiple, varied activations and reactivations of a memory trace are needed (Mareschal et al., 2007).

From this perspective, it is not the discovery of the strategy or the experience of learning a piece of information that is most important for subsequent success, but the repeated exposure to it and practice at accessing it multiple times and in multiple different ways. Indeed, the initial strength of the learning experience does not actually seem to make much difference to the rate of forgetting (Rivera-Lares et al., 2022). There is therefore nothing wrong with the student learning about functionally specialised areas of the brain by making a jelly and labelling parts with cocktail sticks, provided they are subsequently afforded repeated opportunities to revisit and practise their new knowledge in different contexts. (Such activities may also not necessarily have the motivational benefits that we might assume; see 'Competence', page 37.) There is, however, an opportunity cost in terms of the time required. As a result, we tend to leave the jelly – and the plasticine – in the cupboard these days, but you may decide to use your time differently. That's entirely your prerogative as an evidence-informed teacher, provided you maintain a **WHAT mindset** when you do.

The difference between learning and performance

Andrew covered evaluations of social learning theory (SLT) in his last lesson and gave the class a plenary to check that they could recall them. They could. In the next lesson, he begins to plan an essay comparing SLT and behaviourism, but his students seem unable to successfully use the same information in this new context. Indeed, some of them struggle to list the evaluations of SLT at all.

Both authors trained in the era of Ofsted inspecting individual lessons, where 'outstanding' lessons were deemed to be ones in which students could demonstrate learning and progress within the lessons themselves. This led to myriad performative demonstrations of student 'progress', but sadly ignored the fact that what we (and the inspectors) were actually measuring was just temporary performance, rather than the sustained changes in comprehension, understanding and skills that would indicate true learning (Soderstrom and Bjork, 2015).

Ofsted aside, it remains all too common that the demonstration of a skill in the learned context is taken as indicating mastery of the skill in general, meaning lessons progress after a limited number of demonstrations of any new idea. As we have just seen, however, we often need multiple, overlapping experiences with a new idea to be able to transfer our knowledge to a new context. We therefore need to **check what they know**, and **review regularly**, not just from a single demonstration.

Summary

- We need to think hard about the types of repeated hard thinking that we want our students to do, in order to help them build strong and interconnected schemas.

Motivation drives, and is driven by, learning

Schunk, Meece and Pintrich (2014) offer this definition of motivation: 'The process whereby goal-directed activities are instigated and sustained.' Building on this definition, Cook and Artino (2016) observe:

This definition highlights four key concepts: motivation is a process; it is focused on a goal; and it deals with both the initiation and continuation of activity directed at achieving that goal.

For teachers, it is particularly useful to think about motivation for specific goals rather than as a general state. It becomes all too easy to talk about students who are, for example, 'lacking motivation' in general, when what we actually mean is that they are lacking motivation for a specific set of goals related to what we are trying to achieve as teachers and they are trying to achieve as learners. A useful question to ask of a student is what goals they *are* motivated to achieve, if only to highlight to both you and them that this is not some fixed, unchangeable state. Once we've established that they are in fact motivated in some areas of their lives, then it's just a matter of figuring out what drives that motivation and how to transfer this to their psychology studies.

Intrinsic versus extrinsic motivation

Intrinsic motivation is characterised by the desire to perform specific behaviours or activities for the inherent satisfaction of completing them (doing an essay because they enjoy it), whereas extrinsic motivation is where behaviour is driven by external reinforcers (doing the essay to avoid a detention). Reliance on extrinsic motivators diminishes intrinsic motivation (Deci et al., 1999) meaning that while external rewards and punishments may help to establish a behaviour in the first instance, they will unlikely sustain it in the long term. For example, a student may initially decide to work hard on a piece of work because they will receive some form of reward, such as merit points, but this is unlikely to cause them to work hard all year. Our goal as teachers, then, is to find ways to boost the intrinsic motivation of our students. However, intrinsic and extrinsic motivation don't represent discrete, binary positions, rather they are just the endpoints on a scale. Therefore, our aim might be to move students further along the scale in terms of intrinsic motivation, rather than seeing it as a 'state' to be achieved.

According to self-determination theory (SDT, Ryan & Deci, 2020), for students to be more intrinsically motivated, they need to feel:

- Competence – feeling that what they do is allowing them to be successful.
- Autonomy – feeling in control of their behaviour and goals.
- Relatedness – feeling a sense of belonging.

Let's consider these factors in the context of the classroom.

Competence

Competence derives from a feeling of success and may be the strongest predictor of learning gains of the three components (Yu and Levesque-Bristol, 2020).

In our classrooms, students will feel competent if they can successfully learn new material, correctly answer questions or score well in an assessment. This means we need to **manage cognitive load** by thinking carefully about how we present, chunk and sequence new material to ensure we're not overloading working memory and are allowing students to **secure success**. For example, if you're teaching students about the actions of drugs for depression or schizophrenia, they will need to be confident in describing the process of synaptic transmission in order to be able to explain how antidepressants or antipsychotics work. The relationship between motivation and success is a reciprocal one (Vu et al., 2022), and certainly achievement boosts motivation as much, if not more than, the other way around (Garon-Carrier et al., 2016; Guay et al., 2003; Jansen et al., 2022). Therefore, correctly labelling a diagram showing a synapse may initially build their feelings of competence and give them the motivation to engage and challenge themselves further.

Autonomy

Autonomy is a tricky one in schools; the simple fact is that students have an awful lot of things decided for them. So how can we foster a sense of autonomy in our students when so much is out of their hands? First, it's worth emphasising that, according to SDT, students don't need complete autonomy, just a *feeling* of autonomy. They need to feel like they are taking ownership of their goals and the behaviours they adopt in order to pursue those goals. Second, if students are to feel a sense of autonomy from choosing which behaviours to adopt to achieve their goals, then they need to be confident that they know how to do those behaviours successfully, which also suggests that we should first prioritise competence over autonomy (Birch, 2023). This could mean giving students autonomy only after careful training in how to carry out tasks effectively, or autonomy over a choice of strategy from a pre-approved selection. For example:

- Teaching students a range of effective study strategies and then giving them autonomy over which ones they use (see Section 2, 'STAR tasks', page 179, and also Section 5, 'Encouraging a culture of independent learning', page 449).
- Presenting students with some general guidance about what examiners are looking for (rather than rigid scaffolds) and examples of different ways of effectively answering the same question so they can choose what works best for them (see Section 4, page 381 for more on models and modelling).

Relatedness

Relatedness is the extent to which we feel a sense of belonging; in other words, that we can identify with those around us. One of the simplest things we can do is be mindful of the language we use in the classroom. Referring to our students as psychologists reminds them of their shared bond, along with developing confidence with technical psychological terminology. Narrating our lessons with reference to 'we' and 'us' also helps to foster relatedness by drawing on those collaborative discussions and decisions. Shared in-jokes and humour can also be powerful here too, although we've got to be mindful of the potential for distraction. We don't want them to only remember the (episodic) jokes and none of the (semantic) psychology.

Harnessing the power of social norms is also useful. By highlighting positive norms that we want everyone to adopt, we increase relatedness, as students have a clear group identity. For example, if a couple of students in a class haven't completed homework, the teacher might say publicly, 'I'm really disappointed that two of you haven't done your homework', which is actually highlighting the behaviour they don't want.¹⁰ An alternative phrasing, such as 'It's great that almost all of you have completed your homework', instead signals the positive norm. (Of course, those that didn't complete the homework still need addressing, but perhaps more privately and using the kind of positive framing as outlined above.)

Motivation for 'boring' topics

It can sometimes be tempting to talk about lesson content in terms of how interesting or fun we think a topic is. In psychology, this can happen with topics like research methods or biopsychology. If we say or imply to students, 'This is a bit of a dull topic', then we risk significantly damaging the chances of them learning it well. Tam et al. (2023) demonstrated that expecting in advance that a topic would be boring led students to report feeling more bored. We also risk ignoring the fact that what one student may find exciting another may view as quite dull, and vice versa. So, we should always endeavour to **share the rationale** for studying something, potentially increasing engagement and motivation (Jang, 2008). On the flip side, we should never frame parts of our course as boring – or 'dry', as we often seem to euphemistically call them.

Encouraging curiosity in the material itself can also aid motivation. Curiosity levels may be related to prior knowledge (Kang et al., 2009), and having curiosity can enhance learning (Kang et al., 2009; Gruber et al., 2019). **Checking what they know** and reactivating students' prior learning (as well as modelling curiosity and enthusiasm for the topics ourselves) may therefore allow more students to approach even the somewhat 'drier' parts of our specification with more enthusiasm.

---

10 Teachers make similar mistakes with behaviour management; for example, 'I've asked for silence and some of you are talking' makes some students think, 'Oh, ok, it must be alright to talk then.'

Sharing the rationale

One simple and powerful way to engender student trust – and also create evidence-informed students who understand how learning takes place – is to take every opportunity to share the rationale for activities in your classroom. Why are you doing things this way? What do you expect them to get out of the process? This is a useful tool for creating a positive classroom culture (we will refer back to it throughout this book, as well as providing illustrations of how it may happen in the example teaching segments). It's an especially important and useful tool if what you are doing in class may conflict with some students' previous experiences in classrooms, or with their 'lay understanding' of how learning works.

To pick some examples from the forthcoming pages, sharing the rationale may be useful when not giving extensive written feedback on essays, not grading tests or when asking students to perform effortful retrieval activities that frequently reveal to them things that they have forgotten. All of these can seem initially unfamiliar and uncomfortable to students. A teacher who can confidently share the rationale for why they have chosen to do things this way – and why, as a result, the students should benefit, providing they buy into the process as well – can shape a positive, effective and evidence-informed academic culture in their classroom.

Summary

- Helping students develop a sense of belonging, ownership of their learning and, crucially, a sense that they can be successful is likely to increase their motivation to learn more.

Positive habits free up processing capacity

Because **attention and working memory** are limited, we want to find as many ways as we can to free up space in our students' cognitive resources. One way of doing this is to try to assist students in creating efficient classroom habits.

Habits and routines free up processing capacity, because if we are able to automatically respond to a particular situation with a chain of actions then we don't need to waste any precious processing space to work out how we are going to respond. We therefore have more capacity to think about the material itself. In the words of Peps Mccrea, 'routines redeploy attention' from the process of learning to the content of their learning (Mccrea, 2023).

Classroom routines can be roughly grouped into two broad categories. Think about how many you currently use in your classroom.

1. Instructional routines, which assist students with handling the information presented. For example:
    - Routines for knowing what to do when a student is finding work challenging (e.g. 'brain – buddy – book – boss').
    - Routines for specific classroom activities, such as how to approach different retrieval practice tasks.
    - Routines for answering exam questions, such as highlighting command words and key details.
    - Routines for evaluation, such as using an acronym to systematically work through the strengths and weaknesses of a research study.
    - Routines for paired- or whole-class discussions that ensure equal participation and practice opportunities for all.
    - Routines for homework (e.g. format, setting and submission days).
    - Routines for understanding and responding to feedback.

2. Behavioural routines, which assist students in managing their behaviour productively. For example:
    - Routines for entering a classroom and starting a lesson.
    - Routines for participation in class (e.g. hands up or down? Will cold-calling be used? When and how?).
    - Routines for when, or if, technology such as mobile phones can be used in lessons.
    - Routines governing what sanctions, or other reprimands, will result from different classroom infringements.

In all of these routines, if students are familiar and comfortable with the procedures associated with them, they will be able to redeploy their processing capacity from the 'how' to the 'what' of a task, from the process to the content. This increases the ability to think deeply about the material, and therefore the chances to **secure success**, as students who are seen to be performing the desired behaviours will be more likely to turn them into strong habits if they also feel rewarded for their actions (Fiorella, 2020).

Classrooms as a positive habit environment

Habit formation relies on repeated performances of the action in similar environments, so a positive habit environment will make it as easy as possible to perform the desired behaviour repeatedly, and harder to perform other, less desirable ones. For example, it is far easier to reduce the degree of distraction by technological devices if they are simply banned, rather than if 'responsible use' (and self-control) is encouraged. There is good evidence to suggest that such policies can improve academic performance in the case of both computers and mobile phones (Amez and Baert, 2020; Amez et al., 2023; Huey and Giguere, 2023). This positive habit environment will also allow for the formation of productive working routines regarding technology use, even outside of the classroom.

Other examples of creating positive habit environments that have been shown to benefit educational outcomes include:

- Having clear sanctions for behavioural issues such as attendance (Dobkin et al., 2010).
- Spreading homework assignment deadlines evenly throughout the term, compared to making them due at the end (Ariely and Wertenbroch, 2002).
- Reducing distracting visual displays (Fisher et al., 2014).
- Greeting students positively at the door (Cook et al., 2018).
- Modelling and mandating the use of effective independent learning strategies ourselves in courses and assignments (McDaniel et al., 2021).

Habits and motivation

Because habits are produced automatically in response to an environmental cue – and without any consideration of the consequence of the action – they actually bypass our motivational systems entirely. Motivation affects 'goal-directed' behaviour (as we saw in the previous section), whereas habitual behaviours are, by definition, insensitive to such goals. We don't have to think about whether we *want* to do an action that is habitual – we just do it. In fact, many of us will readily recognise situations where we may actively want *not* to do a certain action that has become habitual, but we still continue to do it.

Of course, this does not diminish the importance of motivation in the classroom. We are never going to fully automate all our classroom processes (see 'The "double-edged sword" of habits' below). It does, however, illustrate another potential beneficial effect of **positive habits freeing up processing capacity**. For some students, one potent source of additional cognitive load will be the motivational wrestling match required to get started on a piece of work. Effective working routines can help to avoid this challenge altogether, because internal factors such as self-control have far less of an effect on forming good habits than the environment does (Van der Weiden et al., 2020). It also works the other way of course; even very highly motivated students can struggle to be productive if they lack the right routines.

The 'double-edged sword' of habits

There are three potential drawbacks to encouraging habitual behaviour in the classroom. The first is the time. Classroom routines, as many of us know, only form with regular repetition and focus. We therefore need to choose our routines carefully. No teacher will have well-established routines for all classroom behaviours – there would be no time left for the content! That said, an effective classroom routine often more than compensates for the time required to create them.

Another reason to choose our desired student habits carefully is that they are hard to break once formed. A common example of this concerns the use of acronyms. Many of us will use acronyms (to help structure paragraphs or to create evaluation points, for example), and these can be very useful tools. However, students may then struggle to adapt to situations where the acronym doesn't perfectly fit the study or theory that is being discussed. (See Section 3, page 233 for further discussion on the use of acronyms for core content.)

One final possible drawback to consider is the trade-off between routine and variety in classroom activities. Variety can be a useful tool to stimulate engagement or attract attention (or to provide overlapping retrieval experiences to encourage reconsolidation), but as Doug Lemov says, 'If they have to learn the rules of a new game every day, that leaves only so much time to actually practise and play it.' (Lemov, 2015). Therefore, think carefully about where you can introduce variety into the lessons, and which activities you may want to keep consistent.

> ## What are *your* classroom habits?
>
> While thinking about student habits in the classroom, why not also think about your own! Experienced teachers perform large numbers of complicated routines, sometimes simultaneously (behaviour management, content delivery, formative assessment, etc). Habits are a crucial part of effective teaching. However, habits can also outlive their usefulness – and be very difficult to break.
>
> What are the classroom behaviours you would like to change but find hard to do so? One of us ran a poll a few years ago that revealed two main categories where teachers reported struggling to break ingrained habits:
>
> 1. Inefficient checks for understanding (e.g. saying 'that ok?', 'everyone happy?' or 'any questions?').
> 2. Talking to a class when students are actually working away quietly. (Research would seem to back up these self-reports, as classroom sound recordings have found that silent thinking or writing tasks account for less than 5% of classroom time in some settings (Owens et al., 2017).)
>
> The development of inflexible classroom habits may be one reason why, on average, teachers' development slows down after the first 3–5 years in the classroom (Hobbiss et al., 2021). It also helps us to explain why so much CPD (which will often target teacher knowledge or motivation) fails, as changes in goals will have no effect on the automatic production of an established habitual behaviour.

Summary

- Thinking carefully about the habits we want our students to develop, and curating the environment to help them do so, will help them become more effective learners.

Prior knowledge is a key predictor of future learning

> The most important single factor influencing learning is what the learner already knows. Ascertain this and teach [them] accordingly.
>
> (Ausubel, 1968)

According to psychologist David Ausubel, knowledge is acquired via the integration of new information with what the learner already knows. The goal of learning is to create bodies of knowledge that are vast, stable, connected, organised and accessible. The point of learning is not memorising facts as 'islands of knowledge', but to create meaning by making a bridge between relevant existing knowledge and new information. If we **make meaning** through *assimilation* of new knowledge with old, rather than just trying to memorise new information, then our bodies of knowledge are more likely to transfer to novel contexts, make it easier to acquire further new knowledge and will be less prone to forgetting.

Assimilating new knowledge doesn't just add it to a body of knowledge; it changes the nature and structure of existing knowledge. Even when we do forget, knowledge that has previously been assimilated is more easily relearned, whereas disconnected knowledge will need learning anew as if from scratch.

Ways of learning

Ausubel suggests that assimilation can occur in different ways. The primary way is subsumptive learning, where we acquire a higher order (generalised) concept (a 'subsumer') first, before adding concrete (specific) details or examples. For example, psychology students often confuse the terms 'external validity' and 'ecological validity' and assume that external validity is only relevant when discussing how 'natural' or 'artificial' the setting of a study is. In reality, external validity is the subsumer here, and so it may help for this to be taught first before introducing more specific terms like ecological validity or population validity as sub-concepts.

Assimilation can also happen in other ways:

- Superordinate learning involves the reverse of subsumptive learning, with the specific details being acquired first before a more generalised concept. This would mean students learning a specific example of a sampling technique before broadening this out to the more general concept of sampling.
- Combinatorial learning occurs when connected ideas do not relate in a hierarchical fashion and must be learned side-by-side. For example, while they are clearly related, reliability and validity are distinct concepts that must be learned separately, but connections must be drawn to help students see the links between them.

As we will discuss below, **psychology is a mostly hierarchical subject** (see page 51), meaning that subsumption may be considered the optimal route to help students **make meaning** of new information. However, there are also cases where this is not possible, and we should consider the importance of building our explanations from the concrete to the abstract. Where it is necessary for superordinate or combinatorial learning to occur, teachers must ensure topics are carefully sequenced, there is adequate opportunity for revisiting material frequently and that links are explicitly drawn between ideas. This helps to avoid students compartmentalising information – what Ausubel refers to as 'the enemy of creating links and avoiding confusion' (Cottingham, 2023).

Subsumptive learning in practice: research methods

The way the research methods unit is organised in most exam specifications is in a fairly compartmentalised way – there is one method called 'experiments', another called 'self-reports', another called 'observations' and so on. Students may vaguely understand that these topics fall under the general subsumer research methods but to all intents and purposes see them as completely discrete sets of information that must be learned separately.[11]

Then they encounter some actual studies conducted in real life and things start to unravel:

> Sir, is Bandura an experiment or an observation? And what about Milgram – my textbook calls it a lab experiment, but I read on a past paper mark scheme that it's really a controlled observation. Which is it?[12]

In this context, the student has yet to understand that the overall methodology of the study is not necessarily the same thing as the method by which data is collected. By explaining this distinction and giving multiple examples from different studies, the student will be able to reorganise their existing knowledge, leading to the understanding that a study may entail multiple methods.

Prior knowledge and curriculum design

Cottingham (2023) suggests four principles that should guide our curriculum design based on Ausubel's work:

1. Define bodies of knowledge – Specify what students need to know and understand.
2. Select subsumers – Identify the general and inclusive ideas that provide an overall framework for the content.
3. Feed subsumers with detail – Make decisions about precisely which content and to what level of detail students will need to learn.
4. Sequence for assimilation – Consider carefully how students will encounter new information to ensure it can build on prior knowledge.

Psychology teachers may argue that they have little say in principle 1, and the extent to which you have much say in principles 2 and 3 may depend on which specification you teach. However, examination specifications are often relatively vague, so there remains a problem of selection. This

---

[11] This is reinforced to some extent by the specifications and exam papers that often assess them as separate entities too.
[12] Some teachers may remember the rather contentious debate around this one!

is why when we **check what they know**, we still need to think clearly about what information we want students to know (for example, through defining core questions and by assessing the prerequisite knowledge for new learning). Principle 4 is certainly within our control and must be considered in light of the other three. Carefully selecting the most important subsumers also means ensuring students encounter them at the right time, to allow for them to **make meaning** and learn more effectively.

> ## The curse of knowledge
>
> It can be very easy to underestimate our own subject knowledge expertise, and therefore to underestimate the amount of prior knowledge that new information may require. It may be easy to believe that the older and more senior students we are teaching seem like experts, but we need to remember that in our subject they are still very much novices (see Disciplinary fundamentals, '**Students have limited prior knowledge**', page 54).
>
> The curse of knowledge is a cognitive bias whereby people with expertise often fail to appreciate the depth of that knowledge, or how much more detailed their schemas may be than other people's. As a result, experts can find it very hard to explain things to people who lack similar levels of expertise, as they fail to pitch their explanation at the right level. We've all had the experience in the classroom of being unable to imagine how a particular explanation or example which to you seemed crystal clear could have been misinterpreted. (Or, if you're a fan of charades at family gatherings, how your perfect reconstruction of a famous movie scene could go unrecognised.) That's the curse of knowledge. Carefully examining prerequisite knowledge can help to overcome this.

A final point to consider is that since **prior knowledge is a key predictor of future learning**, it's clear that more, better organised prior knowledge makes it easier to learn new information. The result of this is that those with rich schemas will make progress significantly faster than those who have limited or impoverished prior knowledge. In other words, prior knowledge helps the rich get richer. This has quite profound implications for what happens in our classrooms and may help to explain how different students in the same lesson, ostensibly with the same starting points, may make wildly different levels of progress in what they learn, and why those gaps may just keep getting wider.

Summary
- To allow students to develop rich schemas, they need to **make meaning** by connecting new information with prior knowledge. This means sequencing learning carefully to build conceptual understanding over time.

Feedback must change the learner for the better

It seems obvious that feedback should change our students for the better, but surprisingly often that seems not to be the case. In fact, some feedback interventions can be actively harmful. In one large analysis, Kluger and DeNisi (1996) found that in 38% of well-designed studies, feedback actually made performance worse. When done well, however, feedback can be one of the most powerful tools for learning that we have (Collin and Quigley, 2021). Clearly this is a complex and nuanced area.

There are a number of different ways that feedback has been defined academically, but we think the most powerful definition comes from Carless and Boud (2018), who write that feedback is 'a process through which learners make sense of information from various sources and use it to enhance their work or learning strategies.'

This is a definition that completely turns many schools' approaches to feedback on their head, as it defines feedback relative to the learner rather than the source. As a result, if nothing is done by the learner, it doesn't even count as feedback at all. This is worse than students simply not improving as much as we would like. If practice (after feedback) makes perfect (allowing students to **secure success**), then *practice (without feedback) makes permanent*. Students' mistakes will become ingrained through habit and become progressively harder to shift. Feedback is therefore much more about what the students do than what the teacher does.

But even providing corrective feedback to students and allowing them the chance to act on your recommendations might not be enough to satisfy the Boud and Carless definition, as the 'enhancement' that students need to show is related to 'their work' generally, rather than a piece of specific work. In other words, true feedback should allow students to **make meaning** by seeing the more generalisable principles and transferable skills beneath each piece of work (our pedagogical implication is that it should **feedforward**, see page 102). Or, as Wiliam (2018) puts it: 'The main purpose of feedback is to improve the student and not the work.'

Summary

- Effective feedback improves learners, not work, by equipping them with the skills to perform better in new pieces of work.

Section 1B: Disciplinary fundamentals

In the introduction, we argued that an evidence-informed approach to psychology teaching looks at both what we know about learning in general and the specific features of psychology as a subject, to try to answer the question of what we should do in our classrooms. What are the fundamental principles of psychology that shape the way in which we are able to apply the learning fundamentals that we have just outlined?

Psychology is a hierarchical subject – mostly!

The sociologist Basil Bernstein differentiated between two methods by which the knowledge of an academic subject can be organised (Bernstein, 2006). 'Vertical' subjects are those in which 'general propositions or theories' are applied to and used to explain new knowledge (which is therefore built on top of these general foundations in a hierarchy, such as in the sciences). 'Horizontal' subjects, in contrast, may use different modes of enquiry, perhaps with different key principles and terminology, in different areas of the subject. English literature is a good example here, with different methods of textual analysis being applied to different texts for different purposes.

On the basis of these descriptions, the fact that within psychology there are multiple competing approaches to the subject, each with their own methodology and terminology, may seem distinctly horizontal. However, most school psychology courses are organised around a theme of repeatedly applying the same core approaches to different applied topic areas. For example, ideas from cognitive psychology can be applied to topics such as memory, development, criminal behaviour and mental illness explanations and treatments. Knowledge of research methods also runs throughout all school psychology courses. As a result, once the initial, slightly horizontal foundations are in place, a good deal of school psychology teaching follows a hierarchical structure.

If we accept this, there are a number of consequences in terms of how we organise and sequence our courses. Hierarchical courses will often begin by aiming to give students a mastery of the foundational ideas, before moving on to applying them in different areas. As psychology teachers, we are therefore faced with the challenge of identifying the most foundational knowledge for our particular specifications – the subsumers that will be required most frequently across different areas for the remainder of the course – and to structure our courses around this (see Section 2, 'Curriculum', page 135). We also need to carefully consider which foundational ideas are prerequisite knowledge for each new topic and **check what they know** from these before we start. Finally, we need to make these features the targets for the feedback we give students, as improvements in these areas are more likely to **feedforward** to improvements in other areas too.

Summary
- **Psychology can be considered a mostly hierarchical subject**. This means we need to think carefully about the foundational concepts that underpin our courses and sequence appropriately.

Research methods, and statistics, really matter

On the one hand this is fairly obvious pragmatic advice, given that research methods form such a large part of psychology courses (up to 40% in total, if we include data analysis skills as well). It therefore makes sense to dedicate at least this amount of our classroom time to research methods, to scaffold students learning even more carefully than we otherwise might so they can **secure success**, and to **review regularly** thereafter. The slightly more black and white factual content of research methods sections also means that, if students can develop high levels of mastery of the content, it is an area of the specification that they can pick up large numbers of marks on. This can be especially valuable for students who find the extended writing or evaluative aspects of the subjects more challenging. Research methods also often play a large role in successful evaluative writing as well, meaning that feedback that specifically targets these is likely to **feedforward** into multiple different areas of the course.

One response to the extensive focus on research methods and data analysis in many psychology courses is for teachers (the authors included) to take a somewhat apologetic tone when introducing it. We don't do this anymore. Instead, we try to now emphasise that research methods are absolutely essential for us to ever discover anything interesting about humans at all. How could we possibly ever learn anything interesting if we can't be sure what we are measuring, or if we don't know what factors may be causing the behaviour we're measuring? Equally, how could we know whether any difference we find between two groups is a meaningful difference, unless we are able to statistically test this difference for significance? Students who understand this are usually able to apply themselves to the study of research methods more enthusiastically.

Summary

- Psychology is, at its heart, a discipline based on research methods, and so we should give this both the attention and enthusiasm it deserves.

Students need a blend of scientific and literary skills

Psychology stands at a crossroads between the arts and the sciences. We attempt to employ the scientific method to study a subject matter that, at times, seems to be as effectively explained by poetry as by experiments. Even within psychological research traditions, students have to grapple with the fact that a single action can be described, and studied, at a number of different levels of explanation, all of which may have some degree of validity. An act such as an aggressive outburst could be explained through molecular (possessing the MAOA-L allele), social (vicarious learning) or almost metaphorical (repressed Oedipal rage) means, and in other ways besides.

In addition, psychology students need to show their understanding using a combination of different skills. Students who want to achieve well need to be equally comfortable writing precise short answers, mathematical calculations, drawing graphs, analysing statistical data and writing a range of different types of essays. This combination of content knowledge and process knowledge for how to structure responses means that even seemingly simple questions may be imposing high cognitive load.

We think this presents two specific challenges for psychology teachers. First, it's hard to determine what prior attainment (and in which subjects) is likely to predict performance in psychology, which makes conversations about entry requirements tricky. Second, the variety of students we find in a typical psychology cohort means everyone may be at completely different starting points and find different skills (such as application or evaluation) relatively harder or easier. All of which underlines the importance of **checking what they know** before we start.

It may seem intuitive that if students will eventually need to juggle scientific and literary skills, then we should start juggling practice as soon as possible. However, our experience is the opposite. We have found that it is more effective to avoid asking students to perform complex literary tasks such as essay writing until later in the course, when they have a much more detailed understanding of some of the course content and evaluation principles. This means that we **manage cognitive load** for essay writing, and increases the chances that we can **secure success** (see Section 3, 'Writing essays', page 349 for a longer discussion of how, and when, to teach essay writing).

Summary

- Psychology students need to develop competence across a range of quite different skills, a challenge compounded by the inherent variety in our cohorts.

Students usually have limited prior knowledge

Psychology is not studied at Key Stage 3 and is far less popular at GCSE than at A-level, meaning that in any new psychology class there is a good chance the majority of the class will have little to no prior experience of the subject. This may mean that the content looks easier than other A-level subjects in some ways because it is more foundational, but this fails to take into account that it is not easier to learn because there is no accessible store of already learned material in long-term memory on which to build. The volume of learning demanded of students, and the speed of their required transition from novice to expert, places a premium on teaching approaches that encourage students to review regularly (to consolidate new learning) and **make meaning**, to the point where they can flexibly transfer core knowledge to a number of different areas. Because we know **prior knowledge is a key predictor of future learning**, much of the early stages of a psychology course involves teaching those building blocks of the subject (to lay the foundations for a mostly 'hierarchical' curriculum, as we have seen).

> ### Experts versus novices
>
> Although any given cohort may have a range of prior attainment in other subjects, they are all usually starting with the basics in psychology. This has significant implications, since novices and experts differ in quite fundamental ways, from the way they process information in the environment (Woolf et al., 2016) to the types of activity that are most likely to help them learn successfully (Sweller et al., 2007). Novices may benefit from more direct instruction, whereas experts are able to learn successfully from activities that are more self-guided.
>
> In feedback, novices may benefit from more immediate, corrective feedback, whereas experts will be more able to benefit from feedback that is delayed, or which focuses more on underlying processes (see Section 4, page 363). All this creates a curricular challenge, given that as psychology teachers we are attempting to take students from novice to relative expert in a very short space of time. What therefore works best at the start of Year 10 or Year 12 may not be ideal at the end of Year 11 or Year 13. This requires the planning of a curriculum that is sequenced – and time-allocated – to allow for a transition from novice to expert (see Section 2, page 133).

Let's take the example of evaluation skills. Evaluation is difficult and probably the most challenging skill to teach. One of the problems is that students initially have neither the knowledge about what to evaluate (the content) nor about what meaningful evaluation involves or how to communicate this (the skills). For this reason, we think it's perfectly appropriate to scaffold this quite significantly, at least until relatively far into the course. Early in our careers, we held the misguided belief that telling students which evaluation points to use represented a form of 'spoon-feeding' that was widely frowned upon. Instead, students were often left to figure out these evaluation points for themselves, which inevitably led to us needing to reteach it all properly anyway. We'll discuss this problem in more detail in Section 3, 'Teaching evaluative writing', page 337.

Summary

- Most psychology students will have limited foundational knowledge on which to build and must acquire a large body of knowledge in a relatively short amount of time. Our teaching methods and curriculum planning must be designed with this in mind.

Conclusions, and language, are cautious

Early on in their psychology courses, many students will be introduced to Albert Bandura's famous research into children learning to imitate aggression from watching an adult role model. When doing so, it can be a good challenge for students to be shown his table of results (see below) and asked to form their own conclusions about the factors affecting the children's behaviour.

TABLE 1
Mean Aggression Scores for Experimental and Cotrol Subjects

Response category	Experimental groups				Control groups
	Aggressive		Nonaggressive		
	F model	M model	F model	M model	
Imitative physical aggression					
Female subjects	5.5	7.2	2.5	0.0	1.2
Male subjects	12.4	25.8	0.2	1.5	2.0
Imitative verbal aggression					
Female subjects	13.7	2.0	0.3	0.0	0.7
Male subjects	4.3	12.7	1.1	0.0	1.7
Mallet aggression					
Female subjects	17.2	18.7	0.5	0.5	13.1
Male subjects	15.5	28.8	18.7	6.7	13.5
Punches Bobo doll					
Female subjects	6.3	16.5	5.8	4.3	11.7
Male subjects	18.9	11.9	15.6	14.8	15.7
Nominative aggression					
Female subjects	21.3	8.4	7.2	1.4	6.1
Male subjects	16.2	36.7	26.1	22.3	24.6
Aggressive gun play					
Female subjects	1.8	4.5	2.6	2.5	3.7
Male subjects	7.3	15.9	8.9	16.7	14.3

Bandura et al. (1961) used the data to conclude things such as:

- Same-sex models have a more powerful influence on imitation compared to the control group.
- Non-aggressive role models reduce aggression compared to the control group.
- Boys are generally more aggressive than girls.
- Girls imitate verbal aggression more from same-sex models, whereas boys imitate physical aggression.

If you look at the table for long enough, you can see where Bandura has drawn the conclusions from, but for every conclusion there is at least one piece of information that does not totally fit the pattern. This is a great example of the difference between data and theory, and a powerful example of why, whenever we attempt to study and describe human behaviour in scientific terms, we are only ever able to do so in conditional and cautious ways. In fact, as you can directly ask the students: 'Would we really ever expect the behaviour of a group of humans (which we all know from experience to be so varied and unreliable) to perfectly follow any pattern of prediction?'

This is another disciplinary fundamental arising from an understanding of the complexity of human behaviour, that theories and models are imperfect approximations and will never be perfectly reflected in any data set. This uncertainty can impose a large amount of cognitive load on students who, especially early on in the course, may just be looking for some simple factual truths to get started with.

How this plays out in the classroom will depend on how the teacher chooses to present key ideas, and the language they use to do so. One common problem with psychology students early in their studies is the tendency to present arguments as very much black or white. Milgram's study *is* unethical; laboratory experiments *are not* ecologically valid; the psychodynamic approach *is not* useful. The teacher's role here is to reframe these arguments in more conditional language to represent the real nuance of the situation, for example:

- 'Milgram's study raises ethical concerns.'
- 'Laboratory experiments could be argued to lack ecological validity.'

- 'The psychodynamic approach may not be considered useful.'

A useful phrase to get students into the habit of saying is 'the extent to which'[13] (or some variation thereof), for example:

- Let's consider the extent to which this theory is supported by…
- The extent to which this can be considered a reliable study is based on…
- To what extent do we think this research makes a useful contribution to…

This is helpful phrasing for all psychology teachers because it automatically suggests that whatever we're discussing does not have a fixed answer but lies somewhere on a scale. It also highlights that there will always be at least two different sides to an argument and making any kind of evaluative judgement is about weighing the relative strength between different points. For example, consider the 'nature-nurture' debate. We know in reality there is very little in psychology that is determined by either nature or nurture alone, yet students are prone to (and encouraged by the specification to some extent) assuming they can neatly categorise things as 'caused by nature' or 'caused by nurture'. Instead, we can talk about *the extent to which* nature or nurture may influence a particular behaviour, which implies that a combination of both is true.

Summary

- The inherent complexity of psychology means we can never draw anything more than cautious conclusions about human behaviour; the way we both present and discuss psychological theory and research should reflect this.

There's so much we still don't know

Being humble in the face of our ignorance is clearly an important characteristic for teachers to demonstrate generally, but in psychology

---

13 We may be borrowing from exam boards here – 'to what extent' is a command phrase used for extended responses in the 2015 Edexcel specification.

there is so much that is still a complete mystery to us. We often make a point of saying that some unknown question may be a thing that the future psychologists in the room are the ones to solve. It hasn't happened yet, as far as we know... but we live in hope!

Even as we were preparing this book, Pang et al. (2023) published a new study in *Nature* that suggests the shape of the brain may place as many (or more) constraints on its processing as on its connections. If true, this would fundamentally alter our understanding of how the brain works... and require large scale rewrites of many of our schemes of work! To be a psychology teacher is to embrace such surprising and challenging findings. If the human brain is the most complex object in the known universe, then we should not be surprised by the odd paradigm shift in our understanding of it, and nor should our students. Being open about our own ignorance and that of the field as a whole can be an important thing to model as we try to create a *culture of error* (see page 100) in our classrooms.

All of this means that psychology teachers have a difficult challenge balancing the cutting edge with the core content. Textbooks will typically deal with a lot of 'historical' research, such as Milgram and Zimbardo. How much 'newer' research should students be exposed to? To what extent will this enrich their knowledge and understanding and inspire them further, or, on the other hand, interfere with their learning of the main core content? We discuss these questions in Section 2 (see 'Psychology in the 21st century', page 183).

Summary

- Psychology is very much a developing subject, and so we need to acknowledge the wonder and extent of our collective ignorance and balance carefully the need to learn established content with newer research.

Section 1C: Pedagogical implications

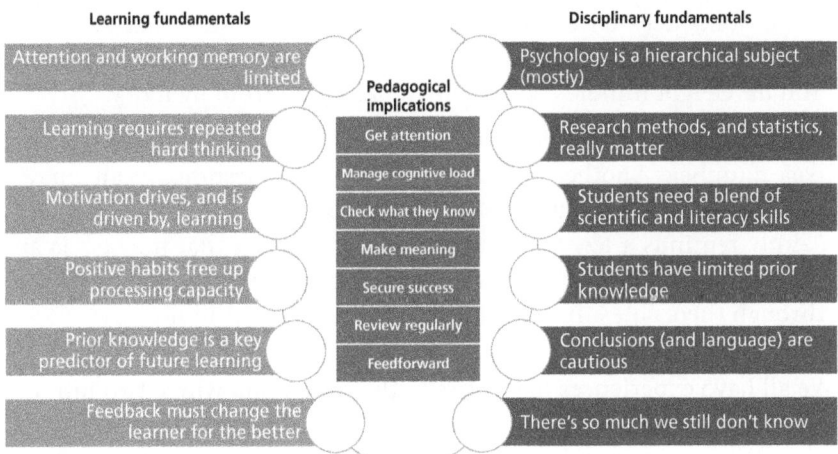

We have now considered some of the key principles of learning and the fundamental disciplinary features of psychology. In this section, we consider the pedagogical implications of what we have discussed so far. In other words, armed with this knowledge, what should a psychology teacher do in the classroom? Importantly, this is a broader question than simply, 'What activities should I do in the classroom?'

The seven pedagogical implications in the above figure help to focus our planning at the level of 'cognitive preparation' (considering the best way to achieve the actual learning aims of the lesson), rather than 'activity preparation' (finding seemingly appropriate activities with which to fill the lesson). What we do in our lessons, what we say, what we display, even how we move and gesture have all been focused and filtered through these seven pedagogical implications, and we have found them powerful tools for classroom improvement. However, as discussed in the introduction, this is not a prescription for exactly how to plan your lessons but rather a guide to the kinds of things that we consider the best bets for teaching, based on what we know about our subject and how students learn.

Get attention

Ensure learners are attending only to the most important things.

> Sara is teaching her class about using case studies as a research method and has just delivered a verbal explanation. She wants to check their understanding and memory of what has just been covered, so she says, 'Right folks, let's check what we know and make sure that everyone here is completely confident. Please complete questions 1–3 on page 47. You have eight minutes. Do it individually, and from memory.'
>
> As the class settles to the task, one student asks for a reminder of the page number. Another student asks, 'All the questions, yeah miss?' Over the next five minutes, as she circulates the room, Sara quietly and calmly reminds a few students who are conferring that the task is an individual one, and tells another two who have started looking back through their notes that it is a task from memory.

We all have experiences like Sara's in the classroom, where two minutes after clearly explaining a task or activity for the third time, a student asks, 'What are we doing again?' Early on in our teaching careers we thought little about them; indeed, we both accepted them as part of the job, or even welcomed them as a sign of engagement. However, increasingly we see classroom segments like the one described above as being indicative of more serious deficits of attention. If students aren't giving full attention to your instructions, then what else aren't they attending to? Given the limitations of attention and working memory capacity, and students' lack of prior knowledge in the subject, it is crucial to **get attention**.

So how can we maximise student attention in the classroom? Thinking chronologically through the learning process, we can prime attention to prepare students to focus, streamline attention by removing distractions from our learning environments and cue attention during learning.

Priming attention

One way that we can make students pay attention is to make them expect that they will *need* to pay attention, for example, by making them expect that their knowledge of new material will be tested. This is known as 'test expectancy', and it makes students attend more closely to the material being presented to them, leading to improved learning both in the lab (Weinstein et al., 2014) and the classroom (Nevid and Armata, 2023). This means that learning segments with tests, quizzes or other checks for understanding not only improve the learning of content covered, but can also prime a pupil to better learn future content (Yang et al., 2018; Hobbiss, 2019). As a result, we now think very carefully about whether any new information that we deliver to a class can be chunked into segments and recall opportunities (or even just 'checks for listening') can be provided to check what the students know after instructions or teaching segments.

Another way of priming attention is to have a combination of very specific goals and regular feedback on how well the goal is being met (Robison et al., 2021). Unlike more general goals (for example, 'Your target grade is…', 'In the next essay try to…'), these are highly specific performance goals, with feedback embedded into the structure of each task. For example:

- 'I can see that most people have recalled at least four key words from the last lesson on their whiteboards. Aim to add at least two more in the next 30 seconds.'
- 'On average students were able to successfully answer 70% of these recall questions last year. See if you can beat that score.'
- 'Write two paragraphs on this topic. Aim to write at least 200 words in the next six minutes. I'll tell you when three minutes have passed, by which time you should have finished your first paragraph.'

A final method of priming attention in students is to encourage them to have a proactive mindset towards attention control. Zedelius et al. (2021) found that participants who believed they could not control their own thoughts reported experiencing more mind wandering. We now remind any students that we suspect of being distracted or mind wandering that they are in control of their own attention and follow that with a request to bring it back to the task.

Streamlining attention by removing distractions

How else can we create a working environment conducive to close, focused attention? Just reduce distractions – simple, right? Well, it depends. We could eliminate many common classroom distractions by teaching in bare, soundproofed rooms and with children at separate individual desks, but, aside from the practical reasons that would make this set-up impossible in most schools, would we really want to?

This is a good example of making evidence-informed decisions as a teacher. We may decide that some distraction is a price that we are happy to pay, given other priorities; for example, group activities or visual displays may bring benefits to our classroom environment even if they provide potential sources of distraction. It's a trade-off. Knowing that **attention and working memory are limited** doesn't mean everything we do has to be slavishly dedicated to this end, but it does mean that we can make more informed decisions about what we do, and when.

Students report being affected by different classroom distractions for different proportions of time (Hobbiss, 2019).

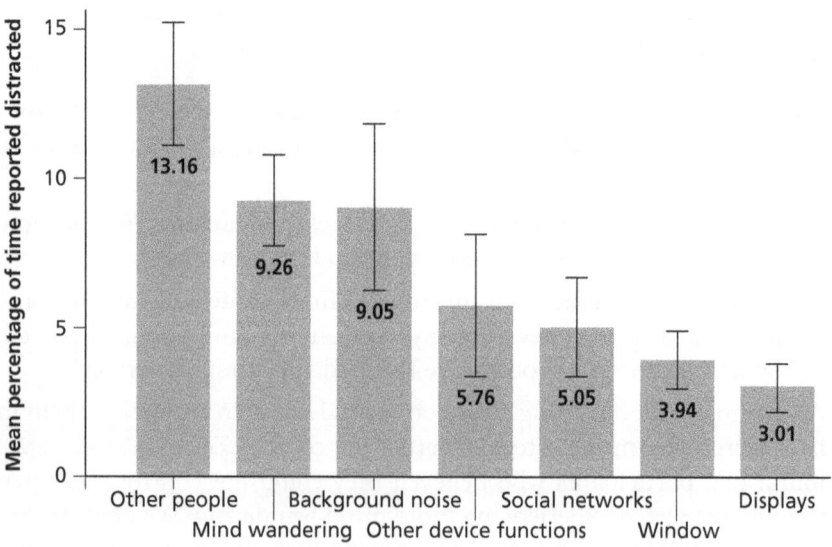

In the order of prevalence, some potential solutions include:

Other people

- Seating plans – even in sixth form!
- Consistent use of the school behaviour policy.

- Tightly structured group tasks, for example, by giving students clearly defined roles and reminding them of good habits of discussion (see 'Paired and self-explanation', page 85).

Mind wandering

- Encouraging students to have a positive mindset towards the control of their attention, and by asking them to think deeply and with interest about the material.

Background noise

- Silence for tasks that will require any level of close concentration or careful thought. (If this sounds obvious, bear in mind that silent thinking and writing tasks have been found to account for less than 5% of classroom time in some settings; Owens et al., 2017.)

Technology

- Use technology in the classroom in a tightly structured context, ideally using devices designed specifically for educational purposes.
- Avoid very open-ended tasks such as 'internet research', as these are likely to open up far more opportunities for attention to be diverted.
- Seat students with laptops or other technological learning aids (such as exam supports) in a place where the screen will be least likely to distract others.
- Phones should be out of sight in bags, as the mere presence of a visible phone – even one switched off – is detrimental to attention (Thornton et al., 2014).

Displays

- Avoid creating over-decorated and visually noisy classrooms that are likely to do more harm than good (Fisher et al., 2014; Godwin et al., 2022).
- As a compromise, remove displays from the front half of the classroom, apart from those that you know you will be referring to regularly as part of a classroom routine (for example, key evaluation terms).

Streamlining attention through 'means of participation' (MOP) and front-loading

This is another term drawn from *Teach Like a Champion* (Lemov, 2015). When we give instructions to students, we may not precisely specify exactly how we want them to do something. For example, saying 'Now answer Q1–5 from the board' may seem clear, but students may be left wondering whether they are to work independently or in pairs, in silence or while talking, in their exercise books or on whiteboards, writing in full sentences or just bullet points. This means the teacher is likely to spend the first few minutes of the task answering, often repeatedly, these 'process' questions, which means neither they nor students are actually grappling with the substance of the questions.

Clarifying the means of participation is about specifying the following: 'Here are some questions on the board to have a go at now. Please do this independently and in silence, writing your answers in your exercise books using full sentences.'

We could make this even more effective by also front-loading our MOP (Boxer, 2020). This means giving the instructions before students have any chance to engage with the content itself, so they are not already starting to think about their answers before you've finished speaking (and therefore may not attend to the instructions you are giving): 'In a moment, I'm going to show you some questions on the board. Please answer these using full sentences in your exercise books, individually and in silence. Here are the questions – go.'

Cueing attention

Cueing attention simply means making it very clear to students what we want them to be focusing on at any moment in time, and it can be hugely powerful for learning (Markant and Amso, 2014; Markant et al., 2016). This can be achieved by explicitly telling students (for example, 'Go to the second paragraph of that page and look at the first sentence only. What specialist terminology is used in that sentence?'), using gesture or body language or by otherwise indicating important information by making it stand out from its surroundings (the technical term for this is 'salience'). Making items more distinctive, for example, by printing a word in a different font, bolding, underlining or colour-coding makes it easier to subsequently retrieve from memory, because it reduces the interference from surrounding information (Dunlosky et al., 2000). We need to be careful, however, that the features we make salient are those directly relevant to the task or information being learned. For example, funny cartoon gifs dancing at the side of your slides[14] are actually serving to make non-task information the salient features of the display.

One powerful attention cueing technique is live modelling, where a teacher creates sentences, images or graphics *during their explanation*, rather than referring to pre-created resources (a visualiser can be a very powerful tool for tasks such as these). Learning information in this way has been found to make students more able to successfully transfer their knowledge and understanding to new contexts (Fiorella and Mayer, 2016a). It also helps to **manage cognitive load** by introducing new elements gradually. The 'example teaching segment' on synaptic transmission at the end of this section (see page 108) demonstrates a live drawing procedure used to both cue attention and **manage cognitive load** in just this way.

Overcoming the embarrassment of demanding attention

It can feel awkward to continually demand attention from psychology students, especially given their more senior status and our inclination to want to 'treat them as adults'. However, this does not mean that we should expect them to simply be able to focus attention successfully, or consistently, for the simple reason that *none of us* can do this. Given this, and our **limited attention capacity**, there's surely no shame in being distracted, and there should be no shame on the part of the student, nor awkwardness on the part of the teacher, at attention being regularly refocused during the course of a lesson.

Here is something that we say to our new students at the beginning of the course (after a brief introduction to the limited capacity of attention):

> As we have seen, the way our attention systems work is that they have very limited capacities, and they are very easily distracted. This is the same for all of us, regardless of age. Obviously, this

---

14 To choose an example we both considered the pinnacle of teaching when we started our careers!

makes it essential that you make every effort to control your attention and to direct it to the right things. During my lessons I will therefore be very clear and specific about where I want you to focus your attention, and I will be checking to make sure that all of you are focusing attention on the right places and in the way that I want it to be. If I don't do this, then the time that we lose as a class adds up very quickly. As a result, if I ask you to redirect your attention, please don't take it personally because I won't hold it against you personally. I am just working hard to create an environment where we are all able to focus most of the time, because then amazing learning happens, especially when you work hard to make it happen too.

What to pay attention to?
Of course, if we are going to work this hard to manage attention, we also need to think really hard about exactly what it is that students should be attending to. We discuss this further in both Section 2 ('Curriculum', page 133) and Section 3 ('Teaching core content', page 199).

Summary
- Attention can be primed in the classroom before information is presented, streamlined by reducing distractions and cued in the classroom during the presentation of information.

Manage cognitive load

Teach with respect to the constraints of working memory.

Working memory and cognitive load
Cognitive load theory (CLT) has been called the 'single most important thing for teachers to learn' (Wiliam, 2017). It builds on the implications of the fact that **attention and working memory are limited** to produce a more education-specific theory of 'instructional design'. The central premise of CLT is that processing information places demands on our attention and memory systems – the level of demand is known as cognitive load. If those demands exceed our capacity (for example, if we are overwhelmed with information) then we experience cognitive overload.

CLT suggests that we can divide the demands placed on our processing capacity into two main categories: intrinsic and extraneous (Sweller et al., 1998). *Intrinsic load* reflects the inherent complexity of information as a function of prior knowledge; in other words, we find more complicated things less overloading the more we already know about them. This is one reason why securing prior knowledge is such an essential part of successful learning. *Extraneous load* refers to any feature of the task design or the environment that places a load on working memory, but that does not facilitate the desired schema construction.

Take the example of drug treatments for psychological conditions, such as schizophrenia. These are often among the most biologically complex details of A-level specifications. A student learning about the action and effects of typical antipsychotic drugs such as chlorpromazine may read the following sentence: 'Typical antipsychotics are dopamine antagonists, which reduce positive symptoms by binding to (and blocking) dopamine receptors without stimulating them.'

This sentence is complex enough (in the terms of CLT, it has high intrinsic load), but now imagine the experience of a student who reads this without a clear schema for synaptic transmission, or the dopamine hypothesis for schizophrenia. Managing the cognitive load of our students so that they become able to access, understand and ultimately use such technical language and concepts is therefore a key challenge of psychology teaching.

Should we aim to always keep intrinsic load as low as possible? No. Because **learning requires repeated hard thinking**, the key to successful learning is to *optimise* intrinsic load (Lovell and Sherrington, 2020), rather than avoid it. While this may mean that we want to reduce intrinsic load for challenging tasks, we may actually want to *increase* the load for simpler tasks, for example, by asking students to do them from memory or by imposing time limits and performance goals. That is, we need to pitch new information at the sweet spot that is not too easy but is not going to cause overload. This requires teachers to **check what they know** because **prior knowledge is a key predictor of future learning**.

CLT: Recommendations for teaching

In 2017, the Australian Centre for Education, Statistics and Evaluation produced an impressively detailed but accessible review of CLT research and distilled the findings into seven key recommendations for teachers (CESE, 2017), which we have also found useful in guiding our own practice. They are specified here along with links to sections of the book where these strategies are demonstrated in other sections. Most of these principles are also demonstrated in both example teaching segments at the end of this section (see pages 108 and 114).

- Strategy 1: Tailor lessons according to students' existing knowledge and skill (as previously seen in '**Positive habits free up processing capacity**', and in the next section: '**Check what you know**').
- Strategy 2: Use worked examples to teach students new content or skills (see Section 3, 'Statistics and stats testing', page 252).
- Strategy 3: Gradually increase independent problem solving as students become more proficient (see 'Levels of scaffolding in psychology' in '**Secure success**' later in this section).
- Strategy 4: Cut out inessential information (see previous section, '**Get attention**').
- Strategy 5: Present all the essential information together.
- Strategy 6: Simplify complex information by presenting it both orally and visually (see Section 3, 'The "shape" of a study', page 286).
- Strategy 7: Encourage students to visualise concepts and procedures they have learned (see 'Advance organisers', page 80, Section 2, 'Mapping the "shape" of a unit', page 164, Section 3, 'The "shape" of a study', page 286).

Cognitive load and practical activities in the classroom

Taking part in practical research in (and beyond) the classroom can be an enjoyable and memorable part of studying psychology. However, practical activities can place a significant burden on working memory. Remembering new procedures, rules for standardisation, how to record results and so on all add to their cognitive load. This is not necessarily a bad thing; conducting research can be overwhelming and often far more complex than students realise until they have a go themselves. This realisation is definitely valuable; however, if we want our students to actually learn about psychology from the experience, then we need to **manage the cognitive load** sufficiently so they are able to also process the theoretical alongside the logistical.

This is one reason why we recommend ensuring that student practicals are carefully structured and managed (see Section 3, 'A "slow" methods practical on counterbalancing', page 267).

Cognitive load, motivation and achievement: A tri-directional relationship

Learning is a complex business, and so it's hardly surprising that many of the learning fundamentals and pedagogical implications that we cover interact with one another. In one really nice example of this, Evans et al. (2024) examined the relationship between teachers' use of 'load-reducing' educational strategies (such as managing the challenge of new learning, scaffolding and providing chances for practice, feedback and independent learning), their students' motivation (by encouraging their competence and autonomy; see earlier in this section, '**Motivation drives, and is driven by, learning**') and attainment. Teachers who looked to employ these load-reducing strategies, and who also promoted feelings of competence and autonomy, had students who achieved better grades in school than those who didn't, and this success works to reciprocally reinforce the students' later learning and motivation. This creates a virtuous triangle on the way to helping our students to **secure success** (see later in this section, page 87).

Summary

- We should seek to optimise cognitive load, which may involve actually increasing it for simpler tasks and reducing it for more challenging tasks by activating relevant prior knowledge and presenting information in a way that respects capacity limits.

Check what they know

Assess and secure prior knowledge before teaching new information.

In the previous section on managing cognitive load, we looked at a sentence describing the action of antipsychotic medication: 'Typical antipsychotics are dopamine antagonists, which reduce positive symptoms by binding to (and blocking) dopamine receptors without stimulating them.'

Undoubtedly, this is a challenging sentence to understand, placing a significant burden on our existing knowledge. In his book, *The Reading Mind*, psychologist Daniel Willingham argues that readers need to know about 98% of the words in a passage for 'comfortable comprehension', and for complex sentences like this it is not just the word meanings themselves but an underlying understanding of their theoretical meaning that is also important (Nation, 2006; Willingham, 2017). If we want a student to be able to not just comprehend, but to *evaluate*, then the figure may be even higher!

In order to be able to understand this sentence, then, students will need knowledge of:[15]

- Neurotransmitters and the process of synaptic transmission (in general).
- The specific features and actions of dopamine, including relevant dopamine pathways.
- The original and revised dopamine hypotheses, including the association between dopamine function and positive symptoms of schizophrenia, such as hallucinations.

---

15   And, of course, each of these points comes loaded with prerequisite knowledge too.

If the student has not already developed a secure schema for synaptic transmission, they are unlikely to be able to integrate the dopamine hypothesis into it. If this is the case, then they have no chance of understanding the effects of antipsychotic drugs. This is why **checking what they know** is an essential feature of effective teaching, as it provides a baseline level for us to respond to, adjusting our explanations and activities to best accommodate the current level of our students. Ensuring that our lessons are pitched at the level of current knowledge means that **motivation can be driven by current learning**. Also, as we saw with the forward testing effect in '**Get attention**', checking what they know also enhances the learning of new material. But what is the most important information to check, and how (and when) should we check?

What to check – the prerequisite knowledge spectrum

Because **psychology is a (mostly) hierarchical subject** and **prior knowledge is a key predictor of future learning**, when we start a new topic, we will usually be able to identify the relevant prerequisite knowledge (PRK) from preceding units. This can sometimes be a long list, especially as students get into Year 11 or Year 13. Ideally, we would check student knowledge of *all* of this prerequisite knowledge (and sometimes we can, as we will see in the following section). However, practically in lessons this often isn't possible. Science teacher Claudia Lewis (2022) therefore suggests that we can arrange PRK for a topic on a spectrum from 'least important', which we'd clearly still ideally like students to know, but is unlikely to derail lessons entirely, to 'most important', without which lessons are likely to fail. Here is a spectrum for the 'forensic psychology' topic of the AQA A-level:

Forensic psychology – prerequisite knowledge

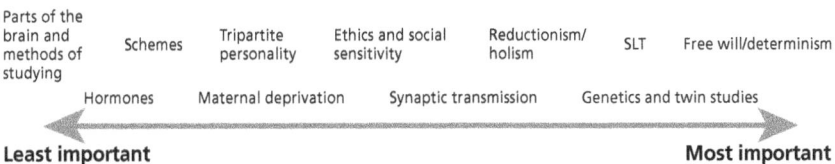

Spectrums like these help us to think more carefully about what information we really need to check the understanding of, as well as how and when we do so. When you make your own spectrums, you may find that they look different from the example provided, and that's absolutely fine. Depending on the specification you teach, curriculum order, teacher preference and a host of other factors, a prerequisite knowledge spectrum will likely look slightly different in different settings.

When, and how, to check what they know

Once we have created a PRK spectrum, we can fairly easily create a rough rule for when to check what students know:[16]

Week before starting new topic	Prerequisite knowledge homework. ALL prerequisite knowledge for that unit checked in some form. Students complete initially from memory but then use notes to complete any gaps (providing rewarming of schemas).
Start of new topic	Prediction exercise, predicting how previously learned theories and concepts will occur in this new topic.
During new topic	Specific prerequisite knowledge required for each lesson, as well as other most important knowledge from the PRK spectrum quizzed at the start of each lesson. Students complete entirely from memory. Student booklets also cue retrieval of relevant prerequisite knowledge.

Of course, the job is not done once the unit is finished either. Memories will fade unless they are reencoded and reconsolidated over time. This is one reason why we also **review regularly**. Therefore, we would recommend always having *some* retrieval questions from other topics present in your lessons, especially for the most important course knowledge that can be used in multiple places (items we call 'nuggets', see Section 2, page 175). Key issues and debates, or research method ideas, are good examples of 'nuggety' information that reoccurs across multiple units. In the example spectrum, therefore, 'ethics and social sensitivity' may actually be checked just as carefully as 'twin studies'.

---

16   NB if you use a core questions curriculum (see page 147) then the selection of questions here is made much more straightforward.

The power of prediction

Another very powerful tool for preparing schemas for new learning, which provides some variety from simple quizzing, is prediction.

When we examined how **learning requires repeated hard thinking**, we saw that memory formation in the brain often moves from the initially episodic to more generalised semantic memories, or schemas. One of the advantages of this shift is that it opens up the possibility of making predictions about the world, which improves the ability to **make meaning**. The theory of predictive coding suggests that our brains evolved to predict what will happen next, and there is evidence for the brain operating in this way in both visual (Rao and Ballard, 1999) and memory (Henson and Gagnepain, 2010) systems.

Asking students to predict how a known theory or concept will be likely to apply to a new, as yet unseen topic area is therefore a very powerful way of encouraging this shift from concrete episodic to flexible semantic memories. For example:

- We know how operant and classical conditioning work. All behaviourist theories are built using one or both of these. So, how would a behaviourist explain a phobia? What about attachment?
- How would SLT explain offending behaviour?
- How would the biological approach explain OCD?
- How would the cognitive approach treat schizophrenia?

If students successfully predict this new application, then as well as reconsolidating and broadening their existing schema through making meaning, they also get the motivation benefits of successful learning and the chance for you to celebrate their increasing ability to think (and predict) like a psychologist. Prediction errors, where there is a mismatch between a prediction from existing knowledge and a new experience, are also a powerful learning tool that can trigger improved attention and memory reconsolidation (Sinclair and Barense, 2018). Predicting and getting it wrong is therefore as useful as predicting and getting it right, provided the student has made a genuine best guess from their existing knowledge. You can't lose!

Doing the thinking in advance – prior knowledge and notes booklets

PRK checks can be built into your resources in advance. This helps you with your *cognitive preparation* for the lesson, focusing you on the learning that you want students to experience and the connections that will allow them to **make meaning** successfully (see Section 3, page 127). In the example below, notes are on the left, with the right-hand side for annotations and student additions, which can then be further scaffolded and directed by pre-planned questions. Here, the question activates prior knowledge.

Other important factors in CBT
• **Behavioural homework**
  ○ Clients are given assignments, such as asking someone out on a date when previously they would have been too afraid to do so.
  ○ This is vital in helping them to test irrational beliefs.
  ○ Also involves a focus on encouraging clients to be more active and engage in pleasurable activities.
• **Unconditional positive regard**
  ○ Ellis emphasises the importance of showing respect and appreciation, regardless of what the client does or says.
	
	Where have we heard this term before?

Another advantage of this format is that it provides a platform for all students to think and write an answer, rather than a verbal question that may only involve one student. It maintains high thinking and participation ratios. Other methods such as think-pair-share or mini-whiteboards could also attain the same aims, however one added bonus of building knowledge checks into resources like this is that it reduces the chances of simply forgetting to do them at the right point in the lesson. We'll discuss the pros and cons of resources like booklets and slides in Section 5, page 430.

Checking for understanding

Checking what students know shouldn't only occur in advance of delivering new content; it is also crucial after delivering new content as a check for understanding. As previously noted, teachers often use inefficient checks for understanding, such as: 'Does that make sense? Are you happy with that? Get it? Are we good with that?' In every case, the likelihood that all students really have 'got it' is very low, but social norms dictate that students are highly unlikely to admit that they are confused. Also, we have to remember that students don't learn what we tell them; they learn their interpretation of what we tell them based on their prior knowledge, so they may *think* they have got it… but actually be way off!

Therefore, it is incumbent on us not to take their word for it; to move from 'do you understand' to 'what do you understand?' (Sherrington, 2021). The way in which we can do this varies depending on whether we want to sample the whole class, the level of depth of answer we are looking for and the extent to which we may want to interrogate the responses we get.

Sampling and whole-class responses

While this will be a familiar term to any psychology teacher, sampling is an important concept to consider in relation to our questioning techniques. Imagine a teacher starts a lesson with a quick retrieval question to activate prior knowledge, such as: 'Name the three stages of social identity theory.' The teacher then cold-calls three students, each one correctly naming the appropriate stage (categorisation, identification, comparison). 'Great,' says the teacher, 'We've remembered the key ideas from SIT, let's move on…'

Let's do some maths. Assuming a class of 20 students, there are 60 possible answers, of which the teacher has sampled three (5%) of them. Can the teacher really infer from this that the whole class is ready to move on? Remember that prior knowledge helps the rich get richer. Making false inferences here hugely increases the likelihood of significant gaps appearing between students.

A better alternative, then, is to get a full set of responses from the whole class. The teacher could easily do this using mini-whiteboards (or more high-tech solutions like Google Forms), allowing them to make a much better judgement about the extent to which the class has secure knowledge or not on this prerequisite knowledge.

What if they don't know? What to reteach, when and how?

There's an obvious elephant in the room here with all this checking what students know and understand: what do you do when it turns out they *don't know*? In the past, without rigorous checking we may have simply moved on in blissful ignorance of the fact that we were simply building on sand and allowing large gaps to form. But since we know that **prior knowledge is a key predictor of future learning**, then we can't ignore it when we realise some (or all) students don't have secure enough knowledge, as we will be making future learning more difficult for them as well.

Essentially, we have a few choices in this situation:

- Do nothing.
- Do nothing *now*, but make note of whatever is going to need reteaching.
- Address it now with the whole class.
- Address it now with specific students.

Which of those choices you make may depend on the extent to which those gaps are important prerequisite content for the material about to be learned, and the proportion of the class that don't have the knowledge required. We may also need time to consider the source of the problem, for example, whether we need to adapt our explanations or resources or find different sources of information.

Finally, we need to remember that once we've retaught the material, we'll probably need to recheck for understanding again. We can't just ask, 'Does that make sense now?' and again assume a positive response is valid. As Doug Lemov suggests, we should *reject self-report*; of course, as psychology teachers, we know about the possible limitations of self-report data already! One strategy that one of us has to deal with regarding student retrieval failure during quiz questions is described in 'Creating a new classroom routine of feedforward accountability' (page 106).

Summary
- Checking what students know, both before and after content delivery, allows us to be responsive to our students' current levels of knowledge and understanding, which is essential for effective future learning.

Make meaning

Help students make connections between what they're learning and what they already know.

As teachers, we know that simply memorising the specification isn't enough to perform well, and that only students who have a deep understanding of the underlying themes and connections within the subject will prosper. It is those students who will be able to think with the necessary flexibility to answer the full range of exam questions, rather than those who have rote learned past mark schemes. It is therefore our job as teachers to weave such meaning making throughout the course. This section will look at some of the approaches that we might use to get us there.

Identifying meaning making concepts

Firstly, we need to identify the concepts that will allow your students to **make meaning** (the 'subsumers' in Ausubel's terminology). What fundamental ideas are the connections between all the various things we do as psychologists; what are the seams holding the subject together? These will operate both on small scales (such as within individual units or applied areas) and also on the scale of the whole subject. The latter category may involve:

- Approaches to psychology.
- Research methods.
- Issues and debates.

Having identified these, we need to place them front and centre in our curriculum planning (see Section 2, page 133), in our teaching practices (see Section 3, page 199) and in our feedback and assessment practices (see Section 4, page 363).

Advance organisers

Advance organisers[17] are a tool to help activate the relevant cognitive structures in learners before they encounter some new information, with the intention of making assimilation of that new information with prior knowledge easier. Given the typically low base of prior knowledge in our psychology students, making those connections and providing those frameworks are even more important. Let's consider different types of advance organiser.

An **expository advance organiser** simply explains or describes what the learning is going to be about. These can be little more than a verbal statement from the teacher (for example, 'Today we're going to learn about the different ways in which researchers obtain the participants for their studies; this is called sampling'), more formally written as the learning objectives or enquiry question for the lesson (for example, 'How reliable are eyewitnesses to a crime?'), a pre-test or a prediction.

Graphic advance organisers can be useful because they can portray the relationship between ideas and the organisation of different concepts more effectively than verbal or written statements (Caviglioli, 2019; Mayer, 2024). Graphic advance organisers may be particularly helpful in showing students where the current lesson fits within the bigger picture and allowing for links to be drawn between topics.

---

17 Advance organisers are not to be confused with knowledge organisers. Advanced organisers are specifically designed to provide an organisational framework for material that is being learned to help students assimilate new information into existing schemas; they should not contain lots of detail. Knowledge organisers are comprehensive resources that detail the core knowledge to be learned in a topic or unit.

Section 1: The teaching framework

Here is an example one of us created for the criminal psychology unit from the Edexcel A-level specification:

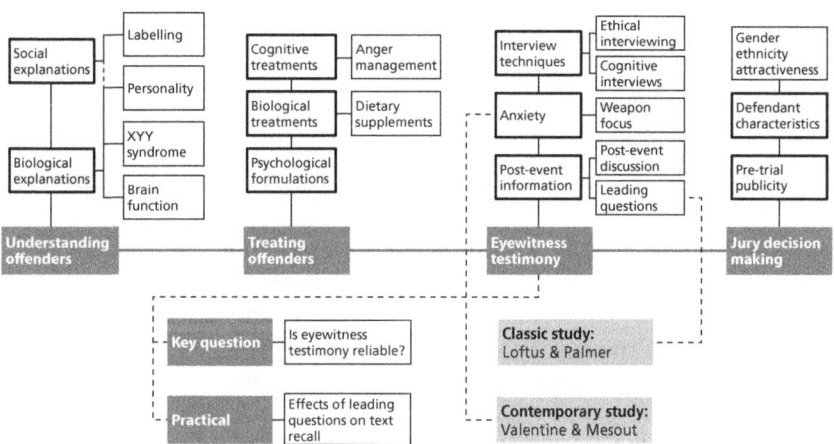

Students would be introduced to this in the first lesson of the unit, although initially this would be presented on screen, with each element animated to control the amount of information students are being asked to process at once to help **manage cognitive load**. This is then presented at the beginning of every lesson (or at the start of any new subtopic if that happens to occur midway through a lesson), and the students also have a copy at the front of their unit booklet for reference. This is used to help place the current topic in the wider context and to see how it fits with what has already been learned or what is yet to be learned (for example, 'Last time we looked at biological treatments for offenders, today we're going to consider an alternative type of treatment: cognitive behavioural therapy.').

Comparative advance organisers are used when introducing new content that is similar to something previously learned and likely to cause confusion between the two sets of ideas. For example, students learning about explanations of prejudice often get confused between realistic conflict theory (RCT, Sherif, 1966) and social identity theory (SIT, Tajfel and Turner, 1979), because central to both theories is the idea of in-groups negatively discriminating towards out-groups. Therefore, when introducing the second theory (SIT) we would need to highlight this overlap – which reactivates relevant prior knowledge of RCT –

before emphasising the key difference between the two. A simple graphic comparative advance organiser could look like this:

	Realistic conflict theory (RCT)	Social identity theory (SIT)
Similarity	Suggests prejudice arises between in-groups and out-groups.	
Difference	Says prejudice only occurs when there is competition between in-groups and out-groups.	Says prejudice can arise simply due to the existence of in-groups and out-groups, without need for competition.

The teacher may start this lesson sequence with some retrieval questions about RCT in order to draw out two key ideas: first, that the concept of in-groups and out-groups is central to RCT, and second, that one of the key flaws in the theory was that it couldn't explain prejudice in the absence of apparent competition between groups.[18]

Meaningful teacher explanations

As the expert in the room, one of the most important things teachers do is explain new ideas to their students. While this may be an obvious point, it can be surprising how little time some teachers spend really thinking about and planning their explanations in advance (this was certainly true for both of us earlier in our careers). The result is that in many cases students don't really understand what we've told them – even if they say they do. Let's consider an example. Megan is introducing social learning theory (SLT) to her class for the first time (we'll assume the class has already studied traditional behaviourist theories of classical and operant conditioning):

> OK everyone, today we're going to learn about a new theory called social learning theory. This was proposed by Albert Bandura and says that people learn by observing models and are vicariously reinforced by the consequences of those models' behaviour.

This is a relatively concise explanation and has some key ideas contained within it, but it may not fully land with some students. Research into

---

18 There is also a key point here about curriculum sequencing, that the teacher has deliberately planned to cover RCT before SIT in order to show how one theory dealt with a shortcoming of the other. See Section 2, 'Curriculum', page 133, for further discussion.

effective explanations, as well as teacher experiences, suggests that effective explanations will often share a number of similar features (Tharby, 2018). They will move from the *familiar* to the *unfamiliar*, which allows for the 'anchoring' of the new idea in **prior knowledge**. This anchoring can also be achieved through the use of metaphor, for example, the use of an iceberg when describing Freud's model of personality. In the same way, explanations will often move from the concrete to the abstract, from the parts to the whole, and from explanations to definitions.

Let's see how Megan could make this better:

> OK everyone, we've learned about two different theories of learning: classical and operant conditioning. Remember that in both cases the organism doing the learning has to experience the association or reinforcement for themselves in order for them to learn. But that's not the only way learning happens, is it? Sometimes we learn from other people. For example, the other day at dinner our eldest daughter made a funny face, and we all laughed. Immediately our younger daughter tried to copy the same funny face. She had learned a new behaviour by copying someone else. This is called social learning.

This time Megan made a connection between previously learned knowledge and the new information and highlighted a key difference between the two to prevent confusion. Then she used a concrete example that would be easily understood by her class, as most would be familiar with this kind of scenario from their own experiences. She hasn't dealt with the idea of vicarious learning yet, but that's OK because she just wants the core idea of learning from observing others before getting into the specific mechanisms of how this happens. She could take this further by giving some more examples (or non-examples) to illustrate, and perhaps asking students to generate their own.[19]

Checking for meaning

While checking for understanding is important, it can often be done in a way that is quite superficial, looking to see that students have given the

---

19   NB this is an example of superordinate rather than subsumptive learning, where it's more helpful to start with specific concrete examples and build up to abstract principles rather than starting with the generalised concept first.

correct answer – or, at least, a close enough approximation of the correct answer to satisfy the teacher. Checking for meaning, therefore, is a more curious and interrogative process (Cottingham, 2023) where we are not just interested in the answer a student gives, but what it tells us about the meaning they've made and the connections between new information and prior knowledge.

Doing the thinking in advance – scripting

When we design resources and activities for our students, the question that must be at the front of our minds is: 'What do we want them to be thinking about?' This should therefore form a key part of the cognitive preparation for our lessons, including which sorts of thought processes they are likely to find more or less challenging. For the most challenging topics (where the clarity of your communication is paramount), scripting can therefore be a very valuable method of helping understanding and meaning making. It also makes sure that as a teacher you don't forget anything important!

Scripts can be either written (into booklets, for example) or verbal. We saw in the previous section ('**Check what they know**') an example of pre-scripted questions to activate prior knowledge. The questions in the right column in the example below are designed to guide student thought in a way that allows them to **make meaning**, through highlighting links to pre-existing knowledge and encouraging the flexible use of evidence in evaluation. This is no different from pre-planning the questions that may be asked verbally in lesson planning, but it has the advantage of keeping the participation and thinking ratio high as every student is required to write an answer.

| **Limitations**
Although it is often effective, there is **research evidence** that systematic desensitisation does not always work:
• **Wolpe (1973)** attempted (unsuccessfully to use systematic desensitisation to treat a woman's fear of insects.
• It turned out that her (estranged husband) had an insect nickname.
• Her 'fear' was simply a displacement of her marital problems.
• By focusing on one level of explanation, behaviourism may miss out on more suitable explanations and treatments. | Which approach does this support instead?

Which debate in psychology is relevant here?

How could you use this point when evaluating the **explanation**, rather than the therapy? |

In addition to notes, you may also wish to script complementary verbal explanations. Indeed, the complementarity with other resources is one of the main reasons why scripting can be so helpful, as it ensures that you can use consistent phrases and explanations throughout. Throughout the book there will be various teaching segments in which the teacher dialogue is scripted (see, for example, the teaching segments at the end of this section on page pages 108 and 114), which may form a useful basis for your own.

Paired and self-explanation

A good episode of teacher exposition and whole-class questioning can be used effectively to introduce new ideas to a class. However, even with a strong classroom *culture of error*, students may be reluctant to expose their thinking initially, and getting responses from every student in the classroom is also an important issue, since every student has their own unique cognitive structure and they all may have made slightly different meaning of the same information.

An excellent approach in this case is to allow students to use self- and paired-explanation. These give students a chance to rehearse their thoughts verbally in a much lower-stakes setting (compared to the public context of a whole-class Q&A session), to hear a peer explain the same idea for themselves, thus reinforcing the shared meaning, and to give and receive feedback (if appropriate).

A further variation on this routine is to incorporate some individual thinking time at the beginning, making the activity *think-pair-share*. While paired explanation is good for rehearsing content just presented by the teacher, think-pair-share may be more effective when you are asking a question that requires students to draw on their prior knowledge or make links between material you've just taught them and other learned content. A simple script for this, which includes modelling and clarifying the means of participation, may look like this:

> OK everyone, in a moment you're going to practise explaining this new idea to each other in pairs. Let's be clear on how this is going to work. Imagine I'm partnered with Jack here. I'm going to take one minute to explain this idea to Jack. I'm going to do this in my own words, without just reading out what I wrote in my notes, although I'm going to use the keywords on the board as prompts to help me. Jack's going to listen carefully to check

what I say is making sense and ask any questions if something isn't clear. After one minute we're going to swap, and Jack is going to explain the same thing to me. Again, it's important that Jack does it in his own words, not just trying to copy exactly what I said. And again, I'll ask any questions if he says anything I don't understand. Right, over to you. In each pair, when I say go, the person sitting on the right-hand side of the table – yes, that's the one nearest the window – is going to go first. 3,2,1 – go!

Although this may seem a lengthy script, in reality it'll only take a minute or so to deliver and is worth the investment if we want this done properly. As this becomes a regular routine, the teacher will simply need to give a very brief cue like: 'Ok, paired explanations, off you go.'

While the students are engaged in their paired explanations the teacher can circulate the room, listening for any obvious misunderstandings or errors, noting any particularly good examples[20] and ensuring students remain focused. If students aren't following the procedure correctly (they are just reading from their notes, for example) then the teacher may need to pause either a pair or the whole class to give some corrective feedback before resuming. At the end of this they could follow up with some questioning or use a whole-class response method such as a question answered on mini-whiteboards to get students to demonstrate their understanding.

Generative learning

'Generative learning' involves students being *active* in constructing their own meaning through integrating it with their pre-existing knowledge. Fiorella and Mayer (2016b) suggest eight useful generative learning strategies, many of which can be easily incorporated into classwork, homework or independent study. Good generative learning activities, as well as being beneficial for learning and making meaning in and of themselves, also provide useful variety in classroom and retrieval activities. The strategies are:

---

20 A helpful tip here is to have something to write on as you circulate. It's hard to remember all the things you have seen when circulating (as we know, working memory is limited!), so keep a note of what to mention, and whose work to highlight, as you go round.

- Summarising (see Section 3, 'Engaging with notes and other texts', page 205).
- Mapping (see Section 1, '**Make meaning**', 'Graphic advance organisers', page 80 and Section 2, 'Mapping the "shape" of a unit', page 164).
- Drawing (see at the end of this section, 'Example teaching segment: Synaptic transmission', page 108 and Section 3, 'The "shape" of a study', page 286).
- Imagining (see Section 3, 'Imagining studies', page 287 and 'Making meaning through predicting study evaluation', page 295).
- Self-testing (see Section 1, '**Review regularly**', page 93, Section 2, 'STAR tasks', page 179 and Section 5, 'Encouraging a culture of independent learning', page 449).
- Self-explaining (see Section 3, 'Verbal rehearsal', page 230).
- Teaching others (see Section 5, 'Encouraging a culture of independent learning', page 449).
- Enacting (see uses of embodied cognition in Section 3, 'Imagining studies', page 287).

Summary

- Richer understanding and more successful learning are achieved when we encourage students to **make meaning** through connecting new information to prior learning and requiring them to be active in the construction of their own knowledge.

Secure success

Allow students to feel competent by setting the right level of challenge.

Barak Rosenshine spent a career researching the features of effective teaching. One key finding was that the most effective teachers (those whose students performed better when practising alone) typically made a greater effort to ensure students succeeded on tasks during lessons. Rosenshine wrote that 'the optimal success rate for fostering student achievement appears to be about 80%.[21] Less than that and student understanding is likely not to be secure enough. More than that, Rosenshine argued, and the material may be too easy. This chimes with research looking at the optimal rate of success for learning from multiple-choice questions, which estimated that 77% was ideal (Butler, 2018), although others have argued for even higher success rates in some areas of classroom life. Brophy (1984), for example, wrote:

> It is important not only to maximize content coverage by pacing the students briskly through the curriculum, but also to see that they make continuous progress all along the way, moving through small steps with high (or at least moderate) rates of success and minimal confusion or frustration. Their [teachers'] questions must usually (about 75% of the time) yield correct answers and seldom yield no response at all; their seat work activities must be completed with 90–100% success by most students.

Other recent research has suggested optimal success rates as high as 94% (Eglington and Pavlik, 2020). Higher initial success increases self-efficacy and motivation in students, improving their ability to perform independently further down the line. Also, slightly easier questions can often be answered more quickly, allowing students to review more regularly and get more practice, maximising the efficiency of learning.

Take a moment to imagine what a class with a 94% (or even 80%) success rate would look like. It's likely very different to most classes we see (where success rates for questions tend to be closer to 40–50% (Still, 2023)). Rosenshine also lists some of the classroom behaviours that teachers can use to increase this level of initial success, such as presenting new information in small chunks to **manage cognitive load**, **checking what they know** very regularly (for example, by asking lots of questions) and then monitoring independent practice closely and giving corrective feedback, which improves future work.

To this, and building on the previous sections, we would add designing hierarchical curricula based around prerequisite knowledge, which provide the best chance of allowing students to make meaningful

---

21 Importantly, though, this does not necessarily have to be initial success. Success following practice and feedback is still success.

connections, and to apply their prior knowledge successfully to new material. Another method of ensuring high success rates is mastery learning, first proposed by Benjamin Bloom (1968), in which learners or the whole class have to reach a defined standard of 'mastery' (often 80% or above), before moving on to the next topic.

Mastery learning in psychology?

While mastery learning approaches may be more effectively applied in primary or maths classrooms, where 'mastery' may be easier to define (EEF, 2021), are there principles from this approach that we could apply to psychology? We think that teachers can aim to achieve mastery levels of learning for selected parts of the specification such as essential foundational or prerequisite knowledge, key research methods, maths skills or evaluation ideas (Shaw, 2023). Because **prior knowledge predicts future learning**, mastery of certain key ideas will also benefit students' ability to assimilate new ideas and topics later in the course.

It can be very freeing for teachers to be able to say (and students to be able to hear) something like:

> This is a really important concept for psychology and so it's important that we all master it. That's why we're going to quiz you on it next week. Fortunately, I know that we are all going to master it, as we'll keep going with it, and I will keep working with individuals until everyone here has achieved at least 80% on the quiz. It doesn't matter at all how many goes that takes, what matters is that I know that everyone has all of this information securely learned, because then as a class we can achieve loads more than we would otherwise.

Students don't want to give up their free time and so will usually make a concerted effort to avoid too many retakes, especially once they see that you are serious and will follow through in holding them to the expected standard (be sure to shuffle the order of items before each retake!). Also, once it has been achieved, it provides a (sometimes all too rare) opportunity to celebrate collective success in the classroom, safe in the knowledge that no-one is excluded.

Productive effort

In order to allow students to **secure success**, they require a level of motivation that can seem out of reach for some. They know they need to study hard in order to achieve it, but this can feel like too much effort for too little (perceived) gain. What can we take from motivational theories to help here?

As discussed in **'motivation drives, and is driven by, learning'**, self-determination theory suggests that competence and relatedness are key drivers of motivation. Therefore, students are more likely to engage in productive effort because they believe they know how to succeed (competence), meaning they are taught effective study strategies that are domain specific. In order to build relatedness, students need to identify as belonging to a group that values independent study.

Expectancy-value theory (Eccles, 1983) also offers some insights here. Students will study harder if they have experienced past success and therefore have higher expectations of success in the future. They will also study harder if they believe that success is worth the effort, which further underlines the importance of a classroom culture in which success is celebrated and that students can see the benefit of regular testing to their learning.

Finally, we also need to consider students' attributions. In order to motivate students to study hard, we need to narrate the outcomes of a test – success or failure – in ways that reinforce attributions around productive effort (Evans, 2023). Some students are excellent at doing precisely the opposite; those that do well claim they didn't really work hard or just got lucky. We need to highlight the productive effort that did occur while framing poor results in the opposite way.

Success (and failure) in different settings

Within a general framework of trying to increase the levels of success in the classroom, there are some differences in success rates that you can aim for in different activities.

Activity	Ideal success rate
Homework and independent tasks	Very high. Student resilience to challenge is lower when you are not there to encourage or scaffold, therefore aim to set homework tasks in which it is possible for all students to be successful the large majority of the time.
Regular seatwork in class	High. We want all students to end all lessons with examples of high-quality work that they can use in revision and as a model of quality when completing later assignments. However, as you are present here, this means there is more scope for initially challenging tasks that can then be scaffolded for success (see 'Levels of scaffolding in psychology' below).
Teacher questions	Mostly high. We want to ask questions that allow the vast majority of students to successfully contribute to the lesson, especially if using techniques such as cold-calling, However, other questioning techniques can, and should, be used to introduce greater levels of challenge.
Essays and exam questions	Initially high. Clearly at some point students will need to grapple with the full challenge of blending scientific and literacy skills – extended writing, timed conditions and all the rest. However, we would argue that this does *not* mean that we expose them to these things as early as possible (see Section 3, page 199). Delay the most challenging tasks until students have secured core knowledge, and scaffold heavily at first to allow all students to experience initial success.

A final consideration is whether there is a culture within the class to **feedforward** (see page 102). The more confident we can be that students will proactively address gaps in their learning and understanding, the lower our initial success rates can be. Bear in mind, however, that a habit of following up on feedback is also more likely to form early on in the course if students have experienced success and have only a small amount of feedback to follow up on.

Levels of scaffolding in psychology

If we are to vary the level of support that we provide our students for different tasks, then it can be very helpful to plan in advance the sorts of strategies that can be used at different levels. This idea is taken from history teacher Rachel Ball, who has written extensively on scaffolding[22] and who advises splitting scaffolding into three levels: heavy, medium and light. Doing this gives us a clear model for how we can fade the level of guidance provided as students develop greater expertise while still

---
22 For example, see Ball's book, *The Scaffolding Effect*, co-authored with Alex Fairlamb.

being confident that we are not fading it by so much that they will not still be able to **secure success**.

Heavy	Medium	Light
• Sentence starters for every sentence in the paragraphs, allowing students to add their own sentences on top of these. • The 'signpost'/topic/point sentence for each paragraph. • Examples of evidence which could be used. • 'Points' and 'so whats' provided for evaluation paragraphs, but 'because' (evidence) section missing. • A list of key words to be used in each paragraph with definitions. • Share detailed success criteria, e.g. as a checklist. • A teacher-created structure strip used to focus each part of the essay. • Detailed shared planning, for example, a whole class 'we write' attempt at a question. • Interrogation and annotation of a model answer, possibly before a 'we write' or 'you write' activity, as above. • Additional time given.	• A choice of sentence starters to choose from for each paragraph. • Evaluation issue for each paragraph is provided. • Page numbers where supporting evidence can be found. • A list of key words to be used. • Share shortened success criteria. • Shared planning used first, for example, a table with evidence that should be used. • A 'we write' question followed by a similar 'you write'. • Annotation of a model answer followed by a 'you write' of a similar answer. • Live marking of student answers to demonstrate good parts of the answer or ensure students do not have misconceptions. • A student-created structure strip used in essay production. • Essay-specific exam mark scheme.	• Number of paragraphs needed, and which assessment objective targeted. • Relevant textbook/booklet page numbers. • Generic exam mark scheme. • Live marking of individual answers during circulation.

Even after the removal of all scaffolding, we do not necessarily leave students to fend entirely for themselves. We want to still support them to learn independently (see 'Encouraging a culture of independent learning' in Section 5, page 449).

In-lesson support and differentiation

One of the most common areas that teachers identify as challenging is differentiation. Many teachers have traditionally been encouraged (or trained) to approach differentiation *pre-emptively*, in advance of the lesson. Planning activities for different sub-groups within our classes (such as target grades or learning styles) would be examples of this, but so are contrasting approaches such as 'teaching to the top'. The danger of all of these pre-emptive approaches to differentiation is that they are essentially backwards; in other words, predetermining the level of support based on presumed (but actually unpredictable) outcomes.

We believe that the most effective approach is one that is responsive, not pre-emptive. Rather than determining what students can do before they start and planning accordingly, we should determine how well students are progressing and then adapt our support accordingly. This doesn't mean we necessarily do everything 'on the fly' – we may still have materials planned and prepared to stretch, support or scaffold in various ways, but the difference is that we choose to deploy them as and when we think they are needed, not in advance.

Summary

- In order for students to feel successful, we need to carefully plan learning with respect to cognitive load and prior knowledge and deploy a range of scaffolding techniques to respond to different learners' needs.

Review regularly

Strengthen memories over time by retrieving and reconsolidating learning.

In Section 1A, we established that **learning requires repeated hard thinking**, and as a part of that we established that retrieval practice has been found to be a highly effective learning strategy in educational settings (Kornell and Vaughn, 2016; Roediger and Karpicke, 2018; Yang et al., 2020). In a classroom, retrieval activities may involve the use of low-stakes testing (written or verbal questions), prediction, pair or self-explanation or other activities designed to actively challenge students to access information from long-term memory. These sorts of strategies increase both storage strength (how deeply integrated and interconnected memories are) and retrieval strength (how accessible the memories are) of learned information (Bjork and Bjork, 1992), including in many studies using real-life educational and classroom settings (Yang et al., 2020) and even specifically in A-level psychology classrooms (Marsh, 2024).

Pan et al. (2023) give four recommendations for successful retrieval practice in classrooms.

- Retrieval must involve 'genuine, effortful attempts to retrieve information from memory'.
- Retrieval is best when it is low stakes. This means not collecting or reporting marks, scores, percentages or grades.
- Retrieval should encompass feedback that includes correct (or high quality) answers (to help ensure that the review can **feedforward** into new learning, see page 102). Retrieval should be repeated regularly.

The WHAT mindset: Why retrieval practice?

Retrieval works for any age, phase, subject or learner, but should not necessarily look the same in all circumstances; this means considering what useful retrieval looks like for psychology specifically. It's also the case that retrieval can happen at any point during a lesson; there are many good reasons to consider starting lessons with some retrieval, but this doesn't mean it should only happen then or that every lesson must start this way (despite what some school policies may state). Teachers' experiences with retrieval practice are often a good example of the importance of the 'W' stage of the **WHAT mindset**: knowing 'why'.

Philippa decides that she would like to start lessons with a regular routine of retrieval practice and opts to spend five minutes every day reviewing the learning from the last lesson. She puts up three questions on the last lesson – which was an introduction to twin studies – and asks her students to discuss the answers with one another.

> As she moves around the class listening to the discussions, Philippa thinks the details recalled sound pretty good, but she finds that when she introduces new information, a number of her students are not able to meaningfully connect that information to the previous topic, and so are only able to provide very superficial answers. Why is the review not helping?
>
> If Philippa doesn't know about why retrieval practice activities are likely to be effective for learning, she may struggle to understand how to adapt her routine. She may even get rid of it entirely. But knowing that **learning requires repeated hard thinking**, and that this hard thinking should involve actively bringing information to mind from memory, will help her to reflect and adjust.
>
> Perhaps not all students are actually retrieving to the same degree, with some pair members dominating the conversation or some looking up the information as they report it to their partner. This could be remedied through more structured discussion routines by banning the use of notes during the quiz or by asking all students to first write answers from memory, prior to the discussion phase. Whatever the right answer for Philippa's classroom, she is more likely to find it through a combination of knowing her class and understanding why retrieval practice is likely to work in the first place.

What to review?

It's simply not feasible for students to have regular retrieval practice of every possible piece of information that they will need over the course of a two-year GCSE or A-level course. As a result, we need to think carefully about what we ask students to review and the amount of information that we include. We recommend:

- Identifying information that forms the 'core' of the subject, and which as a result has the most connections to other parts of the specification. This core knowledge can then form the basis for curriculum building (see Section 2, 'Core and hinterland', page 143) and early assessment (see Section 4', page 377).

- Considering a mastery learning approach for essential foundational or prerequisite knowledge (as seen in the previous section '**Secure success**').
- Codifying broader core knowledge into a 'core questions curriculum' (see Section 2, 'Core questions in psychology', page 147), which allows for targeted lesson planning and learning outcomes (see Section 3, page 199) and helps students to self-test core knowledge in independent learning (see Section 5, 'Encouraging a culture of independent learning', page 449).

When to review?

Retrieval should be from long-term memory. This means we should utilise spaced practice with suitable (and increasing) gaps between learning and subsequent retrieval episodes. We may also consider varying retrieval frequency as a result of:

- The extent to which certain knowledge is required as prerequisite knowledge for new topics (as seen in '**Check what they know**').
- The extent to which new information is liable to become confused with existing information. In this case, retrieval and interleaving of the related concepts with the new information may be useful to help students discriminate between similar concepts they might otherwise confuse. This helps students to **make meaning**.

How to review?

If we want to review information regularly, it is also useful to consider whether you want to vary the form of review (for example, the retrieval practice activity you use). There is a balance to be struck here. As we have seen, **positive habits free up processing capacity**, and as a result, clearly defined lesson routines around retrieval can be hugely helpful. Within this, however, we also want space for variety, not just because students may appreciate a change now and then but also because posing different questions to access the same knowledge helps students to form multiple paths to that knowledge. (In technical terms, it increases 'retrieval strength' as it allows multiple routes to access and makes it more likely that we are observing learning, rather than just performance. This also increases the chances that students will be able to flexibly transfer their understanding to new situations (see Section 2, 'Making meaning and "flexible" exam thinking', page 159). This could therefore mean having a retrieval routine that at times includes (among other possibilities):

- Core questions (see Section 4, 'Formative assessment in psychology', page 371).
- Multiple-choice questions (see Section 4, 'Formative assessment in psychology', page 371).
- 'Goal free' challenges (see 'Making meaning through prediction - predicting research methods questions (and scenarios)' in Section 3B, page 237).
- Mind maps and advance organisers (see Section 2, 'Mapping the "shape" of a unit', page 164).
- Exam questions (see sections 3 and 4).
- Flash essay plans (see Section 3, '"Flash planning" – the ultimate essay challenge', page 355).

You may feel that such variety in retrieval should also include variety in assessment objectives targeted, and we would not disagree with this. However, Badali and Greve (2023) found that retrieval practice of core knowledge also works to improve performance on application questions that use that knowledge, so this suggests that we shouldn't get too bogged down in trying to find questions that target every assessment objective for every piece of core knowledge, as long as we are encouraging regular review of that knowledge.

Using hints to make meaning

Rather than just relentlessly 'testing' students', research suggests that the retrieval strength of schemas (and the ability to successfully integrate new information into them) is maximised if the schema is 'rewarmed' by being reactivated during or shortly before new learning (Guo and Yang, 2023). Importantly, this reactivation does not need to be pure retrieval from memory. Contextual cues can be more extensive for rewarming, as our goal here is simply to reactivate the schema and prepare it for effective further learning (Vaughn and Cornell, 2019), so don't worry too much about giving hints and prompts (at least initially).

How often to review?

In a paper on how to teach for mastery learning, Engelmann (1999) wrote the following:

> A program design that supports mastery does not present great amounts of new information and skill training in each lesson. Rather, work is distributed so new parts in a lesson account for only 10–15% of the total lesson. The rest of the lesson firms and reviews material and skills presented earlier in the program.

A lesson with an 85:15 split in favour of reviewing old content seems completely alien to how most secondary school lessons are structured. As we have already said, we are unlikely to have the capacity to aim for mastery in all but a few select areas, but even without this aim the sheer amount of time that is recommended for review raises questions for us as teachers.

While we would not mandate particular time ratios for retrieval, nor expectations for exactly when in lessons it happens (schools that do this are likely failing at the first step of the **WHAT mindset**), we do think that review should be prioritised at least as much as the delivery of new content. This means being happy to spend up to half of lessons (or more if required) on review. If some of the review has been targeted at prerequisite knowledge, then it should also facilitate the learning of new content subsequently anyway, making the time investment well worth it.

Case study: Creating a culture of retrieval throughout the curriculum

One of us has implemented a system for embedding retrieval throughout the year to counter the problem that, without explicit direction, students in the second year of the course rarely review material from the first year and therefore find themselves with a huge mountain to climb when the mocks come around. This involved mapping out a list of topics against the school calendar, then breaking the topics down into subtopics (in this case based around the Edexcel specification):

Section 1: The teaching framework

Date	Topic	Subtopic	Specified content
12/09	Social	Obedience – Theories	Agency and social impact theory
19/09	Cognitive	Memory	MSM/WMM
26/09	Biological	Nervous system	Neuronal and synaptic transmissions, Drugs
03/10	Learning	CC/OC	Theory and application to phobia
10/10	Methods	Self-reports	Questionnaires and interviews
31/10	Methods	Data analysis	Stats tests criteria
07/11	Social	Obedience – Research	Milgram & Burger
14/11	Cognitive	Memory	Recon/LTM
21/11	Biological	Aggression	Hormones and brains
28/11	Learning	SLT & Bandura	Theory, 3x Bandura variations
05/12	Methods	Experiments	Types, designs, variables
12/12	Methods	Data analysis	Central tendency and dispersion
05/01			
06/01			
09/01	Social	Prejudice – Theories	RCT/SIT
16/01	Cognitive	Research	Baddeley, Sebastian & Hernandez-Gil
23/01	Biological	Aggression	Evol & Freud
30/01	Learning	Research	Watson & Rayner, Bastian
06/02	Methods	Biological methods	Correlation, Brain scans, Twin studies
13/02			

The rationale behind this, and how the process works, is explained to students. Each week in one of their lessons there is a short quiz on the topic specified in the schedule. The schedule is published on Google Classroom (used to set all homework), and it's an easy task to update the deadline each week, so it always shows up on their to-do lists. The topic schedule is published in advance, so it doesn't feel overly challenging for students. The most important purpose here is not to get them to answer the questions in class, but to ensure regular, ongoing and purposeful review of material during their independent study. Knowing it could be *any* material from last year would be way too daunting and ultimately lead to far less success.

The quizzes are always at the start of the lesson and are completed on mini-whiteboards. There are typically only 1–3 questions, ranging in style and including things like straight factual recall ('what is an action potential'), evaluation ('give one strength and one weakness of an independent groups design') or application questions ('Jodi has a fear of clowns, how might this be explained by classical conditioning').

These quizzes are deliberately low-stakes (nothing is scored or recorded), although there is time to go through answers and give corrective feedback. As well as the opportunity for retrieval, this may also help identify any significant gaps or errors in knowledge that can be considered for future reteaching.

'A culture of error': Celebrate mistakes – and forgetting!

Psychology teachers don't need to be told that forgetting is a normal fundamental process in human learning. Firstly, we often teach it in our courses, and secondly, we get the chance to marvel every year at just how comprehensively some students appear able to forget almost anything we think we've taught them!

However, children – and adults – routinely overestimate their ability to remember academic information and complete academic tasks (Xia et al., 2023). As a result, they are often not aware of just how normal, and in fact *essential*, forgetting is to learning (as we lose surface details we gain 'gist', seeing deeper underlying meanings and connections between different memories (Ryan and Frankland, 2022)), associating it instead with failure.

Retrieval activities are challenging because they highlight this so powerfully and could be understandably demoralising if we aren't careful in how they are managed. We therefore need to **share the rationale** for what we are doing when we **review regularly**, and why. This is central to the creation of a *culture of error*, where it is understood by students that error is an essential part of learning and that the response to error is far more important than the initial mistake. Otherwise, students will take easy and less threatening routes, such as leaving answers blank, going straight to their notes or waiting for peers to provide the answers. A positive culture of error also helps to improve our relationships with students themselves (Steuer et al., 2024), as they are less likely to fear negative reprisals for the unavoidable instances where they can't remember something!

Therefore, keeping student participation and thinking ratios high during challenging activities like retrieval requires careful groundwork and structure, and students will need to be helped not to fear failure. Two research findings that we find especially powerful in assisting with this last process are:

- Kornell and Vaughn (2016), who found that retrieval failure with corrective feedback (i.e. getting the answer wrong, but then correcting yourself) was as effective for future learning as retrieval success.
- Kliegl et al. (2023), who found that having a guess on a quiz question for which we don't know the answer is more effective for learning than simply studying later (analogous to leaving an answer blank and waiting for the right answer to be given).

Putting all this together, introducing an activity in class could sound like this:

> We are about to have a go at some retrieval questions on reliability and validity. It's something we covered a while ago but is relevant to what we're about to learn. Make sure you are actively trying to recall the answers from your own memory, as this will help you learn better than looking them up or copying someone else. You may experience retrieval failure but don't worry – that's fine and completely normal. But don't leave blanks – have a go. Even if it's just a guess, then the feedback you get on your retrieval effort will make it more likely you are successful next time. I know and don't care that you will forget things; what's important is that you use this information to take action. When you've identified what you can't remember, this is useful feedback that will direct you to do more self-study on these areas. Ok, here are the questions, five minutes to answer – go.

This then needs to be backed up with action on the part of the teacher. We need to circulate the class and check not just *that* they are writing, but *what* they are writing. This picks up on any 'busy tricking',[23] but it also allows the chance for us to give live feedback, sample the

---

23 A term coined by Adam Boxer to describe student actions like writing the date and title to make it look like they're doing something purposeful.

class understanding of the material and potentially adapt subsequent teaching responsively.

Finally, since retrieval failure will only be helpful if corrective feedback is given, processed and acted upon, it's also important to establish routines to assist with this. Some combination of peer discussion, learning resources and teaching can be used when reviewing answers. Regardless of the exact feedback routine, however, the most important principle is that students then go away and do something with the feedback.

Summary

- In order to strengthen students' schemas, we need to use a range of 'genuine' retrieval strategies that help consolidate core knowledge, identify gaps and provide feedback. Ensuring a culture of error around this will help students engage with the process better.

Feedforward

Provide feedback that moves learners forward in what they know and can do.

Process over task

In the learning fundamentals, we saw that **feedback must change learners for the better** and we introduced the definition of feedback suggested by Carless and Boud (2018) of 'a process through which learners make sense of information from various sources and use it to enhance their work or learning strategies'. The wording here is important; Carless and Boud point to the crucial importance of feedback being used to change something *in the future*, in other words for feedback to **feedforward**. It is, in the words of Hattie and Timperley (2007), about asking, 'Where am I going?' rather than 'How have I done?' Teachers who engage students actively with understanding their errors, rather than spending time simply getting them to the right answer, have students who show larger learning gains (Metcalfe et al., 2024). In order to do this, the attention of both students and teachers needs to be on improving the *process*, rather than the task.

The obvious place to start when thinking about feedback may appear to be how a teacher should give it, but if we want feedback to **feedforward** then we need learners to use the information they receive to make progress. As a result, we need to start with the students themselves. Building on Carless and Boud (2018), we think that there are four key steps to aim for to create 'feedback literate' psychology students (students who will seek out, welcome and act effectively on feedback). When provided with feedback, we want our students to appreciate it, manage emotions, make judgements and follow up.[24]

Appreciating feedback

> Fraser is starting his lesson with a quiz on some previous learning that will be important prerequisite knowledge for a new upcoming topic. He is keen to make sure that students engage with the quiz and identify any gaps in their knowledge. However, the last time he gave students a quiz and used cold-calling to collect answers in class, four of the group came up at the end of the lesson saying they were unsure and asked him to mark their work to 'check that they got it right'.

Sometimes what students view as a perfectly reasonable question can reveal a whole host of misunderstandings and issues. Here, Fraser's students have simultaneously revealed that they have missed the point of the assessment in the first place and that they have not taken any feedback offered on board (or perhaps that they have not engaged with it enough to even be aware of when useful feedback was occurring). Students' ideas about knowledge are often absolutist; in other words, they have a tendency to view nuanced ideas as simply either right or wrong. As a result, they show a preference for 'corrective' feedback, which merely tells them which parts of their work are 'wrong' and gives them replacement answers which are 'right' (O'Donovan, 2017).

Interestingly, even when students are able to accurately report that the purpose of feedback is to improve the process, when reflecting on what their ideal feedback would contain, students still often prefer task-focused feedback (Van Boekel et al., 2023). The feedback our students want may

---

24 If you are interested, you can freely access an academic tool used for measuring students' feedback literacy: Dawson, P., Yan, Z., Lipnevich, A., Tai, J., Boud, D., & Mahoney, P. (2023). Measuring what learners do in feedback: The feedback literacy behaviour scale. *Assessment & Evaluation in Higher Education*, 1–15. https://doi.org/10.1080/02602938.2023.2240983

not always be the feedback they need! In psychology, answers are rarely simple, and feedback is rarely unequivocally corrective. As a result, if we are to avoid the situation that Fraser has experienced here, students must be encouraged to adopt and embrace new and more sophisticated beliefs about feedback, in order to properly understand why they are getting the feedback they are getting and what to do about it. We discuss a number of these in Section 4, including:

- Helping students to understand that feedback is not learning
- Alerting students to the range of experiences that contribute assessment opportunities and provide them with useful feedback
- Giving feedback that encourages students to carefully process and appreciate it, such as:
  - Delayed feedback
  - Partial feedback

Managing emotion

Feedback, as the saying goes, is a gift. Rather more often though, it can feel to many of our students like a curse. Even the most well-intentioned and supportive feedback can easily feel threatening or provoke an emotional response in the recipient. We know this, because it happens to us – all of us – all the time.

As teachers, we need to always bear in mind the power we wield in this regard. And yet the solution is not to shy away from wielding this power, as to do so would be to neglect using one of our most powerful potential tools for student development. Instead, we need to help students to contextualise and depersonalise the more threatening aspects of feedback, in order to manage their feedback emotions. Again, we will discuss strategies for achieving this more in Section 4, for example through:

- Acknowledging the emotion associated with feedback (page 365).
- Reducing competition in the classroom (page 401).
- Using specific strategies to target more severe test anxiety in affected students (page 365).
- Modelling how feedback is received (page 366).

- Encouraging a culture of error (see **Review regularly**, 'A culture of error: Celebrate mistakes, and forgetting!').

Making judgements

We all know that students who are able to make sound academic judgements about the quality of work will be able to produce work of a high standard and will also be well placed to act on feedback provided to them. However, it can often seem that the activities we do in class to encourage students to make judgements put the cart before the horse – the students who are able to peer and self-assess already are the ones who are probably writing the best quality answers and so don't need the practice, while the students who need the practice struggle to assess accurately or provide any useful feedback. Rectifying this situation frequently promises to take up more time than we have available, given the many other constraints of the curriculum, meaning the apparent time savings are never realised.

The struggle with peer and self-assessment is a good example of the 'curse of expertise'. It can seem obvious to us what differentiates a good answer from a poor one, or what extra information will need to be included in order to fully elaborate on a point. As a result, it can be frustrating when students lack these abilities, and also difficult to know exactly how to teach them given that much of our expertise is implicit. In Section 4 we discuss a range of strategies that can help students to more accurately make judgements about the quality of their work.

Taking action

Taking action is perhaps the most fundamental requirement of feedback. After all, if feedback is defined as learners using information to make changes, if nothing changes then no feedback has been provided. Many of the systems described in the previous sections make it easier to support students in acting on feedback (and to hold them to account for doing so). But what else can we do to ensure that, in Dylan Wiliam's maxim, 'feedback should be more work for the student than for the teacher?' We can encourage this by:

- Giving it time (see Section 4, 'Reviewing essays', page 396).
- Carving out time within classroom routines to follow up on feedback, such as providing a chance to 'do it again, better' (see Section 4, 'Reviewing essays', page 396).

- Record keeping or targets carried forward (see Section 4, 'Reviewing essays', page 396).
- Triangulated homework and independent learning tasks that require students to follow up on feedback.

Case study: Creating a new classroom routine of feedforward accountability

How can we get students to **feedforward**, not just for larger written tasks but also on the multiple other sources of feedback that they may receive in a lesson, such as verbal corrections or written annotations? Of course, it's easy to tell students that they should follow up on any gaps that they discover in their knowledge, but can we create a habit environment that allows them to do this more regularly? Here is one method that has proved successful in one of our classrooms recently:

1. Ask a question (or questions) based on the core knowledge that you expect every student to know. For example, this could be in the form of their usual starter quiz (pictured below), but it could also be verbal or in some other form at any point in the lesson. Answers are usually cold-called following individual thinking or writing time, although after writing some time for paired discussion can also be built in as an additional layer of support, providing students know they need to follow up on any useful feedback that they receive in this stage as well.

	Core questions	Question number for reference in case of 'follow-up'
1	Define 'demand characteristics'.	16
2	How did introspection make psychology more scientific?	9
3	What are the limitations of introspection?	8
4	How is the behaviourist approach used to treat phobias (two ways)?	663
5	Explain how a phobia is maintained.	662
6	Explain how a phobia is acquired.	661

2. If a student doesn't have a correct (or high-quality enough) answer, then note the name and question number in your planner in the space for the next lesson for that class. The question can then be bounced around to a few other members of the class. If their answers are also shaky, then I write 'all' instead of the student's name next to the number. The student (or class) is told that they will get that question again next lesson (all students have a copy of all the core knowledge questions and answers in advance, so it is easy for them to refer back to these).

3. In the next lesson, add any 'repeat questions' from the previous lesson onto the end of the starter questions, and direct the appropriate question to the individual written down. If it is an 'all' question, then ask all students to discuss the answer in pairs and then cold-call students to answer in the usual manner.

4. Importantly, once you get a correct (or improved) answer to a question, this provides scope for celebration of new learning and the reinforcement of a culture of error, where you normalise mistakes and shift the focus on to how a student responds to finding a gap in their knowledge.

5. You can also have dedicated weekly homework tasks to 'follow up on feedback', where students are required to show how they have responded to any aspect of the previous week's learning that identified a gap in their understanding. Often, this may include following up on gaps identified from the starter questions (for example, by making flashcards or looking at practice questions on that topic), regardless of whether they were cold-called for the question or not (students should be annotating their answers as they review them and encouraged to follow up on any questions that required substantial annotation). In this way, you hopefully move from only targeting students who happen to be caught out by the cold-calling to a more general culture of accountability and personal responsibility.

Summary
- Feedback, which needs to be delivered carefully to ensure it is well received, should focus on how to improve learning, but is unlikely to have impact unless we build in specific routines to allow students to act upon their feedback.

What does this look like in the classroom?

Let's return to Lauren. How might she apply some of the pedagogical principles in her teaching? We'll consider a couple of different topics that Lauren is likely to cover during the first year of the course: synaptic transmission and schemas. Both topics can be considered pretty foundational as many later topics will draw on these ideas, and students' ability to learn those more complex topics depends on a solid understanding of these fundamental concepts. As noted in the introduction, there is no one right way of teaching any particular area of content in psychology, and so the teaching sequences outlined below represent just two different approaches. After describing each teaching sequence we'll consider what they have in common, where they may differ and how they exemplify various pedagogical principles.

Example teaching segment – Synaptic transmission

Lauren is about to teach her Year 12 class about synaptic transmission. She knows this is crucial for them to learn well, as they will be drawing upon this knowledge in lots of different areas of the course later on, for example, looking at neurotransmitter explanations for disorders like schizophrenia or drug treatments for depression. This topic appears relatively near the start of the biological approach, and in her previous lessons she has covered the major assumptions of the approach, the general distinction between neuronal and synaptic transmission and some key differences, the structure of neurons and the process of neuronal transmission. Lauren got as far as the fact that the action potential reaches the axon terminal.

Lauren starts her lesson with some retrieval questions to activate relevant prior knowledge:

1. What is the major assumption of the biological approach?	That all human experience has a biological basis which stems from the nervous system.
2. Explain two differences between neuronal and synaptic transmission.	Neuronal transmission uses electrical signals within neurons, synaptic transmission uses chemical signals between neurons.
3. Draw and label a neuron. (She's hoping for something that looks like this →)	Dendrites, Axon, Nodes of Ranvier, Terminal button, Myelin sheath, Schwann cell, Cell body, Nucleus, Dendrites

Once she has checked the answers and responded to any obvious errors or misunderstandings, she gives them another task – this time a verbal one – to assess their knowledge and understanding further:

In pairs, turn to your partner and, using your diagram, explain how an action potential travels along the neuron. Partners, you need to listen to what the other person is saying to check for accuracy and ask questions if you think your partner needs to clarify or explain something.

Once Lauren is satisfied that her students are suitably 'warmed up' in terms of prior knowledge, she is ready to start with the new information. She is aware that some students find this material more challenging, and that technical descriptions of biological processes may not seem like the 'kind of psychology' students thought they were signing up for – especially for the second lesson in a row! Lauren needs a nice hook to make it clear to students why this information is both interesting and important, so she says: OK everyone, here's a question. Why do people take drugs?

She's got their interest straight away, so she follows with:

Why are cigarettes addictive? Why does cannabis give you the munchies? Do antidepressants actually make you happy? These are some interesting and important questions, and as psychologists we want to know the answers. But we're not going to really understand those answers unless we get a handle on the biological system that underpins it all. So, what we're learning today is going to help you answer some of those questions. We're going to talk about synaptic transmission – how neurons communicate with one another. This information is crucial for you later in the course. You're going to look at disorders like schizophrenia and depression and learn about the causes and treatments of them. Understanding that starts here.

Lauren uses the board to present the image she used at the end of the last lesson (a zoomed in diagram of the axon terminal with a diagram of a neuron inset) to remind them of the context.

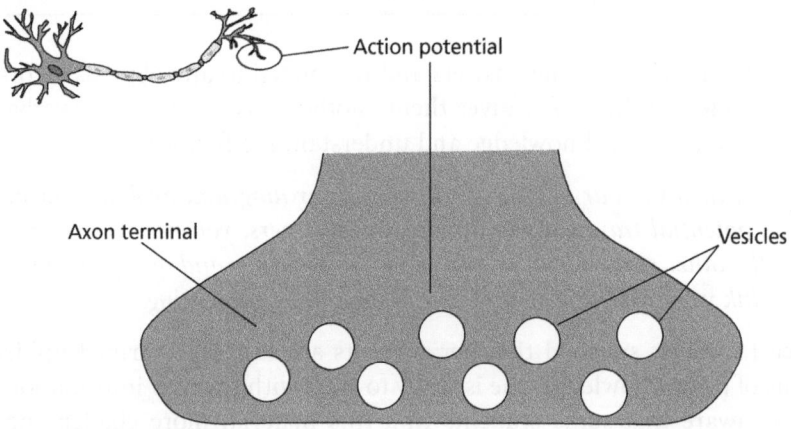

OK, what we're going to do now is pick up the story from here and explain what happens next. We're now moving from neuronal transmission to synaptic transmission. Remember this is about chemical communication between neurons, as opposed to the electrical communication that happens within neurons. In order to do that, we're going to create a storyboard of diagrams to map out the sequence of synaptic transmission.

Section 1: The teaching framework

The students receive a sheet that looks like this:

Synaptic transmission

1.	2.	3.
4.	5.	6.

Lauren quickly divides up the whiteboard into six boxes to match the students' sheet.

Right. Pens down to start, look this way. I'm going to draw something on the board, explain what it is, and label each bit. Then I want you to copy it – don't pick up your pen until I say 'go'.

She draws and labels the first diagram – narrating as she goes – which looks like this:

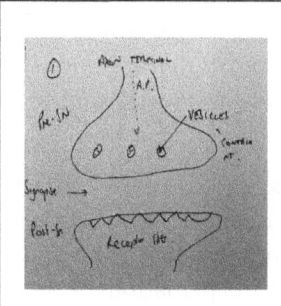	*This is the axon terminal of the pre-synaptic neuron. This contains sac-like structures called vesicles. Here's the action potential that travels down the axon.* *Down here is the dendrite of the next neuron, called the post-synaptic neuron. The gap between them is called the synapse. 'Pre' means before, 'post' means after.* *There are receptor sites on the post-synaptic neuron.* *In a moment you can copy this. Make sure your diagram is labelled accurately. Don't worry about how neat or pretty it looks – this is science, not art! OK, go.*

As the students draw their own version, Lauren circulates to make sure they all look fine and notes any that look particularly good for possible future sharing.

Great job everyone, now onto stage two.

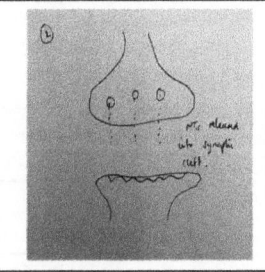	Vesicles synthesise (create) chemicals called neurotransmitters. Examples of neurotransmitters are serotonin and dopamine. When the action potential reaches the vesicles, they release neurotransmitters into the synapse (also known as the synaptic cleft). Your turn – copy that down.

Nice diagrams everyone, what a bunch of lovely neurons!

We're going to pause for a second now for you to recap the story so far. In a moment, you're going to turn to your partner and explain the sequence your two diagrams show. Remember that you'll need to point at your diagrams as you go along to help your explanation. Don't forget to include all key terms and be sure to explain these terms rather than just naming them. Think about the connectives you use – we're describing a sequence here, so you need to say things like 'this leads to' or 'which causes'. Partners, as always you need to listen to what the other person is saying to check for accuracy and ask questions if you think your partner needs to clarify or explain something. Then it's your turn to practise explaining for yourself. Go!

Lauren circulates to listen in on her students' explanations, offering corrective feedback as necessary. She then continues the teaching sequence in the same way, adding two more diagrams to the storyboard and giving another opportunity for students to rehearse their explanations with the new information added on, before adding the final two diagrams in the sequence. The finished storyboard looks like this:

Section 1: The teaching framework

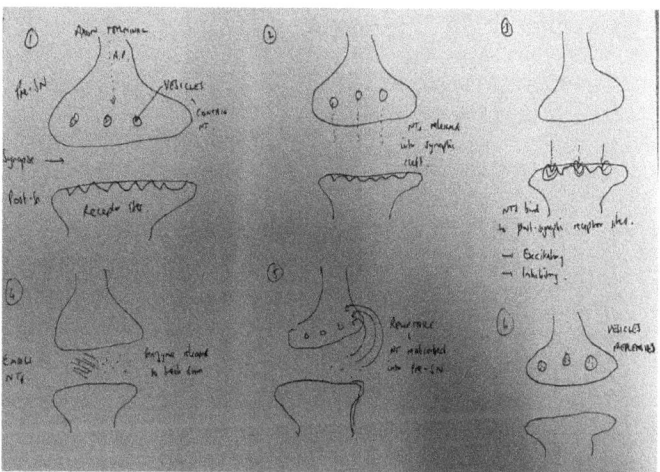

As the students complete their final explanations, Lauren circulates again, looking to fine-tune any points and answering some of the students' questions.

Before finishing the lesson, Lauren wants to do a final summary check for understanding. Depending on the class and time available, Lauren could do one (or more) of the following:

Activity	Example
Some quick mini-whiteboard questions	• What happens when the action potential reaches the axon terminal? • What's the difference between an excitatory and an inhibitory neurotransmitter? • What two things happen to the excess neurotransmitter in the synapse?
A gap-fill (cloze) exercise (NB whether to include the word bank at the bottom will depend on the context of the class; or, it could be a resource made available to students if they need extra support.)	**Synaptic transmission** When an _____ _____ reaches the _____ _____, _____ are released from _____ in the _____ neuron into the _____ _____. The neurotransmitter binds to _____ _____ on the _____ neuron, which either has an _____ or _____ effect, causing the postsynaptic neuron to be more or less likely to fire. Excess neurotransmitter is either broken down by _____, or reabsorbed into the presynaptic neuron through _____. | Vesicles | Receptor sites | Axon terminal | Inhibitory | Neurotransmitters | Postsynaptic | | Synaptic cleft | Action potential | Enzymes | Presynaptic | Reuptake | Excitatory |

Activity	Example
An non-scaffolded writing task (Again, a word bank can be made available if needed.)	Produce a short paragraph explaining the process of synaptic transmission.

These activities may expose some gaps or misconceptions that need to be addressed right away (a very common misconception, for example, is that neurotransmitters actually enter the postsynaptic neuron after binding to receptors), but otherwise Lauren is ready to move on to the next topic. She will be sure to do some retrieval practice on this soon, and to think about reactivating this knowledge whenever students are going to learn about topics like biological explanations and treatments.

Depending on the class or what's coming up in the scheme of work, Lauren could ask some more open-ended, higher-order questions to promote deeper thinking, such as:

- What do you think could happen if someone has too much or too little of a neurotransmitter?
- What do you think could happen if we blocked the process of reuptake?

Example teaching segment – Schema theory

Lauren is planning how to introduce her students to schema theory. In the lesson before, she introduced the cognitive approach (following on from behaviourism and SLT). Although schemas are a topic that do not require extensive prerequisite knowledge, Lauren identifies two core questions from the previous lesson that are especially relevant to the introduction of schemas, and so she includes these in her starter questions (among some others).

Core questions	Suggested answers
What are the key ideas underlying the cognitive approach?	• Behaviour results from cognitive processes, e.g. perception, language, attention, or memory. • Inferences about processes can be made from examining resulting behaviours. • The mind functions like a computer ('the computer analogy'). • Schemas.
Why do cognitive psychologists reject the behaviourist's explanation of learning as a result of random trial and error?	They argue that cognitive processes are important for behaviour (behaviourists thought that the mind was irrelevant), and that cognitive processes operate in an organised and systematic manner.

Having reviewed the starter questions and checked – as carefully as possible – the understanding of the class on the key features and assumptions of the cognitive approach, Lauren divides the whiteboard in two and labels one half 'male' and one half 'female'.

> OK, so the cognitive approach suggests we have thought processes that operate in an 'organised and systematic manner'. But what does that really mean? Let's think about how we can organise information in our minds.
>
> If you are handed a marker pen, I'd like you to write one word on the board that may be associated with either the word 'male' or the word 'female'. These can be based on your own personal opinion, or on characteristics that you think society associates with these categories – I don't mind. Pass the pen on to someone else when you are done, but be ready to add another one if someone else gives you a pen! We'll go for two minutes and collect as many as we can.

After two minutes the board looks like this:

```
  Brave           Tall           Caring                  Small
                                          Teacher
         Football
                                                     Loving
    Confident     Strong

  Unemotional  [ Male ]         Emotional   [ Female ]
                    Aggressive                         Passive

    Soldier      Practical        Weak
                                           Nurse
   Honest                                            Domestic
                                 Childcare
            Energetic
```

You're going to discuss this board with your partner for a little bit. Start with the first contribution from the person on the left of the pair and tell each other how the board makes you feel.

After a minute or so, Lauren brings the discussion to a halt.

OK, great. Walking round the room, it's clear that some of you are made quite angry by this. I heard words like 'stereotype' (which is a great psychological word), 'stupid' (a slightly less technical one!), 'too simplistic' and so on. This is a perfectly natural reaction to seeing something like this, and I feel the same way.

I'm going to give this framework of connected ideas a name, which we will use a lot from now on in lots of parts of our course. We will call things like this a schema. A schema is a set of connected ideas about something. The technical term for this – and I want you to listen carefully as I'll be quizzing you on this soon – is a 'mental framework'.

We're going to have one more discussion, and I would like the other member of the pair to start it off. This time the question is: 'Where does something like this come from? Why do we end up with schemas like this?'

Section 1: The teaching framework

Lauren allows the students to discuss for another minute while circulating. She then cold-calls responses (though this could be informed by what she has heard while circulating), looking to draw out the message that schemas are a product of our *experiences*. Lauren writes the word 'schema' on the board.

That's an important point. The schemas on the board are just examples, but we will all have slightly different schemas, even for very familiar things, because of our different experiences. What was the description for what a schema was that I gave you a minute ago, Delvin? That's right – a 'mental framework'. And where did we say that schemas come from, Evie? Yes – from experience. Let's add those together to make a proper definition.

Lauren then writes on the board: 'Schema: a mental framework, learned from experience, that contains beliefs and expectations about the world'.

Removing the definition from the board, Lauren projects the following question, which allows for a quick check of understanding.

Which of these describes a schema? Pick as many as you think are correct.

(a) Society's ideas

(b) Mental framework

(c) Learned through experience

(d) Beliefs and expectations about the world

It is deliberately vague on the number of answers to select (given they have only just been exposed to the material), and also targets the most likely misconception at this stage: that schemas are 'external' products of society rather than unique internal structures. If students are not confidently answering (b), (c) and (d) (or a number are answering (a)), then Lauren can repeat the above with a different example and re-emphasise the relevant points.

> *Let's have some practice at thinking about what your different schemas may look like. We have looked so far at 'gender' schemas, but we have schemas for pretty much any object, action or concept. Let's take a different example. In the middle of your whiteboards, draw a box and write 'teacher'. Have we all done that? Ok, eyes back on me and pens down. This is a different example to the gender one, but the same ideas apply. Remember, a schema is a 'mental framework of beliefs and expectations about the world', so it should just contain everything that you know – or expect to be the case – about the concept. You have two minutes now to write down your schema for 'teacher'. Be nice!*
>
> [Once two minutes have passed.]
>
> *We call schemas like the ones for 'teacher' (or 'male', 'female', 'parent' and so on) role schemas, as they contain ideas about the behaviour that is expected from someone in a certain role, setting or situation. Another type of schema is an event schema, which contains our beliefs and expectations for what happens in a given scenario.*
>
> *Let's try representing an event schema now. Event schemas are often divided into sequences, so if you find this hard at first, try to break it down into a series of steps. In the next two minutes, write your schema for 'going to a restaurant'.*[25]

Students can then complete a similar process for 'self-schemas'. Lauren introduces a quick check for understanding by asking students to discuss, in pairs, other examples of the three types of schemas, and then cold-calls a selection of these, asking for justification in each case.

> *We've said that schemas develop from experience, but let's think a bit more about how that can happen. There are two important scientific terms to describe how schemas change with experience, so be ready as we will need them later. Imagine a young child out on a walk with their parents and seeing a bird perched on a branch. The parents say 'Look, a bird.' What would their initial schema look like? Probably very simple.*

---

[25] There is a nice, detailed example of a restaurant schema from the 1970s (Shank and Abelson, 1977 – if you Google image search the reference you will find it fairly quickly), which can be an excellent discussion stimulus to compare to what the students produce and draw out the variations in experiences that may have led to those differences.

Section 1: The teaching framework

```
                                    Tail

                              ┌─────────┐
                              │  Bird   │
                              └─────────┘

                                Two wings
```

The bird then flies off. This is new information, and it can be added to our schema quite easily. Importantly, this new information doesn't conflict with anything in the existing schema, so we don't need to change it in any way; we can just add 'can fly' into the existing schema. We call this process assimilation.

```
                                    Tail

                         Can fly

                              ┌─────────┐
                              │  Bird   │
                              └─────────┘

                                Two wings
```

Assimilation – interpreting new information using our current understanding
(adding it into an existing schema)

But sometimes schemas don't work to explain the world around us. On the next walk with their parents, the child sees a plane. They have never seen a plane before. What might the child say when it sees a plane for the first time, Cerys? Yes, they might call it a bird! After all, it fits into the current bird schema that the child has. So, imagine that the child says 'bird?', and their dad says, 'no, plane'. The child will need to adapt its schemas. In this case, they will have to make a totally new one for 'plane'. These schemas will overlap in some areas but will be separate in others. We call this process of changing schemas (or making new ones) in response to conflicting new information accommodation.

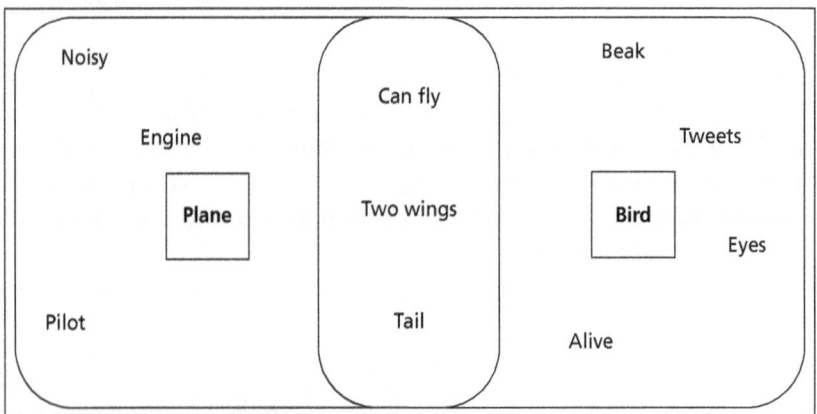

Accommodation – altering an existing schema (or creating a new one) when new information conflicts with existing schemas

Here are three quick mini-whiteboard questions to check your understanding so far.

- *What is a schema?*
- *Name three types of schema, giving examples of each.*
- *Describe two ways that schemas can change as we learn.*

If she feels that the class understanding is sufficient, Lauren can then continue by considering some of the strengths and weaknesses of using schemas in processing information and the applications of schema theory (which will occur later in the course), such as in eyewitness testimony or depression.

The final core question sequence looks like this:

- What is a schema and what purpose does it have?
- Name three types of schema.
- Describe two ways that schemas can change as we learn.
- Describe how schemas may not lead to accurate information processing.
- How might self-schemas be involved in depression?
- How can schemas affect the accuracy of eyewitness testimony?

Lauren then gives students some exam question practice to demonstrate their understanding further. In the next lesson, she replicates simple research into the effects of schemas on cognitive processing (Bransford and Johnson, 1972), following initial retrieval practice of these core questions again.

Analysis of teaching segments

Looking at these two teaching sequences it's clear there are many common themes in the way Lauren has applied various pedagogical principles.

Pedagogical implications	Examples in teaching segments
Get attention Ensure learners are attending only to the most important things.	• New topic is introduced with a 'hook' in the form of an interesting question to answer, priming attention by sparking students' curiosity. • Attention is explicitly cued to the relevant place in the diagram. • The means of participation is explicit (and front-loaded) in every activity, ensuring students are focusing on the right things. • Students are warned to expect checks for understanding to create test expectancy. • A variety of techniques (mini-whiteboards, discussion and cold-calling) are used to maintain the 'thinking ratio'.

Pedagogical implications	Examples in teaching segments
Manage cognitive load Teach with respect to the constraints of working memory.	• Explanations are clear and concise with no extraneous elaboration, and move from concrete to abstract, familiar to unfamiliar and explanation to definition. • New information introduced in small steps, with regular checks for understanding interpolated within the sequence. • The use of diagrams supported with clear explanation takes advantage of the benefits of dual coding therefore boosting working memory capacity. • Labels on the diagrams are situated in accordance with the principle of spatial contiguity, reducing extraneous load. • Activities are clearly modelled throughout, and instructions are kept precise and simple. • Students are given lots of opportunities for verbal rehearsal to increase the likelihood of encoding new information.
Check what they know Assess and secure prior knowledge before teaching new information.	• Prerequisite knowledge is identified and assessed prior to new teaching. • A combination of different retrieval strategies, both straightforward 'quizzing' and some paired explanation or rehearsal, allows Lauren to activate and check prior knowledge.
Make meaning Help students make connections between what they're learning and what they already know.	• Explanations are linked to prior knowledge and concrete examples to help students assimilate new information. • Use of a comparative advance organiser (e.g. neuronal vs synaptic transmission) helps students distinguish between conceptually related ideas. • Links are made to future learning, allowing students to see how this knowledge fits within the broader domain of the subject. • Higher-order understanding tested, as well as lower-order learning (e.g. application by prediction suggesting new examples of the types of schema).

Pedagogical implications	Examples in teaching segments
Secure success Allow students to feel competent by setting the right level of challenge.	• Students are given lots of opportunities for both written and verbal rehearsal to increase the likelihood of encoding new information, with positive habits for classroom discussion encouraged (e.g. turn taking). • Gradual increase in difficulty and abstraction of tasks (e.g. from verbal rehearsal to written core questions to exam questions), along with appropriate scaffolding, to give students further opportunity to rehearse the information in different ways and to practise independently, increasing motivation and self-confidence.
Review regularly Strengthen memories over time by retrieving and reconsolidating learning.	• Retrieval activity checks necessary understanding and allows for activation of relevant schemas to enhance new learning. • Further retrieval practice planned for subsequent lessons.
Feedforward Provide feedback that moves learners forward in what they know and can do.	• Feedback from prerequisite knowledge checks, verbal discussions, teacher explanations and core questions are built into final exam question practice.

In both teaching segments, what looks like a relatively simple sequence of activities – questions, explanation, diagrams and reviews – is actually a pretty complex endeavour. The best teachers make these things look simple and may not even be aware any more of just how hard it is to get all of this right (and that's not to say that it couldn't still be improved).

Lauren hasn't attempted to create any elaborate activities just to engage students or grab their attention; the variation that is there (and these segments would look and feel different in lots of respects) comes from the content itself. Both segments can be considered examples of 'direct instruction' or 'teacher-led', and hopefully it's clear that they are far from the stereotype of a dry, didactic 'chalk and talk' lesson that some people assume of direct instruction, but rather rich with student-teacher interaction. And in both cases, the lesson segments are underpinned by a broad range of evidence-informed principles that increase the chances of students learning the content properly.

This is not to say that these lessons are the only way of demonstrating the pedagogical principles covered in the above table; nor would we prescribe these principles as a checklist for lesson planning, and certainly not for carrying out lesson observations. As soon as we do this, we lose sight of the purpose of what we're doing, meaning lethal mutations are much more likely.

Other methods may successfully achieve these aims in different ways, or you may adapt these examples to suit your own style and context – this is the essence of evidence-informed teaching. When demonstrating the **WHAT mindset** of evidence-informed teaching, the principles above provide our 'why?', and the teaching segments above demonstrate the result of a number of years of adjustment and refinement. Your end result may well look different, so be confident in your professional judgement and expertise – provided you have committed to the intellectual process.

References

1. Amez, S., & Baert, S. (2020). Smartphone use and academic performance: A literature review. *International Journal of Educational Research*, 103. https://doi.org/10.1016/j.ijer.2020.101618
2. Amez, S., Vujić, S., De Marez, L., & Baert, S. (2023). Smartphone use and academic performance: First evidence from longitudinal data. *New Media & Society*, *25*(3), 584-608.
3. Antony, J. W., Ferreira, C. S., Norman, K. A., & Wimber, M. (2017). Retrieval as a fast route to memory consolidation. *Trends in Cognitive Sciences*, 21(8), 573-576.
4. Ariely, D., & Wertenbroch, K. (2002). Procrastination, deadlines, and performance: Self-control by precommitment. *Psychological Science*, *13*(3), 219-224.
5. Atkinson, R. C., & Shiffrin, R. M. (1968). Human memory: A proposed system and its control processes. In Spence, K. W., & Spence, J. T. (eds), *Psychology of learning and motivation* (Vol. 2, pp. 89-195). Academic Press.
6. Ausubel, D. D. (1968). *Educational psychology: A cognitive view*. New York: Holt, Rinehart & Winston.
7. Badali, S., & Greve, M. (2023). Can successive relearning enhance performance on application-based exam questions? *Journal of Applied Research in Memory and Cognition*. Advance online publication. https://doi.org/10.1037/mac0000137
8. Ball, R., & Fairlamb, A. (2025). *The scaffolding effect: Supporting all students to succeed*. Routledge.
9. Bandura, A., Ross, D., & Ross, S. A. (1961). Transmission of aggression through imitation of aggressive models. *The Journal of Abnormal and Social Psychology*, 63(3), 575.

10. Bartlett, F. C. (1932). *Remembering: A study in experimental and social psychology.* Cambridge, UK Cambridge University Press.
11. Bernstein, B. (2006). Vertical and horizontal discourse: An essay. In Barton, L. (ed.), *Education and society* (pp. 53-73). Routledge.
12. Birch, R. (2023). On how to develop independent learners. *Rebecca Birch - on Education.* https://rebeccabirch.substack.com/p/on-how-to-develop-independent-learners
13. Bjork, R. A., & Bjork, E. L. (1992). A new theory of disuse and an old theory of stimulus fluctuation. In Healy, A. F., Kosslyn, S. M., & Shiffrin, R. M. (eds), Essays in honor of William K. Estes, Vol. 2. From learning processes to cognitive processes (pp. 35-67). Lawrence Erlbaum Associates, Inc.
14. Bloom, B. S. (1968). Learning for mastery. *Evaluation Comment, 1*(2), 1-12. (ERIC Document Reproduction No. ED053419)
15. Boxer, A. (2020). A Chemical Orthodoxy. *Front-Loading.* https://achemicalorthodoxy.co.uk/2020/10/14/front-loading/
16. Bransford, J. D., & Johnson, M. K. (1972). Contextual prerequisites for understanding: Some investigations of comprehension and recall. *Journal of Verbal Learning and Verbal Behavior, 11*(6), 717-726.
17. Brophy, J. E. (1984). *Teacher behavior and student achievement* (No. 73). Institute for Research on Teaching, Michigan State University.
18. Butler, A. C. (2018). Multiple-choice testing in education: Are the best practices for assessment also good for learning?. *Journal of Applied Research in Memory and Cognition, 7*(3), 323-331.
19. Carless, D., & Boud, D. (2018). The development of student feedback literacy: Enabling uptake of feedback. *Assessment & Evaluation in Higher Education, 43*(8), 1315-1325.
20. Caviglioli, O. (2019). *Dual coding with teachers.* Hachette UK.
21. CESE (2017). *Cognitive load theory: Research that teachers really need to understand.* Centre for Education Statistics and Evaluation. https://education.nsw.gov.au/content/dam/main-education/about-us/educational-data/cese/2017-cognitive-load-theory.pdf seems to work for me... but also here: https://drive.google.com/file/d/10R0Wc54E7yUXnBj0FZbi8eTmuO4ZLvwR/view?usp=drive_link
22. Collin, J., & Quigley, A. (2021). Teacher feedback to improve learning. Guidance Report. *Education Endowment Foundation.*
23. Cook, C. R., Fiat, A., Larson, M., Daikos, C., Slemrod, T., Holland, E. A., Thayer, A. J., & Renshaw, T. (2018). Positive greetings at the door: Evaluation of a low-cost, high-yield proactive classroom management strategy. *Journal of Positive Behavior Interventions, 20*(3), 149–159. https://doi.org/10.1177/1098300717753831
24. Cook, D. A., & Artino Jr, A. R. (2016). Motivation to learn: An overview of contemporary theories. *Medical Education, 50*(10), 997-1014.
25. Cottingham, S. (2022, January 9). How retrieval practice works part 1. *Overpractised.* https://overpractised.wordpress.com/2022/01/09/how-retrieval-practice-works-part-1/

26. Cottingham, S. (2022, January 30). How retrieval practice works part 2. *Overpractised.* https://overpractised.wordpress.com/2022/01/30/how-retrieval-practice-works-part-2/
27. Cottingham, S. (2023). *Ausubel's meaningful learning in action* (T. Sherrington, Ed.). John Catt.
28. Cowan, N. (2001). The magical number 4 in short-term memory: A reconsideration of mental storage capacity. *Behavioral and Brain Sciences, 24*(1), 87-114.
29. Deci, E. L., Koestner, R., & Ryan, R. M. (1999). A meta-analytic review of experiments examining the effects of extrinsic rewards on intrinsic motivation. *Psychological Bulletin, 125*(6), 627-668.
30. Deuker, L., Olligs, J., Fell, J., Kranz, T. A., Mormann, F., Montag, C., Reuter, M., Elger, C. E., & Axmacher, N. (2013). Memory consolidation by replay of stimulus-specific neural activity. *Journal of Neuroscience, 33*(49), 19373-19383.
31. Dobkin, C., Gil, R., & Marion, J. (2010). Skipping class in college and exam performance: Evidence from a regression discontinuity classroom experiment. *Economics of Education Review, 29*(4), 566-575.
32. Dudai, Y., Karni, A., & Born, J. (2015). The consolidation and transformation of memory. *Neuron, 88*(1), 20-32.
33. Dunlosky, J., Hunt, R. R., & Clark, E. (2000). Is perceptual salience needed in explanations of the isolation effect? *Journal of Experimental Psychology: Learning, Memory, and Cognition, 26*(3), 649-657.
34. Eccles, J. (1983). Expectancies, values, and academic behaviors. In Spence, J. T. (ed.), *Achievement and achievement motives: Psychological and sociological approaches* (pp. 75-146). San Francisco, CA: W. H. Freeman.
35. Education Endowment Foundation (2021). Teaching and learning toolkit. *London: Sutton Trust-EEF.*
36. Eglington, L. G., & Pavlik Jr, P. I. (2020). Optimizing practice scheduling requires quantitative tracking of individual item performance. *npj Science of Learning, 5*(1), 15.
37. Engelmann, S. (1999, July). Student-program alignment and teaching to mastery. In *25th National Direct Instruction Conference.* Eugene, OR: Association for Direct Instruction. https://www.researchgate.net/publication/234713709_Student-Program_Alignment_and_Teaching_to_Mastery.
38. Evans, M. (2023). Motivating productive effort through testing. *Educontrarian.* https://educontrarianblog.com/2023/09/09/motivating-productive-effort-through-testing/
39. Evans, P., Vansteenkiste, M., Parker, P., Kingsford-Smith, A., & Zhou, S. (2024). Cognitive load theory and its relationships with motivation: A self-determination theory perspective. *Educational Psychology Review, 36*(1), 7.
40. Fiorella, L. (2020). The science of habit and its implications for student learning and well-being. *Educational Psychology Review, 32*(3), 603-625.
41. Fiorella, L., & Mayer, R. E. (2016a). Effects of observing the instructor draw diagrams on learning from multimedia messages. *Journal of Educational Psychology, 108*(4), 528-546.

42. Fiorella, L., & Mayer, R. E. (2016b). Eight ways to promote generative learning. *Educational Psychology Review, 28*, 717-741.
43. Fisher, A. V., Godwin, K. E., & Seltman, H. (2014). Visual environment, attention allocation, and learning in young children: When too much of a good thing may be bad. *Psychological Science, 25*(7), 1362-1370. https://doi.org/10.1177/0956797614533801
44. Forster, S., & Lavie, N. (2008). Failures to ignore entirely irrelevant distractors: The role of load. *Journal of Experimental Psychology: Applied, 14*(1), 73-83.
45. Forster, S., & Lavie, N. (2011). Entirely irrelevant distractors can capture and captivate attention. *Psychonomic Bulletin & Review, 18*(6), 1064-1070.
46. Godwin, K. E., Leroux, A. J., Seltman, H., Scupelli, P., & Fisher, A. V. (2022). Effect of repeated exposure to the visual environment on young children's attention. *Cognitive Science, 46*(2), e13093.
47. Gruber, M. J., Valji, A., & Ranganath, C. (2019). Curiosity and learning: A neuroscientific perspective. In Renninger, K. A. & Hidi, S. E. (eds), *The Cambridge handbook of motivation and learning* (pp. 397-417). Cambridge University Press.
48. Guay, F., Marsh, H. W., & Boivin, M. (2003). Academic self-concept and academic achievement: Developmental perspectives on their causal ordering. *Journal of Educational Psychology, 95*(1), 124-136.
49. Guo, D., & Yang, J. (2023). Reactivation of schema representation in lateral occipital cortex supports successful memory encoding. *Cerebral Cortex, 33*(10), 5968-5980.
50. Hattie, J., & Timperley, H. (2007). The power of feedback. *Review of Educational Research, 77*(1), 81-112.
51. Henson, R. N., & Gagnepain, P. (2010). Predictive, interactive multiple memory systems. *Hippocampus, 20*(11), 1315-1326.
52. Hobbiss, M., Sims, S., & Allen, R. (2021). Habit formation limits growth in teacher effectiveness: A review of converging evidence from neuroscience and social science. *Review of Education, 9*(1), 3-23.
53. Hobbiss, M. (2020). Attention in the classroom. My 'best bets' from the research. *The Hobbolog.* https://hobbolog.wordpress.com/2020/01/30/attention-in-the-classroom-my-best-bets-from-the-research/
54. Hobbiss, M. H., & Lavie, N. (2024). Sustained selective attention in adolescence: Cognitive development and predictors of distractibility at school. *Journal of Experimental Child Psychology, 238*, 105784.
55. Hobbiss, M. H. (2019). *Attention, mindwandering and mood: Relating personal experiences in daily life and in the classroom to laboratory measures* (Doctoral dissertation, UCL (University College London)).
56. Huey, M., & Giguere, D. (2023). The impact of smartphone use on course comprehension and psychological well-being in the college classroom. *Innovative Higher Education, 48*(3), 527-537.
57. Jang, H. (2008). Supporting students' motivation, engagement, and learning during an uninteresting activity. *Journal of Educational Psychology, 100*(4), 798-811.
58. Jansen, T., Meyer, J., Wigfield, A., & Möller, J. (2022). Which student and instructional variables are most strongly related to academic motivation in K-12

education? A systematic review of meta-analyses. *Psychological Bulletin, 148*(1-2), 1-26.

59. Kang, M. J., Hsu, M., Krajbich, I. M., Loewenstein, G., McClure, S. M., Wang, J. T. Y., & Camerer, C. F. (2009). The wick in the candle of learning: Epistemic curiosity activates reward circuitry and enhances memory. *Psychological Science, 20*(8), 963-973.

60. Kelleher, J. D., & Dobnik, S. (2019). Referring to the recently seen: Reference and perceptual memory in situated dialog. *arXiv preprint arXiv:1903.09866*.

61. Kliegl, O., Bartl, J., & Bäuml, K. H. T. (2023). Repeated guessing attempts during acquisition can promote subsequent recall performance. *Journal of Experimental Psychology: Applied, 30*(2), 282.

62. Kluger, A. N., & DeNisi, A. (1996). The effects of feedback interventions on performance: A historical review, a meta-analysis, and a preliminary feedback intervention theory. *Psychological Bulletin, 119*(2), 254-284.

63. Kornell, N., & Vaughn, K. E. (2016). How retrieval attempts affect learning: A review and synthesis. In Ross, B. (ed.), *The psychology of learning and motivation* (pp. 183-215). Elsevier Academic Press.

64. Kramer, S. L., Scull, J., Porter, A., Massey, C. M., Merlino, F. J., & Baker, J. Y. (2024). Can either using cognitive science principles or improving teacher content knowledge boost student achievement in middle school science?. *Journal of Research in Science Teaching, 61*(7), 1543-1573.

65. Lemov, D. (2015). *Teach like a champion 2.0: 62 techniques that put students on the path to college*. Jossey-Bass.

66. Lewis, C. (2022). Prereq checks – do they know what they need to know and how do we know? *MDB Science*. https://mbdscience.wordpress.com/2022/06/01/prereq-checks-do-they-know-what-they-need-to-know-and-how-do-we-know/

67. Lovell, O., & Sherrington, T. (2020). *Sweller's cognitive load theory in action*. John Catt.

68. Mareschal, D., Johnson, M. H., Sirois, S., Spratling, M., Thomas, M. S. C., & Westerman, G. (2007). *Neuroconstructivism*. Oxford University Press.

69. Markant, J., Ackerman, L. K., Nussenbaum, K., & Amso, D. (2016). Selective attention neutralizes the adverse effects of low socioeconomic status on memory in 9-month-old infants. *Developmental Cognitive Neuroscience, 18*, 26-33.

70. Markant, J., & Amso, D. (2014). Leveling the playing field: Attention mitigates the effects of intelligence on memory. *Cognition, 131*(2), 195-204.

71. Marsh, L. (2024). Can retrieval practice improve student performance within an A-level psychology classroom? *Impact, 21*. https://my.chartered.college/impact_article/retrieval-practice-vs-restudy-an-authentic-classroom-investigation/

72. Mayer, R. E. (2024). The past, present, and future of the cognitive theory of multimedia learning. *Educational Psychology Review, 36*(1), 8.

73. McCrea, P. (2023). *Routines redeploy attention*. Evidence Snacks. https://snacks.pepsmccrea.com/p/routines-redeploy-attention

74. McDaniel, M. A., Einstein, G. O., & Een, E. (2021). Training college students to use learning strategies: A framework and pilot course. *Psychology Learning and Teaching, 20*(3), 364-382. https://doi.org/10.1177/1475725721989489

75. Merrell, C., Sayal, K., Tymms, P., & Kasim, A. (2017). A longitudinal study of the association between inattention, hyperactivity and impulsivity and children's academic attainment at age 11. *Learning and Individual Differences, 53*, 156-161.
76. Metcalfe, J., Xu, J., Vuorre, M., Siegler, R., Wiliam, D., & Bjork, R. A. (2024). Learning from errors versus explicit instruction in preparation for a test that counts. *British Journal of Educational Psychology.* Advance online publication. https://doi.org/10.1111/bjep.12651
77. Nation, I. (2006). How large a vocabulary is needed for reading and listening?. *Canadian Modern Language Review, 63*(1), 59-82.
78. Nevid, J. S., & Armata, C. E. (2023). Paying attention in class: Using in class quizzes to incentivize student attention. *Teaching of Psychology.* https://doi.org/10.1177/00986283231185136
79. Nuthall, G. (2007). *The hidden lives of learners.* New Zealand Council for Educational Research.
80. O'Donovan, B. (2017). How student beliefs about knowledge and knowing influence their satisfaction with assessment and feedback. *Higher Education, 74*, 617-633.
81. Owens, M. T., Seidel, S. B., Wong, M., Bejines, T. E., Lietz, S., Perez, J. R., ... & Tanner, K. D. (2017). Classroom sound can be used to classify teaching practices in college science courses. *Proceedings of the National Academy of Sciences, 114*(12), 3085-3090.
82. Pan, S. C., Cooke, J. E., Little, J. L., & McDaniel, M. A. (2023). Using online and clicker quizzes to learn scientific and technical jargon. In Overson, C., Hakala, C. M., Kordonowy, L. L., & Benassi, V. A. (eds), *In their own words: What scholars and teachers want you to know about why and how to apply the science of learning in your academic setting* (pp. 473-480). Society for the Teaching of Psychology. https://teachpsych.org/ebooks/itow
83. Pang, J. C., Aquino, K. M., Oldehinkel, M., Robinson, P. A., Fulcher, B. D., Breakspear, M., & Fornito, A. (2023). Geometric constraints on human brain function. *Nature, 618*, 566-574.
84. Rao, R. P., & Ballard, D. H. (1999). Predictive coding in the visual cortex: A functional interpretation of some extra-classical receptive-field effects. *Nature Neuroscience, 2*(1), 79-87.
85. Ritvo, V. J., Turk-Browne, N. B., & Norman, K. A. (2019). Nonmonotonic plasticity: How memory retrieval drives learning. *Trends in Cognitive Sciences, 23*(9), 726-742.
86. Rivera-Lares, K., Logie, R., Baddeley, A., & Della Sala, S. (2022). Rate of forgetting is independent of initial degree of learning. *Memory & Cognition, 50*(8), 1706-1718.
87. Robison, M. K., Unsworth, N., & Brewer, G. A. (2021). Examining the effects of goal-setting, feedback, and incentives on sustained attention. *Journal of Experimental Psychology: Human Perception and Performance, 47*(6), 869-891.
88. Roediger III, H. L., & Karpicke, J. D. (2018). Reflections on the resurgence of interest in the testing effect. *Perspectives on Psychological Science, 13*(2), 236-241.
89. Ryan, R. M., & Deci, E. L. (2020). Intrinsic and extrinsic motivation from a self-determination theory perspective: Definitions, theory, practices, and future directions. *Contemporary Educational Psychology, 61*, 101860.

90. Ryan, T. J., & Frankland, P. W. (2022). Forgetting as a form of adaptive engram cell plasticity. *Nature Reviews Neuroscience, 23*(3), 173-186.
91. Sayal, K., Washbrook, E., & Propper, C. (2015). Childhood behavior problems and academic outcomes in adolescence: Longitudinal population-based study. *Journal of the American Academy of Child & Adolescent Psychiatry, 54*(5), 360-368.
92. Schunk, D. H., Meece, J. L., & Pintrich, P. R. (2014). *Motivation in education: Theory, research, and applications.* 4th edn. Upper Saddle River, NJ: Pearson.
93. Shank, R., & Abelson. R. (1977). *Scripts, plans, goals and understanding.* Erlbaum.
94. Shaw, S. (2023, July 7). Implementing mastery in A-Level psychology: An update. ATP conference.
95. Sherif, M. (1966). *In common predicament: Social psychology of intergroup conflict and cooperation.* Houghton Mifflin, Boston.
96. Sherrington, T. (2021). Check for understanding… why it matters and how to do it. #rEDSurrey21. *Teacherhead.* https://teacherhead.com/2021/10/17/check-for-understanding-why-it-matters-and-how-to-do-it-redsurrey21/
97. Sinclair, A. H., & Barense, M. D. (2018). Surprise and destabilize: Prediction error influences episodic memory reconsolidation. *Learning & Memory, 25*(8), 369-381.
98. Soderstrom, N. C., & Bjork, R. A. (2015). Learning versus performance: An integrative review. *Perspectives on Psychological Science, 10*(2), 176-199.
99. Staresina, B. P., Gray, J. C., & Davachi, L. (2009). Event congruency enhances episodic memory encoding through semantic elaboration and relational binding. *Cerebral Cortex, 19*(5), 1198-1207.
100. Steuer, G., Grecu, A. L., & Mori, J. (2024). Error climate and alienation from teachers: A longitudinal analysis in primary school. *British Journal of Educational Psychology.* Advance online publication. https://doi.org/10.1111/bjep.12659
101. Still, K. (2023, April 29). What if feedback is a waste of time? ResearchEd Berkshire.
102. Sweller, J., Kirschner, P. A., & Clark, R. E. (2007). Why minimally guided teaching techniques do not work: A reply to commentaries. *Educational Psychologist, 42*(2), 115-121.
103. Sweller, J., Van Merrienboer, J. J., & Paas, F. G. (1998). Cognitive architecture and instructional design. *Educational Psychology Review, 10*, 251-296.
104. Tajfel, H., & Turner, J. C. (1979). An integrative theory of intergroup conflict. In Austin, W. G., & Worchel, S. (eds), *The social psychology of intergroup relations* (pp. 33-37). Monterey, CA: Brooks/Cole.
105. Tam, K. Y., Van Tilburg, W. A., & Chan, C. S. (2023). Whatever will bore, will bore: The mere anticipation of boredom exacerbates its occurrence in lectures. *British Journal of Educational Psychology, 93*(1), 198-210.
106. Tharby, A. (2018). *How to explain absolutely anything to absolutely anyone: The art and science of teacher explanation.* Crown House Publishing Ltd.
107. Thornton, B., Faires, A., Robbins, M., & Rollins, E. (2014). The mere presence of a cell phone may be distracting. *Social Psychology, 45*(6), 479-488.
108. Van Boekel, M., Hufnagle, A. S., Weisen, S., & Troy, A. (2023). The feedback I want versus the feedback I need: Investigating students' perceptions of feedback. *Psychology in the Schools, 60*(9), 3389-3402.

109. Van der Weiden, A., Benjamins, J., Gillebaart, M., Ybema, J. F., & De Ridder, D. (2020). How to form good habits? A longitudinal field study on the role of self-control in habit formation. *Frontiers in Psychology, 11*, 560.
110. Van Kesteren, M. T. R., & Meeter, M. (2020). How to optimize knowledge construction in the brain. *Npj Science of Learning, 5*(1). https://doi.org/10.1038/s41539-020-0064-y
111. Van Kesteren, M. T. R., Ruiter, D. J., Fernández, G., & Henson, R. N. (2012). How schema and novelty augment memory formation. *Trends in neurosciences, 35*(4), 211-219.
112. Vaughn, K. E., & Kornell, N. (2019). How to activate students' natural desire to test themselves. *Cognitive Research: Principles and Implications, 4*, 1-18.
113. Vu, T., Magis-Weinberg, L., Jansen, B. R., van Atteveldt, N., Janssen, T. W., Lee, N. C., ... & Meeter, M. (2022). Motivation-achievement cycles in learning: A literature review and research agenda. *Educational Psychology Review, 34*(1), 39-71.
114. Weinstein, Y., Gilmore, A. W., Szpunar, K. K., & McDermott, K. B. (2014). The role of test expectancy in the build-up of proactive interference in long-term memory. *Journal of Experimental Psychology: Learning Memory and Cognition, 40*(4), 1039-1048. https://doi.org/10.1037/a0036164
115. Wiliam, D. [@dylanwiliam]. (2017, Jan 26). I've come to the conclusion Sweller's Cognitive Load Theory is the single most important thing for teachers to know [Tweet]. Twitter. https://twitter.com/dylanwiliam/status/824682504602943489
116. Wiliam, D. [@dylanwiliam]. (2018, March 23). This is why I keep on pointing out that the main purpose of feedback is to improve the student and not the work... [Tweet] https://twitter.com/dylanwiliam/status/977265017279033344
117. Willingham, D. T. (2017). *The reading mind: A cognitive approach to understanding how the mind reads.* John Wiley & Sons.
118. Wolff, C. E., Jarodzka, H., van den Bogert, N., & Boshuizen, H. P. (2016). Teacher vision: Expert and novice teachers' perception of problematic classroom management scenes. *Instructional Science, 44*, 243-265.
119. Xia, M., Poorthuis, A. M. G., & Thomaes, S. (2023). Children's overestimation of performance across age, task, and historical time: A meta-analysis. *Child Development, 95*(3), 1001-1022. https://doi.org/10.1111/cdev.14042
120. Yang, C., Luo, L., Vadillo, M. A., & Shanks, D. R. (2020). Testing (quizzing) boosts classroom learning: A systematic and meta-analytic review. *Psychological Bulletin, 147*(4), 399-435. https://doi.org/10.1037/bul0000309
121. Yang, C., Potts, R., & Shanks, D. R. (2018). Enhancing learning and retrieval of new information: A review of the forward testing effect. *npj Science of Learning, 3*(1), 8.
122. Yu, S., & Levesque-Bristol, C. (2020). A cross-classified path analysis of the self-determination theory model on the situational, individual and classroom levels in college education. *Contemporary Educational Psychology, 61*, 101857.
123. Zedelius, C. M., Protzko, J., & Schooler, J. W. (2021). Lay theories of the wandering mind: Control-related beliefs predict mind wandering rates in- and outside the lab. *Personality and Social Psychology Bulletin, 47*(6), 921-938.

Section 2: Curriculum

Lauren

Lauren has just accepted a post at a new school as subject leader for psychology. She is going to be teaching an unfamiliar specification after having delivered a different one for several years in her previous post. She has been given a scheme of work by the previous post holder, but it appears to be little more than a list of topics taken from the specification and presented in the same order, with page references for the textbook the department has adopted.

Although Lauren has taught a lot of the content before, she is surprised about the sequence of some topics as they are different to what she's been used to. There's also some unfamiliar content, and she is unsure about what students actually need to learn and the detail that is required. She has a look through the textbook, which provides some helpful pointers, although she is surprised to find some sections with quite different examples and supporting studies to the ones she normally teaches for that content. She's also slightly worried that there appear to be some factual errors!

The senior leadership team have asked that subject leaders populate a shared document outlining their scheme of work, and Lauren is considering whether or not she wants to go with what's already there or rewrite some or all of it. The equality and diversity lead has also asked that subject leaders do an audit of their curriculum and highlight where they are promoting diversity by showcasing the contribution of female and ethnic minority subject-specific figures.

> Lauren has also been given the dates that the school runs mock exams, and she is expected to have finished delivering the curriculum by Easter of Year 13 to allow for the school's mandated revision period in the run-up to public exams. Finally, Lauren has been given a copy of the school's homework policy, and has noted the expectations of a specific number of hours of independent study assigned per week.

What are the specific curriculum challenges Lauren is facing?

- She is unsure about the sequencing of units and whether simply following the order of the specification is the best solution.
- There is some unfamiliar content in the specification, and she doesn't know exactly what she's going to need to teach.
- Furthermore, there is some content she has taught before, but she isn't sure the extent to which this matches the new specification.
- The departmental set of textbooks contain information that is unfamiliar even for familiar topics (and, in places, wrong!), and she's not sure about some of the specific subtopics or option choices outlined.
- She is unsure about the level of diversity within the content in the current curriculum and whether she needs to try to do something about this.
- She is already feeling the pressure of making sure she has got through the curriculum in time for the exams at the end of the course, and she hasn't even started yet!
- She is going to need to figure out what kind of homework she should set in order to adhere to the school's policy, while at the same time being meaningful for her students and not over-burdensome for her workload.

Section 2: Curriculum

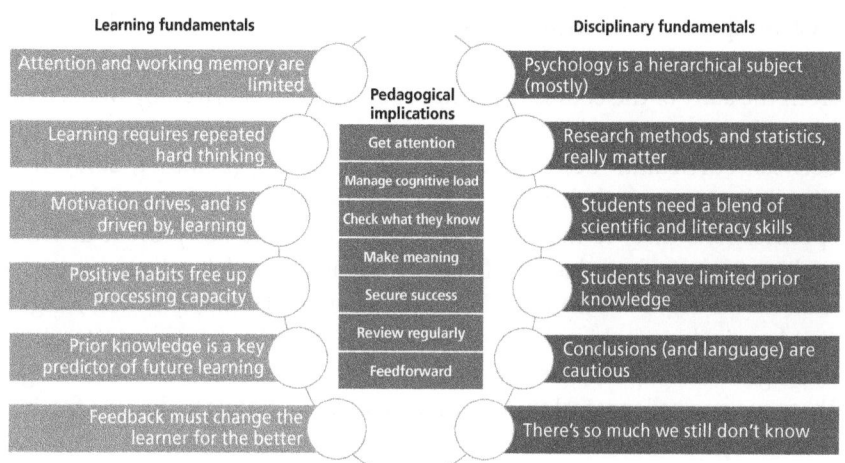

Curriculum making in psychology

In Section 1, we discussed some of the learning and disciplinary fundamentals that have significant pedagogical implications for psychology teaching. They help guide *how* we teach. However, consideration of the 'how' must be balanced with the 'what'; in other words, which bits of psychology are we actually going to teach? Early in our careers, we probably didn't spend a huge amount of time thinking about this because it appeared to be prescribed for us, either officially (for example, laid out in exam specifications and textbooks) or because we left those sorts of decisions to the wisdom of heads of department and subject leaders. Instead, we probably looked at the list of topics to be covered and jumped straight into lesson planning. However, the 'what' and the 'how' are inextricably interlinked, and any decisions about how to teach have to be grounded in what we are teaching. In this section, we will discuss a range of curriculum decisions that should be considered before we think about what we may actually do in our lessons.

The recent focus on curriculum thinking in schools has rejuvenated and energised many in teaching.[1] Having deep and thoughtful discussions about what to teach, when and where, feels exciting. If you only teach an A-level or

---

1 Although for balance it's worth pointing out this has also led to cynicism in other quarters!

a GCSE specification, then many of those decisions may seem to have been made for you (and it can be pretty dispiriting at times to think that) right from the start of the course, and almost everything is driven by what could be in the exams. However, this would be to ignore the distinction made between curriculum design and *curriculum making* (Lambert, 2017). It is true that our curricula have been designed for us (in the form of the exam specifications that we must all follow), but this does not prevent us from making a curriculum that benefits our students; indeed, it remains essential that we do so, as it also benefits us. Lambert and Biddulph (2015) argue that 'curriculum making is key to becoming, and developing, as a teacher'. Taking ownership of our curriculum develops our content knowledge, sharpens our pedagogical thinking and also motivates us to develop further (autonomy, as we saw in Section 1, is a key driver of motivation).

What choices *do* psychology teachers have?

We make a distinction here between macro- and micro-curricular decisions:

- Macro-decisions are those relating to the big picture:
    - Which specification do you want to deliver?
    - Which option topics will you teach?
    - How will you sequence those topics across the whole programme of study?
- Micro-decisions are those at a more granular level, i.e. the fine details of what and how you teach:
    - Within a topic, how will you sequence the various concepts and subtopics?
    - Where there are options, what specific content will you teach?
    - How much do they need to know about each topic?
    - For a given topic, which particular examples will you choose to share with students?
    - Which evidence will you introduce to help assess the different theories that students are learning about?
    - What should you set students for homework to support their learning?

Section 2A: Macro-decisions around curriculum

Choosing a specification or option topics

Unless you are present at your department's inception, it's likely that you will have inherited an exam specification. Adopting a new one is a huge undertaking with significant workload implications, and so the decision to switch is not one that should be taken lightly.[2]

There are a range of different factors to consider when deciding what we want to deliver to our students:

- What we think could have the most accessible (or 'easiest') content for students. For example, we may look at the grade distributions for previous years. In 2023 and 2024, WJEC had a larger proportion of A* and A grades than the other specifications, although the cumulative percentage of students getting a 6 or 7 in IB is also high.
- How clearly specified the content is. For example, the IB specification is less prescriptive about content than most of the others. This may be seen as either an advantage or a disadvantage, depending on your preference.
- Which options are most popular nationally, and therefore likely to be better supported in terms of either teacher networks or resources. At A-level, for example, AQA is currently by far the most popular specification in the UK.

---

2 Our discussion is geared around the delivery of an A-level psychology specification, but the general principles would apply for any type of qualification. However, if you were choosing to deliver the AS, either standalone or co-taught alongside the full A-level, then some curriculum decisions will necessarily look a little different.

- What we think may be of most interest or relevance to our own students.
- What we think may be the easiest to actually teach.
- What we think may be the most enjoyable to actually teach.
- What we think gives our students the best chance of success in the exam.
- Which has the 'best' course content, i.e. the psychological content that we find most convincing, empirically sound, interesting or contemporary.
- Which options avoid us having to deliver content that we ourselves find challenging, or don't like for some other reason.

All of these factors are important to consider, and perhaps that in itself is one of the most important messages here – that it is a considered decision, rather than simply a result of defaulting to whatever has gone before. Careful thought needs to go into the relative weight of factors that may be considered more in the students' interests (topics we deem more relevant to them) versus those that are more in teachers' interests (what we think is easier to teach). It may be worth spending time looking at things like grade boundaries as these do vary significantly between specifications, although it's also worth remembering that grade distributions usually don't vary nearly as much. For example, while the grade boundaries for Edexcel are typically significantly lower compared to AQA (in the order of 15–20% for the A*), the grade distributions are virtually identical.

Ultimately, this is a difficult decision to make, and one that therefore needs to be fully supported by the members of your department (see Section 5, 'Managing a psychology department', page 427) as well as the senior leadership team. There may be significant budgetary implications, and as mentioned above, any curriculum change will certainly increase workload in the short term. Deciding the extent to which the trade-off is worth it is tricky, and it's not a decision that is easy to reverse. It's also worth bearing in mind that specifications are changed (sometimes to quite a significant extent) around about every 7–8 years,[3] and so holding out until the dust settles may sometimes be the wisest course of action.

---

3   As if to underline this, at the time of publication, some exam boards are releasing details of some changes (albeit relatively minor ones) in terms of specification structure.

Sequencing units

There are numerous possible principles that we could use to help us sequence the units in our curriculum:

- Specification order.
- Exam coherence (units from a particular exam paper together).
- Teacher expertise (teaching topics a teacher is most familiar with first, or in split classes, dividing the course up according to expertise and then sequencing the units to fit).
- Engagement first (starting with topics that students find enjoyable to entice them).
- Challenge first (starting with the most difficult or least engaging topics as a means of selecting out the least committed to the subject).
- Interweave units with complementary knowledge (often done in the form of splitting research methods units and teaching it in segments next to appropriate applied content, e.g. teaching experiments at the same time as memory).
- Telling a story (chronological order of units).
- Prerequisite knowledge (sequencing units with the least prerequisite knowledge first, or the parts containing the most essential prerequisite knowledge for the largest number of other units, or just present in the largest number of other units).

When we both started teaching, we typically began at the top of this list. There's something satisfying about ticking off the topics in order, and this makes it easier to see progress throughout the course. Textbooks are almost always aligned to specifications, and therefore this helps students because they will only ever be moving onto the next page rather than jumping around to different topics. We may hope that the people who designed the specification have some sort of expertise and have actually thought hard about the sequence in the first place. However, in our experience, simply following the specification may not help students to **make meaning** and develop the strong schemas that we want; in fact, it can result in significant confusion.

In the Edexcel specification, for example, students learn four 'foundation' topics in their first year: social, cognitive, biological and learning (they are set out in that order). But in order to properly understand the theoretical underpinnings of the cognitive approach, the use of the 'computer analogy' and the information processing model, you really need to understand how this represents an enormous shift in thinking from the behaviourist perspective that was dominant from the early 20th century until around the 1950s. Therefore, it makes more sense from a conceptual point of view to teach students about learning theories first, so that when they do encounter the cognitive approach they can see how one emerged partly as a response to what had gone before (as we have seen **psychology is a (mostly) hierarchical subject**).

Another consideration in this discussion is that our sequencing may also depend on the allocation of teaching. For example, do classes have one solo teacher, or are they shared between teachers? We discuss the relative merits of both options further in Section 5 (page 423), but clearly which option you choose has a significant impact on curriculum sequencing (having shared classes makes this potentially much more complex). Do you simply split the course in half and deliver different units in parallel? Or do you have one teacher delivering 'content' topics like social influence or memory, while the other does approaches and research methods? How do you weave things like exam skills across the curriculum? These are difficult questions to which there are no clear right answers, and it may be a case of experimenting from one year to the next. Again, we find the **WHAT mindset** to be useful here.

Case study: Unit sequencing

Here is an example of how the units for the AQA A-level could be sequenced according (primarily) to a combination of prerequisite knowledge and 'unit coherence'. As ever, this is not to say that the sequence below is the correct one; all of the other factors mentioned above will also play into decisions, and even in a curriculum designed wholly around the same principles there is scope for disagreement. It would be perfectly legitimate to sequence these units in an entirely different order, depending on which pieces of information you decided were most foundational and how you envisaged weaving those into subsequent work. The thought process is king here.

Section 2: Curriculum

Week	Content YEAR 12	Week	Content YEAR 13
1	Induction / Approaches	1	Pyschopathology
2	Approaches	2	Pyschopathology
3	Approaches	3	Attachment
4	Approaches	4	Attachment
5	Approaches	5	Attachment
6	Approaches	6	Attachment
7	Approaches	7	Attachment
8	Approaches	8	Schizophrenia
9	Approaches	9	Schizophrenia
10	Biopsychology	10	Schizophrenia
11	Biopsychology	11	Schizophrenia
12	Biopsychology	12	Schizophrenia
13	Biopsychology	13	Forensic
14	Biopsychology	14	Forensic
15	Biopsychology	15	Mocks
16	Research methods	16	Mocks
17	Research methods	17	Forensic
18	Research methods	18	Forensic
19	Research methods	19	Forensic
20	Research methods	20	Relationship
21	Research methods	21	Relationship
22	Research methods	22	Relationship
23	Internal exams	23	Relationship
24	Research methods	24	Relationship
25	Social influence	25	Issues and debates
26	Social influence	26	Issues and debates
27	Social influence	27	Issues and debates
28	Social influence	28	Issues and debates
29	Social influence	29	Revision
30	Memory	30	Revision
31	Memory		
32	Memory		
33	Memory		
34	Memory		
35	Internal exams		
36	Internal exams		
37	Pyschopathology		
38	Pyschopathology		

In this sequence, the 'approaches to psychology' unit, which is actually from paper 2 in the exam, comes first. This allows students to be introduced in a general way to some of the most important theories for explaining behaviour (the behaviourist, social learning, cognitive, psychodynamic, humanistic and biological approaches), their associated research methods and some of their strengths and weaknesses. The knowledge covered in this unit reoccurs to some degree in every single other unit, and some units (such as psychopathology, schizophrenia and forensic psychology) are almost entirely composed of applications of the different approaches. This means that knowledge of the approaches can lead to *subsumptive learning* in later units (as we saw in Section 1, **prior knowledge is a key predictor of future learning**). The unit also provides a nice overview of the subject as a whole and its historical development. A final point in support of this method is that evaluation of approaches is often easier than for studies or more specific theories. It therefore seems an appropriate unit to begin with.

The other unit that can be subsequently applied to every other one is, of course, research methods. This makes it another good candidate to come early in the curriculum sequence; indeed, it could well come first, and many teachers do choose this option (especially those who also favour a 'challenge-first' approach). Again, the right decision here will be context dependent.

Armed with these two foundational units, a good deal of the prerequisite knowledge for the units can be covered. Why then cover biopsychology in between them? This is where some 'exam coherence' thinking comes in. Adding in biopsychology means that all of paper 2 can be taught in the order it will occur in the exam. It also provides further useful prior knowledge for some of the more biological aspects of the applied units, and comes before research methods because – in our experience – research method concepts are better taught as *superordinate learning*. In other words, it works better when students have some concrete examples they can attach to research method ideas (without these, the concepts are sometimes too abstract for them to understand). Studying biopsychology first allows for some extra examples of research studies to have been covered, which can then be used for this superordinate purpose.

Beginning with the 'approaches' unit (and also covering it in depth and dedicating time to it; see 'The timing of units', page 161) also allows for the introduction of some of the key issues and debates, especially when dealing with the comparison of approaches. These are essential concepts with which to **make meaning** and form useful evaluation points throughout the rest of the course but also have a dedicated unit within paper 3. Having spent time on them in the initial unit and then **reviewed regularly** in the interim, the final unit becomes one of revision, in which no new content is introduced at all but instead examples of the issues and debates are mined from students' prior knowledge of the other units.

Core and hinterland

Once you have selected (or inherited) a specification, chosen your units and decided on their sequencing, it may feel like your curriculum decisions are coming to an end – in actual fact, they are only just beginning. What exactly are you going to expect students to know, or do? What will you do in the lessons to get them there? How long will it take? How will it all fit together? How can you minimise the strain on students? Curriculum making requires considering these questions and, as ever, coming to an informed decision about what would work most effectively in your context, before implementing, assessing and adjusting as you go in accordance with the **WHAT mindset** of evidence-informed teaching. A good place to start is to consider the curriculum's 'core', and its 'hinterland'.

Christine Counsell (2018) uses the concepts of core and hinterland to help distinguish the types of knowledge we want our students to learn. The basic premise is that the core knowledge is the content they *must* learn, whereas the hinterland is the broader context in which the content sits. Counsell considers, for example, the major characters and plot points of a novel as core. You need to know (as in, have committed to long-term memory) these details in order to talk about the novel meaningfully, but these only really make sense in the context of the wider novel – the hinterland – which is just as important. As Counsell explains:

> However, much as pupils may be advised to study or create distillations, commentaries and plot summaries, however much these become decent proxies for (and aids towards) the sort of thing that stays in our heads after we've read the novel, to bypass reading the novel altogether would be vandalism.

In psychology, we can think of the major approaches, theories and studies as core, although there will of course be many debates about which theories and studies should be included here. The 2013 British Psychological Society (BPS) report into the future of A-level psychology suggests that 'the three historical roots of psychology (experimental psychology, biological psychology and social psychology) act as an identifiable core upon which to build a curriculum'. Clearly, the exam boards don't necessarily fully agree with this!

However we've defined the core, these are the bits we want our students to remember and what they will need to have learned to be successful in their exams. But along the way, we need to give them access to the hinterland – the broad context in which every study or theory is placed (for example, knowing how a theory developed from what came before and which methodological challenges a piece of research is trying to overcome). This could mean teaching them things that aren't strictly in the specification, but without which their other knowledge loses value and meaning. We can term this 'psychological literacy' – a broader sense of knowledge and understanding of the psychological landscape that helps us make sense of anything we learn about. Indeed, the importance of hinterland may stretch well beyond the classroom; McGovern et al. (2010) use the term 'psychologically literate citizens' to refer to the outcome of a course in psychology that results in students becoming 'critically scientific thinkers and ethical and socially responsible participants in their communities'.

Why does this matter? If students can learn the core content really well, do they need all this extra stuff? Well, yes. If they get the bigger picture, they are far less likely to make naive, sweeping assertions such as:

- 'Classical conditioning as an explanation for phobia lacks generalisability because it's only based on a case study of a single participant (Little Albert).'
- 'Raine's study of murderers' brains is reductionist because he fails to acknowledge the social influences that may lead to violent behaviour.'
- 'Milgram's studies of obedience don't apply to women as he only studied males.'

For someone well versed in the subject, it's clear that these sorts of claims are flawed. But we have to remember that our students are novices – and we are experts – and the difference between the two is largely to do with depth of knowledge. It's not our students' fault when they make naive assertions if their ignorance is because we haven't taught them what they need to know.

However, given the plague of content coverage in a packed specification, a pragmatic approach is important. There are trade-offs to be made in terms of deciding where students really do or don't need that wider context and department teams need to work together on this. We've all been there when students ask that most depressing of questions: 'Do we need to know this for the exam?' And sometimes the answer to that is something along the lines of, 'No, but we've thought very carefully about this, and we think that if you don't learn this then you won't really understand the stuff that you do need for the exam.' If we want them to become psychologically literate, they need continuous exposure to the wider world of psychology.

Some specific practical suggestions are:

- Giving adequate time for teachers' subject knowledge development. Go back to source materials or original research papers rather than relying on condensed, summarised (and, occasionally, inaccurate) textbook versions. If you can't allocate departmental budget on journal subscriptions, then some professional organisations (such as the Chartered College of Teaching) offer access to journals as part of their membership, or alternatively you can often use open access preprints or contact authors to access papers.
- Giving over department meeting time for discussions around research and theory. A colleague may be teaching a topic for the first time and be unaware of the broader context, so sharing that knowledge is important. A related point is making sure everyone is aware of the depth and detail required for a topic on a particular specification. It can be easy to see something listed that you've taught on a different specification only to discover that the knowledge required is somewhat different!

- Sharing original research articles with students and setting them for reading (where appropriate, as navigating an academic paper can be pretty challenging for some students, especially early on).
- Sharing links to current research via platforms like the BPS Research Digest. The more the students are exposed to research beyond their exam specification, the better they can appreciate how what they're learning fits in the wider landscape.
- Encouraging students to reach out to researchers themselves – many are more than happy to share their work with keen A-level students. One of us remembers with great pride a student who we taught who emailed Eleanor Maguire (author of the famous 'taxi drivers' studies) asking some questions and was delighted to receive a detailed response outlining a range of findings from her further research, including some results that were still to be published!
- Get students to take part in real research studies. Keep an eye out for studies recruiting from the relevant age groups and suggest (or mandate) that students sign up (e.g. set it as a homework task). Off the back of one such assignment to participate in an online working memory study, one of our students recently ended up spending the day in Cambridge to receive an fMRI scan – an unbeatable enrichment experience for an aspiring psychologist!
- Share your own hinterland learning. Communicate what you have recently learned with students, and enthuse them with stories of research – the journeys of discovery that make psychology so fascinating. One of us often allocates five minutes at a suitable 'brain break' point in the middle of double lessons to showing any interesting and relevant recent publications or psychology news they have come across.

Core knowledge – how much depth do you go into?

Although our specifications are typically clear on what to teach, they are less specific about how much depth to go into. The vagueness of terms in the specification can mean that teachers are left to guess as to precisely what, and in how much detail, they are to teach. Exam-board approved textbooks offer some guidance but they, too, vary in how much content they include, meaning teachers have to make a best-guess about which bits to cover or leave out. For example, how many studies should students encounter in order to adequately evaluate a theory? This can be especially challenging if you teach a specification such as the IB, where content is less clearly specified. What teachers are often left to do is to pore over mark schemes and examiners' reports with a fine-tooth comb looking for clues as to what will or won't be credited for a particular question. This clearly raises some issues.

First, with any specification (especially early on), it's going to be a while before the whole syllabus gets covered, meaning the detail is only being revealed in a rather piecemeal fashion. It may take several years of exams before some topics appear on a paper, which means teachers are somewhat in the dark as to whether they are teaching that content at the right level of detail. A second, larger problem is that clearly this is completely the wrong way around. The assessment should be driven by the content, but what teachers are having to do is work backwards from the assessment in order to figure out what to teach! In addition, examiners keen on getting students to demonstrate critical or 'flexible' thinking will sometimes create questions that seem to deliberately stray beyond the bounds of students' core knowledge. As a result, even the most forensic assessment of precisely what knowledge has been required in the past is unlikely to entirely cover each new paper. Core knowledge alone is unlikely to ever be enough.

However, this is not to say that carefully selecting and specifying the core knowledge that you want students to possess has no merit; on the contrary, we think it is an essential and hugely powerful tool for improving teaching and learning. One simple way to identify core knowledge in a curriculum (and to communicate this expectation to your students) is through the use of a *core questions curriculum*.

Core questions in psychology

Core questions are a way of codifying the desired knowledge outcomes of learning in your classroom (the bank that one of us currently uses for AQA A-level consists of 1013 question-answer pairs covering the entire course). They involve the planning of questions and answers before lessons, for example, the below may be the desired knowledge outcome of a lesson on conformity.

Core question	Suggested answer
What is conformity?	A process in which someone's behaviour or beliefs are influenced by a larger group of people (a majority).
What are the types of conformity?	Compliance, identification and internalisation.
What is compliance?	When an individual changes their behaviour in public (so as not to stand out from a group) but *doesn't* change behaviour or beliefs in private.
What is identification?	When an individual changes their behaviour in public in an effort to be accepted by and fit into a group they want to be in. This may *sometimes* also lead to changes in private opinion and behaviour too, but not always.
What is internalisation?	When an individual changes their behaviour or view to that of others in the group, in public *and in private* (because they think that the majority is correct).
What are the explanations of conformity?	Informational social influence and normative social influence.

There are many benefits to having this level of concreteness and specificity in your curriculum planning for both teachers and students, and these benefits have been supported by large-scale evaluations of core knowledge curricula, which have been found to lead to improved learning (Grissmer et al., 2023). We will look at some of these benefits below.

Planning lessons using core questions

Core questions can allow us to plan better lessons. If we have a set of exemplar questions and answers planned in advance, then we already know exactly what our desired learning outcomes look like. This means, for example, that we can focus much more precisely on what activities, scaffolding and questions may be needed in order to create that learning in our students (moving beyond simply having resources that cover the topic). If we already know in advance what we think high quality answers would look like, then we can consider more deeply the processes that may be needed to get students there.

This means it is easier for teachers to **check what they know**, both in advance of a lesson in our prerequisite knowledge checks and after a teaching segment to check understanding. It also makes it easier to adapt.

Once students start to answer questions or do activities, we have a model that we can refer back to, allowing us to more quickly and accurately judge in real time the state of student understanding and to respond appropriately. As a result, core questions make it easier to **secure success**.

Beyond the classroom, core questions allow for the accurate triangulation of class, home and independent work. We can set homework that we know is explicitly linked to our in-class learning outcomes (such as retrieval practice quizzes on a selection of core questions, using online platforms such as Carousel Learning or Quizlet), and we can recommend independent learning activities to our students that do the same. We can also use class activities to reinforce the learning from outside the classroom, as if we have a very clear idea of exactly what students should know as a result of their homework, then we can plan activities that **check what they know** and follow up on any issues much more accurately. Successfully threading the same core questions through all three of these areas therefore allows you to **review regularly** and effectively.

Importantly, however, core questions are not everything! They are a lesson planning tool, not lesson planning in themselves. It would be a pretty miserable lesson that simply revolved around the revealing and learning of a sequence of core questions; in fact, this would be an actively harmful approach, as it would suggest to the students that their learning could be reduced to a series of disconnected facts that did not need to cohere together into a meaningful whole. In the words of science teacher Tom Millichamp (2023), 'Teachers should still teach so that students truly understand the material with the core question acting to effectively summarise that understanding.'

Our teaching, in other words, should still be designed to **make meaning**, which is enriched by hinterland, examples, stories and all the other things we do to make the subject come alive. It is just that we now have a concrete and shared model for the outcome of that process.

Writing good core questions

We can also write core questions that emphasise making meaning over rote learning (Moore-Anderson, 2022). For example, questions that test students' understanding of the *relationships* between different pieces of information, rather than basic factual recall. Consider the possible core questions below on obedience.

Core question	Suggested answer
Name at least two situational factors that affect obedience to authority.	Prestige of location, proximity (to victim), wearing a uniform.
What did Milgram find happened to obedience when he replicated his study in a run-down office block?	Obedience dropped from 65% to 48% (a non-significant result).
What did Milgram find happened to obedience when he replicated his study with an experimenter in plain clothes instead of a white coat?	Obedience dropped from 65% to 20%.

One of the common challenges that students face when learning about obedience is meaningfully connecting the evidence (such as Milgram's variations), the factors affecting it (such as uniform) and the explanations for it (such as agentic state and legitimacy of the authority). The questions above, although accurate, do not help to address this challenge. Rephrasing the questions to look at the relationships between factors, evidence and explanations may help students to **make meaning**.

Core question	Suggested answer
What is the relationship between the prestige of the location and obedience? How do we know? What explains this relationship?	When Milgram changed location to a run-down office block, obedience dropped to 48% (from 65% in the original), but this was a non-significant change. In theory, prestigious locations increase the apparent legitimacy of the authority, so the more prestigious the location, the greater the obedience levels – though this is not confirmed here.
What is the relationship between the uniform and obedience? How do we know? What explains this relationship?	Uniforms increase obedience levels as they are a visible symbol of authority. When Milgram dressed the experimenter in plain clothes instead of a white coat, obedience dropped to 20% (from 65% in the original). Also, Bickman (1974) found obedience to a uniformed guard (82%) was much higher than to someone with no uniform (36%). Therefore, uniforms increase the apparent legitimacy of the authority.

These questions can also lead on to further discussions about which factors seem to have the largest effect, why that may be and how we can know. Naturally, not all of our core questions will look like these. There will always be a need for more basic factual questions that emphasise key term definitions or other 'static', rather than 'dynamic', knowledge (Moore-Anderson, 2023). Where possible, however, extending core questions by emphasising relationships can help to address student misconceptions and facilitate meaning making.

Benefits of core questions for students

As well as helping us plan lessons, there are many benefits to students of having core questions shared with them. Initially, it gives students absolute clarity about the expectations you have of them in terms of their learning, which can be hugely reassuring and motivating for students just starting out into the unknown of a new examination subject. They also provide a ready-made, and high quality, bank of material for self-quizzing right from the start of the course, and therefore make it much easier to get students started with productive study habits from the off. They are a valuable tool for feedback and self-reflection; when comparing their answers to the core question exemplar answers, students are required to make judgements about the quality of their work and what they could improve on, allowing improvements to **feedforward** into new work.

Core questions or exam questions?

We may accept the benefits of core questions in terms of lesson planning but still ask whether students will benefit from having them woven into their work. Why, for example, quiz students on core questions when we could just use exam questions? Exam questions are, after all, the medium through which they will ultimately have to demonstrate their understanding, so they are clearly crucial pieces of the puzzle throughout the course that we should be referring to and using regularly.

That said, we think there are many benefits of prioritising core questions for students, especially early in the course. The variety of exam questions, even those on the same topic, is extensive. They may be phrased differently to each other, target different assessment objectives or cover different numbers of marks, all of which creates additional cognitive load for students. If we have designed our unit sequencing around prerequisite knowledge and have therefore focused on foundational knowledge as a basis for early units, it makes sense to prioritise the acquisition of this knowledge as securely as possible.

As well as content knowledge, a good deal of additional expertise is required to successfully answer exam questions, including knowledge of assessment objectives, mark distributions, command terms and question wording implications, answer structuring, extended writing skills and more. As a result, if a student does not answer an exam question correctly, then it is not always clear to them (or to you!) where the underlying issue is. This makes it very difficult to **feedforward** successfully. Core questions allow us to cut through this uncertainty by allowing us to focus solely on successful knowledge acquisition (initially), *and then* solely on exam skills (once we are fairly sure that the core knowledge is secure). We illustrate this to students using a simple flow chart:

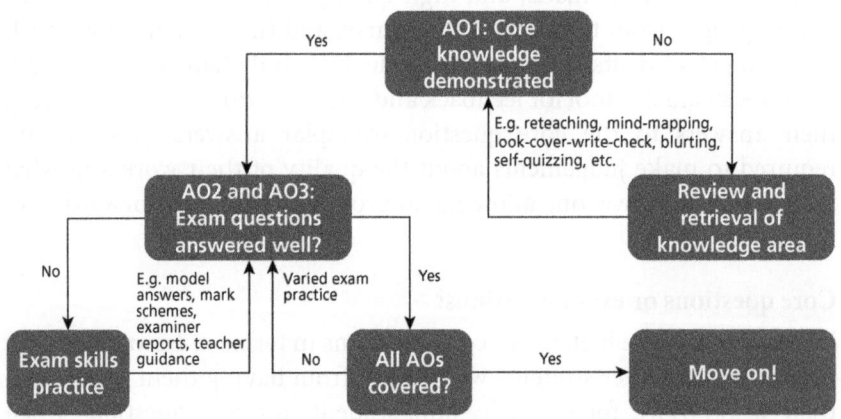

This is a very useful reference tool for students doing independent revision, but it should also be a valuable tool for us as teachers. Sequences such as this allow us to make more accurate formative assessments of our students, by successfully isolating the skills that may be holding them back (see Section 4, 'Formative assessment in psychology', page 371 for further discussion of what this could look like in detail). They also allow students to build effective independent study and revision routines that will prepare them for the final exam, but which also lay the groundwork securely.

Using hinterland to make meaning

As discussed above, core knowledge only really makes sense when placed in a wider context – the hinterland knowledge. What sorts of hinterland knowledge do we want to impart to our students to help them **make meaning** of what they are learning? This is partly dependent on the specification you teach, as what may be considered core by one exam board (by being named on the specification) could be deemed hinterland by another. Putting that practical issue aside, however, we think there are some good general rules of thumb to help us think about the kinds of hinterland knowledge that will be useful to our students and help them **make meaning** of the core.

Study variations or replications

These may not be named on the specification, but they can give a wider perspective on that line of research. For example, no student is expected to have learned all of Milgram's variations, and some exam boards will only prescribe a few. However, being aware of the wide range of factors that Milgram investigated helps students to better understand the complex influences on obedience beyond those they have specifically learned. Furthermore, it helps paint a broader picture of Milgram's contribution to our understanding of obedience and the importance of his methodology as an innovative research paradigm. In addition, studies that have replicated Milgram's findings (in various settings, eras, cultures and with different participants) may also be important to consider (see 'Psychology in the 21st century', page 183). A challenge here is that it is clearly not feasible for teachers to do background reading on every single area of research listed in the specification, but continually updating our subject knowledge, particularly with more contemporary research, is probably one of the most useful forms of subject-specific professional development we can engage in.

Researcher backgrounds and biographies

Sometimes researchers are no more than a name on a long list that students have to learn. Students have no way to differentiate one researcher from another and can be pretty dismissive of some researchers because they don't 'like' the particular study they've had to learn about. Providing a wider context for that researcher can be valuable here. This can include highlighting other things they've contributed to or a wider appreciation of their work so they aren't solely associated with a single piece of research. Some stories could connect with core content that students need to learn as well as adding 'colour' to a name. For example, talking about how Alan Baddeley helped invent postcodes (seriously, look it up!) and how that work fit with his later research on semantic versus acoustic encoding that itself paved the way for first the 'multistore model' of memory and later his own 'working memory model'.

Socio-political and historical context

In order to consider the contribution a piece of research (or theory) may have made to psychology, we need to consider when it took place and what else was going on at the time. For example, major events may have catalysed a particular area of research, such as the backdrop of the Holocaust and trial of Adolf Eichman that triggered lots of the landmark studies in social psychology in the 1960s, especially the work of Stanley Milgram.

Theory development and applications

Students often encounter theories in a very specific context, for example, to explain a particular behaviour like obedience or aggression. This means they rarely consider some of the other ways in which that theory has been applied (what else can it explain?) and also may not learn about the ways the theory has developed since its first inception, or the legacy the theory has had in inspiring the work of others. For example, most psychology specifications feature Freud at some level (although this varies quite significantly) but many students are left with the impression that Freud is somewhat of an embarrassing irrelevance to contemporary psychology and is studied for historical purposes only.[4] However, despite the many theoretical and methodological criticisms, it's also true that Freud has made a significant impact to the landscape of psychology and our cultural landscape. Whether we consider this in terms of the practical applications (such as psychotherapy), the influence on post-Freudians such as Erik Eriksson or John Bowlby or the broader theoretical contributions to psychology, politics, public relations, advertising and even literature, we can't deny Freud's legacy.

---

4 An interesting thought here would be to consider whether we would examine Freud's work at all if it didn't feature in the specification. Perhaps this is a good example of the kind of hinterland knowledge that we may want students to know about to provide context for the core knowledge.

Chronology or development of theories and approaches

We want to avoid students simply compartmentalising every topic without seeing the connections between them, and instead to finish our courses having **made meaning** of psychology as a discipline and not just a random list of theories or studies. Stories such as historical narratives can be an important part of this process and have been found to aid the learning of scientific concepts (Tobler et al., 2024). Some specifications allow for this (for example, the AQA 'Approaches' unit starts with Wundt and invites students to consider behavioural, psychodynamic, cognitive, biological and cognitive neuroscience approaches), but even where they don't, we can provide a narrative framework of the development of psychology to help tell that story (our curriculum sequencing is important here too). This helps students better understand some of the broader synoptic themes such as psychology as a science because they can see how the theoretical body of knowledge and methodological tools used have evolved over time. Similarly, seeing how one theory led to another is important, and students won't necessarily make this connection simply by noting that one date occurs after another.

Residual knowledge – disciplinary thinking?

Other hinterland knowledge that we may explicitly include in our lessons could include the conceptual understanding of the shape of psychology. What does a study generally involve? What is a psychological construct? What do we mean by a theory (and how can this be different to a model or explanation)? What is an approach? If we can answer these kinds of questions, then we can say that we have developed psychological literacy (McGovern et al., 2010) or disciplinary understanding.

By focusing on these disciplinary concepts, not only are we helping our students **make meaning** of the content they encounter in our curriculum, but we are also setting them up for future studies. What specific research or theory that they may encounter in the future is something we can't predict, but the underlying structure of that disciplinary knowledge is something we can provide.

Section 2B: Micro-decisions around curriculum

Sequencing topics within a unit

Some – although not all – of the same decision-making processes that governed the sequencing of units in a curriculum will also be at play when sequencing the learning within a unit, such as:

- Specification order.
- Telling a story (e.g. chronological order of content).
- Existing expertise (i.e. place sections to which students will be able to bring the greatest amount of previous learning earlier in the sequence).
- Prerequisite knowledge (i.e. place sections where students will require the largest amount of prior knowledge towards the end of the sequence).
- Linking content by approach (e.g. by teaching both the biological explanation and the treatment for a condition together) or by type (e.g. teaching all explanations then all treatments subsequently).

How to Teach Psychology

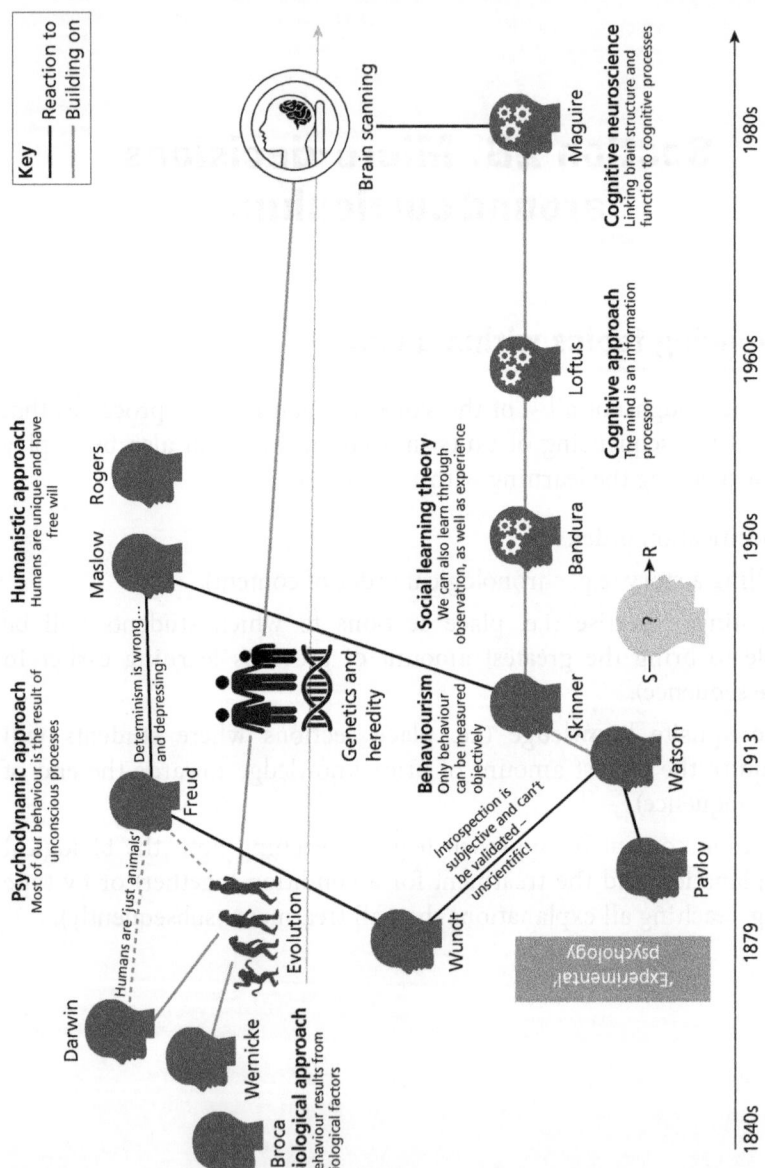

A 'timeline' of the approaches featured in the 'Approaches to psychology' unit in paper 2 of the AQA A-level. How would you sequence the teaching of these areas? How could their sequencing vary according to the different principles above, and which do you think would be most appropriate in this case?

As with sequencing our units, we both began teaching the topics within them by simply following the specification order. Again, we gradually decided that this sequence was not necessarily the one that would best allow students to **make meaning**. For example, in the Edexcel specification, within the topic of 'Memory' the working memory model (WMM) is presented before the multi-store model (MSM), even though the WMM was developed specifically to counter some of the problems with the over-simplistic representation of short-term memory in the MSM.[5] In the same topic, reconstructive memory is presented last, even though this was proposed in 1932, over 30 years before any of the other theories. For students to understand why the MSM represented an important milestone in memory theory, it helps to appreciate the 'loose' theoretical nature of what had come before. A similar example comes in the 'Attachment' unit in AQA A-level paper 1, where the specification order lists Bowlby's later monotropic theory before the preceding theory of maternal deprivation. Therefore, it is an important exercise to consider whether following the specification or textbook sequence is going to help or hinder the students' developing understanding of the course.

Making meaning and 'flexible' exam thinking

Designing a curriculum and lesson experiences that prioritise making meaning is an important enough goal, even when exam questions are relatively predictable, and the required depth of understanding is clearly communicated by the specification. It is even more essential when this is not the case; in some exams in recent years, this has certainly not been the case. Sometimes questions seem to have been designed to explicitly test a students' ability to make connections, and so refer to terminology or combinations of ideas that are not in the specification. The IB paper 3, for example, requires students to think through a scenario and apply their research methods knowledge to a specific unseen study. Edexcel also have a synoptic element in paper 3, in which knowledge of the approaches needs to be applied to a novel topic area. Even outside these specifications, however, there is an expectation that students can draw

---

5 In one textbook, on the pages dealing with the WMM, it actually says: 'You may prefer to read about the MSM first'. Wouldn't it have been easier for them to switch the order?!

links and connections in ways that they might not have predicted. Examiners' reports for these frequently use terms such as 'flexible thinking' in their reviews of students' performance. Indeed, the AQA 2023 paper 2 examiner's report refers to knowledge being used 'flexibly' on no less than five occasions. For example:

> Students should know that, for this type of question, they must demonstrate understanding and be able to **flexibly** apply their knowledge to explain novel scenarios [Question 4]
>
> While it appeared that students had not focused on this topic in depth, those with a good understanding of what the [topic] was were able to use their knowledge **flexibly**, linking this to studies they had covered in other topic areas, and utilised their knowledge of issues and debates to discuss [topic] effectively [Question 6]

What do questions designed to elicit this flexibility look like? Here is an example from the 'Attachment' unit in AQA paper 1, taken from specimen paper 3 (2017):

> Briefly evaluate Bowlby's monotropic theory. In your answer, refer to multiple attachments and the role of the father (6 marks)

The specification content referring to Bowlby's monotropic theory is: 'Explanations of attachment: learning theory and Bowlby's monotropic theory. The concepts of a critical period and an internal working model.'

While 'multiple attachments' and 'the role of the father' are referenced in other points in the unit specification, and while both are definitely relevant to Bowlby's theory, nowhere in the specification is there any indication that students may be asked to combine these specific pieces of information. The aim (one that we are broadly in favour of as a general idea) is to assess whether students have developed a meaningful, interconnected schema of the unit as a whole (allowing them to think 'flexibly'),[6] rather than, for example, rote learning each specification bullet point in isolation.

---

6   The reality is often rather different, however, as we discuss in Section 4, 'Interpreting test and exam results', page 405.

This requirement for flexibility can of course be seen even more readily in the synoptic areas of the course. While the specifics may vary, every exam board expects students to comment on things like issues and debates while drawing on a range of knowledge from across the units they have studied. Sometimes those synoptic links may be really obvious, but in other cases students need to work quite hard to make connections between different areas of their knowledge. We therefore need to plan a curriculum that, wherever possible, encourages cognitive flexibility and **meaning making** and draws out links between different content areas and units.

The timing of units

Another aspect of curriculum building is the time we allocate to different aspects of it. In specifications with a heavy content load, time is a precious resource and the allocation of it needs to be considered carefully. One relatively common strategy is to cover content as rapidly as possible, freeing up time to 'revise' (or, if necessary, entirely reteach) content again towards the end of the course. Indeed, every year a select group of teachers seem to manage to finish their entire specification content by Christmas of either Year 11 or Year 13. However, impressive as this feat of content coverage is, and as seductive as the prospect of so much revision time with classes is, we do not recommend taking such an approach. For one thing, as we have seen, the most effective strategy for forming detailed, well-consolidated semantic memories is to **review regularly**. Review activities are often the first things to make way when the focus shifts to content coverage, not least because we can in theory postpone the review until the end of the process. As well as being less effective for memory consolidation, a lack of interspersed review also limits the students' ability to **make meaning** and draw links between different content areas. If your approach centres on needing the time to potentially reteach large swathes of the course at the end of it, it does also raise the question as to what the point of your initial lessons is!

Instead, we aim to more evenly space out our content coverage over the entire time available, accepting that if we build regular review into most lessons then this will take longer to cover, *at least initially*. If we can be reasonably confident that a good deal of the prerequisite knowledge is secure for most students, then the units with heavy synoptic content can be covered much more rapidly, including retrieval practice activities. This is why, in the scheme below, 'Approaches' gets double the classroom time as does 'Psychopathology', despite it being equally weighted in the exam. The 'Psychopathology' unit draws heavily on 'Approaches' as well as 'Biopsychology' (six weeks) and 'Research methods' (eight weeks), and so having covered those in great detail with regular review, we are able to cover the new unit very efficiently. Increasing expertise with other aspects of 'psychological literacy' (for example, how to make and structure evaluation, answer questions, structure essays and so on) also means that by the end of the course, even units that do not have such a heavy synoptic load (such as 'Relationships') can be covered relatively swiftly. Placing 'Issues and debates' last provides useful revision and still leaves two weeks at the end of the year for some traditional revision lessons that can focus on honing exam skills and looking at whole papers (rather than 'reteaching').

Section 2: Curriculum

Week	Content YEAR 12	Week	Content YEAR 13
1	Induction / Approaches	1	Pyschopathology
2	Approaches	2	Pyschopathology
3	Approaches	3	Attachment
4	Approaches	4	Attachment
5	Approaches	5	Attachment
6	Approaches	6	Attachment
7	Approaches	7	Attachment
8	Approaches	8	Schizophrenia
9	Approaches	9	Schizophrenia
10	Biopsychology	10	Schizophrenia
11	Biopsychology	11	Schizophrenia
12	Biopsychology	12	Schizophrenia
13	Biopsychology	13	Forensic
14	Biopsychology	14	Forensic
15	Biopsychology	15	Mocks
16	Research methods	16	Mocks
17	Research methods	17	Forensic
18	Research methods	18	Forensic
19	Research methods	19	Forensic
20	Research methods	20	Relationship
21	Research methods	21	Relationship
22	Research methods	22	Relationship
23	Internal exams	23	Relationship
24	Research methods	24	Relationship
25	Social influence	25	Issues and debates
26	Social influence	26	Issues and debates
27	Social influence	27	Issues and debates
28	Social influence	28	Issues and debates
29	Social influence	29	Revision
30	Memory	30	Revision
31	Memory		
32	Memory		
33	Memory		
34	Memory		
35	Internal exams		
36	Internal exams		
37	Pyschopathology		
38	Pyschopathology		

A final consideration worth mentioning here is the importance of communicating these decisions to our students, including sharing the rationale. The latter half of Year 13 can feel somewhat like an arms race between subjects to have 'finished the course'. Students start getting rather twitchy in the run-up to Easter because, for example, 'we've already finished history' and yet in psychology we're planning to 'teach' for at least another few weeks. Therefore, we need to ensure students understand our approach and manage their expectations (and anxiety). If we have fostered a strong culture in which we **review regularly** – and explain clearly why we're doing it – then this helps to persuade students that they have actually had the same amount of revision time as history (and in actual fact probably more), just spread throughout the course in a more time-efficient and effective manner.

Mapping the 'shape' of a unit

As well as sequencing, we can also provide other aids to help students see connections and **make meaning** within units. One of the simplest examples of an activity like this is mind mapping. Mind mapping can be a useful retrieval practice technique, allowing students to **review regularly** and consolidate their understanding. However, activities such as this also provide a secondary benefit as mind maps, at their most useful, can become a visual representation of a schema, and can therefore provide a simple overview of all the interconnections between information in a highly accessible and concrete form. It can also be a very useful tool for keeping information separate, such as in the case of theories which are commonly confused or used in the wrong sections. This awareness of the 'shape' of a unit is something that, for all their many benefits, core questions do not tend to provide.

However, rather than simply telling students to draw a mind map, the mapping process needs to be carefully structured so our pre-existing expertise can be brought to bear. Two simple principles to follow are:

- Place information with common connections (where you want students to make links) close to one another.
- Place information that you need students to keep separate as far away from one another as possible.

For example, in the AQA specification, 'Relationships' is an optional paper 3 topic. Students often enjoy studying it but find the examination content challenging. One reason for this is that there are a number of sections of the unit that overlap in ways that are sometimes helpful, and at other times not. Using the principles above, we can therefore plan the framework of a mind map around the following information:

- Evolutionary explanations link to 'physical attractiveness' as a factor affecting attraction – *place nearby.*
- 'Self-disclosure' is both a factor affecting attraction and also a key feature of theories of virtual relationships – *place nearby.*
- The three theories within the 'factors affecting attraction' section are frequently confused with the four theories in the 'theories of relationships' section, and vice-versa. In particular, the 'filter theory' is often used erroneously in essays on theories of relationships (this is entirely understandable, as the distinction between these two categories resides more in the minds of AQA than any coherent academic criteria) – *separate as much as possible!*

The final mind map looks like this:

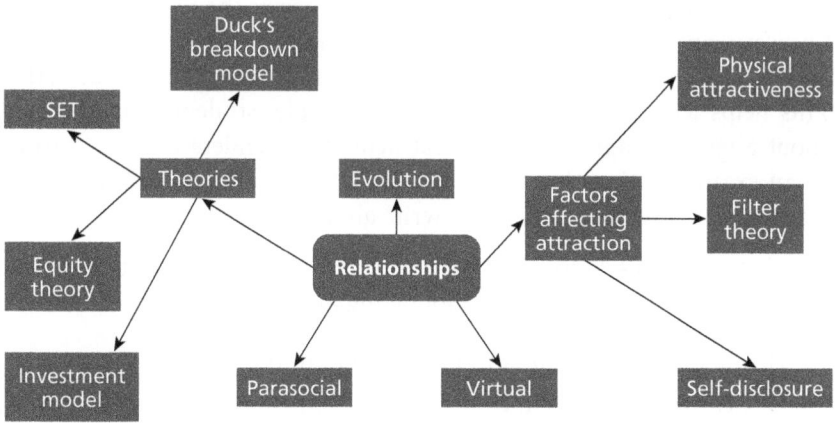

Notice that this arrangement is not simply the arrangement suggested in the specification; instead, this represents what we want the students' schema to look like, if all goes well. Thus, knowing the shape of a unit through mapping it in this way can also help us to avoid misconceptions or common exam technique errors, as well as strengthening student memory in a way that augments other methods of retrieval. It can also help to remind students of the existence of certain parts of the specification that, for whatever reason, commonly seem to be forgotten ('resistance to social influence' in the AQA 'Social influence' unit may be a good example of this).

As we considered in Section 1, visual representations like this can also be used as a form of advance organiser in order to help students **make meaning** of the material they are about to learn. Because new information needs to be connected to prior knowledge, using advance organisers to represent parts of the curriculum gives students an easy way to make those connections. Teachers can help this by 'zooming in' or 'zooming out' as they introduce new material.

Choosing the right content

'Will this come up in the exam?' Although this can be a rather tedious question to field, it is obviously important that students know what material they can be assessed on. One important nuance to clarify is the difference in the specifications between the use of the terms 'including' (indicating prescribed content that could be named in an exam question) and 'for example' (indicating content that cannot be assessed directly). This helps avoid situations where, for example, students have learned about anger management as a treatment for offenders but are thrown by an exam question that refers to a cognitive treatment and they don't realise what they are supposed to write about!

So, what principles do we want to consider when choosing content for our curriculum? One or more of the following aims are likely to be relevant:

- How likely is the content to prove useful in the exam?
- Is it easier to understand or remember (this could be in relation to content that is already included, or it could be extra content that helps to elucidate an otherwise difficult area)?
- How easy is it for you to access the content in enough detail? (Is a textbook summary sufficient? An abstract behind a paywall? A full paper? A book?)

- Can it be used in multiple areas, either within or between different units on the course?
- Does it allow for recap of previously learned material (e.g. through the application of a particular theory, the use of a certain method or even the sharing of a complementary evaluation issue)?
- How relevant is the content in contemporary psychology (i.e. does it better represent where our 'current' thinking is than another option)?
- Does it help to broaden and diversify your curriculum?

As noted throughout this discussion, there is no single right answer, and we have certainly experimented with a number of these factors in the course of our teaching. The context of your own students will be another important factor to consider and may affect the relative weighting of some of these principles.

Where to find the best content

In no particular order, we tend to look for relevant content or research for our curriculum in:

- Mark schemes and examiners' reports, which will often suggest indicative content for a particular question, some of which may be new to you.
- Textbooks, including those written for alternative specifications. Oddly, the same content taught across different specifications can make use of totally different theories or supporting evidence provided, and therefore can provide a really good resource for additional examples (as well as application ideas or practice questions).
- 'Summary' platforms such as the British Psychological Society (BPS) Research Digest, which provides regular updates on contemporary research written in an accessible manner.
- Academic search engines, such as Google Scholar. This has the advantage that you're likely to come across everything out there, but represents a greater investment of time and effort to find what you're looking for. Also, if you don't have journal subscriptions, you may be limited to access to abstracts only (although these are typically far more detailed than the one- or two-line summaries presented in some textbooks).

Choosing the best explanations and theories within a topic

Let's take the example of explanations for disorders. Every psychology course will cover this at some point, and students will typically need to learn at least two biological explanations for a given disorder. While some specifications offer a choice between multiple disorders, it's likely that an awful lot of students will learn about schizophrenia, so we'll use this as our example here. Consider what each specification says that students need to learn (NB in some cases these are suggested rather than prescribed):

AQA	Dopamine hypothesis	Genetics	Neural correlates
OCR	Biochemical	Genetic	Brain abnormality
Edexcel	Function of neurotransmitters	One other biological explanation	N/A
Eduqas	Dopamine hypothesis	Cannabis influence	Enlarged ventricles

Clearly there is plenty of overlap here, but also some significant divergence. Even where there are seemingly the same explanations listed, the level of depth or detail that we choose to go into may vary by specification. For example, AQA and Eduqas explicitly name the dopamine hypothesis, so it may be considered reasonable, therefore, to focus only on dopamine function (both hypo- and hyper-dopaminergia) as the explanation. Edexcel gives the broader heading 'Function of neurotransmitters', which implies consideration of dopamine plus at least one other neurotransmitter (such as serotonin or glutamate), while OCR is even broader still with 'Biochemical', which may include a range of different neurotransmitters and perhaps even consider the role of hormones such as cortisol. If we then consider the 'alternative' explanations listed for each specification, we can see even greater variation, from the highly specific (genetics, enlarged ventricles) to the slightly more nebulous (brain abnormality, neural correlates or even 'other').

A further consideration is the extent to which the chosen explanations map onto the chosen treatments. While it is fairly normal across specifications for there to be multiple explanations taught alongside multiple treatments, these don't necessarily always match up, and where we have choice as to precisely which explanation or treatment to deliver, we need to take this into account. For example, in delivering the schizophrenia topic in Edexcel alongside the biological explanations and treatments, the specification simply prescribes one non-biological explanation. Possible options here are a cognitive explanation or the social causation hypothesis. Similarly, the requirement for treatment includes one non-biological treatment; again, we could look to cognitive treatments such as CBT, or an alternative such as family therapy. The most obvious route to take from a topic coherence point of view would be to teach a cognitive explanation followed by a cognitive treatment.

However, students typically find this explanation quite challenging, and therefore we could also make the case for teaching social causation as our non-biological explanation. It's arguably less abstract for students to understand and remember than cognitive explanations (anecdotally, they certainly seem to prefer it), which helps **manage cognitive load** (especially given the high demand already placed on them by biological explanations). Furthermore, it makes the link to an interactionist view (the diathesis-stress model – that environmental stressors act upon an underlying predisposition, triggering or worsening a schizophrenic episode) more straightforward, which is a useful theoretical position to know about in order to understand the complexity of schizophrenia and also gives students a concrete example to discuss wider synoptic issues and debates like reductionism versus holism, nature versus nurture or the influence of culture.

But now we have a different problem, in that the treatments based on this approach (for example, assertive community treatment, Stein and Test, 1980) are less well established and may present other challenges for students learning them (see Section 3, 'Treatments', page 305), as well as that textbooks that mention them are somewhat light on detail. Therefore, assuming we opt for something more concrete like CBT or family therapy, we are still going to need significant groundwork-laying in order for students to have sufficient prior knowledge to **make meaning** of the rationale behind it (see Section 3, 'Treatments', page 305).

Once again, we do not present a preferred right answer here, nor suggest that there is one. But being alive to this trade-off, making decisions deliberately, taking into account the specific details of your own context and being willing to review, reflect and experiment with different approaches should stand you and your students in good stead.

Case study: Choosing a second 'neural correlate' of schizophrenia

In the 'Schizophrenia' optional unit for AQA A-level, students are required to know 'neural correlates, including the dopamine hypothesis'. Note the use of the plural for 'correlates' – rarely can a single letter have open such a range of choice and confusion! A cursory glance at the research literature or popular science websites reveals an almost overwhelming array of candidate molecules and structures that could be taught as a second neural correlate alongside the dopamine hypothesis.

We choose to teach students about the work of Judith Ford. Ford and her colleagues have conducted multiple studies into the 'corollary discharge' mechanism (whereby planned actions are relayed to the appropriate sensory cortex, inhibiting it and helping us distinguish between internally and externally generated signals). For example, Ford et al. (2001) studied seven healthy men and seven male patients with schizophrenia and used event-related potential (ERP) to measure activity in the temporal lobes when listening to either their own spoken words or a recording of played back speech. Controls showed a reduction in activity when processing their own spoken words, compared to played back speech, but schizophrenia patients showed no such reduction. Ford et al. (2002) later found that this disconnect between frontal and temporal areas was larger in patients prone to auditory hallucinations. Ford concluded that reduced fronto-temporal communication (poorer communication between Broca's area and auditory areas, including auditory cortex and Wernicke's area) may contribute to the misattribution of inner thoughts to external voices in schizophrenia.

This works well as a second neural correlate for the following reasons:

- It does not introduce any new neurotransmitters or brain areas that students will not have previously studied.
- It can be covered using limited new technical terminology. The term 'corollary discharge' can be omitted, for example, in favour of a more descriptive 'poor communication between frontal and temporal language areas', or even 'poor communication between Broca's and Wernicke's areas' (which is a slight oversimplification, but not inaccurate).

- It provides useful links to prior knowledge, such as the functions of Broca's and Wernicke's areas and ERPs as a method of studying the brain.
- It also provides useful links to other explanations within the unit, as the misattribution of internal speech is also an example of impaired meta-representation (i.e. the cognitive explanation). Ford's research can therefore be used as supporting evidence here as well.
- There is also a simple, concrete demonstration of the theory as it is thought to be corollary discharge that explains why we can't tickle ourselves (Blakemore et al., 1998). (Cue lots of entertainment in the classroom as students try to tickle themselves and each other!) Memorably, Blakemore et al. (2000) found that schizophrenics can tickle themselves, a lovely demonstration of the theory that students enjoy and grasp easily.

Choosing which disorders to teach

Although every exam specification features clinical psychology in some form, there is still some variation in precisely which disorders are prescribed, and there is certainly some choice for teachers here. While schizophrenia is often the popular option (and is prescribed on Edexcel and AQA), students could also learn about a range of other disorders including OCD, depression, bipolar, phobia, anorexia, stress and many others. As with the other micro-curriculum decisions we've considered, there are a range of factors to weigh up here, and no clear right answers. However, an additional dimension to consider will be the extent to which this represents a particularly challenging area of content for students with their own potential mental health struggles.

Mental health issues among students are certainly on the rise (Creswell, 2023; Guzman Holst et al., 2023), and so the likelihood of there being students in a given cohort having experience with things like anxiety, depression or eating disorders (or quite possibly some combination of all three) is higher now than ever. The 'prevalence inflation hypothesis' (Foulkes and Andrews, 2023) suggests that increased social awareness and publicity of mental health issues may actually be contributing to this increase, and any experienced psychology teacher will be able to think of students for whom learning about disorders has been a

> challenging, if not outright harmful, experience. This should not necessarily be a reason to steer clear of discussing these disorders, and, of course, learning about them in a safe context can be an incredibly positive experience for many students. But it is certainly a danger that studying complex conditions in the inevitably slightly superficial manner that an A-level unit invites could do more harm than good.
>
> These choices should be approached with caution, and we need to be clear both to ourselves and our students (and to our colleagues) that we are psychology teachers and not mental health professionals. It can also be helpful to have an idea about which areas are likely to be found most challenging by members of each cohort and considering if any adaptations can be made to your curriculum in light of this. Further, it's probably helpful for teachers to have thought about some sort of standard 'health warning' that helps to guide students appropriately whenever we are discussing these sorts of issues.

Choosing the right research and studies

Although most specifications feature a number of 'named' studies that students must learn about, they will typically also require a wider range of research on which to draw (we discuss this further in Section 3: 'Teaching studies', page 284). How many of these you choose to include in your curriculum is extremely flexible. While we could prioritise teaching based on more general principles such as research methods or issues and debates, referring to research is the primary method by which ideas are evaluated within the psychological research literature, so we would therefore argue that being able to use an extensive range of further research is a key part of creating 'psychological literacy'.

The most likely source of research for most (beyond the named studies in the specification) will be the textbook, but there is significant variation here, and we may choose to look elsewhere. The research presented may only highlight a very specific point about a theory – one that doesn't seem to fit with the way you want your students to think about it. It may be that the research provided is restricted in some way due to the sample, design, task or setting. While this may be useful for the students to evaluate, it can lead to an unhelpful view of the theory in which all the evidence is undermined. Students can easily fixate on methodological issues with supporting evidence and use this to erroneously conclude that the theory itself is inherently flawed. It may also be the case that a textbook's evaluation points, although accurate, are too complex or esoteric for students to meaningfully incorporate into their schemas. It may even be that a textbook's report of research is simply incorrect (this is surprisingly common, see Steuer and Ham, 2008).

This is not to suggest that you should immediately reject the choice of studies made by others, just to advise against doing so blindly. As a very simple rule of thumb, only include a study in your curriculum if:

- You see where the study either complements or criticises other evidence or theories provided, without overlapping so much with them as to become redundant.
- You have a very clear picture of the sorts of evaluative points that you would want your students to be writing when using it.

Case study: Using research to make cognitive explanations of mental illness concrete

Due to its abstract nature (representation of cognition is less concrete than, for example, biological processes), students often find cognitive psychology more challenging than other approaches. As a result of this, the choice of evidence is an important part of trying to make cognitive explanations more accessible and familiar to students.

In the 'Psychopathology' unit of the AQA A-level, students cover cognitive explanations for depression, including Beck's negative triad. Beck's own study (which found higher levels of biased thinking in depressive participants; Beck, 1967) could be used as supporting evidence here, but we have found that students struggle to remember this research. In discussions with colleagues and the students themselves, we decided that the likely reason for this was that the study was compounding the difficulties of abstraction that come with cognitive explanations. The cognitive biases measured were slightly nebulous and hard to define, and also don't relate perfectly to the features of Beck's cognitive triad. It therefore didn't allow for effective *subsumptive learning* as the concrete details didn't easily map onto the higher order concept. It was all just a bit too woolly.

We decided that it would be better to find evidence that highlights one specific – and more easily definable – cognitive bias arising from depressive cognition. A search on Google Scholar led to the work of Mohammed Al-Mosaiwi and Tom Johnstone on 'absolutism'. Absolutism is defined as 'words, phrases and ideas that denote totality, either of magnitude or probability', for example, 'every', 'never', 'always', 'totally', 'completely', 'absolutely' and 'must'. Al-Mosaiwi and Johnstone (2018) conducted a content analysis for absolutist language in internet support forums for depression and suicidal ideation, and compared these with control forums for asthma, cancer and diabetes. They found that the depression forums contained more absolutist words than control forums, with the suicidal ideation forum the highest.

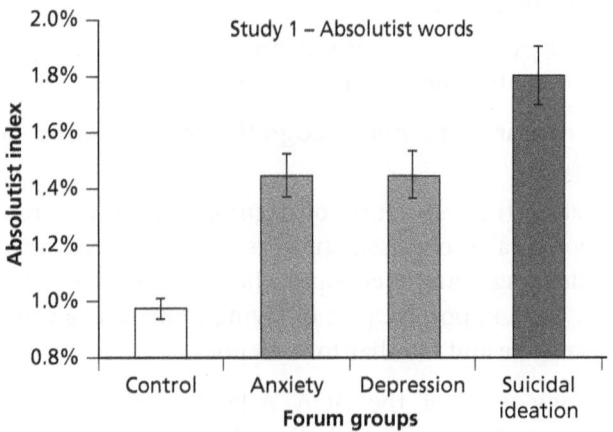

Why is this easier to remember? Now the subsumer – that the cognitive triad leads to biased thinking – can be taught along with some concrete subconcepts that exemplify this, such as absolutist language. The evidence then complements this by providing a specific example of increased occurrence of one of the subconcepts. It also provides a useful recap of a research methods technique (content analysis) that students often find challenging. Students seem able to recall this study much more clearly than the evidence that we previously used and can use it more successfully in their evaluations of the wider explanation.[7]

---

7   Students averaged nearly three marks more than the national average on a 16-mark essay question that examined this knowledge in 2024.

Nuggets

'Nuggets' is the term we might use for areas of content that are 'portable' and can be used in multiple places across the course. A good nugget is worth its weight in gold (pardon the pun…), as not only does it help future learning but it also provides free revision, thus cutting down the volume of information that students need to know. Typically, we would refer to studies here, but some theories or concepts are also quite 'nuggety' in that they may provide prerequisite knowledge for learning about a range of other ideas. To consider something a useful nugget, we think it should:

- Allow students to make multiple points *across* topics.
- Allow students to make multiple points *within* topics.

An excellent example here would be Albert Bandura's classic Bobo Doll studies (1961, 1963 and 1965). While students will no doubt encounter this when learning about SLT in its own right, the research (or SLT as a theory) may also be used in a number of other domains (this selection is by no means exhaustive):

Applications	Methodological features	Issues and debates[8]
Aggression Gender roles Crime Phobia Child development	Experimental design Observational methods Self-report methods Data analysis (quantitative and qualitative) Ethics	Nature versus nurture Social sensitivity Reductionism versus holism Determinism versus free will Psychology as a science

Being deliberate about the use of nuggets is helpful for students. Not only do they reduce the amount of content to be learned, but they also help to **manage cognitive load**, because if the students have encountered a study before then they are only concerned with how it is relevant to whatever specific topic they are trying to apply it to and not all the associated methodological detail. This allows students to better **make meaning** of new ideas because they are anchoring new knowledge in what they

---

8 Each specification varies slightly on which issues and debates are to be covered, but the majority of these should be familiar to any psychology teacher and are even likely to be taught to students regardless of whether or not they actually feature on the specification.

already know. Because they are studies with high utility, we should also ensure they are ones we **review regularly**.

Nuggets across units and topics

Many other studies can also be used as examples in various different places in the specification and therefore may be drawn upon in different sections of the exams. Again, we present what we consider some useful examples here, but there are many more you may think of (and an exercise discussing and generating such a list is probably a pretty productive activity to complete either individually or within your department).

Study	Topic links
Loftus and Palmer (1974) – Reconstruction of an automobile accident	• Memory (reconstructive memory theory). • Crime (reliability of eyewitness testimony). • Research methods (experimental methods). • Issues and debates (application of psychology).
Watson and Rayner (1920) – Little Albert	• Learning theory (classical conditioning). • Phobias. • Ethics.
Raine et al. (1997) – Not guilty by reason of insanity (NGRI) murderers	• Biopsychology (localisation of function). • Aggression. • Crime (explanation for offending). • Research methods (experimental design, brain scans). • Issues and debates (nature versus nurture, determinism versus free will).
Osborn and West (1979) – Family criminality	• Approaches (SLT and biological). • Crime (explanations for offending). • Issues and debates (nature versus nurture, reductionism versus holism).
Bowlby (1944) – 44 juvenile thieves	• Development/Attachment. • Approaches (psychodynamic). • Research methods (retrospective studies, self-reports).
Tienari et al. (2004) – Schizophrenia adoption study	• Approaches (biological approach). • Schizophrenia (genetic/family dysfunction explanations and interactionism). • Research methods (adoption studies, natural experiment). • Issues and debates (nature versus nurture, reductionism versus holism).

Study	Topic links
Ford et al. (2001) – Neural communication in schizophrenia	• Biopsychology (localisation of function). • EEG/ERP method. • Research methods (experimental designs, quasi experiments). • Schizophrenia (biological/cognitive explanations).
Brendgen et al. (2005) – Twin study on aggression	• Biopsychology (genetic explanation for aggression and interactionism). • Social learning theory. • Developmental psychology (shift from physical to social aggression). • Research methods (longitudinal studies, self-reports, cross-cultural issues). • Issues and debates (nature versus nurture, reductionism versus holism).

Nuggets within units and topics

These are studies we may use to support different points within the same topic area:

Type of study	Example study
Studies that can both support and criticise something.	Wolpe (1973) attempted (unsuccessfully) to use systematic desensitisation to treat a woman's fear of insects. It turned out that her (estranged) husband had an insect nickname. Her 'fear' was simply a displacement of her marital problems. However, Wolpe is also noted for treating a patient with fear of cars successfully through flooding (by driving her around for several hours until her fear subsided). Therefore, this study can be used to both support and criticise behaviourist treatments for phobia.
Studies that can be used to support one thing and criticise another.	Shallice and Warrington (1970) reported the case of patient 'KF', who showed impairment for verbal but not visual STM. This can be used to challenge the multi-store model but support the working memory model.
Studies that can be used to evaluate a range of different theories within the same topic.	Fox (1977) studied infants raised in Israeli kibbutzim. The infants were tested using the strange situation. Reunion behaviour was much stronger for the mother than for the metapelet (kibbutz nurse). This could be used to comment on a range of explanations for and influences on attachment, including learning theory, monotropic theory, 'strange situation' and cultural variations in attachment.

A caveat – contextualisation is key!

One potential danger with nuggets is that students can sometimes apply them rather superficially and not make effective links to the context of the question. For example, students may encounter a novel scenario that describes a behaviour they have not studied and be asked to explain it using various approaches or theories. Let's imagine the scenario involves drug addiction (which students haven't learned explanations for), and the question requires students to consider how well learning theories can explain it. It's fairly obvious how social learning theory can be applied here, but when it comes to evaluation, they can come unstuck. It's likely they will draw upon Bandura's Bobo Doll studies to support the idea of imitation of models but may then fail to make appropriate links back to the specific behaviour given in the scenario (addiction). In Section 3, we will discuss the importance of context in students' evaluative writing to try to avoid this problem.

Homework and independent study

As psychology teachers, we often find ourselves reminding students there is no perfect piece of research and that, if we are to have real faith in them, all conclusions require *triangulation* across a number of different methods and evidence forms. The same caution should also be applied to the conclusions that we make regarding our students' learning, and it is therefore important that all the work we want our students to do, whether as classwork, homework or independent learning, is designed to help us triangulate our judgements of their progress, and also to help students **secure success**. This could take the following sequence:

1. In class – teach new content.
2. Independent study – review/self-quiz/self-explain the new content in the following days.
3. Homework (after a suitable delay) – quiz of core questions on the topic.
4. In class (on day the homework is due) – starter questions of the hardest or least successfully completed core questions from the homework.

5. Independent study – follow up on feedback from the core questions quizzes.
6. In class – exam questions on the topic.

Research suggests that homework is becoming less effective for student learning (Glass and Kang, 2022), as more students are simply copying from the internet (or using AI[9]). Therefore, it is even more important for us to **share the rationale** for homework and independent study so students don't simply see them as meaningless chores to be checked off a list, and also to set activities that lead to meaningful learning.

STAR tasks

If we want students to engage in independent learning activities that are effective, and that operate in synergy with classwork and homework, then two things need to be in place:

1. We need to have explicitly taught our students how to perform the sorts of learning tasks that we want them to be performing independently.
2. We need to provide a structure that makes it as easy as possible for students to actually do the tasks regularly (so developing productive study habits).

Building on the ideas of religious education teacher Dawn Cox, one of us has recently begun including tables like the one below into work booklets, with the enjoyably corny acronym of STAR (student taking advantage of resources) charts. Students can record their independent learning across a range of approved activities, mapped against each point of the specification. This can be left entirely to students' discretion and motivation, or a certain number of activities can be required each week (our current preferred method). You can also create some competition or rewards for those with the most (or best) STAR resources. Importantly, however, any activities at the top of a STAR chart need to have been explicitly taught to students, so that they know how to use them for effective retrieval practice (or if you include an 'other' category as below,

---

9 There are other, more useful ways for us to harness the power of AI; we discuss some applications in Section 3, 'Teaching core content', page 199, and Section 4, 'Assessment and feedback', page 363.

that students can at least justify how their preferred method follows effective learning principles).

Specification content	Core questions answered	Mind-mapped	Flashcards (or similar)	Open drive exam questions	Feedback follow-up	Other
Origins of psychology: Wundt, introspection, the emergence of psychology as a science						
Learning approaches: The behaviourist approach, including classical conditioning and Pavlov's research						
Learning approaches: The behaviourist approach, including operant conditioning, types of reinforcement; Skinner's research						
Learning approaches: Social learning theory including imitation, identification, modelling, vicarious reinforcement, meditational processes; Bandura						

Flipped learning – Principles and pitfalls

Another technique that promises to aid the coherent triangulation of classwork and homework is 'flipped learning', in which students learn some new content knowledge (often AO1 skills) independently or for homework in advance of a lesson, and then complete related activities (often focused on more challenging AO2 or AO3 skills, or exam questions) in class with the teacher. Despite the enthusiasm for flipped learning, it's worth noting that the academic evidence in support of it is far from consistent and tends to report higher levels of success at university level than in schools (Kapur et al., 2022). That's not to say it cannot be effective, but the research suggests that it works best in a tightly structured format.

One recently suggested structure for flipped learning, based on a large review of previous research, is 'fail, flip, fix, feed' (Kapur et al., 2022):

- Fail – give part of the task *prior to instruction* (perhaps multiple-choice questions), as this can stimulate 'productive failure' (showing students what they don't know, stimulating curiosity and generating prediction errors).
- Flip – pre-exposure to the ideas in the upcoming class (same as in the standard model).
- Fix – mistakes and misconceptions are identified (through formative assessment methods) and explicitly addressed by the teacher, who also emphasises connections and relationships that may not have been obvious to students in the flipping stage.
- Feed – students **feedforward** by identifying what their next steps for improvement are.

It's clear to see why such a system may be more effective than more traditional flipped learning; indeed, it nicely incorporates some of our pedagogical implications such as **check what they know**, **make meaning** and **feedforward**. However, this comes at a time cost, as the 'fix' and 'feed' phases still need to occur in class, and all this is before even moving on to the other post-flipping activities, such as evaluation and exam question practice. Flipped learning is often touted as a solution to the problem of content-heavy courses and limited class time. If it is to be done really effectively, however, especially for more challenging topic and content areas, we are not convinced that these benefits always persist, hence our tendency to restrict this to the most accessible content areas.

Section 2C: Psychology in the 21st century

Balancing the classic and the contemporary

In 2013, a report from the British Psychological Society (BPS) surveyed more than 400 psychology teachers and nearly 900 A-level psychology students for their thoughts on the A-level curriculum (BPS, 2013). The report concluded:

> There was wide support for the inclusion of both classic theory and research and more contemporary material at A-level. However, there was no consensus about the relative importance of old and new material. It was felt that A-level specifications should be better structured so that old and newer material can be combined in a meaningful way. There was some debate over how to operationalise 'contemporary'. It was widely felt that newer material needs to be carefully selected and that what is important is not publication dates per se but the inclusion of some modern trends in research and theory.

It may feel like the same debates are still happening! However, this may be because such debates are always going to be a part of psychology – or, indeed, any social science. How well do we do this? Consider the canon of social psychology – the likes of Milgram, Asch and Zimbardo who have been, in various combinations, included in our specifications for nearly as long as A-level psychology has been around. Of course, they do represent significant contributions to our understanding of social influence, but recent years have seen much debate over their methods and findings (for example, the views of Perry, 2013, Baumrind, 2015 and Reicher and Haslam, 2006).

To what extent are these debates presented to students? Bartels (2015) carried out a content analysis of the coverage of the Stanford Prison Experiment (Haney et al., 1973) across 17 introductory textbooks and found that of six major criticisms of the SPE, none were explicitly covered by more than two of the textbooks, and most did not mention any of the criticisms at all.[10] Perhaps it could be argued that these studies are important because the ideas they explore are still being debated, so it's not what the findings tell us (or not) that matters, rather the fact they have raised so many important questions.

We would argue that we do therefore have something of a responsibility to introduce aspects of contemporary psychological research and thinking to students. If we allow students to draw conclusions about the value of particular studies based on a narrow frame of reference, then we are doing them a disservice. Importantly, however, this should only be done in ways that will also aid students to access the course content, and we should not see the need for the inclusion of contemporary research as simply another box to be ticked.

Useful methods for including more contemporary research and thought into our courses in ways that are directly relevant include *replication studies, systematic reviews* and *meta-analyses*. These methods provide the opportunity to illustrate how the research has developed since the original starting point (and the sophistication of our conclusions with them), and also all raise the possibility of research findings conflicting with one another and consideration of why this may be (which can then be linked to the peer review and publication process, and the replication crisis, should you so wish). Some nice examples include:

- Fisher and Greenberg (1996) – meta-analysis of 2500 studies of psychoanalysis that found support for the validity of a number of Freud's ideas.
- Shin et al. (2021) – failed to replicate Godden and Baddeley's (1975) study of context-dependent forgetting effects when learning on land and underwater (at least in terms of immediate recall), although using virtual reality rather than the real environment.

---

10 Griggs and Whitehead (2015) found very similar results for textbook coverage of Milgram.

- Joel et al. (2020) – meta-analysis of 43 longitudinal studies of couples to identify relationship-specific predictors of relationship quality.
- Ozden and Glover (2023) – mixed methods review of factors affecting the success of protest movements in creating social change that found that consistency (i.e. presenting a unified front and message) has only a very small effect on social change.
- Jerrim and de Vries (2023) – systematic review of peer review reports that found that inter-rater reliability of peer review had a correlation of just +0.2.
- Franzen and Mader (2023) – successfully replicated Asch's original line length study of conformity and considered further variables impacting social influence as well as testing in more realistic contexts.
- Carlsson et al. (2000) – literature review of neurotransmitter explanations and treatments of schizophrenia that identified the importance of both serotonin and glutamate in understanding symptoms of schizophrenia with implications for drug treatments.
- Wright and Czeisler (2002) – failed replication of the commonly cited Campbell and Murphy (1998) study on the effect of light shone on the skin on circadian rhythms.

Case study: Balancing classic contemporary research – Milgram and Burger

When we're teaching studies such as those carried out by Milgram, it's not hard for students to appreciate the impact they have had on psychology as a field, and their contributions to society in general. However, it's less intuitive for students to appreciate the nuances of experimental design, which may affect our ability to conclude that 'ordinary' people can be made to do terrible things.

To draw out this understanding, a good example to follow Milgram is the work by Jerry Burger (2009), who successfully replicated Milgram's study 50 years later. Burger's findings suggested that situational variables still have the power to make ordinary participants exhibit harmful behaviour towards their fellows.

However, Burger only allowed participants to progress to 150 volts on the (fake) electric shock generator in order to reduce ethical issues. This raises some problems as it means it wasn't a true replication, and it could be argued, therefore, that Burger's results don't really tell us all that much as his participants were never put in quite the same situation as those in Milgram's original studies. We can, therefore, discuss with students how experimental design choices impact the conclusions that we can draw about human behaviour.

Yet Burger wasn't simply trying to replicate Milgram; he was also trying to demonstrate that it was still possible to conduct powerful experiments in social psychology without sacrificing ethical considerations. Taken alongside the work of Reicher and Haslam's BBC Prison Study, for example, this represents a significant new paradigm in social psychology. Without our guidance, students are unlikely to recognise these things for themselves, and so, again, this is an important area of hinterland knowledge that we must take care to impart if we want students to appreciate why they are learning about a particular piece of research.

Embracing diversity

Psychological research relies upon the notion of external validity, which is the ability to generalise conclusions beyond the sample being studied. The extent to which researchers have historically felt able to use often unrepresentative samples to draw conclusions about diverse populations is therefore absolutely central to understanding the strengths and weaknesses of the subject itself; appreciating this is central to developing psychological literacy in our students.

This is why the consideration of diversity cannot be a bolt-on to our curricula, and why it has at times been frustrating to see teachers being directed towards recent resources that, while informative and interesting, do not always tie in coherently with exam specifications. Such resources include the BPS webinar 'Decolonising the curriculum',[11] the e-book, *Hidden Histories: Black in Psychology*[12] (Carmichael-Murphy and Danquah, 2022) and even resources produced by the exam boards themselves, such as AQA's (2023) support guide to 'Culture in psychology'.[13] All of these are valuable and well-produced documents that we recommend to teachers (and to students who are keen to read

---

11   https://www.youtube.com/watch?v=wu9XkmYXjkg
12   https://www.researchgate.net/publication/361552876_Hidden_Histories_Black_in_Psychology
13   https://filestore.aqa.org.uk/resources/psychology/AQA-7182-RSG-CIP.PDF

further), but they do not necessarily assist us with the day-to-day business of making a diverse curriculum through which to deliver the core content.

So how can we approach this for ourselves? As with all of our other evidence-informed decisions, we need a **WHAT mindset** (knowing *why* we are making a change, starting *humbly* with small changes, *assessing* and *tweaking*). The first step in this process, essential to knowing why we might need to change the curriculum, is to work out how big the problem is to start with.

Know the diversity in your own curriculum

'How diverse is your curriculum now?' You may well have a hunch about the answer to this question (and the hunch may well be correct), but how do you actually *know*? Understanding the scale of the diversity problem in our curricula requires – before any corrective measures – assessing the actual extent of it. For example, aware that a number of the key studies and historical approaches are fairly androcentric, one of us recently undertook an audit of all of the studies in their curriculum that were first authored (or co-authored) by women. This required a fair amount of time on Google Scholar, but the results were interesting and are given below.

Approaches:	Biopsychology:
Rosalie Rayner – Little Albert.	Bernadette von Dawans – fight or flight.
Sheila Ross and Dorothea Ross – conducted Bobo Doll studies alongside Bandura.	Evelina Fedorenko – localisation of function.
Karen Horney – psychodynamic approach and issues and debates.	Nina Dronkers – localisation of function.
Eleanor Maguire – 'taxi drivers' study.	Eleanor Maguire – 'taxi drivers' study.
	Laura Danelli – EB case study.
	Patricia Murphy – exogenous zeitgebers.
	Tamsin Kelly – endogenous pacemakers (submarine study).
Social influence:	**Psychopathology:**
Diana Baumrind – Milgram ethics.	Marie Jahoda – definitions of abnormality.
Rosetta Pareyson – cross-cultural Milgram replication.	Susan Mineka – SLT and phobias.
Carol Schmitt – explanations of obedience.	Lisa Gilroy – systematic desensitisation.
	Irene Elkin – CBT appropriateness for depression.

Memory:	**Attachment:**
Phyllis Bahrick – LTM duration.	Peggy Emerson – stages of attachment.
Margaret J. Peterson – STM duration.	Janine Oostenbroek – neonatal imitation.
Brenda Milner – HM.	Karin Grossmann – role of the father in attachment.
Barbara Wilson – Clive Wearing.	Tiffany Field – role of the father.
Elizabeth Warrington – KF.	Mary Ainsworth – 'strange situation'.
Jess R. Baker – cue-dependent memory (chewing gum).	Cindy Hazan – long-term effects of attachment.
Elizabeth Loftus – EWT leading questions.	Marina Rain – parasocial relationships.
Fiona Gabbert – EWT post-event discussion.	
Judith Cutshall – EWT anxiety.	
Kerri Pickel – EWT anxiety and weapon focus.	
Becky Milne – cognitive interview.	
Relationships:	**Forensic psychology:**
Yadika Sharma – mate selection cross culturally.	Aiste Jusyte – hostile attribution bias.
Helen Clegg – intersexual selection.	Jane Ireland – CBT for anger management.
Elaine Walster – matching hypothesis.	**Schizophrenia:**
Susan Sprecher – reciprocal self-disclosure.	Sarah-Jayne Blakemore – cognitive explanations.
Leda Sportolari – self-disclosure in online relationships.	Judith Ford – corollary discharge, neural correlate and metarepresentation.
Natasha Tidwell – filter theory.	Jean Addington – CBT for schizophrenia.
Samantha Joel – social exchange and equity theories.	Neva H. Patel – schizophrenia PET.
Margaret Clark – exchange versus communal relationships.	Fiona Pharoah – family therapy.
Laura Stafford – equity theory.	Carol Anderson – family therapy/interactionist treatments.
Caryl Rusbult – investment model.	Judith Newton – token economies.
Wind Goodfriend – investment model future investments.	
Patricia Frazier – relationship breakdown.	
Debra Oswald – online relationships.	
Lynn McCutcheon – parasocial relationships.	
Marina Rain – parasocial relationships.	
Hannah Schmidt – parasocial relationships.	

Is this an 'acceptable' number? We're not sure that it would be possible to define exactly what such a figure would be. It's certainly not 50% of the total number of studies that are covered in the curriculum, and in some areas (such as social influence, notably an area containing less contemporary research) the representation is poor. In others, such as attachment and relationships (historically research areas where female psychologists found it easier to gain a foothold), the proportion is approaching or over 50%. Rather than have a defined quota to aim towards, it is probably better to use this process to provide targets for areas in which the representation could be improved (social influence, approaches, psychopathology and forensic psychology) as our resources are updated.

Conducting an audit in this way also throws up surprises, mainly in the form of researchers whose names you may have known and used for a while without ever realising that they were female. Thus, when your students (as ours certainly sometimes do) slip into the 'default male' mode of describing a researcher as 'he', we're in a much better position to challenge that with 'she, actually!'

Finding and incorporating diverse research

If this process highlights the need to make changes, the next step is to actually find the appropriate content. An additional choice here, though, will be the form of diversification that you would like to see achieved by the content choice. In the table above, we focused on diversity from the perspective of the gender of the researchers, but we could equally aim for greater gender diversity in samples. We could also aim for greater cultural diversity of researchers, although we must be cautious here as the cultural background of the psychologist is rarely revealed in any great detail, or of samples. All are worthy targets, and so to some degree it is probably desirable to aim to achieve all of them at different points.[14]

A valuable form of research to incorporate into core content, which also assists an understanding of external validity, are *cross-cultural studies*. It is likely that most of us will have these in our curriculum already in a number of places (such as in social influence when discussing Milgram), but with a bit of searching you may find them useful in many more areas of the course.

---

14 A guide by the American Psychological Association provides some useful (and very detailed) questions to consider when aiming to create diverse resources for our students: https://www.apa.org/pi/oema/programs/recruitment/inclusive-textbooks.pdf

A nice example (which features as an optional contemporary study in the cognitive section of the Edexcel specification) deals with development of phonological loop capacity in working memory. Sebastián and Hernández-Gil (2012) studied Spanish children aged 5–17 years using digit span tests and found that while the overall pattern of development looked similar to English-speaking counterparts, mean digit-span was lower for Spanish children. This can be explained by the word-length effect such that Spanish words for numbers typically contain more syllables (quattro, ocho) than English numbers (four, eight). This study presents a good way to discuss the power of cross-cultural research to contribute to things like the nature-nurture debate since it supports both nature (that capacity of the phonological loop appears universal) and nurture (that digit span may differ relative to the speaker's native language). It's also a good example of a nugget (see above) as it can be used to talk about different theories of memory (such as WMM and MSM), research methods (such as the use of cross-sectional studies), synoptic debates (such as nature-nurture), and developmental psychology (the study also included comparison with older patients, as well as those with frontal variant frontotemporal dementia).

Of course, even studies of cultural diversity can be outdated! Some studies of cultural difference consider the distinction between 'collectivist' and 'individualistic' cultures which, while still widely used in some areas of research, is also now increasingly questioned as a valid dimension of difference in an increasingly globalised world. Teaching students from different and diverse cultural backgrounds can also be a real boon here and asking for their personal experience may offer a powerful sense of perspective for the class (although, of course, we should also consider the extent to which their perspective is representative too!) We should therefore be cautious that our attempts to highlight cultural diversity do not tip over into equally flawed and simplistic stereotyping. As noted next, however, this does not mean that we should avoid such research, just that we highlight the possibility for further evaluation of it.

Diversity through evaluation

Enjoyable as it can be to find new and interesting research to include in our core curricula, this is not always possible. The specification is as it is, and the constraints that this imposes (in terms of mandatory studies and so on) need to be accepted. It is surprising how rapidly the current generation of specifications – first taught in 2015 and so prepared in the early 2010s – can seem outdated; indeed, this is probably inevitable given the speed of social change in some areas.

We often see teachers who are wrestling with the challenges of presenting content to students who they worry will find aspects of it unacceptable, particularly in areas such as gender or relationships. As ever, while individual context must be carefully considered and teachers may decide that certain units could incite too much controversy among students to be worthwhile, we certainly think that there is no necessary reason to avoid content that may be deemed outdated or lacking in diversity. If we feel that the specification is not as diverse as we would like, it actually opens up the opportunity to promote diversity through evaluation of the prescribed content. In exactly the same way that we would not teach Milgram's or Asch's results as the absolute last word in social influence processes and would look at later work and evaluations to provide a more nuanced picture, we should not assume that theories of gender or relationships that may date from the 1970s are presented as gospel truth.

Indeed, this can sometimes be a bit of a gift to evaluation, as it provides a running theme that can stretch through the majority of a unit (providing positive evaluations of theories or explanations that *do* generalise more diversely, as well as criticism of those that don't).

Case study: Challenging 'classic' psychology and emphasising diversity in social influence research

Below is a booklet page that aims to guide students to consider how later replications and cross-cultural research may produce a more nuanced understanding of when and how conformity effects may occur. The teacher needs to be responsive here to the amount of scaffolding they think needs to be provided to the class before reading (both in terms of possible historical context and understanding of Asch's findings and conclusions), and also after reading (for example, during paired discussion).

The aim of the research chosen here is to *tell a story* about the extent to which Asch's findings can be generalised more broadly. The research (and subsequent discussion and annotation of the notes) covers temporal validity (showing that the success of Asch replications has been mixed, possibly because of the historical context (Nicholson et al. attributed their results to higher national cohesion in the UK following the Falklands War)), methodological and sampling differences and cultural variation. The page is designed to:

- Illustrate to students that classic studies may often not replicate.
- Demonstrate that successful replication or not may be as much due to cultural, historical or methodological factors as the actual psychological construct being studied.
- Emphasise that **research methods really matter** and **conclusions are cautious**, two of our disciplinary fundamentals.

Evaluation of Asch's research and conclusions

Asch's study may be a 'Child of its Time', low in temporal validity.
- Critics of Asch argue that his findings are unique to the culture and time in which the research took place.
  - During the 1950s (McCarthyism)
  - All participants were American men

What is McCarthyism? Why might this influence the results of conformity studies?

Contrasting research: Perrin and Spencer (1980)
- A repeat of the Asch study in England using engineering students showed conformity in 1/396 trials!
- BUT... when carrying out the study using youths on probation as participants and probation officers as confederates, conformity was similar to Asch's results.

Why do you think the findings for the study using youths on probation were so different?

What does this variation in the results tell you about the Asch effect?

Nicholson et al. (1985)
- They did find conformity levels similar to Asch in a replication using British students.
- When comparing these results to those of Perrin and Spencer, they put the differences down to a greater sense of national cohesion at the time.
- The Asch effect is an unpredictable phenomenon, relying on a number of historical and cultural factors

Why do you think this was?

Asch's conclusions may be culturally biased
- Cross-cultural studies into conformity have shown much higher levels in countries such as Japan and China.
- Such countries are typically called collectivist cultures.
  - Emphasis is placed on behaviour that will benefit the larger group, rather than the individual.
  - 'Selfish' behaviour is significantly frowned upon in such cultures.
- Oh (2013) found that collectivist cultures showed higher levels of compliance. However, there was less cross-cultural variation in internalisation.

What issues does this raise regarding the interpretation of research findings?

Why would different types of conformity be affected differently by culture?

The picture could be further complicated – depending on a teacher's confidence in the class understanding and desire to challenge them – by the addition of cross-cultural research that has *not* found higher levels of compliance in collectivist cultures (for example, Takan and Sogon, 2008), or by interrogating the individualistic versus collectivist distinction in the first place.

Summary

In this section, we've considered a range of key ideas around what we should be teaching our students as part of our psychology curriculum. As we have seen, the view that teachers have little choice in what they teach when delivering a prescribed exam syllabus is quite far from the truth. There are many decisions to be made, and the permutations are almost endless. We hope it's been clear throughout this section that we don't believe there is any 'right' decision in the myriad choices available, but that the most important thing is that decisions are thoughtfully considered with an evidence-informed approach, rather than followed by default. Now that we've considered both the 'how' (pedagogical principles) and the 'what' (curriculum decisions), it's time to look at them together in action.

References

1. Al-Mosaiwi, M., & Johnstone, T. (2018). In an absolute state: Elevated use of absolutist words is a marker specific to anxiety, depression, and suicidal ideation. *Clinical Psychological Science*, 6(4), 529-542.
2. Bandura, A. (1965). Influence of models' reinforcement contingencies on the acquisition of imitative responses. *Journal of Personality and Social Psychology*, 1(6), 589.
3. Bandura, A., Ross, D., & Ross, S. A. (1961). Transmission of aggression through imitation of aggressive models. *The Journal of Abnormal and Social Psychology*, 63(3), 575.
4. Bandura, A., Ross, D., & Ross, S. A. (1963). Imitation of film-mediated aggressive models. *The Journal of Abnormal and Social Psychology*, 66(1), 3.
5. Bartels, J. M. (2015). The Stanford prison experiment in introductory psychology textbooks: A content analysis. *Psychology Learning & Teaching*, 14(1), 36-50.
6. Baumrind, D. (2015). When subjects become objects: The lies behind the Milgram legend. *Theory & Psychology*, 24(5), 690-696. https://doi.org/10.1177/0959354315592062
7. Beck, A. T. (1967). *Depression: Clinical, experimental and theoretical aspects*. New York: 1967.
8. Blakemore, S. J., Smith, J., Steel, R., Johnstone, E. C., & Frith, C. D. (2000). The perception of self-produced sensory stimuli in patients with auditory hallucinations and passivity experiences: Evidence for a breakdown in self-monitoring. *Psychological Medicine*, 30(5), 1131-1139.
9. Blakemore, S. J., Wolpert, D. M., & Frith, C. D. (1998). Central cancellation of self-produced tickle sensation. *Nature Neuroscience*, 1(7), 635-640.

10. Bowlby, J. (1944). Forty-four juvenile thieves: their characters and home-life (II). *International Journal of Psychoanalysis*, 25, 107–128.
11. BPS (2013). *Briefing paper. The future of A-level psychology*. https://efpta.org/docs/FutureOfAlevelMarch2013INF209-A-Le-528312-01-04-2013.pdf
12. Brendgen, M., Dionne, G., Girard, A., Boivin, M., Vitaro, F., & Pérusse, D. (2005). Examining genetic and environmental effects on social aggression: A study of 6-year-old twins. *Child Development*, 76(4), 930-946.
13. Burger, J. M. (2009). Replicating Milgram: Would people still obey today?. *American Psychologist*, 64(1), 1-11.
14. Campbell, S. S., & Murphy, P. J. (1998). Extraocular circadian phototransduction in humans. *Science*, 279(5349), 396-399.
15. Carlsson, A., Waters, N., Waters, S., & Carlsson, M. L. (2000). Network interactions in schizophrenia—therapeutic implications. *Brain Research Reviews*, 31(2-3), 342-349.
16. Carmichael-Murphy, P., & Danquah, A. (2022). *Hidden histories: Black in psychology*. University of Manchester.
17. Cottingham, S. (2023). *Ausubel's meaning learning in action* (T. Sherrington, Ed.). John Catt.
18. Counsell, C. (2018, April 7). The dignity of the thing. *Senior Curriculum Leadership 1: The Indirect Manifestation of Knowledge: (A) Curriculum as Narrative*. https://thedignityofthethingblog.wordpress.com/2018/04/07/senior-curriculum-leadership-1-the-indirect-manifestation-of-knowledge-a-curriculum-as-narrative/
19. Creswell, C. (2023). Editorial perspective: Rapid responses to understand and address children and young people's mental health in the context of COVID-19. *Journal of Child Psychology and Psychiatry*, 64(1), 209-211.
20. Fisher, S., & Greenberg, R. P. (1996). *Freud scientifically reappraised: Testing the theories and therapy*. John Wiley & Sons.
21. Ford, J. M., Mathalon, D. H., Heinks, T., Kalba, S., Faustman, W. O., & Roth, W. T. (2001). Neurophysiological evidence of corollary discharge dysfunction in schizophrenia. *American Journal of Psychiatry*, 158(12), 2069-2071.
22. Ford, J. M., Mathalon, D. H., Whitfield, S., Faustman, W. O., & Roth, W. T. (2002). Reduced communication between frontal and temporal lobes during talking in schizophrenia. *Biological Psychiatry*, 51(6), 485-492.
23. Foulkes, L., & Andrews, J. L. (2023). Are mental health awareness efforts contributing to the rise in reported mental health problems? A call to test the prevalence inflation hypothesis. *New Ideas in Psychology*, 69, 101010.
24. Fox, N. (1977). Attachment of kibbutz infants to mother and metapelet. *Child Development*, 48(4), 1228-1239.
25. Franzen, A., & Mader, S. (2023). The power of social influence: A replication and extension of the Asch experiment. *PLOS ONE*, 18(11), e0294425. https://doi.org/10.1371/journal.pone.0294425
26. Glass, A. L., & Kang, M. (2022). Fewer students are benefiting from doing their homework: An eleven-year study. *Educational Psychology*, 42(2), 185-199.

27. Godden, D. R., & Baddeley, A. D. (1975). Context-dependent memory in two natural environments: On land and underwater. *British Journal of psychology, 66*(3), 325-331.
28. Griggs, R. A., & Whitehead III, G. I. (2015). Coverage of recent criticisms of Milgram's obedience experiments in introductory social psychology textbooks. *Theory & Psychology, 25*(5), 564-580.
29. Grissmer, D., Buddin, R., Berends, M., Willingham, D., DeCoster, J., Duran, C., Hulleman, C., Murrah, W., & Evans, T. (2023). A kindergarten lottery evaluation of core knowledge charter schools: Should building general knowledge have a central role in educational and social science research and policy? (EdWorkingPaper: 23-755). Retrieved from Annenberg Institute at Brown University: https://doi.org/10.26300/nsbq-hb21
30. Guzman Holst, C., Bowes, L., Waite, P., Skripkauskaite, S., Shum, A., Pearcey, S., Raw, J., Patalay, P., & Creswell, C. (2023). Examining children and adolescent mental health trajectories during the COVID-19 pandemic: Findings from a year of the Co-SPACE study. *JCPP Advances, 3*(2), e12153.
31. Haney, C., Banks, C., Zimbardo, P., & Aronson, E. (1973). *A study of prisoners and guards in a simulated prison* (pp. 52-67).
32. Jerrim, J., & de Vries, R. (2023). Are peer reviews of grant proposals reliable? An analysis of Economic and Social Research Council (ESRC) funding applications. *The Social Science Journal, 60*(1), 91-109.
33. Joel, S., Eastwick, P. W., Allison, C. J., Arriaga, X. B., Baker, Z. G., Bar-Kalifa, E., ... & Wolf, S. (2020). Machine learning uncovers the most robust self-report predictors of relationship quality across 43 longitudinal couples studies. *Proceedings of the National Academy of Sciences, 117*(32), 19061-19071.
34. Kapur, M., Hattie, J., Grossman, I., & Sinha, T. (2022). Fail, flip, fix, and feed – Rethinking flipped learning: A review of meta-analyses and a subsequent meta-analysis. *Frontiers in Education, 7*. Frontiers Media S.A. https://doi.org/10.3389/feduc.2022.956416
35. Lambert, D., & Biddulph, M. (2015). The dialogic space offered by curriculum-making in the process of learning to teach, and the creation of a progressive knowledge-led curriculum. *Asia-Pacific Journal of Teacher Education, 43*(3), 210-224.
36. Lambert, D. M. (2017). Powerful disciplinary knowledge and curriculum futures. In Pyyry, N., Tainio, L., Juuti, K., Vasquez, R., & Paananen, M. (eds), Suomen ainedidaktinen tutkimusseura (pp. 14-32). Finnish Research Association for Subject Didactics.
37. Loftus, E. F., & Palmer, J. C. (1974). Reconstruction of automobile destruction: An example of the interaction between language and memory. *Journal of Verbal Learning and Verbal Behaviour, 13*(5), 585-589.
38. McGovern, T. V., Corey, L. A., Cranney, J., ... & Walker, S. J. (2010). Psychologically literate citizens. In Halpern, D. (ed.), *Undergraduate education in psychology: Blueprint for the discipline's future* (pp. 9-27). Washington, DC: American Psychological Association.
39. Millichamp, T. (2023, August 6). Core questions are s***... https://tomchillimamp.medium.com/core-questions-are-s-38fec7713be4

40. Moore-Anderson, C. (2022). Measuring and fostering biological thinking beyond short-answer questions. *The School Science Review, 385*, 103.
41. Moore-Anderson, C. (2023). *Made real: Ways of teaching that inspire meaning-making*. Christian Moore-Anderson.
42. Osborn, S. G., & West, D. J. (1979). Conviction records of father and sons compared. *British Journal of Criminology, 19*(2), 120-133.
43. Ozden, J., & Glover, S. (2022). Protest movements: How effective are they? *London: Social Change Lab*. Retrieved 30 November, 2023.
44. Perry, G. (2013). Deception and illusion in Milgram's accounts of the obedience experiments. *Theoretical & Applied Ethics, 2*(2), 79-92.
45. Raine, A., Buchsbaum, M., & LaCasse, L. (1997). Brain abnormalities in murderers indicated by positron emission tomography. *Biological Psychiatry, 42*(6), 495-508.
46. Reicher, S., & Haslam, S. A. (2006). Rethinking the psychology of tyranny: The BBC prison study. *British Journal of Social Psychology, 45*(1), 1-40.
47. Sebastián, M. V., & Hernández-Gil, L. (2012). Developmental pattern of digit span in Spanish population. *Psicothema, 24*(2), 183-187.
48. Shallice, T., & Warrington, E. K. (1970). Independent functioning of verbal memory stores. A neuropsychological study. *Quarterly Journal of experimental psychology, 22*(2), 261-273.
49. Shin, Y. S., Masís-Obando, R., Keshavarzian, N., Dáve, R., & Norman, K. A. (2021). Context-dependent memory effects in two immersive virtual reality environments: On Mars and underwater. *Psychonomic Bulletin & Review, 28*(2), 574-582.
50. Stein, L. I., & Test, M. A. (1980). Alternative to mental hospital treatment: I. Conceptual model, treatment program, and clinical evaluation. *Archives of General Psychiatry, 37*(4), 392-397.
51. Steuer, F. B., & Ham, K. W. (2008). Psychology textbooks: Examining their accuracy. *Teaching of Psychology, 35*(3), 160-168.
52. Takano, Y., & Sogon, S. (2008). Are Japanese more collectivistic than Americans? Examining conformity in in-groups and the reference-group effect. *Journal of Cross-Cultural Psychology, 39*(3), 237-250.
53. Tienari, P., Wynne, L. C., Sorri, A., Lahti, I., Läksy, K., Moring, J., ... & Wahlberg, K. E. (2004). Genotype–environment interaction in schizophrenia-spectrum disorder: Long-term follow-up study of Finnish adoptees. *The British Journal of Psychiatry, 184*(3), 216-222.
54. Tobler, S., Sinha, T., Köhler, K., & Kapur, M. (2024). Telling stories as preparation for learning: A Bayesian analysis of transfer performance and investigation of learning mechanisms. *Learning and Instruction, 92*, 101944.
55. Watson, J. B., & Rayner, R. (1920). Conditioned emotional reactions. *Journal of Experimental Psychology, 3*(1), 1-14.
56. Wolpe, J. (1973). *The practice of behavior therapy* (2nd Edn) (General Psychology Series) (Volume 1). Pergamon Press.
57. Wright Jr, K. P., & Czeisler, C. A. (2002). Absence of circadian phase resetting in response to bright light behind the knees. *Science, 297*(5581), 571-571.

Section 3: Teaching core content

Lauren

Lauren is thinking about how to plan her lessons for the next half term. She is not sure if she needs to do any planning, given the existence of a full set of resources on the shared network drive, which is populated with work booklets for each unit and slides organised by lesson in the order of the specification. However, she is not sure exactly how to use these. For example, a lot of the slides and booklet pages contain big chunks of information, and it's not clear how whoever created them actually used the resources to impart this information to students. There are also various activities embedded in the resources, but again she isn't entirely clear on the structure of the activities the author had in mind when they wrote them. There are some standardised pages at the end of each section containing tables that appear to cover evaluation using acronyms, some of which she is familiar with – though some are new to her. She also has a large bank of resources for activities she has used in the past saved in her own drive. Lauren feels like she has plenty of things to do with which to fill the time for each lesson. What else does she need to do?

We've considered both the 'how' (pedagogical principles) and the 'what' (curriculum decisions), so now we can delve into the core business of planning and teaching lessons.

From resource planning to 'cognitive preparation'

Lauren is 'resourced', but is she really 'cognitively prepared' for her upcoming lessons? This means lesson planning that moves beyond being led by resources and activities to being led by the actual learning aims of the lesson. In this section, we consider the best way to achieve these through our pedagogical implications.

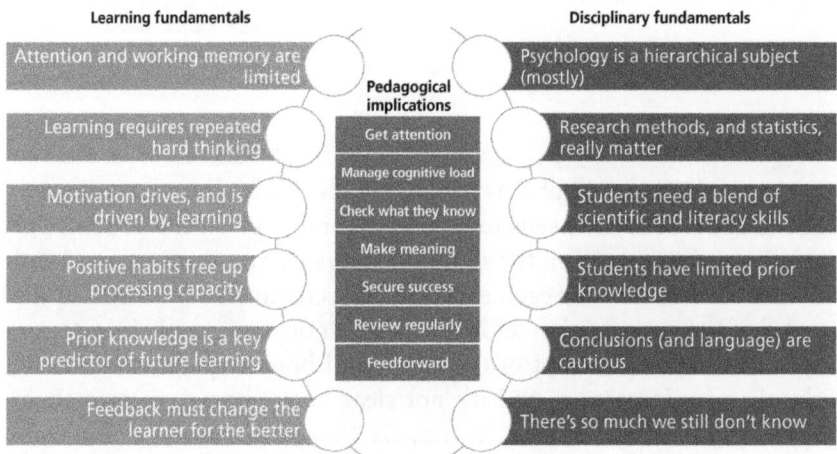

Let's start by thinking about the specific challenges of cognitive preparation that Lauren is facing:

- Thinking about the different assessment objectives and how students can develop a clear understanding of each of them through her lessons.
- Thinking about what she wants students to do with the material. Should they make notes? If so, how? How should they answer questions? How should they revise? Do these processes need to change for different forms of content (such as theories, studies and treatments), or for different assessment objectives?
- Thinking about the knowledge and skills that students will need to have in order to perform the classroom behaviours she wants to see, and how these can be inculcated in advance. This can include both behavioural habits, and prerequisite knowledge.

- Planning specific questions she wants to ask (including follow-ups) and to whom, to allow her to **check what students know** and **secure success**.
- Identifying likely errors or misconceptions that will arise and thinking about how to **review regularly** to address them.
- Deciding whether rehearsing or scripting explanations of some of the content could help her students to **make meaning**.
- Generating or finding plenty of examples (and non-examples) to support explanations, for checking understanding or for independent practice.
- Generating or finding model answers to share and discuss.
- Mapping out evaluation points (and potential conclusions) that she wants to make sure students consider or arrive at.
- Thinking about how she can give feedback which will **feedforward** into future work.
- Thinking about how different specification areas can be connected in students' minds to help them **make meaning**.

Induction - setting up students for success

As we discussed in Section 1, psychology students mostly have **limited prior knowledge**, which means that how we start their psychology studies is really important to help set them up for success further down the line. We need to think carefully about the content they will learn first, and how this will prepare them to learn throughout the rest of the course. We also saw that psychology requires **a blend of scientific and literacy skills**, which, combined with the fact that we typically have very varied cohorts, means that we'll need to spend a lot of time developing those skills. Furthermore, students embarking on a psychology course will have gone through a transition from one phase of their education to another (most typically from GCSE study to A-levels) that necessitates a new range of study skills to cope with the increasing academic demands placed on them. We know that **positive habits free up processing capacity** and so developing some effective study skills early on will help students grapple with the content far more effectively. As well as developing effective instructional routines with the class, the induction is also a place where behavioural routines can be established, and these remain essential regardless of the fact that psychology students are relatively senior within school.

What knowledge should they encounter first?

So, where's the best place to start? There will be a range of views on this, and lots of teachers will probably have their go-to 'intro' lesson. But does it matter what you start with or, is it just about getting them interested from the beginning?

As we saw in Section 1, **prior knowledge is a key predictor of future learning**, and if we want students to **make meaning** then we need to think about our sequencing carefully. In line with our pedagogical principles, it makes sense to identify the general and inclusive ideas (subsumers) that provide an overall framework for the content and start there.

Given that **psychology is a (mostly) hierarchical subject,** we think there are important ideas that ideally should be encountered at the beginning of the course. Which ideas, then? Our disciplinary fundamentals give us one possible answer here: **research methods, and statistics, really matter**. Other high level subsumers that can be good for securing an initial foundation include the approaches, issues and debates or some key theories. Below is an example sequence of lessons that we think will help introduce students to a selection of some of the most important ideas they need to learn. Each one is framed around some key questions as a form of advance organiser to help students think about why this content matters.

Introduction to psychology	• What is psychology? • What's the difference between a construct, theory, method and study? • What are the different views of human behaviour (approaches)?
Psychology and science	• What is the scientific method? • What does a study involve? • To what extent can psychology claim to be a science?
Sampling	• Who takes part in psychological research? • What's the best way to get hold of them?

Ethics	• How should we treat participants in research?
	• What are the challenges of studying people ethically?
Reliability	• How do we know we can trust the findings of research?
Validity	• How do we know if we're actually measuring the right thing?

The precise content of each of these lessons could vary from one teacher to another, but if the lessons are carefully planned and sequenced there will be a clear thread running through them that should leave students with a better sense of what psychology actually is (and isn't!) before they start grappling with too much further content.

That's not to say that introductory concepts need to be taught entirely free of any psychological content. The case study on 'evaluating behaviourism using the features of a science' (see page 35) provides an example of how the features of a science can initially be covered in a general sense and then built into gradually more sophisticated evaluation over the initial topics of a specification.

What skills do we want them to develop first?

An induction period is the perfect time to focus on sculpting students' academic habits, which might include:

- Making notes.
- Engaging with notes and other texts.
- Independent study.
- Engaging with exam questions.
- Regular retrieval.
- How to discuss and contribute in class.
- Behavioural expectations.

Making notes

Students (and teachers) are often very preoccupied with making notes, but sometimes little attention is given to what this actually involves. This can lead to staggering variation in the detail and quality of what students produce, an erroneous belief that having a 'good set of notes' is the key to success and independent study that entails making notes on many pages of a textbook and assuming that learning will just happen along the way. Clearly, we need a more considered and strategic approach.

In this context, let's consider the use of Cornell notes[1] as a strategy for review and consolidation outside of lessons. This method can be used to make notes during lessons, although this requires an additional set of skills that would require further investment of time. Cornell notes are an effective strategy to consider that have a number of benefits:

- For teachers:
    - They provide a purposeful, regular homework task, meaning that you're not trying to endlessly create homework for the sake of it (especially if your setting has any kind of homework policy specifying amount or frequency).
    - They are easy to check because of the standardised format, and while they don't require marking, they are good tools to help **feedforward**.
- For students:
    - They are a useful resource to help them **review regularly**.
    - The process of making them provides an opportunity for students to **make meaning**.
    - Once students are familiar with the process they can focus more on the content itself, so they can be a tool to **manage cognitive load**.

Embedding a Cornell notes system

If you want to embed this method as a habit, you need to make this an explicit expectation from day one. Of course, students will need to learn how to do them properly, which means we need to:

- **Share the rationale** for using the Cornell system.
- Provide materials to explain the different elements and what goes in each section.

---

[1] For specific detail on the form and process of Cornell notes, see this handy guide: https://lsc.cornell.edu/how-to-study/taking-notes/cornell-note-taking-system/

- Provide models from a range of contexts to show what a finished set of Cornell notes may look like.
- Model the process in class, with explicit narration of the different thought processes required for each stage.
- Give students the opportunity to practise in class and get live feedback.
- Take in[2] the first completed set of Cornell notes and provide whole-class feedback, ensuring that students act on that feedback straight away (and repeat as many times as required!).

Engaging with notes and other texts

Another option is to provide students with the information you want them to know, for example, in a textbook summary, revision guide or booklet. These allow you as the teacher to provide pre-prepared notes to students, which guarantees the information in students' notes is of the desired standard. The trade-off is that students are not active in the creation of their own notes, and therefore further support and systems are required to ensure that students think hard about the material and **make meaning** from it (rather than, for example, reading passively and highlighting every other word for no clear purpose). (See Section 5, page 423 for a more detailed discussion of the benefits and drawbacks of using booklets or textbooks.)

Students are sometimes surprisingly bad at actively reading the resources we give them – or, rather, it's not something students have typically developed good habits around if they're expected to take much away from what they're reading. The curse of highlighting is a common issue, which more often than not simply results in handouts, worksheets and booklets that contain extensive passages of fluorescent colour with all the 'ofs', 'thes', 'ands' and 'buts' left blank.

The following guidance for students can help build better reading habits:

- Don't pick up a pen or highlighter until you've read through the whole text. You don't know what's actually important until you've

---

[2] By 'take in' here we mean nothing more than collecting them, having a quick flick through to identify common errors and then giving them back again. This can easily be done with a whole class in about three minutes while they're doing something else like some retrieval questions.

seen the bigger picture, so once you've read it once you can go back through and highlight.
- Anything you highlight, annotate too. If something is being highlighted, it's because you've thought it's important. Adding annotation provides some insight – what makes that piece of information significant? Annotations could include key terms, links, conclusions, evaluation and more, and they can help to **manage cognitive load** by providing more permanent records of our thoughts that are helpful if we review material later. Without this, students will look back over the page at a later date and need to reinterpret all that highlighting, often thinking, 'Why did I highlight that bit?'
- Produce mini-summaries and generate questions after reading. Once you've read through a paragraph and perhaps highlighted (*and* annotated!) a few bits, then trying to write your own brief summary of the information helps to **make meaning**, as does generating questions to act as prompts.[3] **Mini-whiteboards** are often useful here, as students feel more comfortable drafting their ideas first before committing something to the page.

Case study: Engaging with a notes booklet

One way that this can be done is through targeted questions in the notes, which scaffold students to make connections and think more deeply about the material in the way you might want them to. An example of this is as follows, from an introduction to the behaviourist approach.

---

3 NB both strategies are included in the creation of Cornell notes, which is why they can form such an effective note-making system.

Section 3: Teaching core content

The behavioural approach

Assumptions
- **Behaviour is learned.**
  - All behaviour (apart from reflexes in newborns) is learned from experience.
  - We are essentially born 'Tabula Rasa', or as blank slates.
  - This is known as empiricism.
- **The mind is 'irrelevant'.**
  - We can't directly observe what people are thinking.
  - The only measurable data is gained from observing behaviour directly.
- **Environmental determinism.**
  - There is no free will. Our behaviour is controlled by forces in the environment and can only be changed by changing the environment.
- **Animals and humans learn in the same ways.**
  - Humans learn in the same way as other animals, through simple stimulus-response associations.
  - We learn to drive in the same way that a cat learns to use a cat-flap.
  - Therefore, animal studies can be used to make generalisations about humans.
  - Experimental results can be used to make laws about human behaviour (a nomothetic approach).

The behaviourists 'changed the subject matter of psychology from the study of conscious experience to the study of behaviour'. Why might they have wanted to make this change?

If these are what the approach focuses on, then what does it ignore?

What are some drawbacks of making these assumptions?

Another approach can be to ask students to immediately recall or discuss the material they have just read in as much detail as possible (and make sure they are aware of this requirement before they start reading). We call this the 'blurt box'.

Activity 1: BLURT BOX! Cover notes, blurt and then check back against the notes when asked.
Activity 2: Paired summarising – Cover notes and take it in turns to verbally summarise the material you have just read and blurted.

The two activities at the bottom of the notes section allow for generative learning, which facilitates meaning making through summarising and self-explanation. As with all induction strategies, these engagement tools will require explicit training from the start, and involve narrating the classroom you are looking to create. Make it clear how you want students to interact with the resources, interact with each other in discussion, report back to you, make notes of areas that they need clarification on and so on.

Independent study

It is very common for students at the start of their psychology course to struggle to develop good independent learning habits. This may partly be because they have never been taught effective learning techniques explicitly (how to make and use a flashcard, for example), but another problem is that they often report 'not having enough to review yet'. In the first few weeks of a new course, the students may not cover a huge amount of information, and what they do cover may seem very fresh in their memory.

Why do students need to be reviewing information already? We would offer two justifications:

1. If students don't develop good working habits initially, less effective habits will form in their place – and habits once formed are hard to shift! A few weeks of using spare time poorly, or not at all, may not seem too harmful initially. Once the volume of work begins to rise, however, students can find themselves already struggling against such harmful habits. A priority, then, is that they are learning to use their time well. As an example, rather than psychological content, the first few questions in a core questions curriculum could be questions about effective learning techniques.

Core question	Suggested answer
'Attention is the gateway to cognition' and 'Memory is the residue of thought' – what do these statements mean for your learning?	We can't think about what we don't pay attention to. We don't learn things we haven't thought hard about.
What is retrieval practice and why is it important?	Retrieval practice is a strategy in which we 'bring out' information from our memories. Deliberately recalling information forces us to pull our knowledge 'out' and examine what we know. This is important because it has been shown to be an effective way of learning.
Name three good retrieval practice techniques.	Example answers: 'brain dumps', flashcards, self-quizzing, look-cover-write-check, explaining (from memory) to yourself and others, mind maps (from memory).
What is 'spaced retrieval' and why is it important?	Spaced retrieval means spreading out retrieval practice activities over periods of time. This is especially useful for improving the memory of items over long periods of time, which means that we need to regularly review past work in order to cement it in our memories

2. Overlearning is fine! As noted in Section 1, mastery for some elements of the curriculum may be extremely helpful. After the questions above, for example, the core questions can incorporate some of the features of a science, which will be useful for the remainder of the course. In the absence of much other work, if students **review regularly**, they can pretty much learn these answers word for word. This not only helps students to **secure success** early on – it makes them more likely to be able to successfully recall and apply these ideas to subsequent parts of the course.

Example question	Example answers
What features make something a science?	Replicability, standardisation, control, reductionism, generalisability (NB that 'falsifiability/hypothesis testing', 'objectivity' and others are often also given as features of a science in other sources, so they're fine too).
Define 'replicable'.	If a research procedure can be repeated accurately (in the same way as the original).
Define 'standardised'.	If the same thing is done or said to each participant throughout a research procedure.
Define 'controlled'.	If other variables (other than the independent variable) are removed or kept constant during a research procedure so they don't affect the results.
Define 'generalisable'.	If the results of a research procedure can be applied more broadly, not just to the sample (the people who took part).
Define 'reductionism'.	The belief that human behaviour can be explained by breaking it down into simpler component parts (as followed by most scientific psychologists).

Having some overlearning built into the early part of the course is a way to help students see the benefit of effective learning strategies. The KBCP framework (McDaniel et al., 2021) suggests that students will only independently engage with learning strategies if they:

- (Have) **K**nowledge of them.
- **B**elieve they will work.
- **C**ommit to their use.
- **P**lan how they will be used.

Often students are told 'how' to work independently while not being provided with the structure to see the success of their efforts and build the ideas into their personal routines (for more on this see Section 5, 'Encouraging a culture of independent learning', page 449). Overlearning some early material allows students to see the success of the learning methods you coach them to use, and to commit to their use at a slightly less busy and cluttered point of the calendar. All this helps them to build effective and lasting independent learning habits.

Engaging with exam questions

Although we don't want to gear our teaching entirely towards the exams nearly two years in the future, we also want to establish some basic habits around exam technique as soon as possible. Given that reading the question is the first task, it's unsurprising that some of the guidance provided in this section for engaging with texts is basically the same: read everything through once, before picking up a pen and annotating the question to get your thoughts down on paper. However, an additional skill we want students to learn is to be able to decode exam questions, which partly means analysing command terms but also involves learning to parse the construction of exam questions (actual instructions) to figure out what they're being asked to do.

Section 3A: Teaching assessment objectives

Pritesh

It's an early morning in the middle of August, and Pritesh is waiting to find out how his students have done in their psychology A-level exams. As he waits for the results to arrive, he's thinking about the various students he's taught over the past two years. A couple of names spring to mind: Lisa and Sarah. Lisa was one of those rare students who was an utter privilege to teach. Hard-working, keen as mustard, full of insight, bursting with interesting questions and always willing to go beyond the syllabus, whether from additional reading that Pritesh provided or her own research. Her writing was original, and she worked hard to break free from the shackles of any restrictive paragraph structures. She totally 'got it'.

Sarah, on the other hand, didn't. She literally told Pritesh she 'didn't get it' virtually every lesson and in after-school clinics. When Lisa made some thoughtful synoptic connection between two different areas of the course, Sarah's expression made it look like her head was going to explode. She did, however, have an impressive memory, and was able to rote learn vast swathes of information to regurgitate in assessments, even if it was fairly clear she didn't necessarily understand what she was writing.

The moment of truth. Pritesh sees the email with the results attached and opens it. Sarah got an A*, while Lisa achieved a B.

Of course, there will have been many other factors at play here, but this kind of scenario is probably familiar to anyone who's been teaching a while. If it is, then you'll recognise that these kinds of results will niggle away at us. We'll question the value of how we've taught our students and feel that we've somehow let some of them down. We shouldn't begrudge Sarah her grade – she undoubtedly put the hard graft in – but it can be challenging to think that the Lisas of this world – who also worked incredibly hard – have not been rewarded for their ability and enthusiasm, and that the top prizes (in terms of grades at least) have gone to those who simply learn better how to play the examination game. Playing the game, jumping through hoops – these aren't the things we signed up for when we decided to teach psychology!

However, the fact remains that students need to understand how they are going to be assessed if they are going to successfully translate their knowledge to a strong performance in the exams. There are differences of opinion over just how explicitly we should teach this to our students. One argument suggests that if we just teach the content well enough, and our students develop rich schemas with deep and meaningful connections, then the AOs will take care of themselves. Indeed, when the 2015 A-level specifications were launched, the exam boards were at pains to suggest we shouldn't be teaching by assessment objective, and that students didn't need to worry about what AO1 or AO3 meant. We'd be fascinated to know if any teachers have managed to maintain this position – and we're prepared to bet a good deal of money that they haven't! We feel this is idealistic and perhaps somewhat naive; our experience has shown that the vagaries of examination mark schemes are such that leaving it to chance may do our students a disservice.[4]

Therefore, our aim here is to present ways of teaching that accommodate both the Lisas and Sarahs of the world. We need to teach in a way that respects the nuances of the discipline, sparks our students' passion for the subject, allows them licence to be creative in their responses but, ultimately, still allows them to achieve well in their exams. In this section we consider the different assessment objectives that students have to master in order to do so.

---

[4] A further challenge we should be aware of is that the labelling of assessment objectives is not consistent across different subjects (for example, where AO2 is application for one subject, it could mean evaluation for another), and some subjects may have either fewer or more AOs than psychology. This makes it doubly important for us to take time to explicitly teach this to students, and check they know it.

AO1

AO1 refers to knowledge and understanding, and makes typically around one third of the marks available. It is often somewhat downgraded as 'mere knowledge', but AO1 forms the building blocks for the other assessment objectives – application (AO2) and evaluation (AO3).

What does good AO1 look like?

To score well on AO1, students need to be able to:

- Demonstrate detailed knowledge *and understanding* of psychological content.
- Select the right amount of relevant knowledge to answer given questions.
- Select the *most relevant* knowledge to assist with answering particular questions (for example, knowledge that links most clearly to a given scenario, or which sets up subsequent evaluation most successfully).

Students often struggle to get AO1 right because they fail to demonstrate understanding, rather than simply remembering the knowledge. Consider this definition of operant conditioning:

> Operant conditioning is learning through the consequences of your actions - reward or punishment.

This definition shows knowledge and has some appropriate key terms. But does it demonstrate understanding of what 'learning through consequences' actually means? Here's a more developed version:

> Operant conditioning is learning through the consequences of your actions, through reward or punishment, which either increase or decrease the likelihood of a behaviour being repeated.

When we want students to demonstrate their knowledge and understanding, there are a few key features that can be good indicators that they have done it successfully:

- Inclusion of relevant key terms used appropriately and with technical accuracy (e.g. selecting exactly the right key term for a given context).
- A good level of detail while still being relatively concise.

- Thoroughness (e.g. describing the whole 'story' of a study from aims to conclusions, or the full sequence of stages in a theory).
- Accurate use of examples.

Teaching AO1 (using the pedagogical implications)

One of the mistakes we made early in our careers was to mistakenly assume that knowledge was easy to transmit to students, and that we should be focusing more of our time and energy on 'higher order' skills like application, analysis and evaluation. As such, we presumed that if we just talked students through some content in what we perceived as a clear way, then they could get straight onto the more sophisticated stuff. However, since we now know that **prior knowledge is a key predictor of future learning, learning requires repeated hard thinking** and **psychology is a mostly hierarchical discipline,** we can see why we were wrong to relegate knowledge in this way. Crucially, if AO1 is taught well, then it makes things like application and evaluation easier for students because they have something concrete to apply and evaluate. This also helps to reduce the likelihood of more generic responses, free of meaningful context.

The precise nature of AO1 will depend on the specific content to be taught (such as theories, studies and treatments), but we think there are some general principles arising from our pedagogical implications that are applicable in most areas.

Check what they know

Ensure prior (prerequisite) knowledge of foundational concepts is secure before adding further detail, to allow students to assimilate new information. For example, if you're teaching the details of a new study, it may make sense to check knowledge of some of the methodological features before starting (assuming students have encountered them elsewhere). When teaching Loftus and Palmer's (1974) classic study on leading questions, it may help if students already know and understand (and can evaluate where appropriate):

- Sampling.
- IVs and DVs.
- Lab versus field experiments.

- Experimental design (independent groups).
- Use of self-reports (questionnaires).
- Demand characteristics.

It may be appropriate to start this learning sequence with some retrieval practice on some of these elements before introducing Loftus and Palmer's study. Which ones you choose may depend on prior learning of the students, or which ideas you want to activate specifically in order to generate good discussion further down the line. For example, a key point of understanding in this study is that the second experiment (where they asked if participants saw broken glass after a week's delay) was conducted in order to determine if the results of the first experiment were due to reconstructive memory or demand characteristics. Therefore, reviewing students' knowledge of this specific methodological idea may be useful here (there may also be relevant prior content knowledge relating to the memory topic that you want to check here too, such as reconstructive memory theory, schemas or eyewitness testimony).

Of course, you may be choosing to use Loftus and Palmer's study as a vehicle to teach these methodological features (or at least some of them). However, this has the potential to impose significant cognitive load on students, which means they may focus more of their attention on the methodology or the actual content of the study – but not both. In our experience, if you want students to learn about a study in relation to some specific theory or key concepts, then ideally there would be minimal novel methodology to process at the same time (of course, this is not always entirely possible).

Make meaning

In order for students to understand new information, they need plenty of opportunities for connecting to what they already know. This may be their prior learning in psychology but may also be their own life experiences. For example, when introducing concepts relating to operant conditioning, it may make sense to start with reviewing their knowledge of classical conditioning and ask students to generate examples of situations in which they have either been rewarded or punished, so that the more abstract terms in operant conditioning are grounded in concrete examples.

Students also need plenty of rehearsal of new ideas to build their own understanding, and in varied forms; for example, paired talk and visual organisers such as mind maps (to show connections between ideas), or flowcharts and storyboards (to represent sequential information such as the stages of a theory or study).

Secure success

We want to build students' confidence with plenty of low-stakes checks for understanding and meaning, which can include:

- Mini-whiteboard quizzes.
- Multiple-choice questions.
- Matching tasks (e.g. key terms to definitions).
- Gap-fill exercises.
- Simple application tasks.

Review regularly

Students will need lots of retrieval of key ideas, in varied forms. This could include incorporating concepts that cause confusion to improve accuracy of recall.

Teaching key terminology

In vocabulary research, 'Tier 3' vocabulary is defined as subject-specific vocabulary that learners need to understand in order to communicate like experts across the curriculum. In psychology, terms like 'anxiety', 'depression', 'phobia', 'biological approach' and 'psychodynamic approach' are all examples of Tier 3 vocabulary, as even though some of these terms may be used in more everyday language, students must learn their specific psychological meanings.

As noted in Section 1, one reason to check what students know is that it has been suggested that readers need to know up to 98% of the words in a text to be able to understand it properly (Nation, 2006), so what chance does a student have who is not very familiar with all of the Tier 3 vocabulary in this question? We estimate that our Year 12s learn around 120 new Tier 3 words and phrases in their first unit alone! That's a lot, and given the importance of using key terminology effectively, it deserves a strategic approach.

Science teacher Ian Taylor writes superbly on teaching science like a foreign language, employing many of the tools that our modern languages colleagues have been using effectively for years (Taylor, 2019). Many of his ideas are immediately applicable to psychology, such as:

- Get students using key terms as often and as confidently as possible. For example, this can be through verbal rehearsal of a process prior to writing ('Describe the process of synaptic transmission to your partner using the six terms on the board in the correct order'), choral repetition or individual targeting.
- Get students writing key terms accurately. Vocab tests are a great way to get students familiar with definitions, and the terms can then be incorporated in longer paragraphs (for example, 'Write a paragraph evaluating the cognitive approach using five of the key terms from your quiz'). Vocab tests can be used to ask students to learn the words, learn the definitions (harder) or to learn the terms in relation to their connection to others. They are also a simple way to **secure success**, for example through a mastery learning approach.
- Focus on etymology to help students **make meaning** (e.g. 'anhedonia' vs 'avolition'), make connections across different specification areas (e.g. 'monozygotic' vs 'monotropy') or reveal real insights into the concepts themselves (e.g. 'psychodynamic', which perfectly captures the turbulent inner world that Freud imagined the mind as being).
- **Manage cognitive load**. New terminology can be difficult to remember, let alone adopt and use. This can be made easier, for example, by leaving new terms on the board or providing them in a list in booklets as students practise applying them.
- Use the terms yourself. Exposure to fluent use of high-complexity vocabulary improves language comprehension in listeners (especially for poorer readers, Westbrook et al., 2019). For example, don't describe the corpus callosum as a bundle of connections when you could call it 'a bundle of myelinated axons'.

AO2

AO2 is application, which links psychological knowledge (AO1) to a particular context given in an exam question stem. A stem may describe:

- A hypothetical scenario involving the behaviour of one or more people that needs explaining according to a particular theory or approach.
- A scenario in which a person may require a specific type of treatment or intervention.
- A research scenario detailing a hypothetical study (these are quite often based on or inspired by real pieces of research).

What does good AO2 look like?

To score well on AO2, students need to be able to do the following well:

- Analysis of the question, including command words, to identify what they need to do.
- Correct selection of the key concepts and knowledge they need to talk about (e.g. selecting the most relevant specific aspect of a theory).
- Correct selection of material from the context to exemplify a key idea (e.g. picking out quotations from the stem to illustrate a particular concept).
- Combining knowledge with context in an effective but concise way (e.g. providing plausible applications to a scenario that lacks specific details).

Teaching AO2 (using the pedagogical implications)

- **Get attention.** Make sure students are attending to the most salient aspects at each point in the process. This could mean explicitly directing them to identify specific words or phrases to quote from the question or stem.
- **Check what they know.** Activate relevant prior knowledge (AO1) that students will need in order to answer the question. If it refers to a particular theory, then have some retrieval questions (or other activity) ready that activate the most important ideas they'll need

to apply. Check that the students understand this with probing questions, not that they can just regurgitate some key terms.
- **Manage cognitive load.** Provide appropriate scaffolds, especially early on. This may include annotating a model on the board (or under a visualiser) and writing a bullet point list of success criteria for the students to refer to once they start. If necessary, chunk it up into separate sections and carry out whole-class checks at each point.
- **Make meaning.** Students need to be able to make sense of both the information they need (AO1) and the information in the stem, as well as the connections between the two. Sometimes these are quite obvious; sometimes the students will need more guidance. Use careful questioning to check before anyone starts writing. Where there are gaps, model your own thinking about the connection between AO1 and the stem.
- **Feedforward.** Once students have started, give live feedback (individual or whole-class – see Section 4, page 363), as this helps to offer timely corrections. Refer to success criteria where appropriate. As students get more confident, they can use these criteria for themselves to self- or peer-assess their work and provide their own feedback for improvement.
- **Review regularly.** Application needs lots of practice with varying contexts so that students are fluent in the process (since **positive habits free up processing capacity**), skills become embedded and they can tackle novel contexts. This is also a good way to embed ongoing retrieval practice that develops higher order thinking rather than just knowledge retention.

Application questions typically feature a scenario that portrays a particular example of behaviour that students are required to explain using a specific theory or construct from within a theory. For example:

> A researcher conducted a study into obedience in a hospital setting. The researcher, posing as a doctor, asked a number of nurses to prepare a drug for a patient, well beyond the safe dosage. When the doctor gave the instructions in person, 75% of the nurses complied with the request. When the doctor gave the instructions over the phone, the obedience rate was 43%.

> Explain how social impact theory (SIT) could be used to explain the findings from this study.

In order to teach students how to answer this kind of question, we may want to do a number of things:

- Check prior knowledge of SIT, including appropriate key terms.
- Identify, highlight and annotate different elements of the scenario and the question to determine exactly what they are being asked to do or include (and *not* include!).
- Identify the specific details of the scenario that should be used to contextualise answers.
- Model the planning process to demonstrate how to organise the information into a clear set of points relative to the number of marks available.
- Model the writing process to produce effective (and concise) exam answers.

AO3

AO3 is evaluation, most commonly in terms of explaining strengths and weaknesses of psychological ideas, but also sometimes in terms of comparing ideas to each other, drawing reasoned conclusions from information given or suggesting improvements.

AO3 is difficult. Students consistently find this the most difficult assessment objective to achieve the marks for – and that's because it is! It is, however, essential, both in terms of opening up the possibility of the highest grades for our students, and more generally in terms of developing psychological literacy. In this section, we're going to talk about evaluation in terms of how to develop the type of evaluative thinking that we want students to engage in, generate a good list of strengths and weaknesses of whatever they're learning about and discuss their relative importance. This requires some slightly more specialised planning and structuring than AO1 and AO2, in our experience, and so this section is somewhat longer than for those assessment objectives.

(In Section 3C (page 337), we'll consider how to develop students' ability to write evaluatively.)

What does good AO3 look like?

To score well on AO3, students need to be able to do the following well:

- Understand relevant evaluative ideas for psychological concepts and methods (e.g. generalisability or demand characteristics).
- Communicate this understanding in a way that shows an understanding of the *contextual detail* of what they are evaluating (i.e. in a way that avoids genericism).
- Structure writing to allow the clear communication of this contextualised understanding.
- Maintain focus on one evaluation issue until it has been thoroughly discussed (and avoid conflating different issues, such as reliability and validity).
- Select relevant supporting evidence (if appropriate).

In this context, it's worth thinking about some important principles of evaluation that underpin the kinds of thinking we want to engender in our students. It's relatively easy to get students to learn a list of key evaluation terminology such as 'reliability' and 'validity' with reasonably good definitions, and after a few attempts, students will develop some basic heuristics about when to use some of them. For example, if the students are evaluating a study, they need to consider the level of control and talk about the effects of extraneous variables on validity or for a theory to say something about some supporting evidence. However, what they struggle to do, especially in writing, is really demonstrate that they know what this means, in context.

This can lead to very circular exchanges in lessons, such as the following example:

Teacher: *What's a strength of this study?*
Student: *It's reliable.*
Teacher: *OK – what makes it reliable?*
Student: *It uses a standardised procedure.*
Teacher: *Alright, why does that make it reliable?*

Student: *Because it can be replicated*

Teacher: *Good – so what?*

Student: *So that means it's reliable.*

Teacher: *Why?*

Student: *Because it's standardised.*

In this example, the student has not really grasped why the use of a standardised procedure affects reliability, and certainly hasn't applied this effectively to the study at hand (would you have any idea which study was being discussed here?). Therefore, in order to evaluate effectively, we need to get students to think about evaluation in two specific ways.

First, students need to be able to support the claims they're making about the particular thing they're evaluating, with some evidence from the thing they're evaluating. Imagine that students are studying an experiment which investigated the effect of background noise on memory for a list of words:

> This study is replicable because it used a standardised procedure, as all participants completed the same memory task in the same conditions with the words being projected on the screen for the same length of time.

Now we've got some specific contextual details to support the claim being made. But the student still isn't explaining why this is actually a strength of the study. Sometimes students presume that simply saying 'so this makes it reliable' is enough.

Therefore, the second thing they need to be able to do is explain how this particular aspect affects the ability to make specific assertions about the thing being evaluated:

> This increases the reliability of the findings, because the experiment could be replicated to see if similar effects of music on memory are found consistently in other samples.

Now we are clearly adding another layer of *context*, which shows why this particular issue is relevant for this particular study, as opposed to the totally generic evaluation point we started with. Let's put this altogether and consider what we're really looking for in evaluation:

Section 3: Teaching core content

Paragraph section	Function
This study is replicable because it used a standardised procedure, as all participants completed the same memory task in the same conditions with the words being projected on the screen for the same length of time.	This is a contextualised point, because it shows knowledge of the specific details of the study and makes clear why the claim (the study is replicable) is true in this particular instance.
This increases the reliability of the findings, because the experiment could be replicated to see if similar effects of music on memory are found consistently in other samples.	This moves on to explain why this can be considered a strength of the study. How does this affect the overall conclusions presented by the study?

So, there are two levels of context at play here. The first is about identifying why the claim being made in the point is true in this specific context. We'll call this 'context 1', or C1. The second level of context is about suggesting the broader implications of the claim – how does the claim affect our ability to assert something. We'll call this 'context 2', or C2.

Question	Statement	Context
Explain the claim being made about X.	*This study is replicable because it used a standardised procedure, as all participants completed the same memory task in the same conditions with the words being projected on the screen for the same length of time.*	C1
What is the effect of C1 on the ability to assert Y?	*This increases the reliability of the findings, because the experiment could be replicated to see if similar effects of music on memory are found consistently in other samples.*	C2

We'll return to this idea of different layers of context in Section 3C (page 337) on evaluative writing, as this is where students particularly struggle to move away from generic responses. However, it's important to have these two ideas in mind as we consider the specifics of evaluating different elements of the core content, namely studies, theories, treatments and methods.

Evaluation points – anything goes?

Students need to understand what constitutes valid evaluation for a given context. Unfortunately, they sometimes fail to consider what the thing they're evaluating is actually saying, trying to do or trying to claim, and consequently include irrelevant or incorrect evaluation points. There are a few ways in which this can manifest itself.

Firstly, let's consider a couple of examples that students commonly claim:

> A strength of correlations is that they tell us about a relationship between two variables.

This statement makes no sense, because it claims that a strength of something is that it simply does the thing it's intended to do. That's like saying that a strength of a chair is that you can sit on it – it wouldn't be a chair otherwise! Different (and equally common) manifestations of this problem are assertions like 'a strength of theory X is that it explains behaviour Y' or 'a strength of this study is it successfully achieved its aim of testing X'. Well, yes!

> A weakness of the working memory model is that it doesn't explain what happens to information in long-term memory.

This statement is essentially the reverse position, in that it claims that the working memory model falls short for failing to do something it was never intended to do. That's like criticising your sofa because it doesn't have an engine! This is why it's important to ensure that students understand the 'big idea' behind a particular theory, study, treatment or method.

A second consideration comes specifically when students are discussing research as supporting evidence for a particular theory or treatment. In search of more developed lines of argument, they introduce counterpoints which critique the evidence they've cited. All well and good so far, but students sometimes have a tendency to do this indiscriminately. For example:

> The role of the prefrontal cortex in aggression is supported by evidence from Raine et al. (1997), who showed using PET scans that...

However, PET scans are invasive as they involve injecting people with a radioactive tracer, and therefore this is unethical.

In this instance, the student has gone into their schema for 'evaluating PET scans' and just picked the first (or possibly only) point they can remember. But, clearly, the ethical issues around the use of PET scans have absolutely no bearing on whether or not the evidence presented to support an explanation for aggression is valid or not. This is quite a nuanced point for students to grasp, and so telling students they can just critique the evidence without discussing *why* they are critiquing it is likely to send many of them down the wrong path.

A final problem to consider is that students make evaluative points that only make sense from the very narrow perspective of what they've learned in their studies. Consider these examples:

Classical conditioning as an explanation for phobia lacks generalisability because it's only based on a case study of a single participant (Little Albert).

Milgram's studies of obedience don't apply to women as he only studied males.

In both cases, the student has written something that is only true according to what they have learned so far on their syllabus. This is a problem, as students can't know what they don't know, and so underlines the need for us teachers to ensure they develop a wider appreciation of the context in which the research they're learning about took place, to help students avoid making these kinds of assertions.

Teaching AO3 (using the pedagogical implications)

Teaching the first evaluation points

It's probably a relatively uncontroversial statement that evaluation is the hardest part of psychology courses, and that teaching it well is challenging. What we should do about this state of affairs, however, is rather less clear cut. If it's the hardest part of the course, should we start with it right from the very start? Alternatively, perhaps we should wait until we are sure that other foundations are in place (such as knowledge and application abilities) until we broach evaluation. In an ideal world, we think we would like to follow the second model of these, but this would require not evaluating the topics that occur early in a curriculum and then looping back to cover evaluation of them at appropriate points later in the course.

This creates a challenge of curriculum planning that we have never quite been able to surmount. The compromise is to introduce evaluation ideas from the beginning of the course (although carefully scaffolded and sequenced), but to wait until later in the course to tackle independent writing of evaluation paragraphs and especially full evaluation essays. 'Carefully scaffolded and sequenced' is a crucial feature here, as both provide students with the best possible opportunity to **secure success**. Early in the course, we are not in the business of stratifying or assessing our students. We want high success rates, motivation and positive mindsets. We would go so far as to say that it is almost impossible to over-scaffold early evaluation! Here's how you could go about this process:

Pick some evaluation ideas

So far, so obvious... but which ones should you pick? As a rule of thumb, good early evaluation issues will ideally be:

- Easily applicable to (at least) the first few topics that appear in your curriculum sequence.
- Relatively accessible as ideas in and of themselves.

The second point is important. Applying evaluation ideas to psychological research is challenging enough without also having to struggle to remember or understand the issue that you are trying to apply. For this reason, we would suggest that jumping straight into complex concepts such as validity may not be ideal for an introduction to evaluative thinking, as students then have to juggle both the concept of validity and the application of the concept to a piece of research. For a new student, that is a severe demand on cognitive load. Better perhaps to start with something more familiar to them and build on these through *superordinate learning*. One good example of this, given that many of the terms will be familiar to them from KS3 and GCSE science (or indeed from an induction to the subject like the one at the start of this section), may be 'features of a science'.

In one of their first lessons of the course, one of us provides students with a table like the one below and structures some discussion activities around how easy or difficult it would be to meet these standards in psychology. This provides a nice introduction to the general debate about psychology as a science, but also provides some useful, and in some cases relatively familiar (such as 'replicable', 'standardised' and 'controlled'), evaluative terminology.

Feature of a science	How easy do you think this would be to achieve in psychology?
Replicable – the procedure can be repeated accurately.	
Standardised – the same thing is done or said to each participant.	
Controlled – other variables are removed or kept constant, so they don't affect the results.	
Reductionist – breaking down human experience into more easily measurable parts.	
Generalisable – the results can be applied more broadly beyond the sample who took part.	
Falsifiability (hypothesis testing) – theories should generate predictions (hypotheses) that can be tested and proved either correct or incorrect.	

One thing to emphasise through this discussion is that the cumulative aim of all of these features is to allow us to discover *cause and effect relationships*. This point will be useful when we think about the wider implications (the 'so what?') of evaluation points.

From this base, one of the first big theories that we then tackle (and evaluate) is the approach of behaviourism. At the end of the segment, we can introduce evaluation by assessing how well behaviourism achieves the various features of a science using an adapted version of the previous table (using the terms we introduced in the previous section, this will give us the information needed for C1), which, when completed, may look something like this:

Feature of a science	How well does behaviourism achieve this aim? Give examples (C1)
Replicable – the procedure can be repeated accurately.	Very replicable as they use consistent procedures (e.g. schedules of reinforcement), which can be repeated exactly.
Standardised – the same thing is done or said to each participant.	Highly standardised procedures (e.g. systematic desensitisation, or Skinner's box reinforcement/punishment schedules).
Controlled – other variables are removed or kept constant, so they don't affect the results.	Very controlled (e.g. Skinner's box allows complete control of the environment).
Reductionist – breaking down human experience into more easily measurable parts.	Very reductionist. Control of other variables, so only the effect of one change (e.g. reinforcement) is measured.
Generalisable – the results can be applied more broadly beyond the sample who took part.	Less strong. Use of animals (e.g. in Skinner's box) is assumed by the behaviourist to be generalisable to humans, but this is probably not true in all cases.
Falsifiability (hypothesis testing) – theories should generate predictions (hypotheses) that can be tested and proved either correct or incorrect.	Very falsifiable. Skinner box-tested hypotheses, which could be falsifiable.
Given all of the above, how 'scientific' overall do you think behaviourism is? Justify your answer	Overall very scientific, although there are some problems with generalisability in some cases.

Verbal rehearsal

We could skip straight to writing evaluation paragraphs after the exercise above, but one extra quick and easy step that maximises student practice opportunities (especially before the more nerve-wracking step of actually committing thoughts to paper) is verbal rehearsal. This provides a form of self-explanation, which is a generative learning activity that can help to consolidate new learning. Students can pair up and take it in turns to verbally create evaluation paragraphs with each other. If you wish, you could scaffold this activity using a prompt, such as:

One strength of the behaviourist approach is that it is highly scientific.

It uses research practices that are _____ [*insert feature of a science that behaviourism does well*], for example by _____ [*give specific example – for C1*]

This allows cause and effect relationships to be discovered between stimuli and behaviour, such as between _____ and _____ [*give specific example – for C2*]

After this, students could also be challenged to turn this paragraph around to form a criticism for the one feature of a science (generalisability) where there were more questions.

Scaffolded paragraph writing

The final stage is for students themselves to produce a high-quality written evaluation paragraph (in a place that they will be able to easily refer back to). This could involve providing the same sentence starters as for the verbal rehearsal practice (or some other 'heavy' scaffolding method, page 353).

Put it all together, and we may end up with two short evaluation paragraphs on behaviourism, based on the features of a science:

> One strength of the behaviourist approach is that it is highly scientific. It uses research practices that are highly controlled, for example, the Skinner box, which allows complete control over extraneous variables in the environment. This means that cause and effect relationships can be discovered between stimuli (such as a reinforcement) and behaviour (such as pressing a lever).
>
> However, results from animals in a Skinner box may not be generalisable to humans. Human behaviour is far more complex than that of a rat or a pigeon, and our environments are more complex than a Skinner box, meaning that we may not respond to reinforcement and punishment in the same way.

Both of these paragraphs fulfil the C1 and C2 criteria, although they are deliberately kept relatively brief for simplicity in order to **manage cognitive load** as appropriate for students new to the subject. The C2 element especially is very brief in both, and both paragraphs lack technical terms in places (for example, the term 'internal validity' could easily be added into the first paragraph). However, if we aim to **secure** success so that students are confident writing a slightly simpler paragraph about 'generalisation' initially, then they will be in a much better position to understand and incorporate new terms (since **prior knowledge is a key predictor of future learning**) that provide more specific reasons for issues of generalisation, such as ecological validity or population validity.

Building on the foundations

The next step to scaffolding evaluation skills is to identify the points that can also be applied to the next topic in the curriculum sequence. For example, a teaching sequence covering 'Approaches to psychology' could run as follows:

Behaviourism – Social learning theory – Cognitive approach – Cognitive neuroscience

Each of these offers an opportunity to regularly review the issues of control and generalisability, applied to a new topic, while also slowly drip feeding in new technical terminology to increase the depth and elaboration of the evaluation understanding. For example:

Approach	Known issue	New application	New terminology
Social learning theory	Control	Bandura's setting	Population validity
	Generalisability	Bandura's sample	
Cognitive approach	Control	Memory experiments	Internal validity
	Generalisability		Ecological validity
Cognitive neuroscience	Generalisability	'Taxi driver' sample in Maguire's study	Population validity

This is not to say that other evaluation ideas cannot be included alongside these ones if you so wish (Bandura's experiment can be a good introduction to the concept of demand characteristics, for example), but even covering other unrelated evaluation ideas will benefit from students having a core of well-understood evaluation issues that they can discuss and write about repeatedly throughout the early part of their course.

A note on introducing C1 and C2 terminology to students

Although we have used the terms 'C1' and 'C2' in this section, you may want to think carefully about when you introduce these terms with students. Evaluation can be cognitively overloading enough at the start of a course without also having to juggle new abstract terminology. We try to introduce some concrete examples of good evaluation paragraphs over the course of a number of weeks, initially to provide students with a model, but without referring to C1 or C2. Following this, the terms can be introduced in a lesson that uses several examples from contexts they're familiar with (perhaps with some good – and bad – models to compare), and then used to draw out the C1 and C2 elements in the good answers. After this, the terms can be used in lessons and in marking feedback; they will quickly become second nature.

TAONTAIE: To acronym or not to acronym in evaluation?

It's pretty common for teachers to have a range of acronyms to act as prompts for students as they learn how to evaluate each of the ideas in turn. Probably the most widely used is 'GRAVE' for evaluating studies (**G**eneralisability, **R**eliability, **A**pplications, **V**alidity, **E**thics, sometimes converted into 'GRAVEE' by the addition of 'Economic implications'), but there are many out there ('GRENADE', 'MERVS', 'SIR NEDG', 'MER', 'CODA', 'DREAMS', 'SCOUT(S)', 'DINOSAUR', 'SODA', 'SAVED' – even 'ANUS'!) They can be a useful scaffold, giving students a clear set of ideas to use when discussing content in class, and a mental checklist with which to plan answers in exams.[5]

As a further scaffold, students may often complete evaluation tables based around these acronyms, whether on a worksheet, in a booklet or just drawn out on paper. For example:

---

5   To be clear, here we are referring to acronyms for lists of evaluation terms, rather than those based around writing structures such as 'PEEL' (**P**oint, **E**xplain, **E**vidence, **L**ink). We will deal with the related issues around these kinds of acronyms when we look at evaluative writing in more detail later in Section 3, 'Scaffolding evaluation paragraph structure using acronyms', page 346.

Evaluation of Asch's conformity study (1951)	
Generalisability	
Reliability	
Applications	
Validity	
Ethics	

While the actual terms themselves are helpful for students (particularly those students who struggle to really get 'how to evaluate'), overreliance on them can have a negative impact on their thinking and their writing. They can lead to students producing very superficial answers where the evaluative points feel disjointed and lacking any coherence; all too often, it can seem that students have just really missed the point. In other words, leaning too much on these acronyms prevents the students from making meaning.

Therefore, we have to be really careful that *the scaffold doesn't become the schema*. That is, that we don't unintentionally create incorrect ideas about how or what to evaluate based on the supports we have put in place, such as the acronyms or the design of the tables themselves. Some potential problems that can arise are:

- The evaluation issues are in a sequence based on the acronym (to make it easier to remember) rather than in any meaningful arrangement of importance. This means that students tend to prioritise those at the beginning because they're the ones they think of first. For example, students often spend too long evaluating the sample of a study simply because generalisability is at the top of the list.
- The boxes are of equal size (because the table would look weird otherwise), which means that students tend to assume that points are of equivalent weight. This then leads them to think that it doesn't really matter which points they include, and therefore select and write about them indiscriminately.
- The boxes can lead to students forgetting or excluding anything, perhaps of far greater significance, that doesn't neatly fit in one of them (and inevitably just get scribbled elsewhere and ignored). These

tables can *literally* be stopping our students from thinking outside the box! Furthermore, students can get bogged down in discussions around where something fits in the table, rather than properly considering the implications of the issue itself

- Students often find that the options in the acronyms are easier to apply to criticisms than to more positive evaluations. For example, the greatest contribution of many of the major studies covered in our specifications will be that they helped to advance our theoretical understanding of behaviour; this is not usually an option in most acronyms. Students can therefore find themselves writing somewhat facile points about reliability or the like, rather than grappling with the larger implications of a study.

- Students can also neglect properly revising specific evaluation ideas, because they have developed the idea that they can create good evaluation 'on the fly' in exam situations simply by following the acronym. As with many of the problems above, this can lead to superficial evaluation.

What should we do instead, then? We are not advocating ditching the use of acronyms altogether, but perhaps a more careful approach is required. Use acronyms early on, but like all scaffolds, aim to reduce students' reliance on them over time. At the very least, it should be clear that the acronym represents a *partial* list of *possible* evaluation ideas, of which *some* (but rarely all) may be appropriate for a given study.

It can certainly feel more challenging for students if they cannot rely on generic, pre-learned lists of points that they can use for any essay on any topic; they'll have to revise harder, because the arguments are individual to each theory or study. This is certainly more daunting for some students, as their evaluation schema needs to be much richer and more complex. But in the long run, perhaps that's doing them a favour too; let's not forget that **learning requires repeated hard thinking**. The biggest criticism of students' evaluation in exam answers is genericism – that they fail to really link to the context of the question. By rooting the evaluation much more clearly in the content, rather than in generic checklists, the students should end up writing far more convincing, contextualised (showing C1 and C2) answers.

Section 3B: Teaching core content

So far, we've considered the general principles around the various assessment objectives and the different knowledge and skills we want to impart or develop, and how our teaching framework can give us suggestions for effective ways to do this. Now we turn our attention to the domain-specific content of psychology – what is the body of knowledge that we want students to learn? In this section, we deal with the substantive disciplinary knowledge in psychology – the range of methods, theories, studies, treatments, approaches and issues and debates that students will learn about regardless of which specification or qualification you are teaching. Although our teaching framework provides some good general guiding principles, we explore each of these areas of knowledge separately and consider both knowledge and evaluation in turn.

Teaching research methods

As we established in Section 1, **research methods, and statistics, really matter**; arguably, they are the most important thing that students learn. Therefore, we need to ensure that students develop a strong underpinning of research methods knowledge. To foster the kinds of disciplinary thinking we want in our students, they'll need to develop underlying schemas for each type of content they encounter (such as theories, studies or treatments) and the same is true of methods.

One helpful way to frame research methods is around a set of trade-offs that researchers make when working out how to conduct their investigation. For example, when looking at experimental research, we can consider the decision to conduct the experiment in a controlled or naturalistic setting (such as laboratory versus field experiments) or the decision to have different groups of participants completing different conditions of the IV or the same group being tested repeatedly (such as independent groups versus repeated measures designs). Students should understand that whatever decision is made with respect to a particular feature of a method brings both advantages and disadvantages.

In order to **manage cognitive load**, we ideally want to introduce each of these decisions in turn, with the opportunity for students to **make meaning** of them individually before thinking about the entire picture. Research methods, even more so than other areas of psychology, is replete with technical (and often very similar) terminology that can be extremely abstract, especially in the eyes of students who do not have much experience of conducting practical psychology studies. As per our principles of good explanations, this will be best achieved by moving from concrete to abstract, and so plenty of examples are needed to ensure students appreciate the underlying structures of each set of features or decisions, and not just the surface details of a particular example. Because they are so fundamental, these concepts will need to be **reviewed regularly**, and we should take every opportunity to include some research methods retrieval where we can. Every piece of research encountered, in whatever context, provides a chance to review one or more methodological features, as well as providing a wide range of different contexts.

Example teaching segment: Explaining research methods ideas

Joyce is teaching research methods. She begins with a concrete example of a confounding variable in action. She tells students that they are going to investigate whether people can jump higher when listening to rock music compared to listening to classical music. The students are asked to jump and post sticky notes on the wall as high up as they can. Joyce allocates students to one of the groups, making sure that most of the taller students are in the rock music group and the shorter students are in the classical music group.

Of course, the students immediately pick up on this and complain, and Joyce is able to have a lot of fun playing dumb for as long as possible, before getting them to explain what the problem is. In the discussion, Joyce can carefully draw out both parts of the problem – that there is an extraneous variable, height, which is not controlled, but also that height varies systematically with the conditions of the IV. This then allows her to introduce the definition of a confounding variable: 'An extraneous variable that varies systematically between the conditions of the IV.'

Joyce goes on to give a number of examples of confounding variables. For example:

> A researcher conducts an experiment to investigate the effects of sleep deprivation on concentration. One group of participants is allowed a normal night's sleep, while the other is made to stay awake all night. Both groups are given a wordsearch puzzle to complete and are timed on how long it takes them to find all the words. For convenience, the researcher conducts each condition on different days in the week. The control group (normal sleep) are tested on Tuesday morning, while the sleep-deprived group are tested on Friday afternoon (having not slept on Thursday night). Unfortunately, the room the researcher uses for testing is also next to an area where some building work is being done all week, so there is quite a lot of drilling noise in the background.

Let's represent the shape of this study visually:

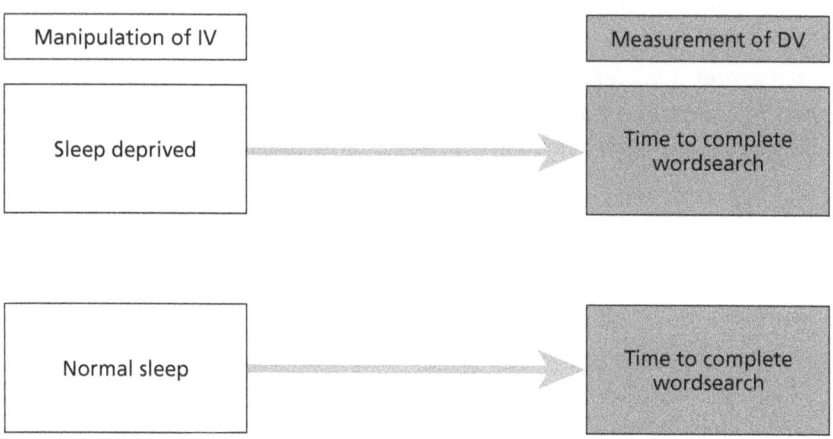

Which group would we expect to complete the wordsearch faster here, given our hypothesis? Exactly – the normal sleep group. But there is more to this study, isn't there? What other variables, other than the IV, are we told about that could affect the DV? That's right. The drilling. Let's add that in.

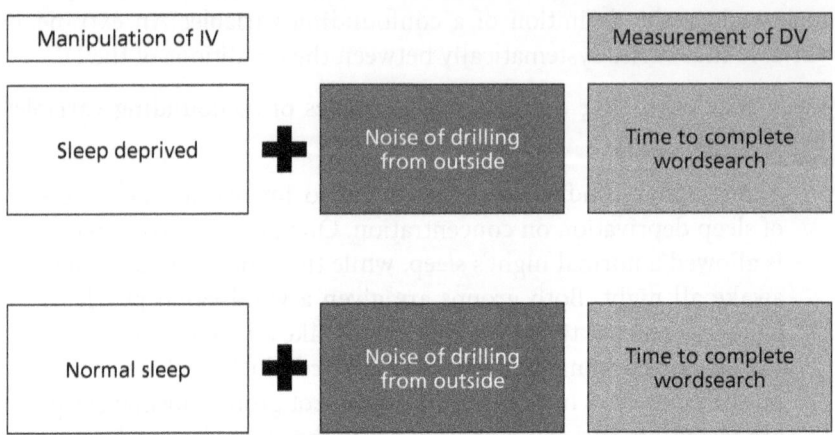

Now the drilling noise is a variable that is not the IV, and I think we can all imagine that it could have an effect on the DV. Tell the person next to you, what do we call these kinds of variables? Krishna? Yes – extraneous variables.

Let's think about the possible effects of extraneous variables. Tell your partner, which condition would we expect to complete the wordsearch faster here, given our hypothesis? Tiffany? Yes, I agree – still the normal sleep group. OK, let's imagine that's what we find… now here's the big question. Would we still be justified in concluding that sleep deprivation affects concentration? Is this experiment still valid as a test of this?

Students may reflexively reject the validity of this design, and need some coaxing to trying to compare the relative effects of the variable in each case.

In other words, why wouldn't we be too worried about the extraneous variable here? Exactly – it's likely to be the same for both conditions. What's the technical term for this? Yes – controlled. Was that the only extraneous variable in this study? Ok, yes – time of day. Let's add that in.

Section 3: Teaching core content

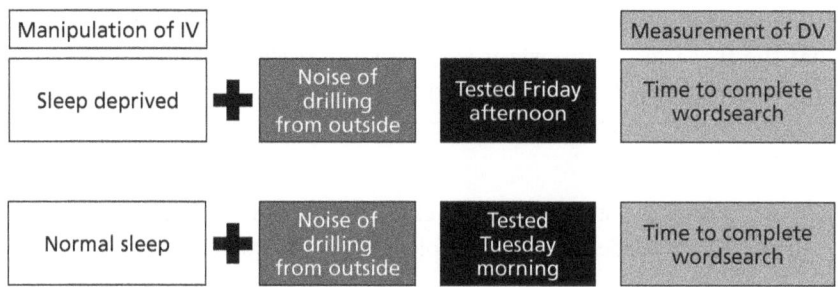

Now, same questions again. Would we still be justified in concluding that sleep deprivation affects concentration? Is this experiment still valid as a test of this? No? Why not? The time of day is an extraneous variable, just like the drilling, isn't it?

From this, Joyce draws out the distinction between the two variables and applies the correct terms.

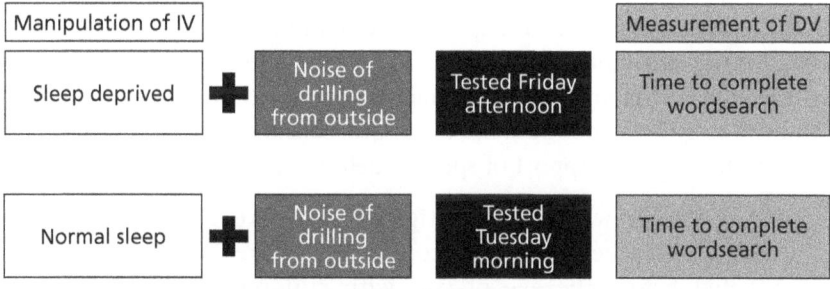

An extraneous variable is any variable other than the IV that **could** affect the DV. A confounding variable is a kind of extraneous variable that **varies systematically** with the conditions of the IV.

OK folks, over to you. I'm interested in the effect of energy drinks on running speed, compared to water. In your books, represent the shape of the study visually, as we did last time. Then try to identify possible extraneous variables for this study, and how they could turn into confounding variables.

Applying research methods

Application marks occur frequently in research methods questions, as many questions will be linked to a stem describing a research study that students need to then link their knowledge back to. We tell our students that the three most important words in any research methods question are 'in this study' (or variations on this), as this is the crucial reminder to them that everything they write needs to be explicitly linked back to the study.[6]

Application to the stem is not too challenging when all the information is provided for students. For example, a question such as:

> A psychologist wanted a sample of 20 children from a nursery school to take part in an experiment. She wrote down the names of all the children at the school and put them into a hat. She then drew out 20 names and used those children for her sample.
>
> (a) Explain which sampling technique the psychologist used in this study. (2)

Here the stem provides the students with information that clearly links to the theoretical concept of random sampling; they will therefore find it quite easy to use information from the stem in justifying their answer. Much more difficult are questions in which the information provided by the stem is incomplete, and where the application therefore requires students to go 'beyond the stem' to suggest sensible *possible* applications, without having the support of specific details in the stem. For example:

> A psychologist wanted to investigate the effects of age of adoption on aggressive behaviour. He compared children who had been adopted before the age of two with children who had been adopted after the age of two. The children were observed in their school playground when they were six years old.
>
> (a) Suggest two operationalised behavioural categories the psychologist could use in his observation of aggressive behaviour. (2)
>
> (b) Explain how the psychologist could have carried out this observation using time sampling. (4)

---

6   Different exam boards may vary in the extent to which this application is enforced; Edexcel is far stricter than AQA, for example, with almost every mark requiring contextualisation.

One of the big challenges in questions like this is getting the students to feel confident in making specific applied suggestions. For example, it doesn't actually matter what the behaviour categories are (so long as they are relevant to aggressive behaviour, and reasonably clearly operationalised), or what the time intervals chosen may be (within reason). Students can find it very difficult, however, to have the confidence to go beyond saying things like, 'Take snapshots of aggressive behaviour after a suitable time interval' to saying something like, 'Take a snapshot of the behaviour categories of "punching (hitting with a closed fist)" and "kicking" after a one-minute interval. Then wait for one minute and take another snapshot using the same behaviour categories. Continue to take snapshots of behaviour in this way after one-minute intervals until the end of the breaktime.'

The challenge of application here is actually the same as the challenge of C1 in evaluation; namely, finding specific contextual details to illustrate a particular psychological concept. In both cases we are asking the question, 'What does concept X look like *in this case*?' If we can get our students used to justifying exactly how ideas are demonstrated in different specific contexts, we therefore stand a good chance of improving both their application and their evaluation skills.

Practising analysing research methods

Given its importance, students don't spend nearly as much time on research methods as they probably should. Whether it's delivered as a separate unit (AQA) or embedded within topics (Edexcel), it's hard for students to gain enough exposure to different research methods in different contexts to fully appreciate the true complexities of studying psychology.

When students do encounter each method, it's often in a very 'prototypical' fashion, which means they develop a somewhat limited schema for the method and may struggle to identify different elements of methodology in different contexts. For example, think about how many times they come across experimental designs that are about things like memory, almost always involving presentation of word lists and comparing the effects of things like type of music or level of alcohol consumption on recall. Think, too, about how often students encounter pieces of real research that don't neatly fit in one methodological 'box'. Students can deal with this better if they have sophisticated schema for the features of different research methodologies, as well as broader 'study' schemas that include the idea that studies may make use of multiple methodologies.

Therefore, in order to help **make meaning**, it's important that the students get lots of practice with multiple examples across a range of contexts. These can be time consuming to write but are a good use of department time, and a discussion about sequencing – working out what makes some examples trickier than others – is often valuable when drawing out the precise features of different methodologies and unpicking the various likely misconceptions that students may have. Alternatively, past paper scenarios (especially ones from old versions of your specification, or from other specifications) can work well. Another option here can be to use AI to write research scenarios for analysis. For example, one of us used the following prompt on an AI platform:

> You are an expert psychology teacher. Generate a set of example research method scenarios that can be used to help A-level psychology students practise identifying different features of research, such as independent and dependent variables, experimental designs and different sampling methods.[7]

This prompt produced numerous examples, including:

- Scenario 1 – Imagine researchers want to see if different types of music affect how well students remember things they learn. They play classical, pop, or no music at all while students study, then test their recall shortly after.
- Scenario 2 – Another research team wants to know if practicing relaxation techniques helps students feel less anxious when giving presentations. They compare students who practice these techniques beforehand to those who don't, measuring their reported anxiety and physical responses.
- Scenario 3 – Researchers observe students working on different sized assignments in the library, recording how long it takes them to actually start working after receiving the task. They wonder if the perceived size of the task (number of items) influences how likely students are to procrastinate.

---

7   Of course, you may need to play around with the prompt to get exactly what you want.

This whole process took about 60 seconds, certainly a lot faster than it would have been to write ourselves or find in past papers! We may want to tweak a couple here and there, but that's still a much more effective use of time. A final thought here is that teaching students how to do this process for themselves also gives them a powerful tool to use for independent study.

However you choose to generate your examples, a good way to implement this is to use it as a vehicle for some retrieval practice at the start of lessons. A research scenario can yield a number of different avenues for analysis and has two clear advantages over straightforward factual retrieval questions. First, it's likely more challenging, which may help improve future recall (the retrieval effort hypothesis states that 'difficult but successful retrievals are better for memory than easier successful retrievals', Pyc and Rawson, 2009). Second, it's closer to the types of questions that students will encounter in the exam, which has been shown to have retrieval benefits (Yang et al., 2021; Agarwal et al., 2021). A good scenario can also be used repeatedly over time, and the teacher can decide to quiz students on concepts covered previously (if retrieval had low success rates) or explore new concepts – or a mix of the two. Let's look at an example.

Example teaching segment: Retrieval practice of research methods

Barney is keen to do some retrieval practice on research methods with his Year 13 class, who he feels have started to forget some of the key ideas, especially the more challenging content such as methods of improving reliability and validity. Barney finds the following scenario in a past paper from a previous specification and presents it at the start of the lesson in which he knows that some of the new content will also involve evaluating the research methods of a study.

> A psychology student was asked to design an investigation to see whether taking exercise could increase feelings of happiness. She proposed to do an experiment. She decided to recruit a sample of volunteers who had just joined a gym, by putting up a poster inside the gym. She planned to carry out a short interview with each volunteer and give each one a happiness score. She intended to interview the volunteers again after they had attended the

gym for six weeks and reassess their happiness score to see if it had changed.

The psychology student's teacher identified a number of limitations of the proposed experiment. Explain two limitations of the student's proposal and suggest how the investigation could be improved. At least one of your suggestions and improvements must deal with either reliability or validity. (6 marks)

NB Barney slightly adapted the question to add the final sentence specifying that either reliability or validity must be referred to, given that these are concepts that students often find difficult to apply.

OK folks. First, I want you to just read the question thoroughly. Then reread and note down any possible issues, and why they occur in this study. If we're going to 'explain' the issues like the question asks us to, then we will need specific context from this study and specific details about what the problem actually looks like in this case, so include this detail in your notes. Three minutes to read and identify some possible issues. Don't limit yourself to two issues at this stage. Note as many as you can. Go.

Barney circulates to check understanding and answers. Three minutes later...

OK, well done. Now when I say go, you will share what you have written with your partner. See if you identified the same thing or something different to each other. Push each other to make the context of the limitation really clear – what does the problem look like in the context of this study? Also, see if your solutions are the same.

Barney circulates again to listen, and then cold-calls some students for suggestions of issues and improvements.

Here's a table of things I thought may be relevant issues in the scenario. It's not an exhaustive list though – you may well have identified other things. As we go through them, note how the issues are explained specifically in the context of the study.

Possible validity issues	Possible improvements
The independent variable (exercise) is not operationalised. There is no attempt to specify the amount of exercise taken, frequency or intensity. These could vary substantially, reducing internal validity.	Clearer operationalisation of IV.
No controls suggested for possible extraneous variables such as initial happiness level, amount and type of exercise undertaken, sleep, diet, etc.	Control extraneous variables (e.g. suggest that all participants do 30 minutes on the treadmill three times a week).
The DV (happiness) is measured through an interview. Interviews are prone to social desirability bias (SDB) (e.g. participants saying they are happier than they actually are, as being happy is socially desirable). This could affect the internal validity of the measurement.	Use a different measurement of DV (e.g. using a questionnaire). Not face-to-face, so SDB is reduced.
Possible reliability issues	**Possible improvements**
The DV (happiness) is measured through an interview. If this is unstructured or semi-structured, then different participants may end up being asked different questions, which will provide different results.	Use a structured interviewing process, or another more standardised DV measurement.
As the student is unlikely to have received training to carry out interviews of this nature, she may not be consistent in her ratings.	Provide training to the student in advance (e.g. interview training and training on classifying different participant responses).
Other possible issues	**Possible improvements**
Ethical issues – there is no mention of informed consent, confidentiality, debriefing, etc.	Ensure all ethical guidelines are explicitly met.

Barney then continues with the taught lesson as normal, making sure that at some point the students are once again required to use their newly reviewed skills of analysing research methods in a new scenario.

Making meaning through prediction – predicting research methods questions (and scenarios)

One way to take this further is to provide a scenario and ask students to predict what questions they could be asked based on the information they've been given. Allowing students free rein over this process also takes advantage of the 'goal-free' effect (Paas and Kirschner, 2012), a finding whereby problems with a nonspecific goal impose a lower cognitive load (and so lead to better learning) than practising by solving problems with a specific goal (i.e. giving them the specific questions that *were* actually asked in relation to the scenario). A goal-free scenario helps students to think about all the possible things they can figure out from the stem and get good at spotting the clues examiners leave – those hooks that students need to use to be able to contextualise their answers. It's also useful preparation for those extended methods questions where a scenario may be followed by a significant number of different questions. Learning to engage with and annotate the stem first – outsourcing working memory to the page – helps further **manage cognitive load** and saves the students from having to go back and reread the scenario anew for each separate question.

For example, take the following research scenario:

> A researcher is investigating the effectiveness of the cognitive interview. A group of 50 undergraduate participants are all shown a video of an incident on a local street. Half of them are questioned using standard interview questions, half of them are questioned using cognitive interview techniques. They are compared on accuracy of recall measured by a score out of 20.

Section 3: Teaching core content

What questions could we generate from this?

- Identify the independent and dependent variables.
- Give one problem with the way the DV has been operationalised.
- Write a suitable alternative/null (directional/non-directional) hypothesis.
- Give one strength/weakness of the sample used in this study.
- Describe the experimental design used in this study.
- Give a strength/weakness of the design used in this study.
- Give a strength/weakness of the use of a laboratory experiment in this study.
- Suggest one way the researchers have used a standardised procedure.
- Identify and justify which inferential statistical test the researchers would use to analyse their findings.
- Suggest one way the researchers could have improved the reliability/validity of this study.

An even more challenging test is to have students write their own research methods scenarios and before suggesting questions for them (or passing them on to other groups to suggest questions). Creating plausible research scenarios and the likely questions that could arise from them requires a very high level of understanding; creating examples from memory also aids learning (it is more effective than standard retrieval practice, Endres et al., 2024). If your students can rise to this challenge, then there is likely to be little in the actual exam that can throw them off.

Evaluating research methods

The sheer number of different research methods that students can be required to know (as well as their respective evaluations) can seem very intimidating at times, especially to the average psychology student for whom a fascination with the intricacies of research methodology is unlikely to have been the primary motivation for taking the course. One way that we can help to cut through this apparent morass of different techniques and evaluations (and to help students **make meaning** through revealing the underlying systems behind the techniques) is to help them understand that research decisions are almost always a trade-off.

Methodological decisions that bring certain benefits will almost always also bring concurrent (and consistent) drawbacks. Two notable examples that occur throughout psychology courses are:

- *Control* – How much control are we able to (or do we want to) have over the research situation. Control trades off against *naturalism* (how we want the research situation to resemble the settings in which the psychological variable of interest actually occurs).
- *Simplicity* – This refers to the delivery of a research procedure or analysis of the results. Simplicity trades off against *complexity*.

Armed with knowledge of these kinds of trade-offs, students should appreciate that there is no such thing as a perfect study, and more usefully (in terms of answering exam questions), they should be able to make both positive and negative evaluations of any piece of research they encounter.

Example teaching segment: Evaluating research methods using C1 and C2

Sam is teaching sampling methods, and displays the following question:

> Marcus is a health psychologist working at his local hospital. He decides to do a study into people's perceptions of smoking using a questionnaire. He uses opportunity sampling to collect his data.
>
> a) Explain one limitation of using opportunity sampling for this study. (3 marks)
>
> b) Explain why stratified sampling may be a better choice for Marcus to use. (3 marks)

Before they get started, Sam may want to remind the class of the trade-offs involved with different sampling techniques, such as how easy they are to do versus how likely they are to produce a representative sample.

While the class are working on these questions, Sam quickly prepares an example answer to spark discussion. (Student examples could also be used here if appropriate ones are noticed during circulation.)

OK folks. I've seen some nice answers so far. How about this one? Is it any good? Tell the person next to you.

> One limitation of opportunity sampling is that it may not produce a representative sample. Whoever is willing at the hospital may not be representative of the wider population. Therefore, the results of the survey may not be generalisable.

What did we think? Shai, what did you two say? [Students may initially report that this is quite a good answer.] OK, yes – I can see what you mean. It's certainly accurate, and it explains what the problem is. So, is there anything that could be improved here? Alice? The link to the study could be more detailed. Can you explain that in a bit more detail? OK, brilliant. Let's highlight the parts of this answer that actually link to the study in the question.

> One limitation of opportunity sampling is that it may not produce a representative sample. Whoever is willing at the hospital may not be representative of the wider population. Therefore, the results of the survey may not be generalisable.

So now we can see the problem a little more clearly. If a research methods question asks us to refer to a study, then it's crucial we do that – which we haven't done here. But there's another reason as well. Remember that good evaluation contains specific context about the thing you are evaluating – C1 and C2. Context about what the problem looks like in this specific case (C1) and what the specific implications of the problem are (C2). So even if the question didn't ask for them, we'd need these details just to write a good evaluation paragraph. Let's break the C1 and C2 down here.

Firstly, C1. Why would an opportunity sample at the hospital not be representative? Tell the person next to you. Evie? Yes, that's a nice idea – there may be doctors and nurses around. Can you take that a step further for me Evie? Remember everyone, we're surveying their perceptions of smoking here. Why won't they be representative? Great, thanks Evie. We may expect them to not be representative in their level of medical knowledge. What would that mean for their likely views on smoking? Let's fill this in on a little table.

C1 – Why would an opportunity sample at the hospital not be representative?	There may be more doctors and nurses who understand the medical dangers of smoking and have a more negative attitude as a result.
C2 – Why would it not be generalisable (and to who)?	

What is the C2 here? We know the 'so what?' – it's that the results may not be generalisable. But why might the results that are collected not be generalisable? Aniqah? Nice – let's write that down.

C1 – Why would an opportunity sample at the hospital not be representative?	There may be more doctors and nurses who understand the medical dangers of smoking and have a more negative attitude as a result.
C2 – Why would it not be generalisable (and to who)?	It may not be representative of average attitudes in the general population, who may know less about the dangers.

Working with the notes above, a more detailed paragraph can now be created, which uses the study information to fulfil the C1 and C2 requirements. For example:

> One limitation of opportunity sampling is that it may not produce a representative sample. Whoever is willing at the hospital may not be representative of the wider population, as it may, for example, include doctors and nurses who have very negative views of smoking. Therefore, the results of the survey may not be generalisable to the wider population who know less about the health risks of smoking.

Statistics and stats testing

Any specification you decide to teach will feature the use of inferential statistics. Statistics underpin quantitative research methods, and so are critical for students to get right. Although you could argue that it only represents a small amount of the overall content they need to learn, it's worth doing well for a couple of reasons. First, it is fairly predictable that questions on inferential tests do reliably come up in some form, and likely on more than one paper (quite possibly all three). Second, if the students intend to study psychology or any other scientific disciplines at university (which a good number do), then confidence in statistics will be of much more use to them than whether they learn about a specific theory or study in a given field. However, there are a couple of important challenges to also consider here.

Firstly, the varied nature of psychology cohorts means we will have a very wide range of mathematical ability and confidence in any given class, from the further mathematicians to those who find the whole thing rather intimidating. Even those confident mathematicians and scientists sometimes struggle, as the specifics of applying inferential statistics to psychological research often looks quite different to the 'pure' calculations they are used to. (Getting students to remember to use *n-1* in a standard deviation calculation can take some practice!)

Secondly, some psychology teachers aren't fans of statistics either! Research methods, and especially statistics, can sometimes be presented as a rather dry necessity; something we *have to learn*, but not as fun as learning about, say, Milgram's research on obedience or offender profiling. As we saw in Section 1A, however, **motivation drives, and is driven by, learning**, and if students expect a topic to be boring they generally report being less motivated to study it.

We therefore think it's important to demonstrate that we do value statistics. While we won't necessarily try to pretend that statistics is our favourite part of the course, we will endeavour to show them that we think it's immensely important. We remember having quite heated debates with research colleagues (and peer reviewers!) about the correct way to analyse particular data – it matters! It's worth reminding students that statistics is the 'exciting' bit of research; the time when you get to find out whether your hypothesis is right or wrong. A significant (or even an insignificant) result can mean a lot, so students need to understand that this is a crucial part of the research process. As their name suggests, inferential statistics are where we get the chance to really make *inferences* about behaviour – where we move from just measuring to *explaining*. Sure, some students won't buy it, but modelling that this is something we value – that is valued by psychology – goes a long way to bringing them on board. With all of this in mind, there are some important pedagogical implications to consider here:

Check what they know

As we have discussed, the varied nature of psychology cohorts usually results in a wide range in mathematical ability and knowledge of statistical testing. Mathematicians will most likely have knowledge of the underlying concepts around probability, while geographers or biologists are likely to have experience conducting tests like Chi² or Spearman's Rho from their studies. Others may have very little knowledge or experience of statistics in the first place. This means we will want to assess their prior knowledge before we start and ensure gaps are filled appropriately.

For example, when presenting students with a formula for, say, the standard deviation, we can expect that some but not all students are familiar with the convention of using n to represent the number of datapoints and not everyone will immediately know that Σ means 'sum of'. Equally, we can't guarantee that students will have a clear grasp of probability notation (or what probabilities really mean, either in general or in psychological research), so before we start actually doing any tests we need to establish, and check, a good deal of prerequisite knowledge. As an example, we would suggest that there is more chance of being able to use and interpret statistics tests correctly if the following core questions are understood.

Core question	Suggested answer
What is the 'significance level' that is used most in psychology? What does this mean in words?	0.05 (5%). We accept results as significant if the probability that the results were due to chance is less than 5%.
Why do we often use the 5% level of significance in psychology? When would we not?	p=0.05 represents a compromise between the risk of type 1 and type 2 errors. When investigating sensitive topics or ones that may affect an individual's health (as in clinical trials), we may want to avoid false positives (type 1 errors) as they could have serious consequences. Therefore, we may set a more stringent significance level (e.g. p=0.01).
'The probability that the results are due to chance', 'The probability that the null hypothesis is true' and 'The probability of making a type 1 error' all mean the same thing. Why?	The 'null hypothesis' predicts that there will be no relationship between IV and DV (in an experiment) or co-variables (in a correlation study). If this is true, then any relationship we see must just be due to chance. If we decide that our results are significant when the null hypothesis is true, then we are making a false positive (or type 1 error).

Core question	Suggested answer
Define 'type 1 error'.	Rejection of the null hypothesis when it should have been accepted (also known as a 'false positive', i.e. finding it significant when it wasn't).
Define 'type 2 error'.	Failure to reject the null hypothesis when it should have been rejected (also known as a 'false negative', i.e. finding it not significant when it was).

Get attention and manage cognitive load

Competence with statistics requires focus, attention to detail and precision. Therefore, it's important that we ensure students are attending to precisely the right bits of information at every step of the process. For example, if we are teaching students to use critical values tables to determine the significance of an inferential test result, then we need to guide their attention carefully. This could mean covering up a section of the table to avoid distraction, highlighting specific columns and rows on the board or getting students to use a ruler to guide them as they read across multiple rows of critical values.

Similarly, when introducing statistical ideas and procedures, it can be tempting to frame everything in a real-world context to help students see the application of what they're doing. While this may be a good way to start, we probably want to strip out some of that detail once we get into the specifics. For example, if we want students to become well versed in giving the correct justification for different inferential tests, then getting them to learn these free from a specific context will avoid distracting them with extraneous information.

Review regularly and secure success

Because statistics is an area that some students find so challenging, we want to ensure they learn to feel competent as quickly as possible. This means providing lots of opportunities to practise with new information, with examples and problems that are carefully scaffolded to ensure students can complete them successfully. It's a topic that can also be added to regular retrieval quizzes easily and in a variety of forms to ensure students develop fluency with some of the important concepts.

Example teaching segment: Inferential statistics and levels of measurement

Asif is planning a lesson on inferential statistics for the Edexcel specification. He wants to provide his students with lots of practice identifying and justifying inferential statistical tests, as he knows it's something they're still not confident on. He has put together a whole range of example research scenarios for the students to have a go at, and he knows that in order to do this successfully they will need to understand that each test has a set of specific criteria. These relate to:

- The type of relationship the researcher is looking for in the data (e.g. difference or correlation).
- The design of the study (e.g. independent groups or repeated measures).
- The level of measurement or data (e.g. nominal, ordinal or interval).

Asif has previously taught this content to this group, and the students have been tasked with learning the criteria for each of the tests they need to know about (indeed, the previous week he used a mastery learning approach, setting a homework task to learn the statistics test table like the one below with a pass mark of 100% – and retests until all students had achieved this). Asif decides to start his lesson with some retrieval practice to check, asking his students to complete a blank version (with row and column headings only) of the table below on their mini-whiteboards.

	Type of relationship	Level of data	Research design
Mann-Whitney	Difference	Ordinal	Independent groups
Wilcoxon	Difference	Ordinal	Repeated measures
Spearman	Correlation	Ordinal	Paired scores[8]
Chi²	Difference/Association	Nominal	Unrelated data/independent groups

---

8   Technically this does not represent a research design per se in the way that we may consider independent groups or repeated measures for experiments. However, it does help to get students to understand the 'shape' of correlational research more clearly, and so it is worth inclusion here even if it's not a specific criterion that they will be required to describe for an exam question.

Asif circulates the room as students complete the task and notes that while most students are successfully filling in the correct criteria, they particularly struggle to identify the correct level of data (i.e. level of measurement) for each test. As he reviews the answers, Asif can tell from the students' responses that even with those who have learned the criteria, many don't really understand some of it properly.

Asif decides that he needs to address this problem now, as the students simply won't be able to access the next task properly otherwise. (NB for the purposes of this sequence, we'll just consider nominal, ordinal and interval. As explained below, it's the nominal/ordinal distinction that students typically find most problematic, so worrying about interval vs ratio is less of an issue here.)

Right, let's look at a really simple, concrete example. Imagine you've got a big group of people taking part in a race – let's say it's a marathon. You want a way to measure their performance. One really simple measure could be whether or not they finish the race – marathons are pretty tough after all! So that would just give you a tally of all the people who did or didn't finish.

Asif writes the word 'tally' at the side of the board.

But that's not going to tell you much about how the runners got on. So, we could also look at those who finished and record their position – first, second, third and so on. This would tell you about how well each runner did relative to everyone else based on their rank.

Asif writes the word 'rank' on the board, underneath the word tally.

But this is still not very precise. The person who won may come in just a few seconds ahead of the person coming second, but the person in third is another two minutes behind. Our rank positions tell us about the order of competitors, but not about their actual performance. For that, we'd need to measure the time in which they completed the race – using hours, minutes and seconds as standardised units of measurement.

Asif writes 'standardised unit' underneath the word rank.

So, each of these is a different level of measurement. Each one tells us something different about the data, and they are increasing in the level of precision. We can now match these up with our levels of data: nominal, ordinal and interval.

Asif shows the students a summary that looks like this:

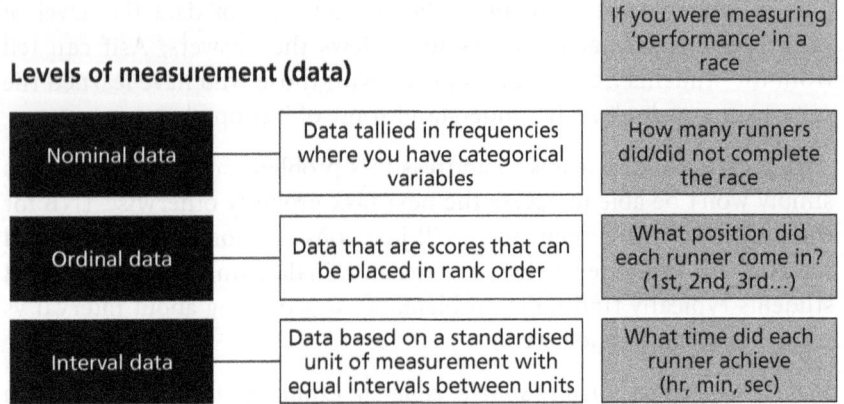

Asif knows that identifying nominal data accurately is the key to this, and the one topic students really struggle with. He has written a set of practice examples for them to work through but first needs to set the class up with the right tools to be able to analyse them.

Let's take our example further, but just focusing on the nominal data. Imagine someone is interested in whether running for charity makes it more likely that you'll finish the race. We already have one categorical variable: whether people did or didn't finish. Now they could look at all the entries and identify those who are being sponsored and those who aren't. This is another categorical variable. We can put those data into a table like this:

	Finished the race	Didn't finish
Running for charity		
Not sponsored		

This is called a contingency table. Each cell in the table represents a tally of people in the different categories. There are two columns and two rows, so we call this a 2x2 table. Each runner can only be tallied in one cell in the table – they can't be both sponsored or not sponsored, or both finish and not finish. This is called independent – or unrelated – data. Let's look at some more examples.

Section 3: Teaching core content

Asif brings up a document that includes more examples. He underlines and annotates the first one, narrating his thinking as he goes.

A researcher is investigating if there is any truth in the stereotype that there are differences between males and females in terms of preferences for cats and dogs.	*Here's the first categorical variable, gender. I'll underline both categories, male and female. Here's the second variable, type of pet. Two categories – cats and dogs.*
A researcher is investigating if there is any truth in the stereotype that there are differences between <u>males and females</u> in terms of preferences for <u>cats and dogs</u>. M F Cat Dog	*Asif draws the contingency table.* *Each participant only gets to vote for either cat or dog, not both, so each tally mark in a cell only represents the data from one participant. Remember, this is what we mean by unrelated data.*

Right, let's do another one together.

A researcher is investigating if there are any differences in mood between supporters of different football teams. They recruit 20 Liverpool fans and 20 Manchester City fans and administer a questionnaire that rates their mood. They are then split into two groups: high mood and low mood.	*What is my first categorical variable, Kyle? That's right – the football team the participants support, either Liverpool or Manchester City.* *And my second categorical variable is… Jade? Mood, yes. And what are the different categories? High and low.* *What do I need to draw now, Carmel? Good – the contingency table.*

259

Asif hands out a sheet with these and more examples.

Right, first thing everyone, I want you to copy the first two examples from the board exactly as I have done them. You need to include the underlining of the different categorical variables, and the contingency table. This is to make sure you have an accurate model to follow when you do them yourself. Once you've done that, you're going to have a go at doing this yourself for more examples. For each one, I want you to highlight the variables and categories first, then draw the contingency table, just like the two examples. Don't skip this bit out – it's really important! This will start to feel a bit samey after you've done a few – this is a good thing! We need to be able to do this accurately, fluently and in any research context, so we need to practise until we can't get it wrong. Right, off you go.

Asif waits at the front of the room while the students settle into the task. After a couple of minutes he starts circulating, checking progress and looking for any problems or misunderstandings. If he spots something occurring more than once, he could pause the class to address the issue with everyone. Naturally, some students progress faster than others, so Asif will need some additional questions to challenge them.

By the end of this task, Asif should be fairly confident that his class have understood what nominal data looks like and are reasonably confident in identifying categorical variables. Since this is a concept that students find challenging and often confuse with other levels of measurement, now is a good opportunity for some *interleaving*. Asif presents his class with a further set of example scenarios, but this time some of them have nominal data, some have ordinal, and some have interval. Again, he models the process of analysing the scenario, and loops back to the original keywords and definitions from earlier (tally, rank, standardised unit) as cues to guide students.

Asif will also need to **review regularly** and so plans in some retrieval practice for future lessons – predominantly scenario-based application questions, since this is the way in which this material is most likely to be encountered in exams.

Doing the maths!

As well as the choice, justification and interpretation of statistical tests, students may be required to actually calculate one for themselves in the exam.[9] While a handful of students are perfectly happy with this, it's something that many find challenging and, if the mountains of mock papers and assessments we've marked over the years are anything to go by, will simply skip straight past in the exam. But we argue that it's well worth taking the time to teach the students how to do this properly. It's one of the few areas in psychology where there actually are definitely correct answers, and the calculations themselves really aren't that difficult. Fiddly, yes, but not hard!

We can also sprinkle in mathematics skills whenever and wherever we can throughout lessons (for example, never collect data without asking students to calculate a mean, median and mode of it). Never work out test or quiz percentages for the students; instead, give them raw scores and make them calculate the percentage. At the same time, only provide the pass mark in percentages, or even as a fraction ('the pass mark was ⅝ of the total marks available'), and make them convert it back to raw scores. The students will hate you for it (though, of course, you will explain the rationale), but it doesn't take long and ensures that every quiz or assessment comes with some simple mathematical analysis.

When it comes to learning the slightly more complex mathematical procedures such as calculating a standard deviation or conducting an inferential test, there are some useful principles to follow. Until they develop fluency, doing a complex calculation will place a high load on students. We can help **manage cognitive load** by:

- Providing clear modelling (e.g. using 'I-We-You') to demonstrate the steps.
- Presenting worked and partially completed examples.
- Use additional scaffolding to support students initially, for example, a crib sheet that provides a key with all the different signs or symbols in a formula (this will need to be withdrawn over time).

---

9   Even if they aren't required to complete the calculations for inferential tests, there is other prescribed mathematical content on all specifications, and so we think the principles we discuss here apply more generally to any mathematical procedures that students may need to learn.

- Reducing extraneous load by initially having 'context-free' problems, where the students are focusing purely on the mathematical operation and not worrying about what the data actually means.
- Giving lots of practice with a range of different examples using different contexts, gradually increasing the complexity.

For example, AQA A-level students are required to be able to calculate the sign test. Once the process has been explained and modelled explicitly to the class, students can be given a worked example to follow step by step, such as the one below.

Sign test: A worked example

A researcher has tested participants on the number of words recalled in a memory test in the morning and afternoon, believing that more words will be remembered in the morning.

Participant	Morning results	Afternoon results	Sign of difference
1	110	122	-
2	59	45	+
3	206	135	+
4	89	90	-
5	76	42	+
6	141	87	+
7	152	131	+
8	98	113	-
9	198	56	+
10	56	62	-

Procedure

1. We have to convert the data to nominal data (categories) so we subtract the afternoon score from the morning score. If the answer is negative, we record - and if the answer is positive, we record +.
2. Then we add up the pluses (6) and minuses (4) and take the less frequent sign and call this S (if any values are the same in the two data sets, they are ignored and N is adjusted).
3. Therefore, S = 4 (this is our calculated value).
4. Now we compare the calculated value with the critical value in the table (remember, we want 0.05 significance, N = 10 and our hypothesis are one tailed).
5. The critical value is 1 when N is 10 at 0.05 significance for a one tailed test; S must be equal to or less than the critical value.
6. The calculated value of S (4) which is greater than the critical value of S (1) = 4 > 1.
7. Therefore, the difference is not significant at the 0.05 level.

Subsequent examples can then gradually remove the amount of scaffolding, such as:

A. Providing all the steps up to and including calculating s but requiring the students to determine whether the s value is significant.
B. Calculating signs of difference, but not the s and n values.
C. Performing the full test.

A few examples at each stage are likely to be needed (and more at stage A if the students have not previously become used to using critical values tables, for example, if the other stats tests have not yet been taught).

Practical activities in psychology

While some specifications (such as Edexcel and Eduqas) prescribe that students complete a set of practical activities, others simply make this a recommendation – something students really ought to do but don't actually have to. Even in the specifications where it is not mandated, examiners' reports emphasise the importance of students having undertaken their own practical investigations. The message here is clear: that practicals are considered inherently valuable for psychology students to conduct or take part in. This raises a problem, however, as if students are not going to be assessed then we could argue that practicals often represent a significant investment of time that would otherwise be used to teach other material.

We think it's worth making a distinction between two different types of practical activity that we can engage students in:

1. Theory practicals are primarily aimed at supporting students' understanding of a particular area of theory or research. For example, conducting a digit span experiment to demonstrate the limited capacity of short-term memory when learning about the multi-store model.
2. Methods practicals are primarily aimed at supporting students' understanding of research methods and data analysis. For example, getting students to conduct their own observation of students'

behaviour around school to learn about the process of creating behavioural categories and gathering observational data.

One clear benefit of practicals is that they provide a bridge from abstract to concrete and help students to root new knowledge in their own experience. This is particularly the case when conducting theory practicals, as a brief description of a research method in a booklet or textbook may not fully enlighten students as to what the participants of a study actually experienced. Furthermore, practicals provide a much better insight into the practicalities of research methods and help expose issues that are otherwise taken as read but not fully appreciated by students. For example:

- The difficulties in recruiting a representative sample of participants in an unbiased way.
- The challenges of collecting observational data (especially if trying to do so covertly).
- The level of planning and attention to detail required to run a controlled experiment using a standardised procedure.
- The importance of pilot studies as a way to iron out problems with the study design.
- The impact of having a relatively small dataset on the reliability of results.

Recent research concurs – practical demonstrations of features of the scientific method have been found to be more effective for understanding than explanation alone (Morris et al., 2024). There is therefore clearly a strong argument for students having these kinds of experiences in order to appreciate what the discipline of psychology actually looks like in the real world. We agree and have always endeavoured to include practical activities in our teaching.

However, we should think carefully about what practicals are useful for in terms of teaching students about research methods. For example, practicals are often not an effective vehicle for introducing more than one single idea (be that methodological or theoretical). This is because practicals place a significant burden on students' working memories, and does not guarantee that they will attend to, or remember, the things we want them to.

For example, imagine you want to teach a class about features of experimental methods such as independent and dependent variables. You could conduct a simple memory experiment in which students listen to either rap music or classical music while learning a list of words and then test their recall. What we may find is that students struggle to dissociate the methodological component of the experiment (the IV and DV) from the thing that the experiment was about (music and memory). The students may pay more attention to what is likely to be the more interesting aspect (the music, or their memory performance), and so they won't really think about IVs and DVs in the way we want them to. Furthermore, without exposure to more examples in a varied range of contexts, their knowledge of IVs and DVs may be too closely tied to the surface features of the experiment they have participated in for them to be able to apply this knowledge elsewhere.

We think, therefore, that practicals are often better suited to demonstrate and review aspects of research methods that students have already learned. This means we can more carefully **manage cognitive load** and allows us to use practicals as an opportunity to check what the students know and practice applying this to a new context. For example, having already taught a range of different features of experimental methods, we could run our rap/classical music experiment as above and then ask a whole range of questions to test their knowledge and understanding, such as:

- What was the IV?
- What was the DV?
- What type of experiment was this (lab/field)?
- What was the experimental design?
- What extraneous variables were controlled for in this experiment?
- Which statistical test would we use to analyse our findings? Why?

Alternatively, we could task students with designing and conducting their own practical and use this as a way to consider all of the different design decisions they'll need to make along the way. A caveat here is that we should probably provide some fairly tight parameters around what students can do and aim to keep things as simple as possible. Students may come up with some highly complex and innovative research designs, but our experience suggests that these will not be feasible to conduct. We can foster a sense of autonomy by including them in the decision-making process but may still choose to steer them in a certain direction.

To conclude, we think practical activities are an invaluable experience for students, and regardless of the extent to which they are required by your exam specification, we should endeavour to include them in our planning. However, we must also be mindful of opportunity-cost, and realistic about what exactly it is that students will learn from them (or what we *want* the students to learn).

In his book, *Teaching Secondary Science: A Complete Guide*, Adam Boxer introduces the 'slow practical' method as a means for **managing the cognitive load** of practical work, which increases the level of understanding that students can access (Boxer, 2021). Boxer's suggestions can be roughly reduced to three recommendations:

- Where possible, do practical work after teaching the content, so that students are not having to learn new content at the same time as trying to negotiate a practical.
- Split practicals into discrete stages.
- Model or explain each new step in the practical explicitly before students carry it out.

Not all of the load imposed by practicals in psychology will be directly equivalent to science (complicated equipment is rarely required for psychology practicals at school level, for example). However, there is enough overlap to merit attention, especially the potential for cognitive overload when students are faced with the dual challenges of trying to learn practical methods skills and new conceptual understanding at the same time. Thus, both of us are increasingly adopting a 'slow' approach to practicals (at least to methods practicals) that are aimed at supporting students' understanding of research methods and analysis. Theory practicals can also benefit, but there are times when the point of a theory practical is to demonstrate the actual psychological effect, which can be undermined by regularly stopping and explaining the process.

Example teaching segment: A 'slow' methods practical on counterbalancing

Trevor is teaching his class about experimental design. During the last lesson, they covered the three designs and the strengths and weaknesses of these. After reviewing their knowledge of experimental designs, as well as features of experiments like IVs and DVs, Trevor says:

Right. We're going to do an experiment. I want to learn how people respond to having an audience. In psychology, doing something better when you have an audience is known as 'social facilitation'. I want to see if we show social facilitation effects for drawing. Specifically, drawing a mouse [use any object for which there are simple step-by-step guides to follow]. *Tell the person next to you. What would your hypothesis be here? Would you expect social facilitation effects or not? OK. Now, actually what you could have said in answer to that question was: 'How can I make a hypothesis when I don't know what the operationalised variables are?' And you would have been right to do so. We can't really predict until we know what we're going to manipulate and measure. So, how would you operationalise 'having an audience'? What about 'performing better'?*

Trevor ends up with a directional hypothesis of 'participants with an audience will draw a mouse more quickly (in seconds) than participants without an audience'. Depending on time and inclination, a null hypothesis could be created as well.

OK, great. Now before we start, what variables do we want to control in this experiment, which you may be worried could affect the DV otherwise? [A number of options may be suggested, but it is likely that 'drawing ability' will be suggested relatively quickly.]

Yes, definitely. Some people are better at drawing than others. That's what we may call a participant variable – a characteristic of the participants that could affect the study's results. What could we do about that? Tell the person next to you.

We would hope, given the previous lesson and the starter questions, that the possible solution of controlling the variable through the experimental design would occur to students, but as we have seen, applying research method ideas to new scenarios is often challenging for students. Some prodding may be needed!

Brilliant. I think a repeated measures design would be an excellent way to control for the participant variable of drawing ability. So, we'll all draw a mouse individually first, then we'll all draw one again with an audience, and we'll see which one was faster. [Dramatic pause, in which hopefully a student points out the problem...] *Ah, yes – good point Jake! I want to make sure everyone has had a chance to think about this carefully. Based on what Jake said, tell the person next to you why everyone doing the drawing without an audience, and then afterwards with an audience is a bad idea.* [20 seconds.] *OK. What did you say, Kate? Great. We'd probably get better through practice, not because of the audience. And I heard some of you also using the technical term for this. People on the right of a pair, tell people on the left what that term is. Brilliant. Order effects. Finally, what would the problem be for our experiment if we didn't control for these order effects? What would that do to the validity of our experiment, and why? Left partner, tell the person on the right...*

This is a more challenging question and may need to be bounced around a few students to build an answer along the lines of 'if the order effects are not controlled, then practice will become a confounding variable and reduce the internal validity of the study as a measure of social facilitation'.

Amazing. Well done. So, we have a problem before we can start. What can we do about it?

If students haven't been taught about counterbalancing, then this solution may not be immediately obvious, but repeated emphasis that the problem is about the *order*, so 'how could we change the *order* of the conditions' is usually enough to get there.

Brilliant. So, we're going to follow that suggestion and use a technique called counterbalancing in our experiment. Counterbalancing is where one half of the participants complete condition A and then condition B, the other half complete condition B and then condition A. Tell the person next to you what that would look like in our experiment? Bilal? Yes, great. Half start with an audience condition, and half start with a no audience condition. Lovely. Here's how we can arrange that, with the group not completing a condition of the IV providing the audience each time.

Trevor quickly sketches the following table.

Group 1	Group 2
Audience	
No audience	No audience
	Audience

It would be easy to simply set students off here, but Trevor now takes the opportunity to demonstrate the procedure.

If we're going to standardise the procedure here, then we need to make sure we perform the task in the same way as everyone else. Gather round the front and watch me. Here's what I want you all to do.

Trevor can now demonstrate a procedure to standardise it – where to have the timer, when to start it, how to ensure that all the steps on the drawing instruction sheet are properly followed, etc. He can also lead a discussion on the role of the audience, and fun can be had in standardising exactly how distracting (or hostile!) the audience should be, depending on how well the group know each other.

Right. We're ready to start. Before we do, though, I want you to tell your partner how we have designed our experiment, and why. The left partner should describe the design of the experiment, using the terms 'repeated measures' and 'counterbalancing'. Do that now. OK, great. Now right partner, please tell your partner why we have done this, using the terms 'order effects', 'practice', 'confounding variable' and 'internal validity'.

This gives Trevor an opportunity to check that students are not so distracted by the prospect of the experiment that they have taken their attention away from what they are supposed to be learning.

Teaching theories

Since psychology aims to understand human behaviour, at its heart is a set of different ideas that try to explain that behaviour. Sometimes these are just referred to as explanations, whereas more formally we may refer to theories or models. Although there are meaningful categorical distinctions to be made here they aren't particularly helpful for students, and so for the purposes of simplicity we'll use 'theories' as an umbrella term here.

> Cerys is marking a set of practice questions her students have completed on the multistore model of memory. In recent lessons, she's been making a real effort to emphasise to her students the importance of using key terms in their descriptions, and she's encouraged to find that her students have indeed included these.
>
> However, she is a little disheartened by their answers; they don't really flow, and just seem to miss the point. Lots of them have just listed the different elements of the model in their descriptions ('There is the sensory register, which is... then there is the short-term store, which is...'). It becomes clear to Cerys that while her class have diligently learned the features of the model, with correct key terms, they don't actually have a meaningful understanding of the model. They don't really get what it says about how memory works.

This is likely a familiar scenario for any experienced teacher of psychology. Students get that they need to learn key terms and embed them in their answers, but this cannot come at the expense of their actual understanding. If they really get what a theory says about a particular construct (memory), then their descriptions will flow. Further, when they get to evaluation, if they really understand what the theory is proposing, then their evaluation points will be couched in that context rather than just a randomly selected list of strengths and weaknesses.

Describing a theory

An effective approach to teaching a theory may start with considering three key questions:

1. What is the essence of the theory, the big idea?
2. How much do your students need to know about it?
3. What are the common misconceptions that students have about this theory, or the mistakes they make when using it?

Section 3: Teaching core content

The big idea

For any given theory, it's useful to be able to condense the main idea into a single sentence. This provides a good starting point, a headline on which to hang the detail. For example, Milgram's agency theory says all sorts of things about why people are obedient, but at its heart is the simple idea that destructive obedience occurs when people defer responsibility to those who they perceive to be in positions of legitimate authority. Here are some other theories in psychology that appear on many exam specifications with a headline summary.

Theory	Headline summary
The multistore model of memory (Atkinson and Shiffrin, 1968)	Memory is made up of a number of different stores, each with varying characteristics; information moves between stores via different processes in a linear fashion.
Classical conditioning (Pavlov)	Learning occurs via association, through the pairing of a neutral stimulus with a learned response.
Social learning theory (Bandura)	Learning occurs through the observation of others.
Social identity theory (Tajfel and Turner)	Our self-concept is determined by membership of different social groups; we favour those like us (in-groups) and discriminate against those not like us (out-groups).
Working memory model (Baddeley and Hitch)	Working memory is an active process comprising limited capacity and modality specific sub-components, which are controlled by a central executive that allocates attention between them.

You may look at these summaries and not entirely agree. Maybe you think you can write a better headline summary yourself. That's fine, and in fact a useful thing you can do as part of your planning (whether individually or, even better, collaboratively) is to have a go at drafting these. It may also be helpful to provide students with these headlines before diving into the specifics. Having a sense of the general shape of a theory is going to give them something useful to hang the details on.[10]

Writing headline summaries is also a pretty good opportunity for some challenging retrieval practice. For a given topic, students can be asked

---

10 Think of this as helping them see the woods, rather than the just the trees.

to write a summary sentence for a few different theories, for example, the three different theories of memory. You can't write an effective summary without genuinely deep knowledge of the theory itself; the process requires you to think hard about the different elements of the theory, strip out the most important concepts and then write about them in a way that really conveys the relationship between them in a meaningful fashion.

What do they need to know?

Here we may need to distinguish between how much students need to know to properly understand the gist of the theory and how much knowledge they might reasonably be expected to demonstrate for an exam question. Ideally, the former should drive our teaching rather than the latter, but a pragmatic view is important. The reality is that what could take two or three lessons of delivery, along with a couple of hours of independent study, may require 10 minutes of students' attention in the exam, at most. We may think we're enriching their understanding with all the enticing details and nuance, but we may only be distracting them from the core of the theory. Therefore, a key guiding principle should be to *know thy specification*. Determine what students are actually required to know, how could this be assessed, and then figure out how much hinterland is needed in order for them to understand it.

For example, the Edexcel specification requires that students learn a psychodynamic explanation for aggression as a non-biological counterpoint to the other biological explanations learned (brain function, hormones and evolution). To get to the point where ideas about sublimation and catharsis make any sense, you need to give a decent grounding in basic Freudian theory (the iceberg model, the psyche, ego defence mechanisms etc). But it would be tempting to dive into a whole range of other ideas from the approach like the psychosexual stages and the Oedipus complex (that some students may have heard of in other places). Of course, it may be possible to make some of this relevant to the topic at hand, but it's a lot of additional information and it's quite possible that students will only remember some of the seductive details and completely forget the important bits they actually need to know.

What are the common mistakes and misconceptions?

One common mistake that students make is not understanding the limits of the theory (i.e. what it does or doesn't actually describe or explain). This is important, as it can lead them to evaluation points that are simply unwarranted. For example, as described previously, students commonly criticise the working memory model because it doesn't explain long-term memory, when it's clearly not trying to.

More specifically, there are concepts within different theories that students typically struggle to understand properly. Knowing these in advance (through experience, asking other colleagues or just thinking of the areas that you yourself find most challenging), can give us a head start in targeting when and how we **check what they know** (or what they don't know!), and adjusting our teaching as a result. Let's look at an example.

Example teaching segment: Operant conditioning

Operant conditioning is something of a touchstone theory in psychology, due to its foundational importance to many later theories and ideas across a wide range of applied areas. It is therefore likely to be something that students can expect to see multiple times in the course. It is also, however, easily confused and is frequently inaccurately applied in exam settings, and so requires careful teaching. As covered previously, we can start with the three key questions for a theory:

1. What is the essence of the theory, the big idea?

   - That behaviour can be altered by its consequences.

2. How much do your students need to know about it?

   - *Know thy specification*, as this can vary! Reinforcement and punishment will definitely be required (some boards differentiate reinforcement into 'positive' and 'negative', but not punishment, while other boards differentiate both). Knowledge of schedules of primary or secondary reinforcement (and the use of token economies) may also be required in some places.

3. What are the common mistakes/misconceptions?

   - Confusing operant and classical conditioning.

- Confusing negative reinforcement and punishment.
- Confusing different schedules of reinforcement.

These answers can guide our planning. For example, an initial aim of teaching operant conditioning could be to communicate the big idea clearly (that behaviour can be altered by its consequences), while also clearly distinguishing it from classical conditioning. It may therefore be sensible to start with recapping the main features of classical conditioning (assuming that most teachers will have dealt with these chronologically and so taught classical conditioning first). This could be in the form of a comparative advance organiser, such as the following example:

Classical conditioning	Operant conditioning
Learning by association	
Reflex response to a stimulus	
No new behaviours produced (existing behaviour produced to a new stimulus)	

Diana is teaching her class using this advance organiser as a base.

Let's recall how these key features worked for Pavlov's dogs. Take it in turns to tell the person next to you how Pavlov's experiments demonstrated each of these three features of classical conditioning.

Right. That's great. But classical conditioning is quite limited as an explanation of a lot of behaviour. For example, looking at our table, all classical conditioning can do is to produce existing reflex behaviours in response to a new stimulus. What about learning new *things? We're now going to look at a form of learning that can create brand new behaviour.*

Classical conditioning	Operant conditioning
Learning by association	
Reflex response to a stimulus	
No new behaviours produced (existing behaviour produced to a new stimulus)	New behaviours can be produced

Let's stay with dogs. Has anyone ever tried to train a dog (or any pet) to learn a new behaviour? Tell the person next to you how you did it.

Students are usually very comfortable discussing principles of operant conditioning (without initially using the technical terms) from the perspective of animal training. This provides a familiar, concrete introduction to the concept. Discussion of the mechanism of this will usually involve students using words such as 'reward' or 'punishment' without much difficulty (they may even do this naturally without knowing they are using the right terms), but they will often need to be assisted in categorising these as examples of learning by consequence.

In all of your examples, the learning for the animal is happening because of the consequences of its actions. Therefore, we have a form of learning that works not by association of stimuli, but through consequences.

Classical conditioning	Operant conditioning
Learning by association	Learning by consequences
Reflex response to a stimulus	
No new behaviours produced (existing behaviour produced to a new stimulus)	New behaviours can be produced

Because we have to process whether the consequences of an action are positive or negative, this doesn't work for reflex responses like classical conditioning. Instead, it works on what we call 'voluntary' behaviours, which just means 'non-reflex' behaviours. Be careful though! Remember that one of the key assumptions of behaviourism is environmental determinism – that behaviour is entirely determined by the environment and that we have no control over it. 'Voluntary' here, therefore, does not mean that we choose it freely; it just means 'not a reflex'. We call this type of learning operant conditioning.

Classical conditioning	Operant conditioning
Learning by association	Learning by consequences
Reflex response to a stimulus	Voluntary (non-reflex) responses
No new behaviours produced (existing behaviour produced to a new stimulus)	New behaviours can be produced

Students should make a copy of this table somewhere in their notes for reference, and practise combining the three features in the table into a full definition of the process.

Right, taking it in turns to tell your partner, we're going to think of some examples of operant conditioning in our own lives. When have the consequences of your actions changed how you acted next time? These could have been good or bad consequences, I don't mind. Two minutes. Go.

In the subsequent discussion, Diana can draw out the ideas of reinforcement and punishment, and also (if the right examples are provided by students) the distinction between positive and negative. These can be written into a table (either pre-prepared or live drawn), and students can then be invited to think of at least two examples of each type of operant conditioning process.

	POSITIVE Stimulus added to the environment	NEGATIVE Stimulus removed from the environment
REINFORCEMENT Increases the likelihood of the behaviour being repeated	Positive reinforcement	Negative reinforcement
PUNISHMENT Decreases the likelihood of the behaviour being repeated	Positive punishment	Negative punishment

Diana follows this up with a scenario that gives students practice identifying and applying the process of operant conditioning to examples. Following this, students could have further practice with additional scenarios featuring either (or both) operant or classical conditioning to provide further examples (and non-examples) of each, again targeting the known misconception of getting the two theories confused. Some good examples to challenge student thinking can include:[11]

- A baby cries, the mum goes to pick them up and the baby stops crying. (If students haven't studied attachment, they may struggle with situations where both positive and negative reinforcement may

---

11   Choosing examples that foreshadow later applied content can provide some free pre-exposure to later units.

be occurring. Here the baby's crying is being positively reinforced, and the mother's caregiving is being negatively reinforced.)
- A student doesn't do their homework and is given a detention. The next time they are set homework, they complete it. (Students may debate whether this scenario illustrates positive punishment, as a detention is being added into the environment, or negative punishment, as freedom is being taken away. Either would be fine, as long as the justification is correct. They may even give a classical conditioning account of it, which would be more challenging, but again could be done successfully.)
- A child gets bitten by a dog and now has a phobia of dogs. (Students who have not studied phobias often struggle to provide a classical conditioning account of this and confuse it with operant conditioning, as they find the idea of generalisation from a specific incident (bite) to the more general category (dogs) difficult.)

Finally, Diana asks students to create their own examples.

Right folks, over to you. Being able to come up with your own scenarios is the ultimate test of understanding. If you can do this, then you are unlikely to be stumped by anything you are provided with in an exam. I'll give you one to start you off:

1. I want to teach my dog to sit. How could I do so using:
    a. Classical conditioning?
    b. Positive reinforcement?
    c. Negative reinforcement?
    d. Positive punishment?
    e. Negative punishment?
2. I want to get my child to eat vegetables. How could I do so using each of the above processes?
3. Pick your own scenario or behaviour and explain how these different learning scenarios might work for that one.

Evaluating theories

Once students have grasped the key ideas of a theory then the logical step is to move onto evaluation. In many cases, students will already have identified a number of relevant ideas as they learn about the theory in the first place, particularly as they become more knowledgeable about psychology and have a range of other theories they have already learned with which to make comparisons.

What kinds of evaluation points should students make about theories? Until students have a fair amount of experience evaluating, they're going to need some clear guidance on what constitutes evaluation. Some important principles that we think are useful to bear mind (and communicate to students):

- In general, the most important consideration is the extent to which a theory is supported by evidence, with the caveat that this depends on:
    - How strong the evidence is (e.g. how robust the methodology is) and how varied it is (are there multiple studies of different types all supporting the theory?)
    - How directly the evidence supports the specific construct the theory is being used to explain (i.e. does it support the general principles of the theory, or has it been applied to specific contexts).
    - Whether there is counterevidence.
- Not all evaluation points can necessarily be considered equal – some are more important than others.[12]
- Which ones are more important may change depending on which particular theory you're evaluating.

Other evaluation points that may be relevant for any given theory include:

- The extent to which the theory provides any practical applications (beyond just explaining something).

---

12 This may be an important consideration for specifications where the mark schemes require that students weigh up the significance of different points when reaching an overall conclusion or judgement.

- Whether it is based on observable processes or makes falsifiable predictions.
- The extent to which tools used to measure concepts within the theory are valid or reliable.
- The extent to which it challenges, improves on or is refuted by other related theories.

As discussed previously, using some kind of acronym may be a useful scaffold for evaluation, at least initially. Acronyms that we've come across that may be used for evaluating theories include:

- **SCOUT** – Supporting evidence, Critique of evidence, Other factors, Useful applications, Testability.
- **USED** – Useful applications, Supporting evidence, Evaluation of evidence, Different theories.
- **CODA** – Credibility, Objections, Differences, Applications.
- **SCALE** – Supporting evidence, Competing evidence, Application (to health, education, etc), Limitation, Explanation (alternative or contrasting theory).
- **GRENADE** – Gender bias, Reductionism versus holism, Ethical issues, Nature versus nurture, Approach, Determinism versus free will, Ethnocentrism.

However, we still need to be careful to avoid letting the scaffold become the schema. One way to avoid this is to have more context-specific evaluation questions that guide students' thinking as to the sorts of evaluation points we want them to make. For example, for students learning about agency theory as an explanation for obedience, we could use a list of questions like this:

1. Is there evidence (from studies) to support specific aspects of agency theory:
    a. Agentic shift.
    b. Moral strain/displacement.
    c. Socialisation into hierarchy.
2. Are there any studies that may contradict or challenge this explanation?

3. Do you think agentic shift can be directly observed and measured?
4. To what extent do you think this theory explains the actions of Nazi soldiers during the Holocaust, for example?
5. How could someone in authority (e.g. military leaders) use these ideas to increase obedience?
6. Are there other factors that may better explain why people do or don't obey an authority figure? (Other social theories? Dispositional factors? Learning theories? Biological influences?)

The eagle-eyed may spot that these questions are essentially derived from the SCOUT acronym outlined above. However, the questions direct students' attention and thinking more clearly to the specific kinds of points we may want them to make for this particular theory. By answering specific questions like these, the students are less likely to end up making the sorts of overly generic evaluative points that we're trying to avoid, and more likely to show C1 and C2. Once these questions have been answered, and using whatever resources students have access to (such as textbooks or booklets), the teacher can then feedback responses and use them to draw out a list of strengths and weaknesses.

A key priority here is to probe and develop students' thinking to avoid them making assertions that are not substantiated (because, for instance, they may have limited hinterland knowledge) or over-emphasising a specific strength or weakness that, in the grander scheme of things, may not actually be that significant (or, similarly, underplay something really quite important).

Evaluating a theory using C1 and C2

The most common (and most important) positive evaluation of any theory in psychology is the degree to which it is supported by research evidence. However, the use of supporting (or contrasting) research is often poorly done. For example, in response to an essay question requiring evaluation of the multi-store model of memory, a student could write:

> Baddeley (1966) found that participants made more mistakes when recalling acoustically similar words from STM, but more

mistakes when recalling semantically similar words from LTM. This supports the MSM.

What is wrong with this paragraph? How well does it demonstrate the key principles of C1 and C2? Before reading on, try to evaluate it yourself and see how you would improve it.

Does this paragraph demonstrate C1? It describes a specific study's findings, after all, so isn't that enough? Not really. Remember that the key question we are asking for C1 is: 'What does claim X look like in this case?'. In the answer above, there is no claim X being made. The answer is not really (at least not explicitly) evaluation at all. This illustrates an important feature of evaluation writing, namely that C1 and C2 both require that a clear evaluation claim is made.

Let's add in an evaluative claim:

> A strength of the MSM is that it is supported by some research evidence. Baddeley (1966) found that participants made more mistakes when recalling acoustically similar words from STM, but more mistakes when recalling semantically similar words from LTM. This supports the MSM.

This makes an evaluative point at the start of the paragraph (albeit a relatively generic one that now repeats itself at the end of the answer), making it clearer why the subsequent research evidence is being mentioned. The details of the research now make a lot more sense, as they occur in the context of the evaluative claim. In this new formulation, the answer provides C1 – what the issue (research support) looks like in this case (Baddeley's study). The final sentence now functions as something of a 'so what'. However, it's still not clear *why* the results of Baddeley's study support the MSM, or which of the claims of the model are strengthened by it. In other words, C2 is missing. Let's add it in.

> A strength of the MSM is that it is supported by some research evidence. Baddeley (1966) found that participants made more mistakes when recalling acoustically similar words from STM, but more mistakes when recalling semantically similar words from LTM. This supports the MSM's claim that STM and LTM are separate stores with different forms of encoding (acoustic and semantic respectively).

Here we have a fully contextualised evaluation of a theory using research evidence.

Extending evaluation: Counterpoints

Consider the answer we created in the previous section – can we take this further? How can we develop the discussion here? One way is for students, where appropriate, to bring in some form of further argument, be that further supporting research, further analysis or implications of the research, or perhaps most simply, counterarguments. However, if they are worth doing, then these arguments need to be laid out in as much detail (and structured as clearly) as the initial answer above. For example, it is common to see attempts to 'extend' evaluation paragraphs that look like the below.

> A strength of the MSM is that its predictions regarding the features of the different stores have supporting evidence. Baddeley (1966) found that participants made more mistakes when recalling acoustically similar words from STM, but more mistakes when recalling semantically similar words from LTM. This supports the MSM's claim that STM and LTM are separate stores with different forms of encoding (acoustic and semantic respectively). However, this research lacked ecological validity.

Let's make sure that the countercriticism is as detailed as the original, containing contextual explanation of the problem (C1) and an analysis of why this is a problem (C2) for the model. (A common mistake that students make is to assume that evaluation of a study is also automatically criticism of the theory that it supports, without making the link clear.)

> A strength of the MSM is that its predictions regarding the features of the different stores have supporting evidence. Baddeley (1966) found that participants made more mistakes when recalling acoustically similar words from STM, but more mistakes when recalling semantically similar words from LTM. This supports the MSM's claim that STM and LTM are separate stores with different forms of encoding (acoustic and semantic respectively), at least under laboratory conditions. However, this research lacked ecological validity, as recalling lists of semantically and acoustically similar words is not an everyday task, so it may be

harder to apply the features of the MSM to memory tasks in real life.

This is a thorough and effective answer that successfully discusses the relative strengths and weaknesses of the evidence supporting the model and considers the implications for the model as a whole. The slight change to the first answer prefaces the subsequent criticism, acting as a 'signpost' for the counterpoint to come. This is the sort of link that students will only be able to make if they are carefully planning the content of their evaluation points and spending time thinking on the best order and structure for them.

Comparing theories

Depending on which specification you teach, students may be asked to compare theories. Even if they aren't going to get a direct question on this, it's a useful addition to the evaluation ideas listed above. However, making decent comparisons is something that students often struggle with, for a few reasons:

- They tend to simply make side-by-side descriptive points rather than making any genuine comparison.
- They assume that one theory is *de facto* better than another simply because it explains something in a different way.
- They overlook the scientific progression of theories (i.e. that later theories typically build upon and improve earlier theories).

An important point here is that teaching chronology is quite significant in this context. While obsessing over precise dates is not that important (although it can preoccupy students more than it should!), understanding a sense of sequence is. This is particularly important since exam specifications sometimes list content in a non-chronological order, with textbook publishers following suit. Therefore, we need to first think carefully about the sequencing of theories in our curriculum, and second, think about how we help students **make meaning** by communicating this sequencing to our students clearly.

Teaching studies

Canvas the views of psychology students midway through or at the end of their course, and a common theme often emerges: 'There's a lot of studies to learn!' While we may argue that the approaches, methods, theories or treatments represent the substantive content in psychology (what the discipline is about), each of these areas is underpinned by research. Regardless of specification, students are expected to know about a large range of evidence, sometimes in quite phenomenal detail, and it's no wonder that many are left presuming that this is the important stuff that they need to know.

Describing a study

Students may start a psychology course with a very limited view of what constitutes a study or research,[13] so this will require explicit teaching. This will initially involve explaining (and identifying in examples) the common features of most studies, such as the aim, sample, method, procedure, results and conclusions. It's also worth explicitly teaching that if the students want a general term for a piece of research then 'study' covers everything!

In the early days of the course, it's probably best to limit students' exposure to studies that, as much as possible, fit a fairly narrow version of this definition so they can build a reasonably strong study schema that allows them to both analyse research and learn the details of new studies. For example, while Bandura's (1961) classic Bobo Doll study is certainly worthy of discussion in many ways, it doesn't represent a particularly simple and prototypical study. Among other things, there are multiple independent variables, the study uses a mixed experimental design, and it collects data via both self-reports and observation. For a novice student this is a lot to take on, and it's not going to help them understand the basic shape of a study to begin with.

Therefore, we may want to stick to simpler studies, or at least present slightly simplified versions of some studies to **manage cognitive load** and avoid adding unhelpful confusion in the early stages. Once this is

---

[13] It can't just be our experience that they will call *everything* either an 'experiment' or 'case study' to begin with!

established, we will want to start to introduce more variety so that their schema develops to encompass a wider range of different methodologies. This will include studies with more complex designs (Bandura et al., 1961), those that involve multiple phases or experiments within the same study (Loftus and Palmer, 1974) or those that gather data in quite different ways, such as meta-analyses or literature reviews.

Something we also need to be mindful of is the level of detail required for different studies. Students can get rather obsessive over studies and therefore need some guidance as to which ones they *have* to learn, which ones they *ought* to learn and which ones could be considered *optional* extras. And for each type, what level of detail should they learn them in? It is useful, therefore, to differentiate between the following:

- Named studies – Students *need* to learn these; they are prescribed by the specification, which means they can be directly assessed in an exam question. This could take the form of details of one element of the study (e.g. sample or findings), a description or evaluation of the main points of the study (e.g. Aim, Procedure, Findings, Conclusions (APFC)) or an extended response (e.g. 'Evaluate…'). Therefore, students need to learn these studies in lots of detail, and they deserve our attention when we are planning retrieval practice.[14]
- Significant studies – Students *ought* to learn these, as they are typically used as supporting or contrasting evidence for a theory or treatment. The emphasis is more on students knowing the overall gist of the study, especially the findings. Where relevant, we can expect students to also learn some specific methodological details to allow them to critique the research itself.
- Minor studies – These may be more optional for students to learn, but they do include additional supporting evidence (on top of the significant studies) that helps the students produce more developed answers. They may also include evidence that can be used to make counterarguments. We can expect students to learn these in no more detail than can be given in a sentence or two, to summarise the main ideas, findings and implications.

---

14 Remember, *know thy specification*. Precisely which specific variations do they need to know?

The 'shape' of a study

Understanding how a psychological study works is a good example of the *curse of knowledge*. We as subject experts have a good deal of tacit knowledge about what a psychology study may 'look' like, and as a result we may only need a relatively short description of the aims and findings of a study to have a pretty clear idea how different groups may have been used, how variables were manipulated or controlled (and which ones), likely strengths and weaknesses and so on. Students, especially early on in their courses, do not have this prior knowledge to call on.

One way that we can help students to have a more concrete conception of the design or findings of a study is to find ways to represent them visually. Diagramming how the full sample for an experiment may be divided into groups that perform the various conditions is not only useful for the understanding of the details of a particular study; it can also help to develop students' research methods understanding, such as how IV conditions can be compared to one another to test a hypothesis and the importance of control groups. Consider the below representation of the original Bandura, Ross and Ross (1961) experiment, for example:

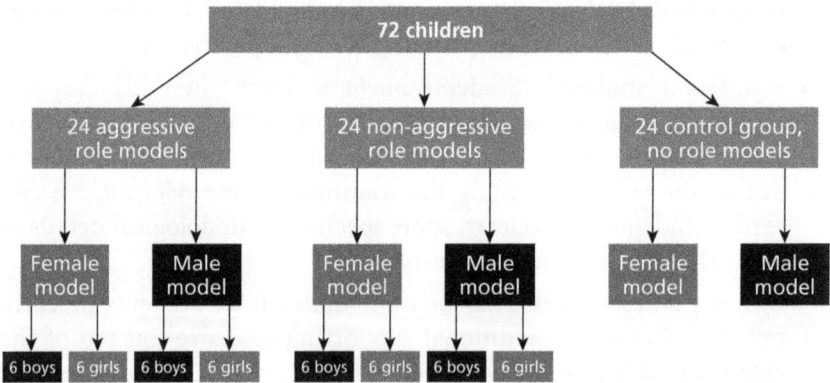

The diagram here functions as a graphic advance organiser that depicts the arrangement of a study (especially a relatively complex one) much more clearly than a written summary.

Another way to consider the shape of a study can be to consider what the results will look like. The vast majority of psychological research that students may encounter can be characterised in one of three ways, which will be presented using particular methods:

Type of research	Presentation method
Looking for a difference in performance on some variable between two groups or conditions (i.e. an experiment).	Bar chart
Looking for a correlation between two variables that have been measured in a group of participants.	Scatterplot
Looking for an association or difference between categorical variables.	Contingency table

We can discuss with students what we can expect the results to look like, and why. If you've got a bar chart, for example, then you can label the different bars with the different conditions of the IV (and add the heading 'IV'), or note the specific measure used for the DV on the y-axis. The point of this is adding contextual detail that students may need in their answers.

As well as in lessons, sketching out how the data can be presented is a useful technique in exams. Research methods scenarios can be quite lengthy and contain lots of detail, and even if they are well annotated it can take time scanning back through the text to find the information you need. With a well-annotated graph all the information is in one clear place, and the layout of the graph adds its own layer of meaning.

Imagining studies

Another technique for helping students to develop an appreciation for what psychological studies are like is to take the time to get them to really imagine what it actually looked like. What would the experimenter see? What would the participants see, and experience? Doing this helps students turn a description of a study (such as a series of written steps) into more of an actual experience. This takes advantage of the *imagination effect*, a cognitive load related effect whereby students learn better from imagining concepts and procedures rather than from restudying them (Mguidich et al., 2025), thus taking an imaginary journey through a research procedure is likely to be more useful to our students' understanding than simple rereading.[15]

In addition, visualising studies can also provide students with important clues as to potential evaluation issues. Telling students that Bandura's results may have been affected by demand characteristics is unlikely to make much sense to students initially, so getting them to properly imagine the experience from the perspective of a participant makes this much easier to comprehend (along with prompts such as: 'Having seen the adult beat up the bobo doll, you are now taken into the exact same room and left on your own. What would you think?').

Visualisation does not simply have to involve picturing the researcher or participant perspective. We can also visualise the flow of a process. For example, students learning about Roger Sperry's famous split-brain studies (Sperry et al., 1969; 'split-brain research' is named on the AQA specification) often find predicting and explaining the results extremely challenging. This is not surprising; the cognitive load of such a task is extremely high, requiring students to simultaneously manipulate the scenario details (what was presented, and where?), details of contralateral organisation of the hemispheres for sensory and motor processing *and* details of specifically lateralised functions such as speech or object recognition. It's a lot, and it's no wonder that some students simply shut down in the face of this. Visualisation of the journey that the information takes can help to **manage cognitive load** by breaking the process into stages.

We also encourage students to close their eyes and physically trace on their foreheads the directions of the information flow, as they seem to find this more effective than using pure imagination. This could be because 'embodying' cognition in this way creates additional spatial and motor representations of the information that can aid understanding (Macedonia, 2019).[16] Students can take one side of space at a time as they follow the information flow, for example, in the following scenario where a face has been presented to the left visual field:

---

15 Of course, there are other ways of achieving this (such as role play), and we can still use these tools as well (especially when the interaction between people is a crucial feature), but visualisation is often more time effective in many cases.
16 Teaching localisation of function can also take advantage of this embodied method.

1. What is presented, and to which visual field? (Students point the left visual field and imagine a face as a stimulus.)
2. Which hemisphere's visual cortex will it go to? (Students trace from left visual field back to right visual cortex.)
3. Which specialised area does that hemisphere have? (Face recognition. Extra points here if you show students the location of the fusiform face area to point to – we've never done that bit!)
4. What can the students do to respond to the stimulus? (Students trace to the right motor cortex, then move their left hands to show that this would be able to move in response.)
5. What can the hemisphere *not* do to respond to the stimulus? (Use language. Some of our students have found it helpful to use their other hand to physically 'block' the other hand from crossing to the other side, representing the information being unable to cross. NB the follow-up idea that, in the absence of a stimulus to right visual field, a split-brain patient may report 'I didn't see anything' is something that students find very difficult initially, but doing this process in reverse for the other visual field, and multiple rounds of practice, can help to illustrate the concept.)

The results of a study

The coverage of the results of a study will again depend on whether you are dealing with a named study or not. Named studies may require results to be understood in a lot of detail, for example:

> Describe the findings and conclusions of Raine, Buchsbaum and LaCasse's (1997) classic research, 'Brain abnormalities in murderers indicated by positron emission tomography'. [12] (Eduqas, AS Paper 1 2022)

> From the study by Dement and Kleitman (sleep and dreams): Describe one result about dream recall in REM sleep and one result about the estimations of dream-duration time in REM sleep. You must use data for one of these results. [5] (CIEA, Paper 1 2019)

Studies not named in the specification will most commonly be included in the curriculum because their results allow students to draw some sort of useful evaluative conclusion. It is therefore useful to consider how much information students actually need to be able to draw the conclusion required. Results can be complex, and may contain specific figures, percentages or other quantitative information that students will understandably baulk at in the context of learning potentially hundreds of other studies. It's therefore always worth considering the question, 'What level of detail do students actually need in order to make the argument we want them to?' Take the following example, taken from the results of Cheniaux et al. (2009) into the reliability of diagnosis in schizophrenia by giving two psychiatrists' descriptions of 100 patients to diagnose using either the DSM-IV or the ICD-10:

- One psychiatrist diagnosed 26 out of 100 patients with schizophrenia using the DSM, and 44 out of 100 using the ICD.
- The other psychiatrist diagnosed 13 using the DSM and 24 using the ICD.

According to our earlier categorisation, this is a significant study for one of us, it plays an important role in the evaluation of the reliability and validity of diagnosis of schizophrenia, and it would therefore be expected that students are familiar with it. That said, do students really need to know (or would it be feasible to expect them to remember) the figures here? Can we make it any simpler, while still allowing students to make the substantive evaluation point (that both diagnostic congruence and inter-rater reliability can be low)? We could take the following, simplified approach:

- One psychiatrist diagnosed schizophrenia at nearly twice the rate of the other.
- The ICD diagnosed patients at nearly twice the rate of the DSM.

This is a much simpler formulation that still allows students to write a detailed evaluation of the reliability of diagnosis, while reducing the burden on their memory and the chances of interference from other figures learned for other studies. Another example, also looking at schizophrenia, is the Tienari et al. (2004) adoption study. Instead of remembering percentage figures, the results could be presented like this:

Risk of developing schizophrenia in Tienari et al. (2004)		Adoptive family 'criticism and conflict'	
		Low	High
Biological family schizophrenia vulnerability	Low	Low	Medium
	High	Medium	High

However, we need to consider a caveat here. While it's important to consider the level of detail we think students need to be able to report in an exam answer, we also don't want to accidentally constrain their broader knowledge and understanding. We may want to present the findings in full to give a complete picture before zooming in on specific aspects or reducing the findings to a more easily digestible summary. Presenting the wider findings contributes to the students' hinterland knowledge and general sense of psychological literacy, and it also helps both satisfy and further spark curiosity.

The 'shape' of a study's results

We can also use visual representations for the results of some studies. Take the example below, based on the results of Maguire et al. (1997), who used PET to investigate which brain areas were most active for different types of memory tasks:

- Topographical sequencing memory (i.e. memory for routes) retrieval is associated with increased activation in the right hippocampus.
- Different brain regions are activated during topographical (routes and landmarks) compared to non-topographical (film plots and film frames) memory retrieval. Topographical tasks use the hippocampus, whereas non-topographical tasks do not.
- The cerebellum was active for all tasks.

These are complicated results, and students may understandably struggle to initially recall them clearly. Contrast that, however, to the formulation below (originally designed by a student of one of ours, so thank you Sajid!):

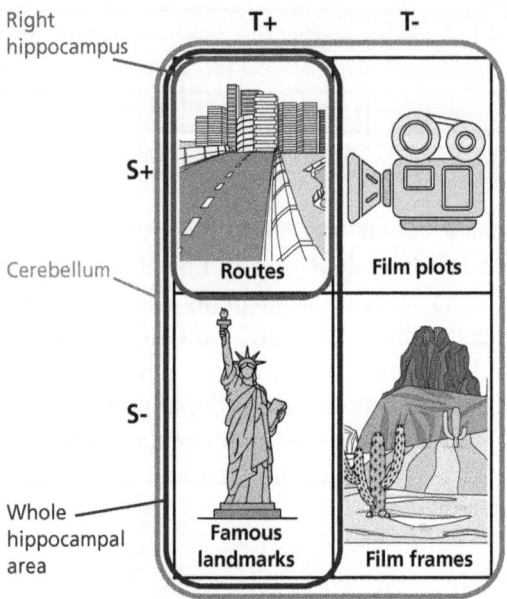

Evaluating studies

How (and even if) we evaluate the studies in our curriculum will depend on a number of variables:

- The type of study it is (i.e. named, significant or minor).
- The position it has in our curriculum sequence (e.g. studies encountered early in the course may be used as a vehicle for more 'basic' evaluation ideas rather than the broader debates that can be brought in later on).
- What we want our students to do with it.
- Whether the evaluation ideas we have taught our students map onto the particular study conveniently.
- Whether we think it's important for students to evaluate it as part of their wider psychological literacy or hinterland knowledge, even if not directly course relevant.

Certainly, then, there is no one size fits all approach to evaluating a study. As we have said already, acronyms can be helpful in some circumstances, but they need to be used with caution. Common ones include:

- **GRAVE(E)** – Generalisability, Reliability, Applications, Validity, Ethics, (Economic implications).
- **SAVED** – Scientific, Applicability, Validity, Ethics, Debates.

Although acronyms may give a good general guide as to the sorts of points we want students to think about, the more concrete and specific we can be in our teaching the better we can support the students to make really meaningful evaluation points. Therefore, guided evaluation questions, which are tailored to a specific study, may be more useful in helping students generate a good set of evaluation ideas. This allows us to carefully select which specific features of the study are suitable for evaluation, which ones may afford good development in the form of counterpoints, and which ones should be avoided as dead ends.[17]

What does good written evaluation of studies look like?

We'll start with a typical example of evaluative writing involving Milgram's baseline study of obedience. Here's a fairly common point that a student may produce while evaluating the sample:

> One problem with Milgram's study is that the limited sample reduces the study's external validity. This is because he used a sample drawn from one area. This means the results cannot be generalised to other populations.

This answer lacks both C1 and C2, so despite a clear structure (point, evidence, explain (PEE)), it's a completely generic paragraph. Let's add some context:

> One problem with Milgram's study is that the limited sample could be considered to reduce the study's external validity. This is because Milgram used all males from the New Haven area of New York. Due to cultural influences, the participants could have similar levels of obedience to one another as they may have had similar experiences of socialisation. This means the results of the study may not necessarily represent obedience levels in other populations, for example, people from different cultural backgrounds.

---

17 Ethics is a good example here. For many studies, it's really not an interesting or important point to consider, but is one frequently used by students regardless!

Examples: Evaluating studies using internal and external validity

Let's look at some further examples in action. One commonly misused evaluation point is the concept of ecological validity (so much so that we have considered banning the term from our lessons!), a classic issue for inviting generic responses. Let's take a look at one possible example of this, from one of the named pieces of research in the AQA specification:

> One advantage of Schaffer and Emerson's research is that it is high in ecological validity. This is because it was conducted in a natural environment.

You will immediately recognise a lack of either C1 or C2 in this example. Let's fix both:

> One advantage of Schaffer and Emerson's research is that it is high in ecological validity. This is because it was conducted in the families' own homes. The infants are likely to be comfortable with their surroundings, and therefore any behaviours displayed, such as separation or stranger anxiety, are likely to be realistic ones [C1]. This means that the results of the study are more likely to be generalisable to the development of real-life attachment behaviours, such as separation or stranger anxiety, in other infants [C2].

Now consider the following paragraph on the Stanford Prison Experiment. Decide for yourself the extent to which C1 and C2 are present here:

> One criticism of the Stanford Prison Experiment is that there were investigator effects. Zimbardo had a dual role as researcher and prison superintendent, which could have introduced investigator effects; indeed, recordings made at the time suggest that he actively encouraged the guards to behave in a more extreme manner towards the prisoners. This reduces the internal validity of the study.

The contextual detail in the central part of this answer is detailed, accurate and supports the initial evaluative claim (C1). The final sentence is also accurate; after a few months, many Year 12s will be able to report that investigator effects are one factor that can reduce the internal validity of a study. But ask the students the follow-up question, 'And what does "reduced internal validity" mean for this study?', and you are likely to be met with a sea of blank faces. This is a problem with the answer above – the 'so what?' section does not address C2. Thorough evaluation of a study needs to show an awareness of the specific conclusions that the research makes, and how the evaluation point relates to the ability to draw these conclusions. Let's add it in:

> One criticism of the Stanford Prison Experiment is that there were investigator effects. Zimbardo had a dual role as researcher and prison superintendent, which could have introduced investigator effects; indeed, recordings made at the time suggest that he actively encouraged the guards to behave in a more extreme manner towards the prisoners. This reduces the internal validity of the experiment as a study of conformity to social roles, as it seems likely that the guards' behaviour was influenced more by pressure from the researchers than their social role.

Making meaning through predicting study evaluation

As we've hopefully made clear by now, getting context right in evaluation is key. One useful tool for helping students to have the confidence to grapple with the specific contextual issues raised by a study is *prediction*. Predicting possible evaluation issues is a low-stakes activity that requires high levels of cognitive engagement with the minutiae of the study being examined. Two specific tricks for setting up prediction in students, both of which have been found useful in previous research (and which we use in our lessons) are:

- *Imagining* – forming a mental image of a study, and what the experience of it might be for both participants and researchers.
- *Professorial thinking* – Thinking 'like a psychologist', for example, in answering the questions, 'What would a psychologist say about this study?', 'What would I [the teacher] think or say about this study?' or 'What else would I want to know about to trust the results?' Amsel et al. (2014) found that representing questions in this way could allow students to think about psychology in a more sophisticated way that was distinct from their own misconceptions. This also depersonalises the students' responses (compared to 'What do *you* think?'), and so can help them to have more confidence in speculating.

Both of these tools can of course be used together, along with appropriate hints and scaffolding to help students make links to instances of similar issues in other research they have previously encountered.

Comparing studies

Some specifications (such as OCR and Edexcel) require students to make explicit comparisons of studies in various ways. The command term 'compare' means that students are required to talk about both similarities and differences between two things. It's helpful first to make the distinction between descriptive and evaluative comparisons:

- **Descriptive comparisons** relate to the features of a study, such as the sample, method or procedure.
- **Evaluative comparisons** involve making relative judgements about a particular evaluation issue (e.g. validity) between two studies.

Both may be fair game, and which type students give will depend on the specific wording of the question. However, there are some points to consider here. Descriptive comparisons are inherently easier to make and will typically be quicker to write, so may be preferable on short answer questions where time is of the essence.

However, students can also easily fall foul of a couple of mistakes when making such simple comparisons. Consider this example:

> Milgram used a volunteer sample, whereas Loftus and Palmer used opportunity sampling.

Although the comparison point here is fairly obvious, it hasn't actually been explicitly stated. It's pretty common for students when making comparisons to simply present two descriptive points side by side, stick a 'whereas' in the middle and hope that will do! Some exam mark schemes will penalise students for this, and so it's worth stating what the comparison point is first:

> One difference between Milgram and Loftus and Palmer is that they used different sampling techniques to obtain their participants. Milgram used a volunteer sample, whereas Loftus and Palmer used opportunity sampling.

This is better, as the point is now clearly signposted. However, it's still lacking context (C1), as it doesn't present any specific details from either study to support the claim being made. Therefore, a more complete version could be:

> One difference between Milgram and Loftus and Palmer is that they used different sampling techniques to obtain their participants. Milgram used a volunteer sample by placing adverts in a local newspaper as well as via direct mail, whereas Loftus and Palmer used opportunity sampling by recruiting students who were available from the psychology department at Washington University.

The same principles apply for evaluative comparisons, although students may have to work a bit harder with their examples because they will also need an additional layer of context (C2). However, these are likely to be higher tariff questions, or even extended response questions, which therefore warrant the further elaboration.

Even where comparison is not explicitly required, it is still a useful skill to teach. Asking students to compare the samples of different studies can help them appreciate some of the nuances around sampling; this may include points about practicality (how hard it can be to obtain a decent sample of the target population) or bias (how different sampling techniques may lead to different types of bias in the sample selected).

Using the example answers above, we may see students initially make the same general criticism of both studies – that 40 males (Milgram) or 45 undergraduate students (Loftus and Palmer) represent limited samples from which we can't generalise. Asking students to consider which they think is a more representative sample requires them to think much more deeply about the issue. They may think about the relative importance of gender, age, background or occupation in relation to what each study is investigating (obedience versus memory), or even the different forms of bias found in different sampling techniques (volunteer versus opportunity). There is, of course, no right answer to this question, but forcing them to justify their judgements with specific, contextual details means they are far more likely to make meaningful and contextualised evaluation points.

Using a study to evaluate other concepts

A key piece of psychological literacy is the ability to use research evidence to draw informed conclusions; this is, after all, the measure by which theories are truly judged in the academic literature. However, students can sometimes find writing well-elaborated paragraphs about research support challenging. If we remember our C1 and C2 distinction:

What is the claim being made about X? = C1

What is the effect of C1 on the ability to assert Y? = C2

When using research support, C1 and C2 may involve explaining:

How do the methods and results of study X appear to support the theory Y? = C1

What can we now say about (some or all) the ideas of Y in light of the C1? = C2

Students find the C2 part particularly challenging when writing about research support. Frequently, it is hard to see how to avoid simply rephrasing the initial point in C2. For example:

There is research support for interference as an explanation of forgetting. McGeoch and McDonald (1931) asked participants to learn a list of words, then learn a second list. When the second list was similar to the first list (words meaning the same thing, as opposed to nonsense syllables or numbers), recall of the first list was worse. This shows interference.

Students can get very stuck here, so it can take a bit of gentle questioning to tease out some of the nuances of the conclusions that we can and cannot make from this research finding. For example: 'Does this show that interference always happens?' 'When, and when not?' 'Does it show that all types of interference happen?' With a little exploration, students will usually be able to identify, for example, that this is a case of retroactive information between stimuli that were very similar to one another. Adding that back into our answer now gives the C2:

There is research support for interference as an explanation of forgetting. McGeoch and McDonald (1931) asked participants to learn a list of words, then learn a second list. When the second list was similar to the first list (words meaning the same thing, as opposed to nonsense syllables or numbers), recall of the first list was worse. This suggests that retroactive interference can impair recall, at least in situations where the information learned is very similar.

This answer has retained a 'point – because – so what?' structure, but there is no need to do so. If you are keen to show your students that the scaffold should not become the schema, then you could show how an equally effective paragraph can involve combining the 'point' and the 'so what?' into a much more detailed opening sentence:

There is research support for retroactive interference impairing recall, at least in situations where the information learned is very similar. McGeoch and McDonald (1931) asked participants to learn a list of words, then learn a second list. When the second list was similar to the first list (words meaning the same thing, as opposed to nonsense syllables or numbers), recall of the first list was worse.

C2 can also be achieved through showing an awareness of the key feature of the theory, which would help explain the results (and so is supported by them). For example:

There is research support for some of the ideas of the behaviourist approach. Gilroy et al. (2003) found that systematic desensitisation reduced fear of spiders compared to a control group who didn't receive the therapy, even 33 months after the treatment. This supports the behaviourist assumption that behaviour is learned from the environment through processes such as classical and operant conditioning and shows that the theory of classical conditioning can be usefully applied to create effective treatments for phobias.

Here the research finding does support behaviourism, but specifically it involves an application of the theory of classical conditioning. Therefore, C2 involves highlighting which specific part of the theory is supported. Here's another example, using the Al-Mosaiwi and Johnstone (2018) study into absolutism in depression:

There is research support for cognitive explanations of depression. Al-Mosaiwi and Johnstone (2018) conducted a content analysis on absolutist language in internet support forums. They found that the depression forums contained more absolutist words than control forums, with a suicidal ideation forum containing the highest number. This supports the idea of cognitive biases such as absolutism playing a role in the symptoms of depression, especially as the biases became most frequent in the most severe depression cases.

Again, the C2 comes from drilling down deeper into the specific aspects of the theory that are supported by the research findings. This is relatively easy for large theories (such as approaches or explanations of mental illness) with lots of constituent parts and different assumptions, but is much harder when the theories are narrower in scope. For example:

There is research support for retrieval failure as an explanation of forgetting. For example, Godden and Baddeley (1975) asked participants to learn lists of words either on land or underwater, and then tested their recall in either the same or the different context. Participants who recalled words in the same context as they learned them (i.e. land-land or water-water) remembered more words than those who recalled in a different context (i.e. land-water or water-land). This supports the theory that retrieval failure can be caused by a lack of shared cues between the learning and recall environments.

It would be easy to include the term 'retrieval failure' again in the final sentence, but this would miss the chance to show an understanding of exactly which aspect of the theory of retrieval failure it is that has been supported.

When planning lessons and creating resources we therefore need to be asking ourselves 'What level of detail do students actually need to know in order to make the evaluative C1 and C2 that we want them to?' For example, in the above answer on McGeoch and McDonald (1931), the desired C2 requires students to be presented with the method in enough detail to know that it involves retroactive information and similar stimuli, so we need to make sure that this is covered in our notes. As we said in Section 2, only include a study in your curriculum when you have a very clear picture of the sorts of evaluative paragraphs that you want your students to be writing when using it.

Evaluating methodology of supporting evidence

A further consideration regarding the level of detail required for significant or minor studies is how much of the methodology students should know about. Again, this rather depends on what kinds of evaluative points we want our students to make when referring to this evidence; while the main point we expect students to make may be how well supported something is by research evidence, how strong that supporting evidence may be is also an important consideration. This allows further development for students writing in the form of extension or counterpoints. For example, let's say we are evaluating Bartlett's (1932) reconstructive memory theory; the starting evaluation point (using supporting evidence) could be:

> Bartlett's theory is supported by evidence such as Loftus and Palmer's (1974) study on leading questions. Participants asked about the speed of a car involved in a crash with the word 'smashed' in the question were more likely to later report seeing broken glass (when there was none) than if the question used the word 'hit' instead. This supports the idea that post-event information (the leading questions) interacts with pre-existing schemas (the expectation of seeing broken glass in a car crash) to produce distortions in memory.

Now let's consider the methodology. This study used a laboratory experiment with lots of controls; clearly, that's plenty of scope for some additional evaluation. We could start with a positive:

> This was a rigorous study that controlled for extraneous variables such as the position of the critical question about the speed of the cars in the questionnaire, which was randomised across participants. Therefore, this study has high internal validity because we can be confident that it was the leading question that led to memory change, rather than something else.

This answer is mostly well contextualised (it includes both C1 and C2), but the student has forgotten what they were actually meant to be evaluating, which is reconstructive memory theory rather than the study (this is an incredibly common feature of student answers). Therefore, we need some additional development of our C2 here:

> This was a rigorous study that controlled for extraneous variables such as the position of the critical question about the speed of the cars in the questionnaire, which was randomised across participants. Therefore, this study has high internal validity because we can be confident that it was the leading question that led to memory change, rather than something else. This provides robust evidence to support Bartlett's idea that memory is an active, reconstructive process rather than a passive and objective recording of events.

We could, if we wanted, take this further still and add some counter-argument by considering the artificial task or setting (and, again, note the importance of linking back to the original theory):

> However, because it was a laboratory experiment, the participants were given an artificial task of watching car crashes on video rather than in real life. This reduces the external validity, because videos of car crashes may not elicit the same level of physiological arousal that would be experienced witnessing a car crash for real, which could impact the accuracy of their recall. Therefore, we may question the extent to which memory is reconstructed outside of tightly controlled laboratory conditions.

Of course, we could take this even further still by adding some counter-evidence such as studies that have tested the effects of leading questions with real witnesses (Yuille and Cutshall, 1986), or perhaps a corroborating study with a different research method (showing the understanding that there is no perfect psychology study and that strong conclusions need multiple overlapping studies with varying methods). If our students get this far and have remembered to contextualise appropriately all the way through, then they should be on the way to a pretty impressive answer!

Extending evaluation: Counterpoints

While there is more of an explicit requirement for balance in evaluations in some specifications compared to others, it is likely that in almost all cases good evaluative writing will consider competing arguments. One clear route to this is to teach students to include counterarguments in their writing.

We'll start by reconsidering our evaluation of Milgram's sample from earlier:

> One problem with Milgram's study is that the limited sample could be considered to reduce the study's external validity. This is because he used all males from the New Haven area of New York. Due to cultural influences, the participants could have similar levels of obedience to one another as they may have had similar experiences of socialisation. This means that the results of the study may not necessarily represent obedience levels in the wider population.

Where could the student go from here? A common strategy (or, at least, what most students seem to default to under pressure) is simply to go back to the compiled list of strengths and weaknesses and pick something from the other side. While this can be done well, it can feel fairly incoherent or rather list-like with no sense of a line of argument. It's better for students to try to keep the same context (C1 or C2) but offer a counterpoint.

This could take a few different forms. We can reverse the point by suggesting why the feature that leads to a weakness could actually be considered a strength from a different perspective (for example, that having a relatively homogenous sample is a good way to control for individual differences, thus increasing internal validity). Alternatively, we could argue that the weakness isn't as much of a threat to the conclusions of the study as there is evidence to the contrary (for example, that later replications with different populations found similar results suggesting that the results can in fact be generalised).

Before we apply this to our earlier example, let's also think about making a small tweak to the original argument. The general thrust here is that obedience in Milgram's participants may not represent obedience in the wider world. This makes it slightly harder to make a direct counterpoint, because 'the wider world' is so big and so vague. Instead, the original point could be made more specific:

This means that the results of the study may not necessarily represent obedience levels in participants from other cultural backgrounds.

Now the counterargument is much easier to make, because there is evidence of similar obedience rates in studies conducted around the world and in different cultures:

> One problem with Milgram's study is that the sample could be considered to lack external validity. This is because he used all males from the New Haven area of New York. Due to cultural influences, the participants could have similar levels of obedience to one another as they may have had similar experiences of socialisation. This means that the results of the study may not necessarily represent obedience levels in participants from other cultural backgrounds. However, Blass (1999) reviewed findings from replication studies conducted around the world and found an average worldwide obedience rate of 61%, remarkably similar to Milgram's original results.

As with our original point, this is a well-explained counterpoint made with supporting evidence. C1 is definitely present – what about C2? The counterpoint hasn't gone back to the original claim (that Milgram's findings lack external validity) to finish the line of argument. This is how a final answer could look:

> One problem with Milgram's study is that the sample could be considered to lack external validity. This is because he used all males from the New Haven area of New York. Due to cultural influences, the participants could have similar levels of obedience to one another as they may have had similar experiences of socialisation. This means that the results of the study may not necessarily represent obedience levels in participants from other cultural backgrounds. However, Blass (1999) reviewed findings from replication studies conducted around the world and found an average worldwide obedience rate of 61%, remarkably similar to Milgram's original results. This suggests that Milgram's original findings may be externally valid, and that situational obedience is similar across cultures.

Section 3: Teaching core content

Treatments

While theories and studies make up the vast majority of content that students will learn about, every specification will also consider treatments in some form. This is most likely to be for a clinical disorder such as schizophrenia or depression but may also be applied to things like offending behaviour. Given that treatments are an application of psychological theory, how we both describe and evaluate them is qualitatively different from what we can do with a theory or study. Although there may typically be fewer of them across the specification, having a clear framework for what to describe and how to evaluate is useful here.

Describing treatments

In describing a treatment effectively, we need to consider four key ideas:

- What are the assumptions underlying the treatment?
- What are the general principles on which the treatment works?
- What are the specific mechanisms of the treatment?
- What does the process involve for patients?[18]

In this section, we will draw on examples based around two of the most common types of treatments students will encounter in psychology: drugs and cognitive behavioural therapy (CBT).

Assumptions of treatments

The kinds of treatments or interventions that we look at in psychology are based on the assumption that there must be something 'wrong', and therefore that any given treatment is predicated on a particular causal mechanism. For example, the use of antipsychotic drugs to treat schizophrenia presumes that irregular dopamine function is (at least partly) a cause of schizophrenic symptoms, and the use of CBT to treat violent offenders presumes that those offenders have underlying faulty thinking patterns that cause them to commit crime.

---

18 A note on language. People receiving treatment may variously be labelled as subjects, participants, patients, clients or even offenders; for simplicity, we will just use the term 'patient' here.

This may seem like an obvious point to make, but students often fail to appreciate this unless they are explicitly told. Explanations of and treatments for a behaviour are often compartmentalised by students as two entirely separate and distinct subtopics, and we may need to help connect the dots for them.

Principles of treatments

This concerns the core ideas about what the treatment actually does, which should logically follow on from the assumptions but still needs to be stated explicitly. For example, if CBT is based on the assumption that a behaviour is the result of maladaptive cognitions, then its core principles are that treatment should aim to identify, challenge and replace those maladaptive cognitions. Laying these principles out clearly helps students understand what the treatment is actually intended to do, which is important in two ways.

First, sometimes students get too bogged down in the specifics (the 'mechanisms') that they forget to think about the overall aim of treatment. For example, students may know and write a lot about the actions of serotonin-specific reuptake inhibitors (SSRIs) as treatments for depression but say little about how this could actually change how a person feels.

Second, a strong understanding of general principles allows students to **make meaning** and transfer learning more easily. If the students have already learned about the fundamental principles of CBT as applied to offending behaviour, then it should be easier to learn about CBT as a method of treating obsessive-compulsive disorder (OCD), and generating evaluation points may be easier as well. That's not to say students don't also need to understand the specific nuances of how the treatment is applied differently in these contexts (anger management won't look the same as CBT for OCD), but the shared principles can provide them with introductory AO1 and AO3 for a range of related topics.

Mechanisms of treatments

Now we get down to the specifics – how does the treatment actually work? This is distinct from the principles, because it's about how those principles are enacted. For drug treatments, this is likely to concern the specific neurochemical changes and their effects on a person's functioning (for example, the actions of serotonin-selective reuptake inhibitors like fluoxetine (Prozac) used to treat depression). For CBT, this may be about how a therapist goes about identifying those automatic negative thoughts and getting the patient to provide evidence to challenge how much those thoughts are congruent with reality.

It's also important to explain to students here that there are many different versions of similar treatments. For example, there are a plethora of different antidepressant drugs that may all share the same basic features (addressing a neurochemical imbalance), but may work via quite different mechanisms (for example, SSRIs and monamine oxidase inhibitors (MAOIs) both ultimately increase serotonergic activity but in different ways). It is important to ensure that students can accurately describe how a particular treatment works *and* are aware that the one or two versions of treatment named on their particular exam specification are only specific examples from a huge range that is out there in the real world.

Processes of treatments

A final consideration here, and something easily overlooked by students, is what treatment actually looks like from the patient's perspective. Important questions to consider here are around the practicalities. How do patients actually receive the treatment? For drug treatments, this typically means taking pills of some kind, but the treatment could also be delivered via injection. This may seem a trivial difference, but it could actually be important if we're talking about the likelihood of patients continuing with a treatment (and therefore the likelihood of long-term benefits). CBT involves regular meetings with a therapist, but patients may also take part in group sessions (such as for role-play) and be asked to keep diaries to record thoughts or mood in between sessions. Furthermore, courses of CBT may be of different lengths for different disorders (for example, depression versus schizophrenia).[19] Knowing about these kinds of specific details gives students much greater insight into patients' experience of psychological treatments and also provides more concrete ideas for evaluation where issues like practicality and likelihood of relapse are important considerations.

---

19 See recommendations from NICE (National Institute for Health & Care Excellence, 2014 and 2022).

When teaching treatments, it's not only helpful to use this framework to delineate and sequence what we want students to learn, but sharing the framework itself with students gives them a useful tool with which to **make meaning** of both current and future content. For example, after teaching whichever treatment you've covered first, you could show a partially completed version of the table below (with the right-hand column left blank), which acts as an advance organiser for the second treatment. Alternatively, you could have much briefer details in the second column to provide a comparative advance organiser or get students to complete their own version once you've taught the treatment, to summarise what they've learned. Since we know that students need to **review regularly**, this could also be used as a helpful scaffold for some retrieval practice. This framework should also enable them to learn about other treatments further down the line much more easily, since it can be assimilated into an existing treatments schema.

	Drugs (e.g. SSRIs for depression)	CBT
Assumptions	Psychological disorders are caused by an imbalance of neurochemicals such as neurotransmitters. Depression may result from low levels of serotonin.	Psychological disorders are the product of maladaptive cognitions (faulty automatic thinking patterns); depression stems from automatic negative thoughts.
Principles	SSRIs aim to increase serotonin levels.	CBT aims to identify, challenge and replace those maladaptive cognitions.
Mechanisms	SSRIs prevent reuptake of excess serotonin in the synapse, which increases binding of serotonin to receptors (therefore increasing serotonergic activity) and causes vesicles to synthesise more serotonin (therefore increasing the amount of serotonin).	CBT involves discussion with the patient to identify those thinking patterns; presenting evidence that challenges those beliefs and teaching alternative ways of thinking. This is coupled with training in behavioural strategies such as...
Processes	Usually taken in pill form, daily dosage. Takes around 2-3 weeks to have effect (though patients may report effects more quickly). Course of treatment typically lasts around six months.	Typically, weekly sessions with a therapist involving discussion and, possibly, some form of role-play. Patients may keep diaries to record their thoughts in between sessions and monitor progress. Typical course of treatment may last around 6-8 weeks, though could be much longer.

Evaluating treatments

As with theories or studies, there is no one-size-fits-all approach that's going to work in evaluating all treatments. That said, it is still possible to generate a list of specific themes that are likely to be useful across a range of types of treatment.

In most cases, the most important question we should be asking of a treatment is whether it actually works or not. This means looking at the supporting evidence that the treatment improves or reduces whatever it's meant to be targeting. As ever, the quality of that evidence is important, so students should be asking things like:

- What was it that actually changed for the patients?
- How was this change measured?
- To what extent are those measures deemed valid or reliable?
- To what extent does the treatment deal with the root cause of the problem (to the extent that we might actually know what the root cause is)?
- Is it 'curing' a patient or just helping manage symptoms?
- What happens once a course of treatment ends? Maintenance of improvements or relapse? What are the long-term outcomes?
- How does this compare with an alternative treatment?

Once we've established how well a treatment does (or does not) work, then it's worth asking other questions like:

- What are the practicalities?
- How easy is it to administer the treatment?
- Does it require trained professionals to supervise, or can it be self-administered?
- How much does it cost?
- Are there any risks, such as potential side-effects? How common and severe are they?
- Does the risk outweigh the potential benefits of the treatment?

We could use a scaffolded system like an acronym to support evaluation, but the same caveats apply. Remember that we are just concerned with how to get students to think evaluatively and generate a strong set of strength-weakness points to use in their answers. How to turn this into effective evaluative writing will be dealt with in Section 3C (page 337).

Example teaching segment: Evaluating treatments

Let's look at a potential teaching sequence for evaluation of anger management as a treatment for offenders. This sequence presumes that:

- Students have previously learned the features of the treatment (the AO1).
- This is not the first time they've evaluated a treatment.
- Students have a teacher-produced booklet to support their learning (a textbook or handout could just as easily support the same approach).
- Students are used to spending time in lessons reading and annotating summaries of research.

Jeff begins his evaluation with a recap of knowledge of the treatment. He puts a set of retrieval questions on the board and students are expected to respond individually, in silence, on mini-whiteboards.

> 1. What is the underlying assumption of this therapy, i.e. what causes offending behaviour?
> 2. What are the three phases of the stress inoculation model?
> 3. What are offenders asked to do in between sessions?

Jeff circulates while the class are answering to check responses, noting any obvious issues to address, and then does a quick run-through of the answers, cold-calling different members of the class and asking plenty of follow-up questions to probe their understanding further. Assuming Jeff has established that a sufficient proportion of the class have remembered a sufficient proportion of the detail (leaving aside the thorny question of what is 'sufficient' in both cases here), it's now time to move on to the evaluation.

OK everyone. We know what this treatment does and how it works, so the important question is whether it's any good. What do we think the most important question we need to answer here is? Rosie? Yes, correct: 'Does it work?' No point having a treatment that doesn't actually work! But let's be clear precisely what we mean in this context. What do we mean if we say that anger management works? That's right, Jon – that it reduces anger in offenders. That's clearly the specific aim of the treatment, but what's the overall goal? Keon? Good – to reduce offending. So, we need to keep that in mind when we start to look at the research – is there evidence that anger management actually reduces offending behaviour?

This discussion is important because students can get fixated on particular issues relating to treatments (often practical or ethical concerns) and may lose sight of either the bigger picture (the point of the treatment, which is to reduce offending) or the main mechanisms (reducing maladaptive cognitions).

Jeff then directs his students to the page in their criminal psychology workbook, which summarises a range of research into anger management. He also shows the same page from the electronic version on the whiteboard (or visualiser).

OK, first job is to read through these study summaries and annotate as you go. Remember, your annotations are there to help you make sense of the information. You can identify key ideas or concepts, summarise main points from the study into a couple of words, identify the extent to which they support anger management as a treatment or critique the methodology of the studies.

Jeff circulates as his students work quietly, reminding them to annotate rather than highlight as required, and answer questions to clarify anything arising from the studies. Students who finish quickly are given some prompts to push their thinking further, such as identifying methodological criticisms of each study. Once everyone has got far enough through, Jeff pauses the class.

You're going to move on to the questions on the next page in a moment. You should work through these questions in pairs, but both of you need to write down your own answers in your booklets. You don't need to write in full sentences – bullet points are fine – but there should be enough detail there to make sense when you refer back to it. For some of the questions, you're expected to refer to specific studies that you've just reviewed; the others are more for you to think about for yourselves. OK, go.

Again, Jeff shows the questions on the board.

> **Anger management discussion questions**
> 1. To what extent does anger management work for the majority of offenders?
> 2. Are some offenders more likely to be motivated to engage with the therapy? Could there be any problems with a 'motivated' participant?
> 3. Do you think anger management works in the long term, including once released from prison?
> 4. To what extent is it possible to really determine how successful anger management programmes are?
> 5. To what extent are anger management programmes cost effective (think about training, staffing, etc.)?

Jeff circulates again while students work through the questions, prompting them to develop their points as required and using questions to direct them to relevant studies or ideas if they're struggling to make connections. Where some students have finished faster than others, Jeff gives them further (verbal) questions to consider to develop their evaluation ideas, for example, getting them to consider counter-arguments and make comparisons to the other treatments they've learned about. As he's doing so, Jeff makes a few mental notes of those that have given particularly good or different responses that he wants to share with the rest of the class.

Once Jeff is happy that the class has made sufficient progress through the questions, he wants to draw it all together and help the students summarise their ideas. He runs through the questions on the board and cold-calls students to give their responses, clarifying and probing with further questions as he goes.

OK everyone, now let's pull it all together. Turn to your evaluation table on the next page (Jeff also scrolls down on screen so the same table is projected on the board).

Section 3: Teaching core content

Evaluation of cognitive treatments for offenders	
Strengths	Weaknesses

We'll start with a strength. What's the most important question we said we needed to consider? Does the treatment actually work? Well, does it, Freya? That's right – there's plenty of supporting evidence that suggests that anger management is effective. Which studies, Abdul? Good, let's note that in our table then.

Jeff writes in the table as students do the same.

Evaluation of cognitive treatments for offenders	
Strengths	Weaknesses
Supporting evidence – reduces anger – e.g. Ireland (2004), Howells et al. (2005).	

What do we mean by effective, though? Charlie? OK, so it reduces anger – great. Does that mean it reduces offending then? Henry, any evidence on this? That's right, none of the studies actually measure reoffending. So, can we determine whether anger management is an effective treatment? OK, let's note that down too.

Evaluation of cognitive treatments for offenders	
Strengths	Weaknesses
Supporting evidence – reduces anger – e.g. Ireland (2004), Howells et al. (2005).	No measures of reoffending – may not work!

Jeff continues with this, working through the ideas generated from the previous task and asking lots of questions to probe students' thinking and make connections between points. By the end of the exercise, his evaluation table looks something like the below[20] (and hopefully students' versions do too).

---

20 In reality, it's likely to look much messier than this with abbreviations, annotations and various lines or arrows drawing connections between ideas to help students link their points or see lines of argument and counterargument.

Evaluation of cognitive treatments for offenders	
Strengths	**Weaknesses**
Supporting evidence – reduces anger – e.g. Ireland (2004), Howells et al. (2005). *Helps manage behaviour in prisons e.g. reducing violent incidents.* *More 'ethical' compared to drug treatments e.g. no negative side-effects.*	*No measures of reoffending – may not work!* *Role-plays may be unrealistic – don't give strategies that can be used in real-world.* *Most effective for 'treatment-ready' offenders so not applicable to all.* *Offenders may be motivated to participate for wrong reasons e.g. early parole.*

Students now have a good list of evaluation points and have also made strong connections between different ideas. This sets them up well for writing about treatments, as they can extend their evaluation with development points ('furthermore…') or counterpoints ('however…').

Approaches

The term 'approaches' refers to the main disciplines within psychology such as behaviourism, cognitivism and biopsychology. The key idea is that each represents a significantly different way of trying to understand human behaviour; each has its own assumptions about the causes of behaviour, favoured areas of study and preferred methodologies. However, a significant challenge for any psychology teacher is that there are significant differences around the structure of that knowledge. Indeed, the different approaches represent entirely different beliefs around the nature of knowledge. Jumping between different approaches in psychology, therefore, is not the same as simply comparing different research methods; it requires the adoption, and comparison, of entirely different worldviews. No wonder students find it hard! And perhaps it's also no wonder that none of us can really agree on what constitutes an 'approach', or how many of them there are.[21]

This issue is probably as much the result of the inherent messiness of psychology as a discipline as it is the idiosyncratic choices of specification writers, and not one that humble teachers may have much bearing upon.

---

21 This includes exam boards. There is significant variation in which (and how many) approaches each board covers, and even in the terminology used to classify them.

But it's important to be alive to these distinctions and to be clear that the 'version' of psychology we are teaching our students doesn't necessarily map onto how psychologists in the real world view the subject.

For example, a student could feasibly study the 'Approaches' topic in AQA and come away thinking that the psychodynamic, humanistic and cognitive approaches are equally popular and important to modern psychology, when in fact the former two are now only of relatively minor importance to some types of therapy, whereas the latter is the dominant paradigm in contemporary scientific psychology. It's incumbent on us to make students at least aware of this issue – that what they are learning is just one version of psychology (this represents the kind of hinterland knowledge that we need to provide our students with in order to make sense of what they're learning). What is also crucial is that you are clear which approaches are included in your specification and what the exam board expects them to be able to say about them – *know thy specification*!

Making meaning using the approaches

As the fundamental theoretical building blocks of the subject, the approaches to psychology are clearly important to master in and of themselves. However, encouraging students to **make meaning** when studying the approaches also pays dividends later on, when approaches knowledge becomes essential prerequisite knowledge for understanding many of the applied areas in the subject.

We have already described a number of systems that will assist with making meaning from the approaches, such as:

- Give the students time. In Section 2, we looked at a curriculum plan that dedicated twice as much time to an initial approaches unit as to some units later in the course.
- Emphasise the relationships between approaches. In Section 2, we described how challenging core questions could go beyond static knowledge testing to examine the relationships between ideas. For example, the questions below are specifically designed to help students understand how the cognitive approach (and subsequently cognitive neuroscience) represents a development on behaviourist ideas of learning.

Core question	Suggested answer
Why do cognitive psychologists reject the behaviourist's explanation of learning as a result of random trial and error?	They argue that cognitive processes are important for behaviour (behaviourists thought that the mind was irrelevant), and that cognitive processes operate in an organised and systematic manner (e.g. using schemas).
What is the relationship between inference and cognitive models?	Models will be made drawing together lots of individual studies (i.e. lots of separate inferences) into a single model of a whole cognitive process (e.g. the multi-store model in memory). The model then provides hypotheses for further testing.
Why could using brain scanning (in cognitive neuroscience) allow us to make better cognitive models?	Brain scans allow us to make better inferences about how the brain processes information. For example, if different areas are active for different tasks, this suggests that the brain treats them differently and they need different boxes in a theoretical model (like STM and LTM in the MSM).[22]

- Test prerequisite knowledge. A good deal of the prerequisite knowledge for applied topic areas will often be from the approaches in some way; this therefore ensures that students begin any new unit as well prepared as possible to make meaningful connections back to the underlying ideas.
- Mapping approaches using *advance organisers* to show both the connections within and between the approaches, including the *timeline* of their development relative to one another
- Foreshadow later knowledge and applications. This is the opposite of prerequisite knowledge testing, in that we are telling students that the knowledge they are currently learning will be important for something later on as well. In doing so, you are illustrating exactly why students need to work hard to understand the present material. For example, in the teaching sequences for synaptic transmission, we saw how Lauren made deliberate links to future areas of the curriculum by highlighting the importance of synaptic transmission to topics such as explanations and treatments of psychological disorders.

---

22 This question also helps to target a common misconception, which is to see brain scans as an end in themselves (which therefore provide a definitive answer to a question), rather than as a piece of extra evidence that still needs to be linked back to a cognitive model through a process of inference.

Approaches: The power of prediction

The study of the approaches often occurs relatively early in many psychology curricula. It may seem that it would be hard to use prediction early on in a course, but right from the start students will be able to predict aspects of theories from a set of initial assumptions. For example, students can be presented with a thinking frame such as the example below. Then, provided with only assumptions of an approach (such as behaviourism), the students can be challenged to predict the answers to the various questions in the diagram.

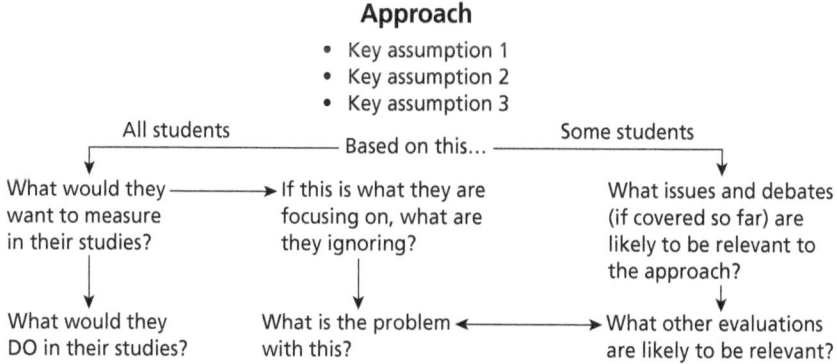

Once the students have covered a couple of approaches, encouraging the use of prediction can be a good way to assess their understanding, as well as to practise the also important skill of applying them to new contexts: 'What would a biological psychologist say about this behaviour?' 'What would a cognitive psychologist?' and so on. The key here is that we shouldn't be expecting precise responses, but that the students show they can draw upon the key assumptions of each approach to guide their thinking. If you're stuck for examples of behaviour, a good source is to go for topics featured in alternative specifications. This has the advantage that, should you or students want to pursue the answers in more detail than you know, there is already some accessible content out there written on it.

Students can also follow the same process to 'predict' the content of each applied area (such as the learning theory explanation of phobias, for example), based on their existing knowledge of the approach and its assumptions.

Applying the approaches

There are variations between the specifications, but typically students are expected to be able to apply their knowledge of any given approach to a particular behaviour or set of behaviours. For example, Edexcel students learn about biological explanations for aggression, AQA students have to apply the behavioural approach to explanations and treatments for phobia, and OCR students learn about memory and attention as part of the cognitive approach.

In each case, it's possible to teach students a very reductive version of a behaviour, and tell them only what they need to know to talk about that specific example. This is certainly more time efficient and decreases the likelihood of students including extraneous material in their exam answers but is flawed for a few reasons.

First, while students may learn the details well, they are less likely to really understand them properly. Without placing that knowledge in a wider context, seeing how it is derived from more general principles, we are giving the students a poor grounding in the subject. Second, we want to develop the student's ability to think synoptically and see connections between different topic areas. They can't do this without a solid understanding of fundamental principles. And third, they may be asked to apply their knowledge of different approaches, etc to novel contexts.

A simple way to support students building a meaningful schema for an approach is to use a range of concrete examples, which allow you to clearly highlight the different elements of the approach. For example, we could present a simple scenario like the following:

> Brad is addicted to gambling and cannot stop himself from going into a betting shop or playing on a fruit machine whenever he sees one.

We could then explain that the biological approach would:

- Suggest there is a neurobiological basis, for example, atypical activity in specific brain regions.
- Investigate this using scientific methods such as brain scanning techniques.
- Try to treat this using a biological intervention such as drugs.

At a simple level, we could then either do the same for a different behaviour to reinforce the principles of the biological approach or look at the same behaviour using a different approach (such as cognitive). Whichever approach you choose – and the extent to which the responses are driven by the students or the teacher – will depend on where you are in the curriculum and the prior knowledge of the students.

Evaluating an approach

There are a number of different angles from which to evaluate an approach:[23]

- Critique the underlying assumptions about the causes of behaviour.
- Critique the typical or preferred methodologies.
- Critique the suggested interventions arising from the approach.

This variety can be very useful as it provides a range of possible sources for contextualisation (C1 and C2) of evaluation points. Of course, this is not to say that students will find this easy or can immediately do it successfully. That's never the case for evaluation!

Let's look at an example for the psychodynamic approach. Students often feel safe evaluating this as they have a strong sense of its major flaws (although they rarely fully grasp or even accept that it isn't all bad!):

> A criticism of the psychodynamic approach is that it is seen as unscientific. This is because its theories are unfalsifiable. This means that there is no evidence that can prove them right or wrong.

As you've undoubtedly spotted, this is technically 'correct' and well structured but entirely generic (lacking both C1 and C2). A better version could be:

> A criticism of the psychodynamic approach is that it is seen as unscientific. This is because it suggests that behaviour is a product of unconscious processes that cannot be directly observed or measured. This means that psychodynamic theory

---

23 If you prefer to use acronyms here, then the same options used for theories (e.g. SCOUT, USED, CODA and GRENADE) can also be used here, given that approaches are essentially large-scale theories.

is unfalsifiable, as there is no way of producing evidence to show that behaviour either is or isn't caused by unconscious drives.

Comparing approaches

In specifications that specifically examine knowledge of the approaches as a standalone topic (such as AQA), comparison of approaches is a relatively common exam question; certainly, it appears in these sections more frequently than comparison questions in other parts of the exam. The extent to which comparison is required will vary depending on the question, and it can be a good introduction to the area to get students to think hard about what different questions may be asking them to do. For example:[24]

1. Outline and evaluate the behaviourist and biological approaches. (16)

2. Outline and evaluate the behaviourist approach. Compare the behaviourist approach with the biological approach in your answer. (16)

3. Outline the behaviourist approach. Compare the behaviourist approach with the biological approach. (16)

The first of these examples is not a comparison question, and the two approaches can therefore (if the student so wishes) be described and evaluated entirely separately (although comparison could be used to extend evaluation). The second example does require some comparison, but this would not need to happen in all cases and so the answer could contain a mixture of standard evaluation and some comparison. The third example is explicitly a comparison question, and so all AO3 marks would need to be phrased as comparisons.

Once students are able to recognise the question requirements, they need to know (or be able to work out) some comparison points, such as similarities and differences between the different approaches. This could, for example, involve giving students a Venn diagram such as the one below, and then getting them to place statements such as 'Animal

---

[24] This is not to say that all of these question types would definitely occur in a real exam – the exercise here is to get the students thinking carefully about what would be required if they did.

behaviour can inform us about human behaviour', 'Internal processes are important in shaping behaviour' or 'People learn from their experiences' in the appropriate locations.

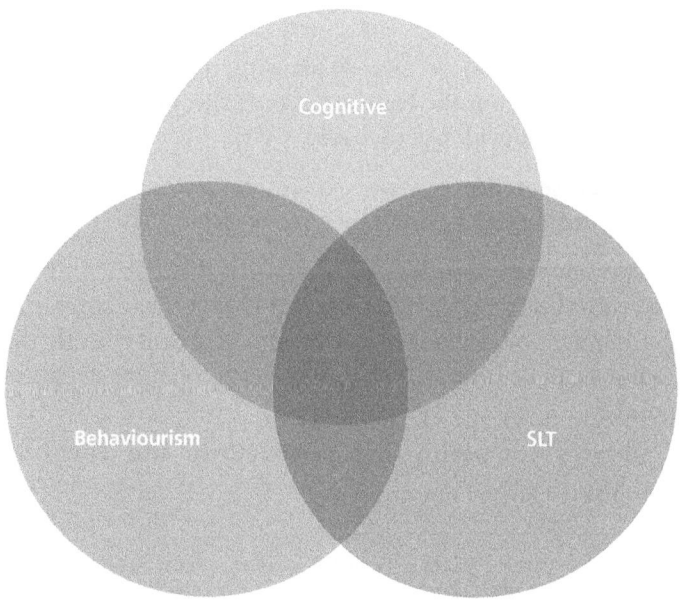

Another method is to place the relevant approaches on the spectrum of a particular issue or debate. Approaches that end up close together can be described as similar, and those far apart as different.

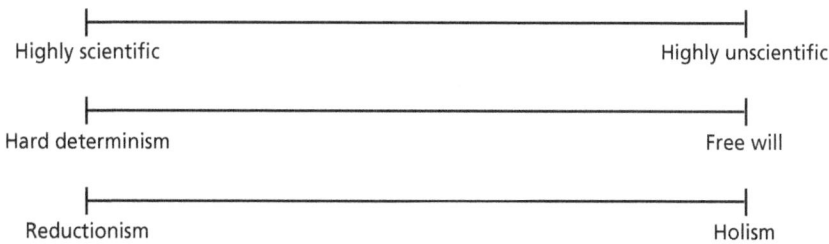

Having identified potential points of comparison, students may also need assistance in fitting these into their 'regular' evaluation answer structure. Comparisons involve looking for similarities and differences, but it's important that they are actually evaluative, not just side-by-side description. The 'so what?' part of the answer could therefore easily be neglected by students. The framework below may help:

1. Write a sentence explaining how the theories/approaches are similar/different [Point].
2. Add a further sentence or two explaining the similarity or difference by pointing out the features of each theory/approach, or by giving an example/evidence [Because + C1].
3. Write a further sentence or two explaining a consequence or implication of the similarity/difference [So what? + C2].
4. If appropriate, identify a difference/similarity that relates to the one you have discussed but which contrasts with it (i.e. a similarity within a difference or a difference within a similarity). (NB the order of 3 and 4 can be reversed if it gives a more coherent structure to your point.)

Put together, answers comparing the behaviourist and cognitive approaches could look like this:

Comparison identified

One similarity between the behaviourist and cognitive approaches is that they both take a scientific approach to the study of human behaviour. An example from behaviourism is the Skinner box, a highly controlled environment that Skinner used to shape the behaviour of animals. In cognitive psychology, Bransford and Johnson (1972) used an experiment with a standardised stimulus (a piece of writing about washing clothes) to investigate the effect of schemas on understanding and memory. Therefore, both approaches conduct experiments in which they aim for control of variables, replicability and objectivity. This allows them (in theory) to discover cause and effect relationships between variables.

Examples from each approach

'So what?' made clear – the implications of the comparison point for each approach

Another similarity between the cognitive and behaviourist approaches is that both believe that people learn how to behave through their own experiences. For cognitive psychologists, experiences help to shape our schemas, which are mental frameworks that help to shape how we perceive and remember things that happen to us. Our experiences therefore affect how we process information, which impacts on our behaviour. For behaviourists, our behaviour is directly determined by classical and operant conditioning, without any need to examine cognitive processes. Therefore, experience is important for both approaches, but for different reasons.

Extending evaluation of approaches: Comparisons

Comparisons also offer students the chance to develop a line of argument further when performing regular evaluation of an approach. Let's return to our previous evaluation paragraph regarding the psychodynamic approach:

> A criticism of the psychodynamic approach is that it is seen as unscientific. This is because it suggests that behaviour is a product of unconscious processes that cannot be directly observed or measured. This means that psychodynamic theory is unfalsifiable, as there is no way of producing evidence to show that behaviour either is or isn't caused by unconscious drives.

What next? If the student is looking to make a comparison, then looking at a very different approach (such as biological) seems a good bet here. However, students don't often do this well to begin with:

> A criticism of the psychodynamic approach is that it is seen as unscientific. This is because it suggests that behaviour is a product of unconscious processes that cannot be directly observed or measured. This means that psychodynamic theory is unfalsifiable, as there is no way of producing evidence to show that behaviour either is or isn't caused by unconscious drives. On the other hand, the biological approach can be seen as more scientific because it uses lots of controlled laboratory experiments, which means that results are more reliable and valid.

There are a few problems here: the comparison point is not really contextualised (beyond the inclusion of the word 'biological'); there's no real sense that the student knows why the biological approach prefers laboratory studies; and there's no sense that they understand why laboratory studies are more reliable and valid (or that they haven't just hedged their bets by chucking both evaluation terms in!).

But a bigger issue is that the student has essentially gone off on a completely different point to the one they started with, which makes the line of argument feel less coherent. To use our contextual analysis, the student has changed C1 from one context to another. A better approach would be to stay with the same focus of falsifiability and link that to the biological approach:

> A criticism of the psychodynamic approach is that it is seen as unscientific. This is because it suggests that behaviour is a product of unconscious processes that cannot be directly observed or measured. This means that the theory is unfalsifiable, as there is no way of producing evidence that can prove it right or wrong. On the other hand, the biological approach can be seen as more scientific because it assumes a biological basis for behaviour and physiological responses can be directly measured.

This is a well-contextualised (C1) point, and the student may leave it there, but if we're really looking to develop a line of argument then it should go further. Just like the original point, some evidence to support the claim being made would be helpful here:

> A criticism of the psychodynamic approach is that it is seen as unscientific. This is because it suggests that behaviour is a product of unconscious processes that cannot be directly observed or measured. This means that the theory is unfalsifiable, as there is no way of producing evidence that can prove it right or wrong. On the other hand, the biological approach can be seen as more scientific because it assumes a physiological basis for behaviour and physiological responses can be directly measured. For example, if you want to look at the effects of testosterone on aggression, it's possible to directly measure levels of circulating testosterone from a saliva swab.

There is some concrete evidence to support the claim in this answer (note that evidence here doesn't have to mean 'research'). Students sometimes worry that evidence requires a named study and find the prospect of learning so many studies completely overwhelming. As discussed, while supporting evidence does make for effective evaluation in many cases, it's not the only possible tool that students have available, and a concrete example that illustrates the point effectively will suffice in many instances. However, if you really do want to go to town with this answer, then inclusion of some research (and the implications of that for the approach – C2) will certainly develop it even further:

A criticism of the psychodynamic approach is that it is seen as unscientific. This is because it suggests that behaviour is a product of unconscious processes that cannot be directly observed or measured. This means that the theory is unfalsifiable, as there is no way of producing evidence that can prove it right or wrong. On the other hand, the biological approach can be seen as more scientific because it assumes a physiological basis for behaviour and physiological responses can be directly measured. For example, if you want to look at the effects of testosterone on aggression, it's possible to directly measure levels of circulating testosterone from a saliva swab. This was demonstrated by Dabbs et al. (1995), who found that violent offenders had higher levels of testosterone than non-violent offenders. This shows that it's possible to falsify claims that, for example, testosterone increases aggression by finding individuals with high levels of testosterone who don't exhibit high levels of aggression.

Issues and debates

Issues and debates are a strange thing. To read some student essays, you would think that they are *the* central feature of psychology, and certainly the primary way that we would ever evaluate a psychological idea.[25] The vast majority of psychological literature, however, pays absolutely no attention at all to issues and debates. It's not necessarily that the concerns raised by them aren't present in the research, it's just that these concerns are generally seen as far less of an issue.

The true debate – if there is even one to be had – is about the relative importance afforded to different levels of explanation, in combination with others, and the degree to which theories can be successfully triangulated with other ones at different levels of explanation into a coherent whole. This is a far more nuanced and difficult position, of course (which is why we don't tend to teach it!), but it is also a far less *urgent* position, in that it presents a problem far less in need of solving. *Of course*, looking at neurotransmitter levels in cases of mental illness is reductionist, but it's only a problem if you believe that we'd never

---

25 And if you've attended some training courses, you may reach similar conclusions.

look at anything else or never try to combine a biological explanation with other levels (which is the precise misconception that we accept our students having for the sake of having a debate and writing evaluations). In fact, it's not really bad at all to be reductionist; it's an essential feature of scientific investigation! The same thing goes for determinism (at least in a low-level experimental sense), or for taking a nomothetic approach. This is why psychology research is generally silent on the issues and debates; they just aren't as important when you know more about how research and theory building works.

Moving beyond the debate: Psychology as a science

Another problem with issues and debates is that students may not appreciate when – and if – there actually is consensus in psychology. Take the 'psychology as a science' debate. The dominant paradigm within psychology is a scientific one, but students may not grasp this fully when they have been exposed to, for example, the humanistic approach, unless we do a good job in explaining how this represents a minority view. Some students, particularly those attracted to psychology by what have been called the 'practitioner aspects' (the more interpersonal applied areas such as therapy, education and nursing) may find the scientific nature of psychology less engaging, and perhaps more challenging.

In practice, academic psychology *is* a science, and therefore the true debate should be about the relative benefits (and costs) of psychology attempting to use a scientific method to try to study a subject matter (human behaviour) that does not always lend itself easily to scientific investigation. We should therefore be emphasising to students that this *is* a scientific discipline and modelling the thinking processes that result from that. We should be discussing how these applied fields develop best practice by drawing on the best available research – as we have attempted to do in this book! As well as simply providing a more accurate picture of the academic discipline, the possession of scientific beliefs about the subject has been found to correlate to students' academic success in psychology courses (Amsel et al., 2014).

Making meaning using issues and debates

Despite what we have said above about the slightly artificial nature of much of the issues and debates coverage in our courses, the fact remains that they do form a key element of our curricula. For example, they form a consistent thread that runs throughout all topics and units, meaning they are a crucial vehicle for making meaning. This process is assisted if we:

- Introduce early (and interweave throughout). In the curriculum sequencing case study for the AQA specification Section 2, page 141), 'Issues and debates' occurred last in the teaching sequence (as something of a revision unit), but began with an extended 'Approaches' unit that allowed for issues and debates to be introduced and subsequently referred to throughout.
- Emphasise the relationships (but also the distinctions) between issues and debates. Many of the issues and debates in our courses are conceptually related to one another. For example, issues like reductionism, determinism and taking a nomothetic approach all stem from attempts to follow a scientific method. Students can therefore quite quickly grasp that in most cases an approach being reductionist is also likely to be deterministic. However, it is also crucial that the students understand the differing implications of each issue in order to avoid the sorts of 'evaluation salad' sentences that conflate different issues entirely, mix them up or treat them as interchangeable, such as '...this means that it is reductionist and deterministic'.
- Test prerequisite knowledge. When planning to cover prerequisite knowledge for a new topic, it pays to identify, and quiz in advance, relevant overlapping knowledge from the issues and debates.

Describing issues and debates: The use of examples

Students often struggle with the C1 section of answers that use issues and debates as evaluation issues. In essays that specifically ask students to discuss issues and debates, this problem can be magnified as this content becomes the AO1, and so can require some quite extensive description and explanation. This can be a challenge for students who have become accustomed to writing 'but the behaviourist approach is reductionist':

> Reductionism involves the idea that human behaviours can best be understood by 'reducing' them into simpler explanations at a particular level of explanation. One example is the behaviourist

approach. It displays environmental reductionism as it reduces all behaviour to the effect of the environment, for example, through classical and operant conditioning.

Students can often get a bit stuck here and be unsure how to extend the description. A good strategy to illustrate the point further is to use an example:

> Reductionism involves the idea that human behaviours can best be understood by 'reducing' them into simpler explanations at a particular level of explanation. One example is the behaviourist approach. It displays environmental reductionism as it reduces all behaviour to the effect of the environment through classical and operant conditioning. For example, the approach provides a reductionist account of phobias that involves them being acquired through classical conditioning and then maintained through operant conditioning, where avoidance strengthens the phobia through negative reinforcement.

A similar example on the idiographic versus nomothetic debate might start like this…

> The idiographic approach to psychology looks to gain an in-depth insight into individuals. It will therefore look to study individuals' subjective experiences using research methods like case studies or unstructured interviews.

… and again, be extended using an example, which in this case comes from a research study:

> The idiographic approach to psychology looks to gain an in-depth insight into individuals. It will therefore look to study individuals' subjective experiences using research methods like case studies or unstructured interviews. For example, Shallice and Warrington (1970) conducted a case study into K.F., who had suffered memory problems following a motorbike accident. By performing multiple different tests on the same individual, Shallice and Warrington were able to conclude that the damage to his auditory short-term memory was much more severe than damage to his visual short-term memory.

As we have established, the C1 here may confuse students who are used to using studies as evaluation, so it's important that they are able to see that the study is just functioning as an example of the approach, rather than the vehicle for any evaluative comment. Depending on the chosen structure of the essay, this evaluation could follow immediately (such as discussing the usefulness of idiographic methods for challenging theories and providing the initial impetus for new nomothetic research programs, in this case contributing to the development of the working memory model). Alternatively, this could be saved for later on.

Evaluating other concepts using issues and debates

Often the first time that students encounter the issues and debates will be when using them to evaluate other ideas, rather than analysing them in and of themselves. This is something that students can latch onto very strongly, as using issues and debates ideas seems to present the possibility of having a relatively small number of evaluative ideas that can be recycled for almost any essay. The problem is that these ideas can often be very difficult to use well. Despite the apparent simplicity initially, the C1 and C2 parts of issues and debates answers can be challenging, and as a result it can be very easy for them to be used in very generic ways. At worst, this can lead to single sentences being tacked onto the end of other paragraphs (such as 'however, biological approaches are reductionist'), but even when there is slightly more development, or when the issue and debate is made the full subject of the paragraph, it is still common to see answers such as:

> One criticism of the psychodynamic approach is that it is deterministic. It does not give us control over our own actions. This means that we have no free will.

This paragraph lacks both C1 (what determinism actually looks like in the psychodynamic account) and C2 (the issue with this for the approach). Before you read ahead, think (or, better still, write) what a better version may involve. There are lots of possible ways that the answer could be improved, so your version does not necessarily need to look like ours, although the C1 and C2 features will need to be present. One improved version could be:

> One criticism of the psychodynamic approach is that it demonstrates psychic determinism. Freud suggested that

behaviour was motivated by sexual and aggressive drives originating in the unconscious id (and therefore out of our control). Adult personality can also be affected by childhood experiences such as fixations in particular psychosexual stages, but these are also out of our control as they result from being either frustrated or overindulged by our parents. This therefore paints a depressing picture of human behaviour as entirely out of our conscious control.

This could be taken further with comparison to other approaches.

Using 'scientific' as an evaluation point

Somewhere along the way, either due to their prior knowledge or experience, or the way in which we induct them into our subject, psychology students pick up the idea that being scientific is generally a good thing (at least for research, even if they struggle to conceptualise psychology as a truly scientific subject). Once they've acquired this idea, it's pretty common to see it used as an evaluation point in all manner of places. Students often don't do this particularly well, however, because they typically fail to demonstrate that they know what this actually means and that this may differ from one context to another.

Students most commonly use the scientific approach when talking about anything biological, presumably because it feels like that's closer to a 'proper' science and so they're safe to make the assumption that biological aspects of psychology are therefore scientific. For example, this could be applied to:

- Neurotransmitter explanations for behaviour.
- The use of neuroimaging techniques (e.g. PET/fMRI scans) to study brain activity.
- Drug treatments.

What students struggle to explain is precisely what it is in each case that is 'scientific' and why this could be deemed a good thing (in other words, the C1 and C2 may be different in each case). For example:

- Neurotransmitter explanations may be considered scientific because you can objectively measure levels of a given neurotransmitter, which allows researchers to accurately test predictions about the association between increased or decreased neurotransmitters and a particular behaviour (e.g. dopamine and schizophrenia). Therefore, being scientific here is about being able to better *make causal inferences* about the behaviour being studied.

- Brain scans may be considered scientific as they allow researchers to gather more objective data, because a participant in, say, a PET scanner cannot deliberately manipulate the activity of different brain regions in response to a perceived cue from the research situation. This means researchers can be more confident that they are getting a 'true' picture of brain activity. Therefore, being scientific in this context is about *increasing the validity* of research.
- Drug treatments may be considered scientific because the active ingredients of the treatment can be accurately measured, which means we can control the precise dosage that the patient receives. This means that drugs can be prescribed with the same dosage for different individuals in a consistent way that would be impossible with a psychological therapy. Therefore, being scientific in this instance is about the *reliability of an application.*

In each of these cases, it's important to note that these aren't the only scientific features or interpretations. For example, drug treatments may also be considered scientific because we can accurately test baseline measures of a particular neurochemical (such as testosterone) and then test again post-treatment to see if it's had any effect. This is useful in the sense that we can use the same base idea ('being scientific') to generate multiple evaluation points. However, this distinction is often confusing for students, who tend towards more generic statements as described above, and so we may want to teach these points explicitly – and possibly even avoid references to being scientific at all!

Evaluating issues and debates

In the specifications where it is required, students often find the process of evaluating issues and debates very challenging. One reason for this is that they often arrive at this point already used to using issues and debates as evaluation for other concepts, and so have developed a habit of thinking that simply introducing the issue or debate is enough.

Take the issue of gender bias (a part of the AQA 'Issues and debates' unit). Students may have used the issue of samples being gender biased (often androcentric), or perhaps they evaluated biases in ways that mental illnesses are diagnosed. We can take the example further by looking at the use of gender bias to criticise the reliability of schizophrenia diagnosis. A student who is able to do this successfully clearly understands the issue of gender bias but can still slip up when the primary focus of the essay shifts onto the issue itself. For that essay, the use of issues and debates worked as evaluation of another concept. Here... it doesn't. In this essay, students need to move from *identifying* the issues to *evaluating* the issues, an extra layer of complexity on what they may have done previously.

Imagine a student is asked to 'discuss issues of gender bias in psychological research'. Evaluation answers like the following are very common:

> One example of gender bias is in the diagnosis of schizophrenia. Loring and Powell (1988) randomly selected 290 male and female psychiatrists to read two case studies and judge them using the standard diagnostic criteria of whether the case studies would be diagnosed. When the case was described as male or given no gender, 56% were diagnosed with schizophrenia, whereas only 20% were classed as schizophrenic if labelled as a female.

This answer has identified the issue of gender bias and provided an example of it. However, in the context of an question that explicitly asks students to discuss issues of gender bias, this is only an AO1 skill. To develop it into AO3, the wider implications of the issue need to be explored, or perhaps the negative consequences arising from it, or the positive developments in trying to combat it.

In order to assist with this process, students can be given a spectrum like the one below for each issue and debate:

Extreme end A   **Extreme end B**

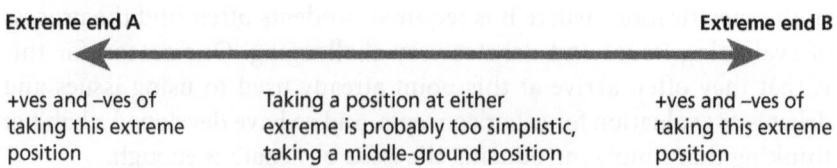

| +ves and –ves of taking this extreme position | Taking a position at either extreme is probably too simplistic, taking a middle-ground position is more sensible | +ves and –ves of taking this extreme position |

Section 3: Teaching core content

Students can annotate examples of the issue above the arrow according to where it fits on the spectrum. Below the arrow, they need to think about the wider implications of establishing a position somewhere on this spectrum. It may be that it is easier to find positives in some places and negatives in others; that's fine (usually there will be more negatives at the extremes and more positives of taking a middle-ground position). For gender bias, we may end up with something like this:

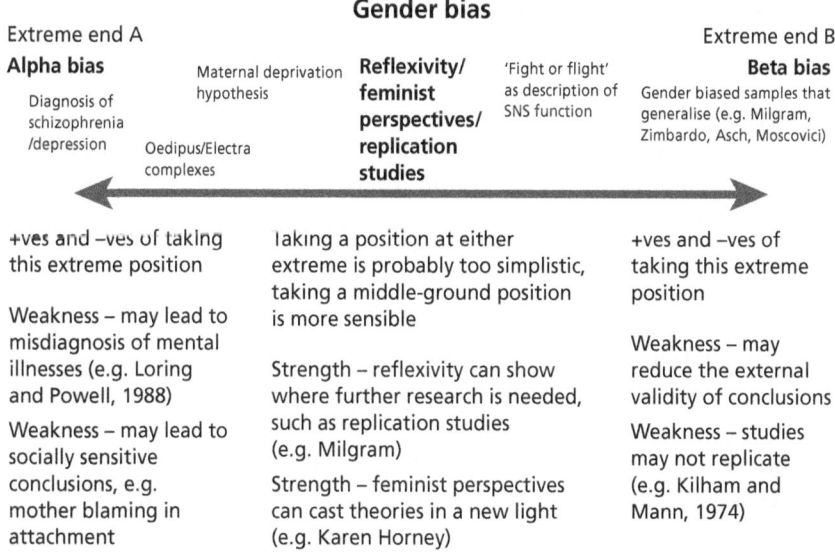

Extreme end A				Extreme end B
Alpha bias	Maternal deprivation hypothesis	**Reflexivity/ feminist perspectives/ replication studies**	'Fight or flight' as description of SNS function	**Beta bias**
Diagnosis of schizophrenia /depression	Oedipus/Electra complexes			Gender biased samples that generalise (e.g. Milgram, Zimbardo, Asch, Moscovici)

+ves and –ves of taking this extreme position	Taking a position at either extreme is probably too simplistic, taking a middle-ground position is more sensible	+ves and –ves of taking this extreme position
Weakness – may lead to misdiagnosis of mental illnesses (e.g. Loring and Powell, 1988)	Strength – reflexivity can show where further research is needed, such as replication studies (e.g. Milgram)	Weakness – may reduce the external validity of conclusions
Weakness – may lead to socially sensitive conclusions, e.g. mother blaming in attachment	Strength – feminist perspectives can cast theories in a new light (e.g. Karen Horney)	Weakness – studies may not replicate (e.g. Kilham and Mann, 1974)

This makes it much easier for students to then organise their information into proper evaluative paragraphs for the particular issue or debate (including C1 and C2). An essay will often follow a pattern of examining one or both extremes, before then finding positions somewhere in the middle of the spectrum for the concluding paragraph. For example:

> One problem with gender bias in research is that alpha biases in gender may lead to misdiagnosis of mental illnesses. Loring and Powell (1988) randomly selected 290 male and female psychiatrists to read two case studies and judge them using the standard diagnostic criteria of whether the case studies would be diagnosed. When the case was described as male or given no gender, 56% were diagnosed with schizophrenia, whereas

only 20% were classed as schizophrenic if labelled as a female. Conversely, women are two times as likely to be diagnosed with depression as men. One possible explanation for this could be an alpha bias in the definition of abnormality and the diagnosis of schizophrenia and depression (due either to gender differences in social norms of behaviour, or perhaps assumptions about biological differences as an underlying cause). This suggests that people may be inappropriately diagnosed (and treated ineffectively) due to these gender biases.

A paragraph for beta bias with a similar structure could look like this:

A problem with beta bias is that it may reduce the external validity of conclusions. Kilham and Mann (1974) replicated Milgram's study in Australia and found that 16% of women obeyed, compared to the 65% of obedience found in the original. This suggests that beta bias in Milgram's original conclusions (based on an all-male sample) may have led to invalid assumptions about women's obedience of authority. However, this study also used a female learner, so this variable could also explain the reduced obedience. This makes it harder to understand the precise effect of any gender bias. In addition, Milgram subsequently replicated his study with all female participants and found almost identical results, which suggests that in this case a beta bias may have been appropriate after all.

The spectrum idea works even more intuitively with the classic 'debates' (such as reductionism versus holism or free will versus reductionism). For example:

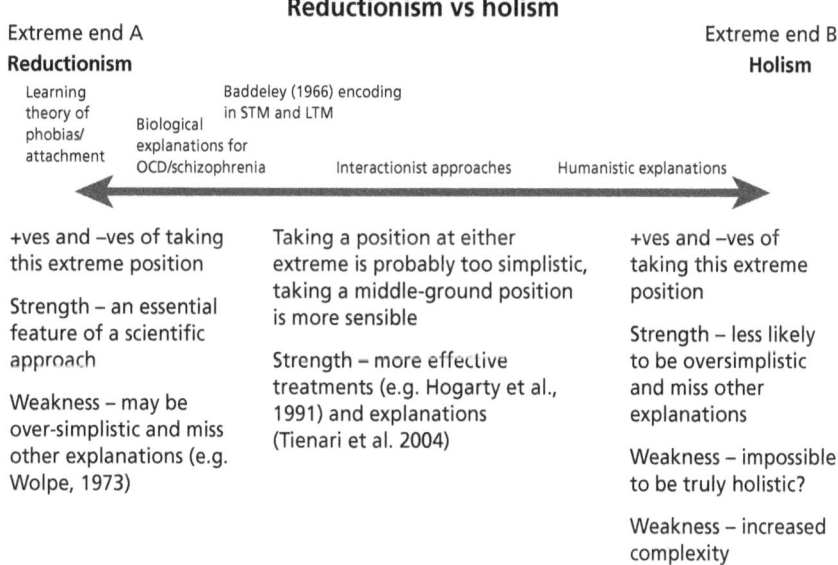

This work can then lead towards a paragraph such as:

> A strength of taking a reductionist approach in psychology is that reductionism is an essential feature of a scientific approach. Scientific methods rely on reducing complex behaviours to simple cause and effect relationships. Experiments, which vary in one variable (the IV) and attempt to control all others to find a causal link between the IV and the DV, are necessarily reductionist. For example, Baddeley's (1966) experiment on encoding in STM and LTM takes a 'machine reductionist' approach, only explaining results in terms of the cognitive processes involved. This allows for inferences to be made about the coding used by each store, based on which conditions show impaired recall.

In the next section we will consider how we can help students to combine these skills to produce effective evaluative writing.

Section 3C: Teaching evaluative writing

We've considered multiple examples of what good evaluation looks like, and the underpinning principles of how to write in context. So how do we get our students to be able to do this? Ultimately, we need our students to be able to combine their various skills into essays. As a result, when considering how we write evaluatively, getting students to write essays would seem the obvious place to start, wouldn't it? Increasingly, we are not so sure. Extended writing is the most challenging part of any psychology course; doing it well requires a huge range of knowledge and skills, both domain-specific and generic. We can see this by considering a *prerequisite knowledge spectrum* such as the example below for a good essay.

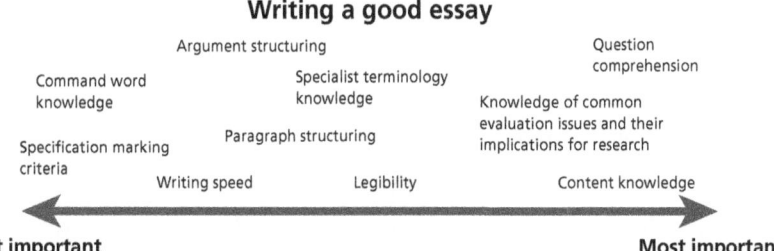

Some of these skills are not really within our control as teachers, but many are – at least to some extent. However, mapping the requirements (and their importance) out like this makes two things clear. First, it shows us where to focus first – on the most essential pieces of prerequisite knowledge that are amenable to teacher intervention. And second, it suggests that there are likely to be too many concurrent skills required for essay writing for some students to do it well early on in the course.

The marathon analogy

In her book, *Making Good Progress?*, Daisy Christodoulou develops an analogy about education and marathon running. Simply put, she suggests that no-one would think that the best way to train for a marathon would be to immediately start running marathons. Training plans involve a gradual build-up of distance and a focus on establishing success at lower levels, before increasing the difficulty of the training. Furthermore, training may involve activities such as intervals, speedwork or hill repeats,[26] which don't resemble a marathon that much. In contrast, a common approach to the 'marathon' of essay writing is to throw students into the full process as early as possible.

Christodoulou suggests that this immediate focus on the end product can prevent us from focusing more on the processes that are required to get to the end product successfully. For example, this could mean:

1. Initially learning to write detailed evaluative sentences (including C1).

2. Learning to write evaluative paragraphs by adding an assessment of the implications (the C2) of the initial evaluation point.

3. Learning to sequence more than one paragraph into a meaningful order.

4. Writing pieces of essay length at speed and legibly.

Alternatively, it could mean varying the level of support given for a task, from very heavy scaffolding early on in the course to light touch assistance later on. The marathon analogy also holds for the ability to learn from feedback, something we will discuss further in Section 4.

Writing paragraphs

In section 3A, we looked at how we could introduce students to evaluative concepts in psychology and how these may be built up into paragraphs.

---

[26] It is, of course, possible to train for a marathon without doing these things – it's just harder!

Students need both explicit teaching of this and practice at applying it. This requires lot of teaching – and a lot of practice!

Example teaching segment: Teacher modelling of evaluation paragraphs

Nadiya is teaching her class about Wilhelm Wundt and his early contributions to introducing a scientific foundation to psychology.

Right, everyone, imagine that a student is asked to write an evaluation of Wundt's contribution to psychology. They write the following:

> One strength of Wundt's contribution is that introspection was more scientific than previous methods for studying the mind. Being scientific means that it is easier to find cause and effect relationships.

Any good? Could you improve it? If so, how? Students, especially early on in the course, may struggle to identify the problem at this stage.

The paragraph is accurate and uses good terminology. So where does it go wrong? Well, read it again, but this time put yourself in the position of an examiner. You have to work out how much the student really *knows and understands about Wundt and his methods. From what they have written, how certain can we be that they get it? If we can't be certain, what do they need to do to make their knowledge and understanding more obvious?*

Remember that good evaluation paragraphs in psychology often follow a rough structure. There is a clear evaluation point that will make a claim about a positive or negative feature. This will often feature a key piece of scientific terminology – here, it was the word 'scientific'. After that we'll need some sort of evidence to back up the claim, and then finally an explanation of why this is a good or bad thing in this case.

The features of well-structured paragraphs can be displayed or written on the board at this stage, to reduce cognitive load.

Has the paragraph on the last page managed this? Tell the person next to you. Jamal? OK, great – I agree. There's a clear point, and a 'so what?', but not really any evidence provided to support the claim.

Nadiya annotates the paragraph:

Point { One strength of Wundt's contribution is that introspection was more scientific than previous methods for studying the mind. Being scientific means that it is easier to find cause and effect relationships. } So what?

Let's add in some evidence. I'll take hands up here: why was introspection 'more scientific'? Kacey? Great – it had a lot of the key features of a science. Tell your partner, and make sure that you each tell the other one at least one of the features of a science introspection displayed. OK, stop. Brilliant. I heard a lot of great answers. I'm going to pick two of the features that I heard people saying: standardisation and control. Let's add that evidence into the paragraph.

Point { One strength of Wundt's contribution is that introspection was more scientific than previous methods for studying the mind. His methods were standardised and controlled. Being scientific means that it is easier to find cause and effect relationships. } Because / So what?

All done? Sadly not! What's still missing? We'll read it again, but pretend that you are an examiner. You have to be absolutely certain that the student really knows a lot about introspection or understands why this had a positive impact on psychology. Can you be sure that they do?

What is still lacking here is some context, some specific information from the idea being discussed that helps to illustrate the evaluation point. Context will often occur twice *in an evaluation paragraph.*

| What is the claim being made about X? | C1 |
| What is the effect of C1 on the ability to assert Y? | C2 |

What would this look like for our paragraph on Wundt?

Nadiya could follow this process by helping students to write their own paragraphs, which may involve further modelling followed by students completing independent practice. Probably one of the hardest lessons learned over years of trying to teach evaluative writing is the sheer number of examples that students need to first encounter and then have a go at in order to develop fluency. All too often, students may get exposed to only a handful of well-contextualised points, and only get to write one or two of their own, often with significant scaffolding.

Case study: I do, we do, you do

A method that incorporates both teacher modelling and student practice is 'I do, we do, you do':

I = the teacher models to the class.

We = the teacher and class complete a model together.

You = the class complete their own independent practice.

It is important to spend enough time on 'I' and 'we' before setting students off onto independent practice ('you'). Tom Sherrington (2020) uses a helpful analogy here of passing on a baton during a relay race. The crucial moment in this process is the brief handover period that – although it may look simple – relies on the incoming runner only letting go when they are confident that the recipient has a steady hold. Similarly, in lessons, students need a secure handover before embarking on the 'you' phase.

A concern that teachers sometimes have with modelling, particularly with the deliberate narration of decision making during the 'I' section, is that it can feel like a slow process, and one in which students are simply passively watching the teacher. For those with more challenging groups of students, this can seem like even more of a risky endeavour as it can be harder to maintain full class 'radar' and the threat of disruption is a concern. However, when done well, modelling should be an interactive and dynamic process. As the teacher narrates their thinking, there are plenty of opportunities for whole-class questioning strategies that ensure high participation and thinking ratios.

Here is an example used to evaluate behaviourism:

How to Teach Psychology

Detailed paragraph of A01 description

The behaviourist approach believes that all behaviour is learned from experience and interaction with the environment. There are two methods of learning for the behaviourist approach. Classical conditioning (CC) involves reflex behaviours and involves associating a previously neutral stimulus with an unconditioned stimulus (which causes a reflex response, called the unconditioned response). Eventually the neutral stimulus becomes a 'conditioned stimulus' and comes to elicit a response (called the 'conditioned' response) all on its own. For example, Pavlov's dogs came to associate the ringing of a bell (NS) with the presentation of food (US), so that the bell caused salivation (CS), a response previously only elicited by the presentation of food. Operant conditioning (OC) controls voluntary behaviour and involves either reinforcement or punishment. Reinforcement, such as a reward (positive reinforcement) makes a behaviour more probable, whereas punishment, such as being shouted at (this would be positive punishment) will make a behaviour less probable. The behaviourist approach argues that all animals (including humans) obey these same laws of learning, and this means that animal experiments can be used to investigate behaviour, and their results generalised to human behaviour. As its name suggests, it is only concerned with externally observable behaviour, behaviourists would say that internal behaviours such as thoughts and emotions were unscientific and not worth studying.

AO3 evaluation paragraph

Clear point made, which is a 'signpost' for the what the paragraph is about, e.g. it can be used to treat phobias, and this is a good thing

One positive of the behaviourist approach is that it has useful applications to real life. The behaviourist principle that the environment can be used to shape behaviours is at the heart of a number of treatments for phobias that are still used today (such as flooding and systematic desensitisation, which are based on classical conditioning). Gilroy et al. (2003) found that systematic desensitisation was effective at reducing fear of spiders compared to a control group who didn't receive the therapy, even 33 months after the treatment. This shows that behaviourist ideas can be successfully used to help people suffering from phobias.

Point backed up and explained using supporting evidence

Explaining clearly 'so what?' and linking back to the question, e.g. what these results show and why this is a positive of the behaviourist approach

AO3 evaluation paragraph (write as a class)

Another strength of the behaviourist approach is that it is highly scientific. It uses research practices that are...

This allows cause and effect relationships to be discovered between stimuli and behaviour, such as between...

AO3 evaluation paragraph (write individually)

However, one weakness of the behaviourist approach is...

If you have the time to do this in lessons, it's probably one of the most useful things students can be doing, but otherwise it can be set as a homework activity provided there is enough practice and scaffolding in the initial 'I do' and 'we do' phases to set students up to do it for themselves successfully. The 'you do' paragraphs don't even have to be on the same topic. Indeed, it's a great way of removing scaffolding to model on one topic or study and then ask the students to write a paragraph on a different, related topic or study, gradually increasing the 'distance' between the model and the new paragraph. For example:

Evaluation of study	Guidance
Weakness of sample in Milgram	Original model – a study that students are typically very familiar and comfortable with, meaning they can focus wholly on the skill of evaluation rather than trying to remember the details of the study.
Weakness of sample in study B	Keeping the same evaluative point but applying it to a new context. This should help students really see how the context (C1) makes points differentiated rather than generic.
Weakness of sample in study C	A third example with the same evaluative focus should help to really consolidate the idea now.
Weakness of procedure in study C	Keep the context but change the evaluative focus.
Strength of procedure in study C	Keep the context and evaluative focus but change the direction of evaluation.
Strength of procedure in study D	Change the context but keep everything else the same.
Weakness of procedure in study D	Change the direction of evaluation but keep all else the same (this could be opportunity to look at counterpoints).

Note that in this sequence the examples have been chosen carefully to only change one feature at a time. This will both help to **manage cognitive load** and also allow the students to **make meaning** of what we mean by context, because they can start to discern the important differences between two apparently similar things (such as criticising the sample of two different studies).

If students are ready for it (especially if looking for some useful revision or independent study activities), then a useful resource may be something to help them generate their own evaluation points. This is just a prompt to give them ideas for the content, focus and direction of their points, for example:

Choose a study	Pick an evaluative focus	Decide a direction
Milgram	Generalisability	Strength
Bandura	Internal validity	Weakness
Loftus and Palmer	External validity	
Bowlby	Reliability	
Maguire	Ethics	
Rosenhan	Useful applications	
	Scientific	

Practising C2s

Since it is arguably the most challenging aspect of evaluative writing, we should probably spend most time on the C2 component. The more time students spend focusing on these, and the more expertise they have in creating them, the better their evaluative writing will be.

C2 development could, for example, involve providing a range of examples (or non-examples) for one specific thing (such as a study) and asking the students what good contextualisation looks like. In the examples below, the left column (shown first) features paragraphs about Loftus and Palmer (1974) in which the C1 is present but the C2 is missing. The right column can then be revealed (or live annotated onto the original) following student discussion or written suggestions using whiteboards.[27]

---

27 NB this could also be used as an effective tool to scaffold some whole-class feedback on students' written answers. We discuss this further in Section 4, 'Assessment', page 363.

Section 3: Teaching core content

Examples lacking C2 – not showing how this relates to what the study is investigating (effect of leading questions)	Examples with C2 included – showing how this relates to memory or eye-witness testimony (EWT)
The sample of undergraduate students may have less driving experience than people in the wider population, which makes the findings less representative.	The sample of undergraduate students may have less driving experience than other people; this means the extent to which they are influenced by leading questions, when asked to consider the speed of cars, may not be representative of the wider population.
Questioning people about videos rather than real car crashes is artificial, so the findings lack ecological validity.	Questioning people about videos rather than real car crashes lacks ecological validity, meaning we can't be certain how much leading questions may affect the testimony of real-life witnesses.
The use of the same video clips and questionnaires meant that this was a standardised procedure, which increases reliability because it would allow for replication of the study to check for consistency of findings.	The use of the same video clips and questionnaires meant that this was a standardised procedure, which increases reliability because they could easily replicate the study to see if leading questions have a similar effect on recall in other participants (which they demonstrated was true in experiment 2).
The use of controls, such as the randomised position of the critical question in the questionnaire, reduced the likelihood of a confounding variable affecting the results, increasing the internal validity.	The use of controls, such as the randomised position of the critical question in the questionnaire, reduced the likelihood of this becoming a confounding variable, meaning they could be confident it was the IV (verb in the leading question) that was causing a change in the DV (estimates of speed).

In addition, booklets can be used when asking students to make meaningful evaluations by considering the 'so what?' of any evaluation point provided (though the teacher also needs to carefully ensure students' answers fulfil C2). For example:

Strengths

There is some (!) research support that top-down profiling can be effective in identifying offenders:
- Ressler et al. (1988) reported a profile (previous page) of a disorganised offender which was created from a murder scene.
- It proved very accurate and was helpful in identifying the perpetrator.   *So what (plus C2)?*

Weaknesses

One criticism of top-down profiling is that it is not generalisable to all types of crimes:
- It is best suited to crime scenes that reveal important details about the suspect e.g. violent crimes like 'lust murders'.
- More common offences, such as burglary do not lend themselves to profiling, as the crime scenes reveal little about the offender.   *So what (plus C2)?*
- This is in contrast to the more widely generalisable bottom-up method (next section).

Another criticism of top-down profiling is that the data on which it is based may lack validity:
- Typology theory is based on the results of interviews with 37 dangerous serial killers, who can be unreliable and deceitful.
- This contrasts with the much more scientific bottom-up method (next section).   *So what (plus C2)?*

Scaffolding evaluation paragraph structure using acronyms

It is common for teachers to help students to structure high quality evaluation paragraphs by using acronyms. Indeed, we do this ourselves. Similar to the use of acronyms used for evaluation issues earlier in this section, there are a range of options to choose from, all with their enthusiastic devotees. Common ways of scaffolding paragraphs include:

- PEEL (Point, Explain, Evidence/example, Link) or PEEEL (with 'elaboration' included).
- PBS (Point, Because, So what?).
- PETE (Point, Explanation, This suggests, Extend).
- IEJ (Identify the point, Explain/example/evidence, Justify).
- PRE (Point, Reason, Evidence/explanation).

Regardless of your preference, it seems that most of these acronyms have the same aims in terms of the paragraphs that they are trying to shape.

Acronym					What's happening?
P(oint)	P(oint)	P(oint)	I(dentify)		Clear evaluation claim made, usually using some form of specialised terminology.
E(xplain) E(xample)	B(ecause)	E(vidence)	E(xplain/example/ evidence)		The evidence for the claim being made (ideally including C1).
E(laborate) L(ink)	S(o what?)	T(his suggests)	J(ustify)		The specific implications of the evidence presented (including C2).

As discussed above, using acronyms can lead to a number of problems:

1. It can lead to a focus on structure rather than meaning, which results in superficial evaluation.
2. It can lead to rigid adherence to the acronym, leading to formulaic paragraphs that aren't tailored to the requirements of the question.
3. It can lead to far more time-consuming writing, since more complex paragraphs are developed slavishly following the acronym rather than by taking a more adaptive approach.

In the example below, there would be nothing wrong with a student producing two full 'PEELs' here (one for the criticism and one for the counterargument), but the result would be time consuming, less concise and probably not as elegant.

Practice evaluation paragraph structuring – example

In this example, there is some countercriticism, as well as a slight change to the usual order.

P (and B), plus C1	One criticism of the Milgram's experiment was made by Orne and Holland (1968) who suggested that participants knew that the experiment was a sham and that they were not giving real shocks.
S (plus C2)	This suggests a major problem for the internal validity of Milgram's conclusions that people will obey authority to the point where they harm others.
B (plus C1)	However, Milgram argued that a majority of participants (70%) in later replication studies reported that they thought it was genuine.
B (plus C1) P/S (plus C2)	Also, Sheridan and King (1972), conducted a replication study using a puppy as the 'learner' and real electric shocks. Most continued to obey and shock the puppy. These findings appear to support Milgram's argument that the experiment was internally valid.

This all requires explicit modelling, and lots of examples, to support students. If we consider what we've discussed about effective evaluation, we can see that the structure of writing is less important than the substance. As well as prioritising meaning (C1 and C2) over structure (e.g. PEEL), there are also some simple shortcuts to make with language choices to avoid the clunky phrasing often seen in students' evaluation points. For example, while starting every new point or paragraph with something like 'One strength of X is...' is a clear way of signposting evaluation, it's often a very inefficient way to write.

Take the following evaluation point:

> One problem with Milgram's study is that the limited sample could be considered to reduce the study's external validity. This is because he used all males from the New Haven area of New York. Due to cultural influences, the participants could have similar levels of obedience to one another as they may have had similar experiences of socialisation. This means that the results of the study may not necessarily represent obedience levels in other populations, for example, people from different cultural backgrounds. (83 words)

Now consider a more concise version:

> The limited nature of Milgram's sample (all from New Haven) reduces the extent to which we can make claims about levels of obedience in the wider population. Differences in culture could influence how likely people are to follow instructions as a result of socialisation, particularly for such a specific, destructive act. (51 words)

The second version does include both C1 and C2, though you may notice the student has switched the order, with C2 being presented first. This kind of flexibility is useful, as we don't want students to feel constrained by a particular structure or order. The detail is reduced, but the key ideas are still present. Similarly, the signposting is reduced but still present – 'the limited nature' clearly indicates that evaluation is happening here. Is it as good as the first version? The honest answer is probably something along the lines of 'not quite, but it's still good enough'. And with a nearly 40% reduction in the number of words (meaning that students may be able to increase the amount of evaluation points in their answers), it's a trade-off that's possibly worth it. As we've discussed, this won't be for everyone, but perhaps something we should consider for some of our students. If we do want students to be able to do this, they'll need a significant amount of modelling and practice to get them there.

Writing essays

Writing full essays, no matter how long we delay and scaffold the process, has to happen eventually. At their heart, of course, good essays require the ability to clearly address the relevant assessment objectives. However, there are also some specific aspects of essay writing which arise from putting everything together.

Structuring essays

One of the things that students can underestimate the importance of in extended essay writing is structure. Having a sequence of information that allows the question to be addressed coherently, each assessment objective to be addressed explicitly, and that (ideally) presents a logical 'flow' of ideas can make a huge difference to the experience of reading an essay.

One way to get students thinking about how to structure ideas is to present them with two archetypal essay structures, which we imaginatively label 'structure 1' and 'structure 2' when introducing these ideas to our students. 'Structure 1' essays contain a single descriptive section followed by a number of subsequent evaluative paragraphs. If required by the question, a section of application can be inserted in between the AO1 and the AO3. 'Structure 2' interweaves these elements more, with shorter sections of description (and if relevant, application) followed by specific evaluation linked to that section. Visually, the essays that may be produced look something like the following examples.

For essays including only AO1:

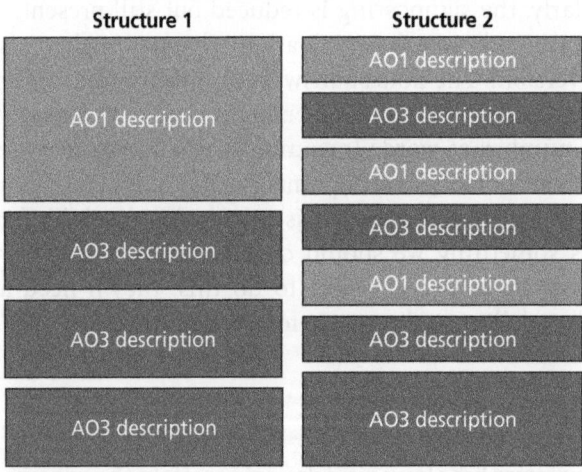

For essays including AO2:

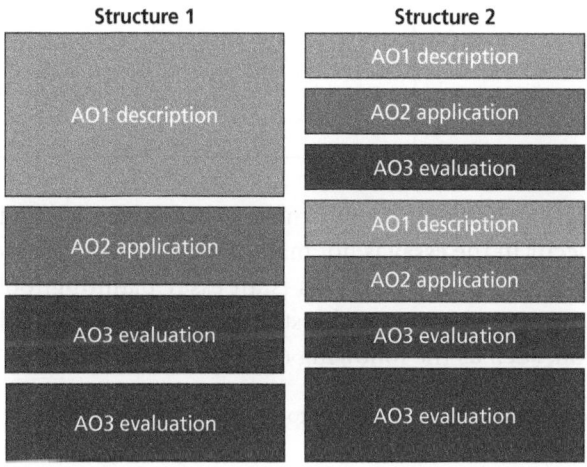

These structures will be more appropriate for some essay titles, and for some specifications. Some titles and specifications may also be more likely to invite deviations from this; for example, they may require that AOs are combined (such as application occurring in evaluation paragraphs as well). As with paragraph structuring, it's important here that the schema does not become the scaffold, and that students are shown how they could deviate from the system where needed.

These two structures still provide a decent starting point though. For example, the question, 'Outline and evaluate the behaviourist approach in psychology', may lend itself to a 'structure 1' outline, as there is a single 'block' of information (the ideas of the approach) to be described, whereas the question, 'Discuss factors affecting obedience to authority', may lend itself more easily to 'structure 2' (as different factors will need to be described separately). This is not to say that these questions could not be answered well using the other structure, just that students are likely to find it easier to write coherent essays using those structures for those essays.

We can also use classroom tools to get students thinking about which structure they could use and how the different parts of the essay may fit together into a coherent flow. For example, we could avoid providing students with planning templates such as this...

A01	A03

... in which the relationship between the information being planned and the order that it will occur in the essay is not made clear. Instead, we can provide students with a 'structure strip'. This is an essay planning tool that allows students to plan an essay in the structure that they would include the information, such as the following example:

> Discuss factors affecting obedience to authority. Refer to research in your answer. (16 marks)

6 A01s, 10 A03s

Roughly 3 A01 points and 3 well-developed (or 4 shorter) A03 paragraphs

Structure strip

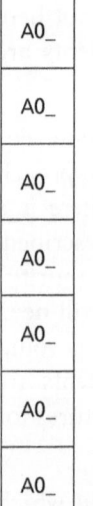

We may also want to use both forms of planning tool but for different purposes. For example, the initial table may be used to simply select and

categorise all the relevant information that students have available to them on a given topic (this in itself can be quite a useful retrieval activity to 'warm up' or check prior knowledge). Once this has been done, a more structured plan (such as using a structure strip) can be put together; however, students are still likely to find the organisation, prioritisation and sequencing of the points challenging. As we've argued already, we think it's almost impossible to over-scaffold this process!

Securing success in essay writing

Clearly, not all of our students are going to experience writing very high-scoring essays, and for many exam boards they may not need to in order to achieve the top grades. This can sometimes, therefore, lead to a fatalism with regard to success in essay writing. We can counter this and increase the likelihood of securing initial success by using:

- Clear success criteria that are provided to students *before* they complete an assessment, such as model answers or mark schemes.
- The very gradual introduction of evaluative writing skills over the first half of the course.
- Heavily scaffolded approaches early on in the course, gradually reducing this until students can write them without assistance some way into Year 13. Our experience – much to our relief – is that the essays at the end of Year 13 are *better* for the students having spent longer on the foundations. In addition, doing fewer full essays earlier in the course frees up more time for this training, as well as focusing on the various core skills of evaluative writing free from the cognitive overload that comes from trying to manage all of them at once.

An example of heavy scaffolding that increases the chances of student success is a pre-submission checklist. Here is an example 16-mark essay question (for the 'Psychopathology' unit in the AQA specification) with a pre-submission checklist below:[28]

---

28 This represents a fairly heavily scaffolded checklist. Over time we would expect this to become less detailed and a more generic version, as presented on page 355, which fits a range of different essay questions.

Rob is a sixth form student who has started hearing voices in his head. The voices come often, are usually threatening and make Rob feel frightened. The voices are making it difficult for Rob to complete his homework properly, and he is worried about how this may affect his chances of going to university. Rob has not told anyone about his experiences, but his parents and teachers have noticed that he appears distracted, anxious and untidy.

Outline and evaluate failure to function adequately and deviation from ideal mental health as definitions of abnormality. Refer to the experiences of Rob in your answer. (16 marks)

Self-assessment checklist

Criteria	Completed? (Yes/Partially/No)
AO1: A definition of failure to function adequately is included and accurate.	
AO1: Reference is made to some of Rosenhan and Seligman's criteria.	
AO2: Application to Rob not completing homework, untidiness and the distress he feels and causes, linked to specific examples of the criteria above.	
AO3: An evaluation point is included and explained with reference to whether it is a strength or weakness of the definition e.g. patient perspective.	
AO1: A definition of deviation from ideal mental health is included and accurate.	
AO1: Reference is made to Jahoda's criteria.	
AO2: Application to Rob's inaccurate perception of reality (voices) and the voices preventing his self-actualisation is included. Link to specific examples of Jahoda's criteria.	
AO3: An evaluation point is included and explained with reference to whether it is a strength or weakness of the definition e.g. it is unrealistic.	
AO3: An evaluation point is included and explained with reference to whether it is a strength or weakness of the definition e.g. it is useful for goal setting in CBT.	
AO3: A final evaluation point is included and explained with reference to whether it is a strength or weakness of either this definition, or both definitions together e.g. ethnocentrism.	

A more generic approach could look like the following:

Psychology essay pre-submission checklist
- Read the list below carefully and tick when you have checked each one has been completed.
- Your work will not be accepted for marking/feedback until ALL of these have been done.

Criteria	Done?
1. You have put your name on it!	
2. Your answer is handwritten UNLESS you usually type in the exam.	
3. You have written a plan before starting the essay and submit this plan.	
4. You have checked your completed answer against your plan.	
5. You have proofread to check for SPAG and that sentences actually make sense.	
6. You have written an amount appropriate to the number of marks available. For 'average' handwriting this equates to approximately: • 8 marks = 1.5-2 sides A4 • 12 marks = 2-3 sides A4 • 16 marks = 3-4 sides A4 • 20 marks = 4-5 sides A4	
7. You have the appropriate balance of AO1/AO2/AO3 material dependent on the marks available for the question. E.g. if it's an 8-mark 'Evaluate' question then there should be approximately equal amounts of AO1 and AO3.	
8. You have balance in your answer by giving at least one positive and one negative evaluation point.	
9. Every evaluation point is linked back to the context of the question.	
10. Your answer has a conclusion at the end, presenting your overall judgement.	

We discuss further the use of success criteria and checklists in Section 4, 'Feedback that can feedforward, page 379).

'Flash planning' – the ultimate essay challenge

If we postpone essay writing in the way outlined above, then we do need to maximise exposure once the students are fully trained and ready.

A great tactic (based on an idea from psychology teacher Lucia Berridge) to get students to wrestle with some of the complexities of essays without taking an excessive amount of class time is 'flash planning'. Give students two minutes or thereabouts to plan an essay, including structure, sequence and content (in brief). The essay can be specifically or randomly selected, depending on your purpose and the level of challenge you want to create.

This is the closest that students can get to the pressurised planning process they may experience in the exam (as well as covertly reminding them *to* plan their essays in the first place). It doesn't guarantee that students will be able to write the essay clearly, of course, but a coherent plan that shows detailed enough knowledge and evaluation ideas, sensibly structured and ordered, is a huge step in the right direction. On the other side of the coin, this sort of activity will often reveal gaps in student knowledge, which can then be followed up as a part of independent study. Flash essay planning forms a regular starter activity in the last few months of our Year 13 lessons.

Combining AOs in extended writing

In some exam specifications, extended response questions may also have an element of application to them. In this context, students may be required to describe and evaluate a particular theory, for example, and apply this to a particular scenario given in the question. These questions are, in theory, more testing for students because they have to use their knowledge more flexibly rather than simply regurgitating pre-learned description and evaluation points.

Here's an example that appeared in the 'Criminal psychology' section of an Edexcel paper 2 in 2020:

> Cassandra is on trial for a recent case of burglary. She is 24 years old, white, of slim build and considered to be attractive. Her lawyer advises her to dress in a smart suit for the trial to leave a good impression on the jury. She has a strong local accent, which is considered to be an unpopular accent. The trial is taking place over 100 miles away from Cassandra's home town, as this is where the alleged burglary took place.

> To what extent may Cassandra's characteristics affect the jury's decision making in her trial? You must make reference to the context in your answer. (16 marks)

This kind of question requires a combination of all three assessment objectives:

AO1: Knowledge and understanding	AO2: Application	AO3: Evaluation
Different defendant characteristics and how/why they may influence a jury's decision.	Links to the scenario – how might these be relevant to Cassandra?	How well are these influences supported by evidence? To what extent may Cassandra's chance of a fair trial be affected?

Students will have studied various defendant characteristics such as gender, race, ethnicity, age, attractiveness or accent. (This is one area where the precise content is not specified, leaving teachers to choose which, and how many, of these characteristics to cover.) The students will also have learned various bits of supporting evidence for each characteristic, and so the construction of an answer for this kind of question is fairly straightforward. The application links are fairly explicit in the question (it's obvious that you can talk about Cassandra's gender, attractiveness, ethnicity or accent), making it a student-friendly question.

While each AO could be dealt with separately, a 'weaved' approach allows students to gain more credit for demonstrating logical chains of reasoning and sustained application, which will score them higher on the mark scheme. The students can construct their answer using paragraphs such as the following example:

AO1: Knowledge	One characteristic of the defendant that may affect a jury's decision is… This is because…
AO2: Application	This may mean that Cassandra is likely to be judged as… which could mean that…
AO3: Evaluation	The effects of _____ have been investigated by _____ who found that… However…

| AO2/3: Link to question – mini-conclusion (if required by exam board) | Therefore, this suggests that... *(must link back to Cassandra)* |

This kind of scaffolding should help provide a clear framework for students who may struggle to organise their thoughts initially, but it should only be there as an initial support that is gradually withdrawn. Stronger students may be able to write more effectively in their own style. We may also want to encourage them to be more sophisticated in their thinking and embrace the complexity of application scenarios, for example, in the scenario above, considering the relative interplay between different factors (since jurors would see Cassandra 'holistically' rather than just as 'white' or 'female') or the interaction between characteristics of the defendant and characteristics of the jurors. However, we also need to be mindful of the potential for this to distract some students from doing the basics well and consider for whom this additional nuance may be most beneficial to think about.

Summary of Section 3

In this section, we've considered the specific areas of content that will feature in any psychology course and how an understanding of our pedagogical principles can guide us in how to effectively teach them to our students. While these are our guiding principles, we also hope it's clear that the specific application of them to different areas of content (such as theories or studies) necessitates subtly different pedagogical approaches. We've also seen that the various skills students need to develop in order to satisfy various assessment objectives require significant thought and attention, and that each one will take time and practice for students to master in isolation (and relative to each area of content), let alone in combination. The next challenge is for us to be able to determine how successfully we've managed to teach all this and what students may still need to do to improve. In Section 4, we turn our attention to this challenge as we consider the role of assessment and feedback in psychology.

References

1. Agarwal, P. K., Nunes, L. D., & Blunt, J. R. (2021). Retrieval practice consistently benefits student learning: A systematic review of applied research in schools and classrooms. *Educational Psychology Review, 33*(4), 1409-1453.
2. Al-Mosaiwi, M., & Johnstone, T. (2018). In an absolute state: Elevated use of absolutist words is a marker specific to anxiety, depression, and suicidal ideation. *Clinical Psychological Science, 6*(4), 529-542.
3. Amsel, E., Ashley, A., Baird, T., & Johnston, A. (2014). Conceptual change in psychology students' acceptance of the scientific foundation of the discipline. *Psychology Learning & Teaching, 13*(3), 232-242.
4. Atkinson, R. C., & Shiffrin, R. M. (1968). Human memory: A proposed system and its control processes. In Spence, K. W., & Spence, J. T. (eds), *Psychology of learning and motivation* (Vol. 2, pp. 89-195). Academic Press.
5. Baddeley, A. D. (1966). The influence of acoustic and semantic similarity on long-term memory for word sequences. *Quarterly Journal of Experimental Psychology, 18*(4), 302-309.
6. Bartlett, F. C. (1932). *Remembering: A study in experimental and social psychology.* Cambridge, UK: Cambridge University Press.
7. Bandura, A., Ross, D., & Ross, S. A. (1961). Transmission of aggression through imitation of aggressive models. *The Journal of Abnormal and Social Psychology, 63*(3), 575.
8. Boxer, A. (2021). *Teaching secondary science: A complete guide.* John Catt.
9. Cheniaux, E., Landeira-Fernandez, J., & Versiani, M. (2009). The diagnoses of schizophrenia, schizoaffective disorder, bipolar disorder and unipolar depression: Interrater reliability and congruence between DSM-IV and ICD-10. *Psychopathology, 42*(5), 293-298.
10. Christodoulou, D. (2017). *Making good progress?: The future of assessment for learning.* Oxford University Press-Children.
11. Dabbs Jr, J. M., Carr, T. S., Frady, R. L., & Riad, J. K. (1995). Testosterone, crime, and misbehavior among 692 male prison inmates. *Personality and Individual Differences, 18*(5), 627-633.
12. Endres, T., Carpenter, S., & Renkl, A. (2024). Constructive retrieval: Benefits for learning, motivation, and metacognitive monitoring. *Learning and Instruction, 94,* 101974.
13. Gilroy, L. J., Kirkby, K. C., Daniels, B. A., Menzies, R. G., & Montgomery, I. M. (2003). Long-term follow-up of computer-aided vicarious exposure versus live graded exposure in the treatment of spider phobia. *Behavior Therapy, 34*(1), 65-76.
14. Godden, D. R., & Baddeley, A. D. (1975). Context-dependent memory in two natural environments: On land and underwater. *British Journal of Psychology, 66*(3), 325-331.
15. Hogarty, G. E., Anderson, C. M., Reiss, D. J., Kornblith, S. J., Greenwald, D. P., Ulrich, R. F., & Carter, M. (1991). Family psychoeducation, social skills training, and maintenance chemotherapy in the aftercare treatment of schizophrenia: II.

Two-year effects of a controlled study on relapse and adjustment. *Archives of General Psychiatry, 48*(4), 340-347.

16. Howells, K., Day, A., Williamson, P., Bubner, S., Jauncey, S., Parker, A., & Heseltine, K. (2005). Brief anger management programs with offenders: Outcomes and predictors of change. The *Journal of Forensic Psychiatry & Psychology, 2*, 296-311.

17. Ireland, J. L. (2004). Anger management therapy with young male offenders: An evaluation of treatment outcome. *Aggressive Behaviour, 30*(2), 174-185.

18. Kilham, W., & Mann, L. (1974). Level of destructive obedience as a function of transmitter and executant roles in the Milgram obedience paradigm. *Journal of Personality and Social Psychology, 29*(5), 696.

19. Loftus, E. F., & Palmer, J. C. (1974). Reconstruction of automobile destruction: An example of the interaction between language and memory. *Journal of Verbal Learning and Verbal Behavior, 13*(5), 585-589.

20. Loring, M., & Powell, B. (1988). Gender, race, and DSM-III: A study of the objectivity of psychiatric diagnostic behavior. *Journal of Health and Social Behavior, 29*(1), 1-22.

21. Macedonia, M. (2019). Embodied learning: Why at school the mind needs the body. *Frontiers in Psychology, 10*, 2098.

22. Maguire, E. A., Frackowiak, R. S., & Frith, C. D. (1997). Recalling routes around London: Activation of the right hippocampus in taxi drivers. *Journal of Neuroscience, 17*(18), 7103-7110.

23. McDaniel, M. A., Einstein, G. O., & Een, E. (2021). Training college students to use learning strategies: A framework and pilot course. *Psychology Learning & Teaching, 20*(3), 364-382.

24. McGeoch, J. A., & McDonald, W. T. (1931). Meaningful relation and retroactive inhibition. *The American Journal of Psychology, 43*(4), 579-588.

25. Mguidich, H., Koudji, B., & Khacharem, A. (2025). Improving tactical learning by imagination: Effects of expertise and time of testing. *The Journal of Experimental Education, 93*(1), 54-68.

26. Milgram, S. (1963). Behavioral study of obedience. *The Journal of Abnormal and Social Psychology, 67*(4), 371.

27. Morris, B. J., Cason, J., Asaro, K., Zhang, Y., Rivers, M., Owens, W., & Dunlosky, J. (2024). Learning the control-of-variables strategy during an informal science lesson on popping popcorn. *International Journal of Science Education, 47*(1), 45-64.

28. Nation, I. (2006). How large a vocabulary is needed for reading and listening?. *Canadian Modern Language Review, 63*(1), 59-82.

29. NICE (2014). Psychosis and schizophrenia in adults: Prevention and management. NICE guideline CG178, recommendations 1.3.9.1, 1.4.2.1 and 1.4.4.1.

30. NICE (2022). Depression in adults: Treatment and management. NICE guideline NG222.

31. Paas, F., & Kirschner, F. (2012). The goal-free effect. In Seel, N. M. (eds), Encyclopedia of the sciences of learning (Vol. 2, pp. 1375-1377). Netherlands: Springer.

32. Pyc, M. A., & Rawson, K. A. (2009). Testing the retrieval effort hypothesis: Does greater difficulty correctly recalling information lead to higher levels of memory? *Journal of Memory and Language, 60*(4), 437-447.
33. Rosenhan, D. L. (1973). On being sane in insane places. *Science, 179*(4070), 250-258.
34. Shallice, T., & Warrington, E. K. (1970). Independent functioning of verbal memory stores: A neuropsychological study. *Quarterly Journal of Experimental Psychology, 22*(2), 261-273.
35. Sherrington, T. (2020). The art of modelling - It's all in the handover. https://teacherhead.com/2020/11/28/the-art-of-modelling-its-all-in-the-handover/
36. Sperry, R. W., Gazzaniga, M. S., & Bogen, J. E. (1969). Interhemispheric relationships: The neocortical commissures; syndromes of hemisphere disconnection. In Vinken, P. J., & Bruyn, G. W. (eds), Handbook of clinical neurology (Vol. 4, pp. 273-290). North Holland.
37. Taylor, I. (2019). TSFL: Teaching science as a foreign language. https://mrtaylorsblog.home.blog/2019/10/21/tsfl-teaching-science-as-a-foreign-language/
38. Tienari, P., Wynne, L. C., Sorri, A., Lahti, I., Läksy, K., Moring, J., Naarala, M., Nieminen, P., & Wahlberg, K. E. (2004). Genotype–environment interaction in schizophrenia-spectrum disorder: Long-term follow-up study of Finnish adoptees. *The British Journal of Psychiatry, 184*(3), 216-222.
39. Westbrook, J., Sutherland, J., Oakhill, J., & Sullivan, S. (2019). 'Just reading': The impact of a faster pace of reading narratives on the comprehension of poorer adolescent readers in English classrooms. *Literacy, 53*(2), 60-68.
40. Wolpe, J. (1973). *The practice of behavior therapy* (2nd ed.). Pergamon.
41. Yang, C., Luo, L., Vadillo, M. A., & Shanks, D. R. (2021). Testing (quizzing) boosts classroom learning: A systematic and meta-analytic review. *Psychological Bulletin, 147*(4), 399-435. https://gwern.net/doc/psychology/spaced-repetition/2021-yang.pdf
42. Yuille, J. C., & Cutshall, J. L. (1986). A case study of eyewitness memory of a crime. *Journal of Applied Psychology, 71*(2), 291-301.

Section 4: Assessment and feedback

Lauren

Lauren has been reading her school's assessment policy, and she notes that she needs to be giving students regular feedback on their work. She decides to set her Year 12 class an essay to complete on explanations for obedience, a topic she's just finished teaching.

When Lauren takes the work in, she notices her students' answers are strewn with errors, and some of them have little coherent structure. She marks them as best she can, writing extensive comments on the work and setting targets at the end, along with a score and a grade that she thinks the work represents. She returns them to the class, admonishing their poor efforts, and then spends some time debating with various students what the marks mean and dealing with 'how can I improve my grade' questions. Some students pore over every comment (and ask what some of them mean), while some look at the mark and then immediately file the essay away in their bag and wait expectantly for the lesson to move on. A week later, Lauren sets the class another essay question for the next topic and is disheartened to find pretty much the same outcome.

Lauren is facing the following challenges:

- How can she set assessments that help her to accurately identify what her students can and can't do?
- How, and when, can she assess her students so that the experience is a useful one for both them and her?

- How can she provide her students with feedback that moves them forward? How much? In what form? When?
- How can she help her students to recognise and be open to potentially useful feedback, in all its many forms?
- How can she emotionally prepare her students for receiving feedback positively and productively, so they are able to put it to use?
- How can she structure her lessons and curriculum so there is sufficient time and focus on feedback for it to have an effect?

We have considered learning and psychology fundamentals and derived our pedagogical imperatives. We have carefully planned our curriculum with these in mind and taught some core content in accordance with the principles. Now, it's time to see what the students have learned. Of course, we are always aiming to **check what they know** in the classroom; most instances of assessment and feedback in the classroom should occur as a natural part of our everyday lesson activities.

However, at some point there will be the need to more formally assess our students, and to provide feedback on this. For both assessment and feedback, the common thread running throughout this section is the crucial importance of *knowing why*. Why are you giving the assessment or feedback that you are? What are you trying to learn from a particular piece of assessment, and what can we expect students to learn from it? What conclusions can (and can't) you draw from it? And will students be able to use their feedback to **feedforward**?

Section 4A: Principles of assessment

Establishing a positive culture of assessment and feedback

Before we look at assessment and feedback specifically, it's worth considering the sorts of conditions and approaches that we can put in place to help make them as effective as possible:

- Appreciate multiple sources of assessment and feedback. Assessment is not just tests, and feedback is not just marking. In fact, in any classroom, there is a huge range of different assessment sources and information resulting from these that students can use to improve their learning. Students need to be alert (and be alerted by the teacher) to this fact.
- Know that assessment and feedback are not learning. Learning is a process that can only happen in the student's mind, and this internal change almost always requires the student to follow up on the feedback given.
- Acknowledge the emotions associated with feedback. In Section 1, we saw that managing emotion was a crucial component of feedback literacy. One way that we can reduce the threat of feedback – especially negative or corrective feedback – is to encourage a culture of error that welcomes mistakes, and which reframes incorrect answers as a process rather than a personal event (e.g. 'retrieval failure' not 'forgetting', or 'learning opportunities' not 'mistakes'). We can depersonalise feedback, for example, through whole class feedback, avoid using grades or delay grading until after feedback has been acted upon. We can also remember to **review regularly**, since regular quizzing has been found to reduce test anxiety (Yang et al., 2023).

- Modelling feedback receipt. Another useful starting point for building a trusting relationship around feedback (including acknowledging the emotions it produces) is for the teacher to also model the receipt of feedback themselves. Being welcoming of feedback from students, and open in your response to them, provides a powerful demonstration of the principles of feedback literacy in action (as well as also being valuable for professional development, see Khoza, 2024).

Let's see this in action.

> Marcia is introducing the topic of statistical testing and statistical significance and has put a starter activity on the board, which consists of six retrieval questions that will be useful prerequisite knowledge for the current lesson. These include questions on experimental designs, probability notation and levels of measurement. Marcia initially asks students to complete the questions individually and without talking, during which time she circulates and looks at the answers being written.
>
> The levels of measurement question in particular has caused problems, with the students frequently confusing nominal and ordinal data and providing incorrect examples. Marcia annotates a few pieces of work with prompts as she circulates and speaks to another couple of students. For the final minute of the activity, Marcia says, 'You have one minute left. Discuss your answers with your partner. If your partner helps you out, add it to your answer in a different colour. If you think they could say more, then push them to explain more clearly or to elaborate.'
>
> Finally, Marcia uses cold-calling to review the answers. She asks three students what they wrote, opens up to the rest of the class to see if there is anything else that could be added, and finishes with a reminder of the definition of ratio data, which the students struggled with.

Marcia's five-minute review activity contains assessment and feedback in multiple forms: written and verbal, teacher and self- and peer-assessed. But it will only be useful if students have been made aware of that fact, and encouraged to see all these different pieces of information as equally useful. It will also only be useful to students if they understand that the process does not end there, and that they need to use the information to **feedforward**.

Marcia could, therefore, have started her lesson by sharing the rationale for what they were doing. Prior to the discussion and cold-calling sections, she could have stressed to students that they will be receiving multiple (equally important) sources of feedback during the exercise. She could have emphasised that feedback is not learning and that learning requires a follow-up, before then providing time for this to occur.

This feels like it could become a fairly long set of instructions to be giving students initially, and Marcia will rightly be worried about cognitive overload. It would therefore be sensible to reduce this to a simple set of bullet points that can be written on the board as a prompt, such as the following:

1. Value all sources of feedback.

2. Feedback alone is not learning; it requires follow-up.

Pretty soon, with some repetition, these ideas about valuing feedback should be encoded into long-term memory, and therefore only require a much shorter periodic reminder, in addition to the above prompts, for students to successfully retrieve all the relevant information.

What is assessment?

The American Psychological Association defines assessment as 'any systematic method of obtaining information from tests and other sources, used to draw inferences about characteristics of people, objects or programs' (APA, 1999). While this is a definition designed to cover various forms of assessment, Joanna Gorin has noted that it is not always applied consistently across disciplines, and especially in education.

> [Current] educational assessments are most commonly based on administration of a single objectively scored, context-free standardised test. In fact, this practice is so widespread that the terms 'educational assessment' and 'educational test' are often used interchangeably. Such practice assumes at least one fact to be true: it is possible to capture all relevant information to answer our assessment questions at a single point in time and in a single context. This assumption directly contradicts the premise of

APA's standards for assessment – that evidence must be gathered from multiple sources in multiple contexts at multiple times. (Gorin, 2014)

Gorin reminds us that assessment provides the basis on which to make reasoned inferences about individual students (or indeed, departments and whole schools). Any test will only measure from a fraction of the overall knowledge domain, and from this sample we draw conclusions about students' mastery of the whole. However, we cannot confidently assume that performance on the fraction will definitely inform us about the domain as a whole, or even much about the specific parts themselves![1] In this way, Daniel Koretz likens tests to political polls, 'in which the responses of a relatively small number of people are used to estimate the preferences of a far larger group of voters.' Similarly, 'test scores are a small sample and are valuable only insofar as they support conclusions about the larger domains of interest' (Koretz, 2008).

Principles of assessment

It is common to divide educational assessments into two broad categories based on their different purposes and the inferences they allow us to make (Wiliam and Black, 1996):

- *Formative assessments* provide information that can be used to *improve performance*. They therefore prioritise context-specific inferences about particular knowledge or skills.
- *Summative assessments* are designed to allow us to infer a *shared meaning* (most commonly a student's position relative to their peers). They therefore prioritise the ability to form consistent judgements over the ability to pass useful information back to the participants.

In education, assessments are often assumed to serve both purposes where, for example, some practice exam questions are used to both summatively assess progress and provide areas for improvement. This is not always as easy as it seems, however.

---

1   See Boxer (2019) for an excellent and highly accessible introduction to these ideas.

Section 4: Assessment and feedback

Carrie has just finished teaching her Year 12 class about the cognitive explanation and treatment of depression. She wants to assess how well the students have understood the topic, and so decides to give them a short test. She finds two past exam questions, which are:

1. Derek is beginning a course of cognitive behaviour therapy (CBT) for depression. In the session, the therapist asks Derek about what sorts of events may lead to bouts of low mood. When Derek says he thinks that 'everyone at work wants me to fail', the therapist empathises with him and says how upsetting that feeling must be, but then asks Derek what evidence he has for this belief. At the end of the session, the therapist gives Derek a list of three behavioural tasks to do before his next session.

   Using your knowledge of the features of cognitive behaviour therapy (CBT) for depression, explain the actions of the therapist during the session. (6 marks)

2. Outline and evaluate the cognitive explanation for depression. (8 marks)

When Carrie gives these questions to her class and takes in the results afterwards, she is disappointed at how poorly her class has done. The average score is 6/14. Looking at the online exam portal for her exam board, Carrie works out that the combined average score when these questions featured in exam papers was 8/14. She decides to spend the following lesson reteaching some of the content.

Based on their performance on the test, what inferences can Carrie make about her students' understanding of cognitive explanations and treatments of depression? The obvious conclusion would be that her students do not understand the topic very well, and (as she herself concludes) that some of it may need to be retaught. But would this inference be warranted?

Validity in assessments concerns the extent to which the inferences that we draw from the assessments are justified. The validity of formative judgements can require a very different evidence base to that required for summative judgements, however, hence the challenge in drawing both types of conclusions from the same assessment. In the example above, Carrie used two questions originally created as (a small part of) a summative assessment, and also drew some summative conclusions regarding the relative performance of her class compared to other students on those questions in exam conditions. This tells her with reasonable confidence that her students have done worse, albeit with numerous caveats about the difference in the contexts in which the questions were answered (classroom versus final exam), their experience (Year 12 versus end of Year 13) and their cohort (comparing the current class to previous students, who they will not actually be compared against in reality).

However, it is far more difficult to make formative judgements from the results of Carrie's class. What do her students need to improve? The questions chosen require a mixture of AO1, AO2 and AO3 skills (in fact, only the first part of question 2 would explicitly target AO1), as well as a certain level of exam understanding to understand the allocation of different marks available and how long the answers should be. The students require time management skills and extended writing skills, as well as close reading skills in order to understand the questions and stem provided. If Carrie is to make accurate formative inferences about what her students can and can't do, and adapt subsequent teaching accordingly, then she needs to be fairly confident what the underlying issue is. Here, so many potential underlying issues *could* be the cause of her students' poor performance that it is likely that any conclusions drawn about what to do next will lack validity. This is not to say that we can't make any inferences at all but, as Daisy Christodoulou writes in her book, *Making Good Progress?*

> The purpose to which an assessment is going to be put does impact on its design, which makes it harder to simplistically 'repurpose' assessments than it may first appear. And while it may be possible for some types of assessment to fulfil both functions, it may also be the case that this involves trade-offs; the assessment that is able to fulfil summative and formative functions may not be ideal for either purpose. (Christodoulou, 2017)

Section 4B: Assessment in psychology

Given everything we have covered in this section so far, what, when and how should we assess our psychology students so we can make the most accurate formative inferences about our students?

Formative assessment in psychology

Formative judgements are made much easier if we are able to assess particular components of psychological ability in isolation, at least initially. As we have just seen, when we are assessing a skill we ideally want to avoid embedding it within a complex text or in questions that additionally require other skills, because then students may fail to solve the problem either for want of the target skills, the additional skills or because of poor reading – and it would be hard to know which. If Carrie wants to assess her students' knowledge and understanding of cognitive explanations and treatments for depression (their AO1 skills), then she may be better off quizzing them initially on just their knowledge. For example, here are a few possible core questions:

- Outline Beck's explanation for depression.
- What sorts of cognitive biases did Beck and Ellis identify as being characteristic of depression?
- What are the strengths and weaknesses of the cognitive explanation for depression?
- Outline Ellis' version of CBT (REBT).
- What are the strengths and weaknesses of the cognitive treatment for depression (CBT)?

Asking these questions (and more) would allow Carrie to make a much more accurate formative inference regarding the understanding of her students. Once she is confident that this is secure, she can then move on to more complex examination questions that require other skills.[2]

Moving in a structured manner like this also allows the exam questions to provide more valid formative information. If, following success in the core questions, Carrie still finds that the application question is poorly answered, this tells her very clearly where the response needs to be focused, as she can now be much more confident that it is specifically application skills that are at fault (although even here there could be some other aspect of exam technique that would also need to be taken into account). This can be an especially important thing to bear in mind when dealing with topic areas in which many, or even most, of the available past paper questions will assess multiple skills (research methods questions that require application to a stem is a common example).

Of course, not all of this has to happen in a formal written manner. The content of student discussions, responses to teacher questions and a host of other more qualitative sources all allow teachers to **check what they know** and provide valuable formative information. This is why the various example teaching segments dotted throughout the book have featured teachers having set tasks that (whether written, verbal or otherwise) are designed to maintain a high thinking and participation ratio, while often circulating the class at the same time. As well as increasing the chances of all students learning, such activities provide the maximum amount of data for the teacher to draw formative inferences from.

Writing (and using) questions for better formative assessment

If we are to use questions to make accurate formative inferences, then it may be better to write our own rather than using past exam questions. Doing so is clearly a time-consuming and labour-intensive process, but it may allow us to target knowledge and skills more precisely. What exactly do we want students to know? And what do we want to be able to learn from their answers? As an example, we looked in Section 2 at how we could write core questions that allowed us to make formative inferences about meaning making, rather than just about rote learning.

---

[2] Although bear in mind that even retrieval practice of definitions can improve performance on application questions (Badali and Greve, 2023), so it's worth prioritising these foundational skills if time is tight.

Another form of question that can be very useful in helping us to make precise formative inferences is multiple-choice (MCQs). MCQs are effective learning tools that provide useful variety in retrieval activities. They might require participants to retrieve not only why the correct alternative is correct but also why the other alternatives are incorrect, increasing the depth of processing and understanding of the material (Sparck et al., 2016). However, they can easily be misused.

Writing good MCQs

Butler (2018) summarised six 'best practices' in multiple-choice question creation. They are:

- Avoid using complex item types or answering procedures.
- Create items that require the engagement of specific cognitive processes.
- Avoid using 'none-of-the-above' and 'all-of-the-above' as response options.
- Use three plausible response options.
- Create MCQs that are challenging, but not too difficult.
- Provide feedback.

Getting more out of MCQs

Some simple methods to increase the challenge or thinking ratio with MCQs are:

- Delaying revealing the options for a short while, so all students have to attempt to retrieve the answer before being cued by the possible options (van den Broek et al., 2023).
- Explaining why each of the distractor options is incorrect. This takes students' thinking further and demonstrates how well they have made meaning of the topic by probing their understanding of connections between ideas.
- 'Reverse engineering' questions (Harvard, 2021) by asking students to suggest a new question for which each of the other options is the correct answer.
- Asking students to estimate their confidence with particular answers (Harvard, 2020). Students who have practised using confidence-

weighted MCQs are better able to transfer their understanding to new but related questions than those who have used standard multiple-choice practice tests, especially if they have been able to discuss and compare ratings with other students (Sparck et al., 2016).

Summative assessment in psychology

As we have said, the aim of summative assessments is to allow us to infer a shared meaning. The norm in most schools is to err on the side of caution with summative inferences by making them as often as we can. The logic for this is clear: it seems preferable that our students 'know where they are' in terms of their current progress and performance level.

However, the level of evidence required to make valid summative inferences from student work is far higher than that required for formative judgements. Formative inferences require only a possible improvement to be identified, whereas summative inferences rely on inferences about how one student compares with another, or with a general standard (such as an exam grade). The latter is a much bigger claim to make, and consequently requires much better evidence to be made with validity. It's hard enough to make valid summative inferences even when using multiple full exam papers, trained examiners and tens of thousands of students to improve reliability. For example, in final A-level papers the probability of a student achieving their 'definitive' grade (a grade confirmed as 'accurate' by a senior examiner) is only slightly over 0.6 (Ofqual, 2018). Think how much harder this is for individual teachers working on the basis of far less information!

We can distinguish between two different levels of summative inference that a teacher may wish to make about their students. The first, which we will term 'school level' summative inferences, involves establishing shared meanings about students within a particular class or cohort within a school. This could, in its simplest form, involve ranking students according to the marks they have received on an assessment. Such a process is simple, requires relatively little data and provides potentially useful information for teachers about students' performance relative to other members of their cohort.

But this won't tell us about the performance of our students in other areas of the course or allow us to judge their performance relative to all other students (such as in their national cohort) or relative to an exam criterion (such as a grade). We can term this second level of summative inferences 'global level'. These are inferences that we are often really interested in as teachers and – let's be honest – the only level of meaning that parents and students are often interested in. Grades and related summative judgements are familiar, and with this familiarity comes the intuitive sense that we know what they mean – even if that is far from the truth.

This is a problem, because global-level summative inferences (usually paired with feedback such as exam grades) require a huge amount of information and standardisation in order to even achieve the relatively unimpressive levels of reliability that Ofqual found in 2018. Often, the best we can do is to give students entire past papers in conditions as closely resembling the exam as possible. Let's say you use one of the 2019 papers. This allows us to make a summative inference along the lines of:

Had you sat this paper with the rest of the cohort who sat it as a real exam paper in 2019, and assuming that there was perfect inter-rater reliability between me and your exam marker, then you would have achieved a 'B' grade'.[3] Note that this is still a very long way away from saying 'you are likely to get a "B" in your exams'. This latter inference would be far less valid, given the fact that the final exams will feature different questions and be taken alongside a different cohort and at a different time within the course (possibly after a lot more revision than the practice paper!). Now consider how much weaker our inferences would be if we try to make global summative inferences (such as grades) using questions collated from different exam papers (such as what can commonly be found in a 'unit test', for example), from different specifications, or even just using single individual essays (as we often see teachers doing). This is highly unlikely to lead to valid summative judgements.

---

3   And even this, of course, is to take the 'nominal' grade boundaries published by exam boards for each paper at face value. In actual fact, the true grade (which is what we are trying to make inferences about) is only based on the total marks across all three papers.

Furthermore, communicating such inferences can lead to what Jerry Muller calls 'metric fixation', where students focus primarily on achieving a grade rather than doing the learning that the grade is meant to represent (Muller, 2018). Global-level judgements distort the learning process because they shift student attention and motivation from learning goals to performance goals. Students who prioritise performance goals are more likely to focus on their ability rather than effort, evaluating their ability negatively and attributing failure to lack of ability (Ames and Archer, 1988). This can therefore actively inhibit the formation of the sorts of resilient mindsets required to **feedforward** and learn from experience. It can also lead to spectacularly self-defeating behaviour such as trying to cheat (or guess a mark scheme to learn) in mock exams.

Grading also increases students' perception of education as a competitive process of social comparison (reducing the point of education to simply beating their peers, Hayek et al., 2014). Balancing knowledge of grading structures as well as the requirements of the assessment also adds to cognitive load, a burden falling disproportionately on the students who need those resources the most (Feldman, 2023). Therefore, the overuse of summative judgements actually impedes both the process and the purpose of learning (through which those results are ultimately achieved).

Delaying and reducing summative assessments

Given all this, we are clear that psychology teachers should aim to reduce the number of summative inferences they make about their students as a result of assessments. In section 3, we introduced Daisy Christodoulou's 'marathon analogy' as an argument in favour of delaying full essay writing in favour of greater 'training' work on the constituent skills; the same also holds for summative assessments. The fact that the final assessment for students is a summative one does not logically imply that we should be giving them summative assessments early and often. Indeed, as we have seen this may well be counterproductive.

Given the extreme difficulty of making valid inferences from summative assessments, coupled with the potential negative effects for students, we should use these cautiously. An early test (or really any test that we might give, even very late in the course) has a different function: a *formative* function (that of assessing the current level of our students and of identifying how they can improve). As a result, we would argue that the vast majority of psychology assessments, and especially those early in the course, should be *purely formative* (accepting, of course, that school reporting schedules may not always assist in this process).

We can go further, though. Why not aim for mastery in early assessments, but set easier, more knowledge-based questions to accommodate this? If we want to assist in the formative process, then the principles of formative assessment established above hold true. If we accept that exam skills usually develop slowly and require extensive prerequisite knowledge, then (following the marathon analogy principle) it follows that we should avoid including these in assessments until later on in the course, when we can be more confident that the skills will have been established. In addition, given the potential motivational benefits, we both now try to set deliberately accessible early assignments that target core knowledge, aim for mastery and are designed to increase motivation. As ever, it is important to clearly **share the rationale** for what you are doing with the students (and if possible, the parents), as it is highly likely that they will be doing other subjects that are assessing them in different ways.

Section 4C: Feedback that can feedforward

We need to take the provision of feedback seriously, both in terms of the effects it can have on the student (as we have argued, feedback is one of the most powerful potential drivers of classroom improvement, Collin and Quigley, 2021) and on the teacher (marking is one of the greatest contributors to teacher stress levels, Jerrim et al., 2021). Therefore, how can we maximise the benefits to students while at the same time reducing the potential costs to teachers?

Feedback before a task

We've all been in that situation where we are marking some work, feel like we've written the same comment on a student's piece of work for the fifteenth time and are left metaphorically (sometimes literally) banging our heads on the desk. Part of the frustration here is because we know that the main feedback is that they just didn't do the things that we thought we'd already told them to do! In these situations, it's easy to bemoan the lack of thought or effort on the part of our students (which sometimes is the case!), but is there anything we can do to prevent this in the first place?[4] In this section, we will look at some strategies that can support students by laying the foundations for feedback that will feedforward *in advance* of completing the task, such as the use of success criteria, models or exemplars and the process of modelling.

Success criteria

Success criteria clarify precisely what students need to do in order to complete a task. These can relate to the type of content to be included

---

4 A nice analogy here was shared with one of us during their teacher training: you've got to fill in the potholes before setting off down the road!

(such as a particular theory or key concepts), the skills to be demonstrated (such as application or evaluation) or the structure to be followed (such as a PEEL paragraph). More complex tasks such as exam questions may include elements of all three.

Success criteria can act as a useful checklist for students before, during or after a task, and may provide a reference point for students to self- or peer-assess their work. Providing success criteria in advance of the work means that students have a clearer idea from the start of what they need to do. This means that feedback may then focus more clearly on the quality of what they have produced, rather than that the students simply forgot to include or do something. For example, using success criteria effectively could mean feedback can comment on the accuracy of the AO1 detail students have provided rather than that they simply didn't include any.

One important consideration here, though, is that we must ensure that we check for understanding when providing students with success criteria. It can be all too easy to give students a clear list and say, 'Make sure you do all of these things', but to make the mistake of assuming that students know what they all mean. Dylan Wiliam captures this situation clearly:

> I remember talking to a middle school student who was looking at the feedback his teacher had given him on a science assignment. The teacher had written, 'You need to be more systematic in planning your scientific enquiries'. I asked the student what that meant to him, and he said, 'I don't know. If I knew how to be more systematic, I would have been more systematic the first time.' (Wiliam, 2011, p. 125)[5]

One way to take success criteria further is to use them as a pre-submission checklist. This means that students are expected to self- or peer-assess their work to ensure that a number of key criteria have been met (or, at least, attempted) before the teacher gives any feedback. This could include whether they've included the right amount of AO1 or AO2 in a question or whether they've included relevant key terms. Ultimately,

---

5   It's certainly our experience that students can, for example, be reminded to follow PEEL structure in their paragraphs, only to be asked two minutes into the task, 'What does the second E stand for in PEEL?'

we want the students to internalise this process and go through their own mental checklist in the exam, so this is a useful scaffold to support them in developing this level of self-regulation.

Models and modelling

While success criteria may be beneficial to students, it's also the case that they often aren't enough to allow students to be successful by themselves. Consider showing someone a recipe with a list of ingredients only but no instructions on how to actually cook the dish. If we want students to learn to do something properly, they need to see what the finished product looks like (models) and how to get there (modelling).

A model is an exemplar of a completed product; to continue the recipe book analogy, it's a photo of the finished dish. This helps guide students more than success criteria because they can see what they're aiming for more clearly. Exemplar work, carefully chosen to illustrate particular features of quality or to illustrate the expectations of mark schemes, is an important introduction for students into high-quality academic communication. Helping students to learn the features of high-quality academic work will help students not only to become better able to make judgements about their own work, but can also help to reduce some of their anxiety associated with assessments (Yucel et al., 2014). Using exemplars provides students with concrete models for reference (which can be returned to), rather than an abstract and transient teacher description. For some students this is enough because they have sufficient prior knowledge and skills to be able to complete it for themselves.

> **Examples and non-examples**
>
> Just as exemplars can be valuable in helping to draw students' attention to the deeper features of academic quality, it is also true that students can benefit from non-examples of quality. Occasional exposure to carefully chosen examples of less successful essays (or the initial drafts of their peers) can be used for contrast and to illustrate to students the boundaries of the concept under discussion. These would ideally be provided side by side to allow students to more deeply understand the similarities and differences between the true examples and the non-examples. In one recent example, one of us found that adapting an exercise that asked students to analyse scenarios to identify which type of conformity was taking place was improved by adding some examples where conformity was not occurring.

Teachers can, however, have the uneasy feeling that providing exemplars before students complete the work will make it 'too easy', and will therefore impede the amount of 'real learning' that will result. However, students very rarely seem to find any aspect of answer writing 'too easy', and extended written questions are consistently the lowest scoring question type across all specifications. The sort of extensive scaffolding that a good exemplar can provide will assist with some of the skills needed for success, though by no means all of them (they are unlikely to have impact on skills like legibility, writing speed, literacy skills or broader content knowledge, for example).

Even if students did find assignments relatively 'easy' in the presence of heavy scaffolding, would this really be so bad? One of the routes to feedback literacy (and reduced feedback anxiety) is to **secure success** (and celebrate it). If students, especially early on in the course, develop the belief that they can succeed and have experience at doing so, then this can only benefit their self-efficacy (even more so if this success is occurring in the more challenging question types). The opposing approach seems to be to throw students into the deep end and ask them to develop all of the skills required for quality answer writing simultaneously.⁶

Another concern that teachers can have is that providing models will lead to students simply mindlessly copying the exemplar answer. However, if we **share the rationale**, then they are more likely to understand the self-defeating nature of such an enterprise. It is also very easy to tell students that they will be asked to repeat the work unless they show a certain minimum number of acceptable changes to the pre-feedback exemplar, for example, altering some evaluation points, using different evidence to illustrate the points or focusing on an alternative approach to psychology. If we provide students an initial exemplar, then we can also perhaps reduce the level of support in other areas (such as introducing time limits), but extended writing tasks are usually difficult enough even with exemplar materials as a guide, especially early on in the course.

Choosing a good exemplar

A good exemplar should provide an example of what you are trying to get your students to achieve (or an example of what you want them to avoid). This sounds obvious, but there are a number of ways to write high-quality answers. It is common to see material shared between teachers without any reference to whether they actually represent the skills that the teacher is trying to inculcate; for example, students who have been taught to write using a PEEL structure may not learn as much from an essay that does not follow this structure. Shared exemplars may well use different research evidence or structure their answers differently to the way that the class has been taught. Even exemplars provided by exam boards may not necessarily follow all the 'rules' of your class. Another recent trend is for teachers to use AI to generate exemplar essays, but this is even more likely to have the same drawbacks.

This is not to say that these approaches have no value, but teachers should be aware that any deviation from the familiar is likely to require some unpacking in order to match it up to the frameworks and evidence our students have been taught. As long as there is enough overlap with your curriculum and desired writing style, and the differences between the

---

6   Previously, we have been guilty of doing this, and in justifying it to ourselves on the grounds that 'they will need to learn to do all of this together eventually'.

exemplar and the taught approach are clearly signposted and discussed, then less targeted exemplars can still have value. However, students can get very easily confused and sometimes quite anxious to see approaches that seem to differ from their usual modes being held up as successful, so we need to ask ourselves whether the benefits of sharing a 'full marks essay', for example, which uses a different paragraph structure and research evidence actually outweighs the cost. If in doubt, the best solution to this is probably to write the exemplar essays yourself.

Another issue is that some students can become rather obsessed with 'model answers' and presume that if we just give them lots of these then that will secure their path to success. This can easily lead to rote learning and inflexible understanding, which does not actually prepare them to think flexibly in exam situations.

Therefore, what many students need is clear modelling of the process itself, to help bridge that gap. Effective modelling involves more than just showing students something being completed; it's also about exposing the thinking that takes place as we do so. This involves narrating the many decisions we are making as we go along to demonstrate the thought processes we expect our students to do for themselves. Doing this, live, in front of a class can be quite a daunting prospect, and is something that many teachers may not feel comfortable with initially. We may want to plan our modelling carefully in advance, possibly to the extent of scripting and rehearsing exactly what we want to say and do. This allows us to manage our own cognitive load and ensure that we are presenting the best quality model we can (or that we are deliberately including specific errors or misconceptions).

One final consideration here is the complexity of what students are often being asked to produce, and the extent to which they need modelling of and practice doing individual components before trying to combine them. Asking students to write an extended response may require them to demonstrate quite a lot of different elements of knowledge and skills together. Even with careful use of models and modelling from the teacher, it's unsurprising that many of our students' attempts go awry because they are trying to do too many things at once.

Furthermore, our subsequent feedback may be of limited value because there are too many things on which to give feedback, and the likelihood of students not being overwhelmed by this is low. This is why we recommend starting with individual elements and building competence before adding complexity. For example, this could mean students writing only the opening point of a range of different evaluation paragraphs until they are fluently producing effective points, before gradually adding more elements of evaluation paragraphs sequentially. It can also involve using systems to gradually relinquish teacher control once we are confident the students have a firm grasp of the requirements, such as 'I do, we do, you do'.

Investing in self and peer feedback

> Ryan has set his class a selection of short answer questions on observational and experimental research methods. In order to cut down on his personal marking time, Ryan asks his students to swap their answers with each other and peer mark them using a mark scheme displayed on the projector. As the students mark the work, Ryan circulates and looks at the marks and the comments being given out. He is disappointed with what he sees. Students are marking their partners much too leniently, and he spots a number of places where errors or misconceptions have been missed and marked as correct (such as 'field experiment' and 'naturalistic observation' being mixed). In the end, he takes the answers in to mark himself.

We've all been there! Making judgements about work, be it the student's own or someone else's, is more cognitively challenging than simply receiving them. However, the process of asking students to make accurate and useful judgements about work is, as we saw with Ryan's example above, a process fraught with challenge, especially in a limited time frame. Investing classroom time into training students to self- and peer-assess can improve their academic outcomes (Yan et al., 2022), especially if given enough time to practise (Falchikov, 2007), but it would be naive to ignore the daunting prospect of trying to train self- and peer-feedback skills alongside a heavy content load.

The solution to this challenge is to start small, with brief episodes of self- and peer assessment built into routine classroom tasks and initially at a fairly low level, before gradually increasing the challenge and the breadth of feedback that students are asked to provide. This could look something like the sequence below, from left to right.

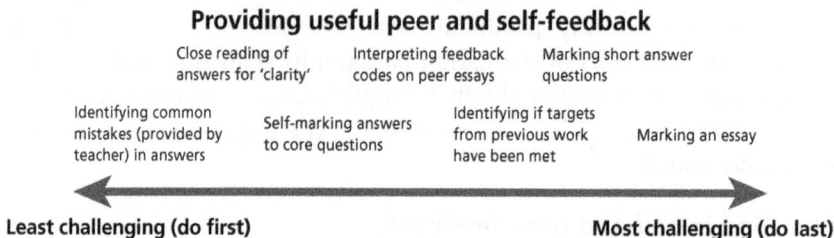

Providing useful peer and self-feedback

Least challenging (do first) ⟵⟶ Most challenging (do last)

- Identifying common mistakes (provided by teacher) in answers
- Close reading of answers for 'clarity'
- Self-marking answers to core questions
- Interpreting feedback codes on peer essays
- Identifying if targets from previous work have been met
- Marking short answer questions
- Marking an essay

Very early on, we want to simply give students the belief that they can usefully assess their own and each other's work, without asking too much of them. This could involve:

- Getting them to check work for predictable misconceptions.
- Encouraging them to read answers slowly and closely, to check clarity. Children naturally overestimate their own abilities (Xia et al., 2023) and will give themselves and each other the benefit of the doubt, unless prompted not to.
- Marking answers to core questions. Self-assessment in this way also allows students to move from rote reproduction to a more nuanced understanding of what constitutes a good answer, understanding the 'range of acceptable meaning' (Cottingham, 2023) for a correct answer.

Moving towards the more challenging end of the spectrum, but before actually asking students to mark work outright, are activities that interpret whether certain specific standards have been achieved in work (either their own or their peers'). For example:

- Seeing whether specific success criteria have been achieved.
- Identifying why certain feedback codes have been recorded.
- Checking whether targets from the previous piece of work have been successfully incorporated into a new piece. This is especially useful for creating a culture of peer accountability, and also for forcing students to actually take action on feedback.

- Comparative judgement, where students are asked to simply decide which answers (from a selection or two or more) are better. Students are usually able to do this with a good deal more accuracy and confidence than when actually applying a mark scheme.[7]

Finally, students can be asked to mark pieces of work. Even here, however, we can build the demands, for example:

- Marking exemplar essays that have been carefully chosen to illustrate the success or failure of a particular skill (as described in the 'choosing a good exemplar' section above).
- Marking whole essays that contain familiar content and formats.
- Self- and peer-assessing work more at the end of units (when there is more extensive prerequisite knowledge).

In all of this it is important to make time to do it properly. This may, for example, involve taking the time to train students to use mark schemes (or some other rubric or marking checklist), and this can be a big investment in the context of a packed curriculum. The evidence suggests that it is worthwhile, however. Students trained to self-assess using marking rubrics show an increased ability to critically assess and improve their own work (Lipnevich et al., 2023).

Feedback and the pedagogical implications

'I've done all that, but they still can't do it!'

You wouldn't be alone if you've ever said or thought something like this. A final thought on how we lay the foundations for effective feedback is that all the best practice in the world will have little impact if students don't actually pay any heed to the information they're being given. As discussed in Section 1, we need to ensure that we **get attention** in order to direct students to the important feedback we are trying to give. We may choose to front-load our means of participation to ensure that students pay attention to the instructions before thinking about the content. We may want to check for understanding by asking questions about process as well as content, ensuring a high participation ratio and sampling appropriately from the class to increase the likelihood that *everyone* knows what they need to do before they start. We need to **manage**

---

7 The same is often true for teachers!

cognitive load by carefully chunking or scaffolding the instructions we give to ensure students don't become overwhelmed with too many things to think about at once. And we need to rigorously **check what they know** and not assume prior knowledge just because we've taught it previously.

Feedback during a task

As discussed, a lot of the time feedback is perceived to be something that is given only after a task has been completed. While post-task feedback has its place, it can often be rather unhelpful at this point, since to act upon it now requires the student to start something anew. Live feedback that is received as a task is being done is more powerful in many ways. Think of this as a driving instructor offering course correction en-route rather than waiting for their learner to crash!

In order to do this effectively, we need to be circulating and monitoring carefully what our students are doing as they progress (or not!) through a task. It's worth noting here that we should try to avoid the temptation to rush in and offer help or feedback straight away. First, this means we are less able to maintain a good radar to ensure the whole class is meeting our expectations. Second, students probably need some time to actually process what we've asked them to do, and so we would do well not to interrupt their thinking at that moment. And third, some students can quickly develop a sense of learned helplessness and low self-efficacy, believing that they are not even able to start a task without our input; this is not going to help develop our students as independent learners.

A further consideration here is whether we plan our path before we start circulating, rather than simply defaulting to the same route, most likely starting with the desk nearest you at the front of the room. We could start with a student who typically works the fastest because we know they have a mindset of 'task completion' over 'hard thinking', and therefore want to ensure they slow down and work with the required care and attention. Or we may go to a typically strong student because we know they're likely to need some additional challenge to stretch their thinking. Or we may go to a student with English as an additional language (EAL) or SEND because we think they're likely to need a little bit of additional support to get them going. Some of these students may be considered useful 'indicators' in that they give us a likely steer as to how the rest of the class is getting on.

There is no correct choice here, and how we plot our path around the room will depend on the context of the lesson, the content, the task and the students. This could be something we deliberately plan before a lesson, when we have time to look at our class lists and perhaps some data to guide our thinking. However, it can also be something decided fairly ad hoc (in fact, we can use our wait time as the perfect moment to make those decisions).

Once we've given sufficient wait time, we then want to know how students are getting on so we can start giving useful, in-the-moment feedback. While many teachers probably do this intuitively, it's actually quite a complex process involving a lot of tricky decisions, and worth breaking down here to consider what those decisions look like. We can represent those decisions visually like the following example:

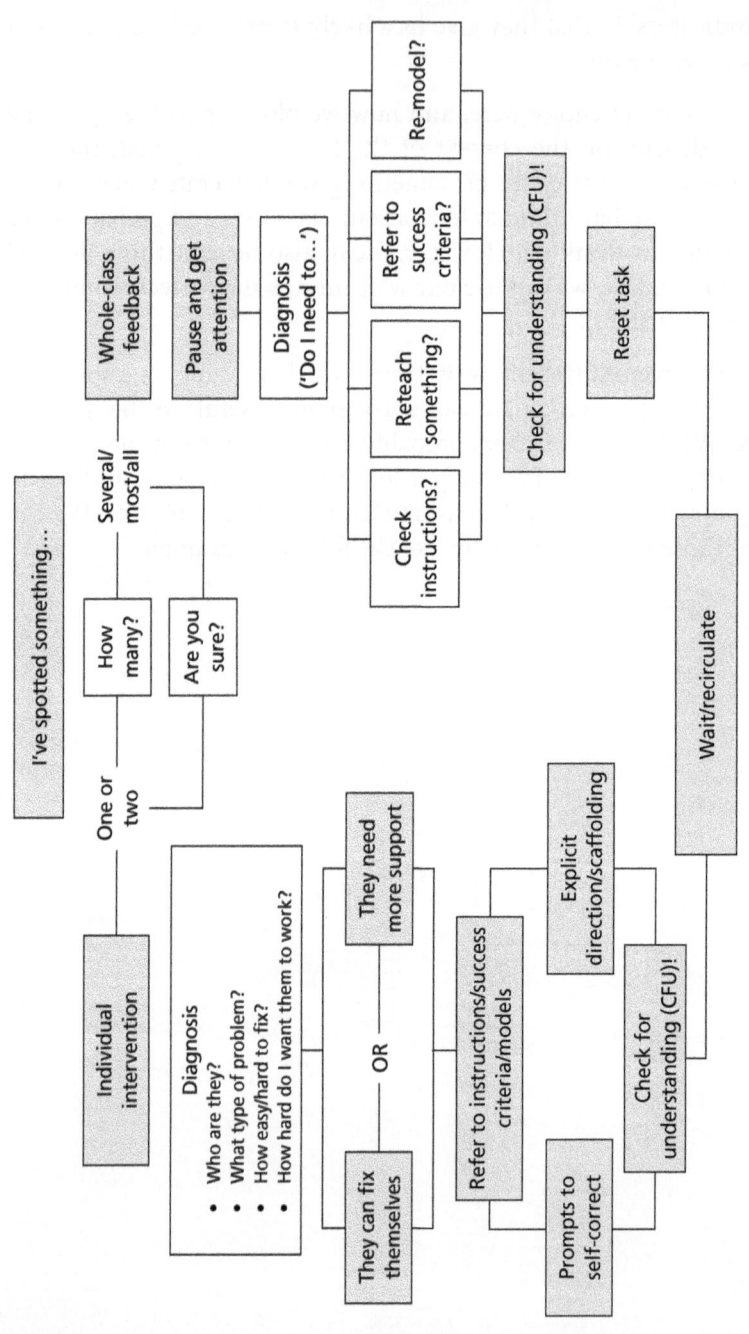

We should note that while we may typically be on the lookout for problems or errors, we may also want to highlight positive work that our students are doing, both to give encouragement and share with the class (remembering that feedback can come from multiple sources, including work completed by others). However, for now we will assume our feedback is corrective. If we've spotted something that we think needs feedback, then our first assessment is the extent of the problem around the room. Is it just one or two students, several, most, or all of them? This will determine what we do next – individual intervention or whole-class feedback – so it's worth making sure.

Individual intervention

We now need to make a quick diagnosis of exactly what the problem is. This could mean consideration of who the student is (including their prior attainment or any learning needs) in order to determine the likely extent of support needed. We need to think about the type of problem that we're seeing, potential causes, how easy or hard it could be to fix and how hard we would be willing to make the student work to fix it. Following this, we could determine whether we think the student can fix the problem for themselves or is going to need more support, and we may choose to refer back to our instructions, success criteria or models before providing appropriate prompt questions or more explicit scaffolding or direction.

Following our feedback, it's important that we once again check for understanding. Just as asking the whole class, 'Do you get that?', is unlikely to yield a valid response, doing this on a one-to-one level is equally fruitless. Students may simply want you to stop bothering them at this point, so saying, 'Yes that makes sense, thank you', may be a quick escape for them! Instead, we need to adopt a more meaningful strategy, such as asking them to explain it back to us, answering a quick question or providing a new example from a different context.

Whole-class intervention

If we've identified that this is a more widespread issue, then we probably want to deal with this with the whole class. If it's that significant an issue, then even the one or two students who aren't struggling with it may still benefit from this feedback, so we need to pause the class. It's important to ensure we do fully get their attention, rather than simply offering our feedback over the class while they continue to work, since there's a good chance they simply won't even notice our input.

What now? Is it just a case of referring back to instructions and checking that students understand the task? Reteach a bit of content that they haven't properly understood? Refer back to our success criteria or models to remind them of what they should be including or aiming for? Or perhaps remodel something for them to remind them of the thinking we're expecting from them? It may well be more than one of these things, and again, whatever we choose to do needs to be supported by rigorous checks for understanding before we let them carry on for themselves.

All of this places a significant burden on our working memory, which means we may not have much capacity to think about other things. This underlines the importance of having well-established expectations and classroom routines in order that we can manage our own cognitive load appropriately. Furthermore, this sort of live feedback process also helps significantly reduce workload in the form of more traditional 'marking'. Rather than waiting for students to complete something and collecting piles of books or paper to take away to mark, much of the feedback has been done in real time. In doing so, we may find that we have a much better sense of how well our students are doing because we spend more time actively reviewing and giving feedback on their work than if we simply wait to take it in; even better, this feedback is more likely to be acted upon by our students.

Finally, we think this form of live feedback represents one of the best forms of responsive teaching there is. A common problem in psychology classrooms with groups of students who vary significantly by academic profile is that they can progress through tasks at very different rates, and we've all found ourselves in the awkward situation whereby some students have already finished before others have barely started. By carefully planning our path and our interventions, this process of live feedback allows us to responsively support or stretch students based on exactly where they are right now, giving them precisely what they need to move them forward. This still requires a certain level of cognitive preparation in our planning (the questions, examples, scaffolds or resources you may need to use in the moment).

Feedback post-assessment

Dawn is returning a set of class essays on the multistore model of memory. They were set for homework last week and she has spent two hours in her evenings marking them. She has annotated each essay with corrections, comments and suggested improvements, and added an overall comment and a mark at the bottom of the essay. Upon returning the essays to the class, she notices that the students tend to immediately turn to the end in order to see the mark, and then compare this mark with those around them.

Some students are obviously very happy with their mark; others take one glance at the paper and put it into their bags rather sheepishly. One or two students ask Dawn, 'What can I do to improve my mark?', and she responds by directing them to the comments that she has made on the essays. Another suggests that Dawn may have made a mistake with the marks and asks her to reread a section. Dawn spends a few minutes at the end of the lesson talking to the class. She tells them that the average mark was quite low, and highlights a couple of common mistakes and comments that she had to write on a lot of their essays.

After students have completed an assessment of some form, a number of questions present themselves. What feedback should we give the students? How should we give it? How much of it should we give? How much time should we spend on it? Dawn is grappling with these questions here, and, as ever in teaching, the answers are not always easy. There are two key general messages to begin with for giving feedback following assessments, before looking in detail at how we can tailor our feedback routines for specific types of assessment.

Give it time...

Actions speak louder than words. If we tell students that feedback is important without providing sufficient time for them to process and act on it, we are actively undermining our own message. Given that feedback is one of the most powerful (and cheapest) tools that we have for student improvement, we as teachers also need to appreciate the giving of it and prioritise it in our classrooms. In the seemingly inevitable annual rush to complete the content-heavy psychology curriculum, feedback can sometimes be the first victim when we look for fat to trim. Siegfried Engelmann (1992) wrote that for most students, 'the amount of practice required is five times what teachers expect', so if we accept that practice plus feedback is required for students to make progress, then this also implies that we may be providing, on average, significantly less feedback that students may actually need.

How can we carve out the time for more feedback? Compared to when we first began teaching, we both now set fewer longer assessed pieces but provide more class or homework time for the feedback to be digested and then fedforward into improved processes. A designated weekly homework to 'follow up on feedback' can help prompt students into taking action on feedback, as well as demonstrating your commitment to the process to the students. Finally, it helps to have clear routines for how to follow up on gaps in knowledge with students and regularly check up on these.

... and give it at the right time

Some student work (such as for essays or tests) will inevitably involve a delay between submission and feedback. In other circumstances, however, there is the potential to provide much more immediate feedback. Which is better? While simple or corrective feedback may be more useful when given immediately, delayed feedback can lead to improved learning for more experienced learners, or when feedback is more evaluative (Carpenter et al., 2012; King et al., 2000). Delaying feedback in more experienced learners has, for example, been shown to improve learning of vocabulary (Metcalfe et al., 2009). Therefore, we suggest that on items such as key vocabulary tests, core questions and multiple-choice questions (for which corrective feedback is likely to be given), teachers should aim for feedback to be as prompt as possible. For more complex, longer written tasks (such as essays and longer exam questions), delayed feedback may prove more effective *once learners are experienced enough*. Given that feedback for such tasks will inevitably be delayed, this is another reason to delay the introduction of essays until you are more confident that delayed feedback will have a more positive, rather than detrimental, impact.

At the very least, marks or grades should be withheld until feedback has been processed and acted upon, as this can improve students' engagement with feedback and their overall academic performance (Kuepper-Tetzel and Gardner, 2021).

Reviewing quizzes and knowledge checks

Quizzes and other knowledge checks will often lend themselves to relatively straightforward corrective feedback. Exactly how absolutist your feedback is (how much you demand word-for-word accuracy, for example) can vary depending on the context and the question. However, the process of giving feedback for such questions would seem to be a pretty simple one; we just tell them the right answer, don't we?

But, what then? Do we suggest that the students go away and *'make sure they know it'*, because *'you will need this stuff'*? Do we get them to write it in their notes in a different colour pen to cue their attention to its importance? Fine – but what then? The big challenge of any feedback is creating lasting change. Sometimes, when the feedback we are giving is relatively simple (as with knowledge quizzes), it can be easy to imagine that the change in students is also easier to create – but this is an illusion.

If we want to **feedforward**, we therefore need to think carefully about how the feedback we provide, and the systems we use to provide it, creates the space for follow-up. Simply getting students to annotate corrections, for example, is unlikely to lead to learning on its own. Tom Sherrington has written critically of routines like this, which he terms 'green-penning':

> Teachers use this with all good intentions but, with my view from the back, I often see that the technique just doesn't work at all for students with significant gaps in knowledge – i.e. lots of green pen – or where any particular correct answer doesn't make any sense to them at all. They go through the motions of writing down the correct answers in their green pen [...] the teacher assumes this has been done successfully and that a knowledge gap has been addressed [...] but all that has happened is that the student has added to the list of things in their book that they don't know or understand. (Sherrington, 2023)

Creating opportunities for follow-up, or further practice (which will help to close the knowledge gap rather than simply identify it), is therefore essential. We need classroom routines about what to do next. In our classes, we aim to:

- Create accountability routines that will facilitate students independently addressing knowledge gaps. If students know that they will be required to demonstrate the learning they have 'green-penned', then they will find it far easier to do something proactive about it.
- Attain mastery for foundational core knowledge through repeated practice until a desired standard has been achieved by all.
- Triangulating classwork, homework and independent work to provide the time and structure for students to address issues revealed in knowledge quizzes, and more generally creating a proactive culture of independent learning (we will discuss this further in Section 5).

Reviewing essays

Following Dawn's disappointment with her students' essays on the multi-store model, she decides to discuss some of their common areas for improvement as a class before setting them another essay as practice. Dawn tells her class that their use of evidence was limited; for example, many students said that the MSM is challenged by case studies such as Patient K.F. (Shallice and Warrington, 1970) but failed to explain how this specifically challenges the model.

Dawn tells them they will be writing another essay (on the working memory model) for homework over the weekend. She makes sure to point out that some of the same evidence (such as the case study of K.F.) could also be used in this new essay, and so it provides the perfect chance to improve. On collecting this second set of essays, she is disappointed to discover that they are generally not an improvement, and many students are using the same study (as supporting evidence this time) but still failing to explain the link back to the model properly.

Most psychology teachers will have had an experience like Dawn's. What more could she realistically be expected to do in terms of providing feedback?

In Section 1, we argued that feedback must **feedforward**, changing the learner for the better. In doing so, we emphasised first that feedback is about what students do, not about what you do as a teacher, and second that the purpose of feedback is not to improve the work but the *learner*, putting the student in a better position to succeed at different challenges in future (for example, avoiding similar errors on new questions). We also introduced a definition of feedback from Carless and Boud (2018): 'A process through which learners make sense of information from various sources and use it to enhance their work or learning strategies.'

If we return to Dawn and accept Carless and Boud's definition, it would seem that, despite all her efforts, Dawn has not really provided her students with feedback at all! Importantly, however, this does not mean that she was entirely at fault. Defining feedback as the process by which students use information provided to enhance their learning immediately places the onus of feedback onto the student and shifts the focus of the teacher from the simple act of 'giving' feedback to creating the conditions and routines where feedback can be acted upon as effectively as possible. This is a hugely powerful shift in our thinking around feedback from what *we* will do, to what *they* will do.

Partial feedback

Paradoxically, one way to make students appreciate feedback more is to give them less of it! Think of a student receiving an essay covered in diligent red pen annotations by the teacher. The cognitive load of digesting all those different comments is huge, and likely to be well beyond the processing capacity of the student in one go. In fact, using eye-tracking, Bouwer and Dirkx (2023) found that students demonstrated superficial processing of many comments, and responded to less than a third of those comments on average, with some students failing to address a single one. Therefore, fewer comments that focus only on the most important improvements are likely to be processed and understood more.

We can also go further. Partial feedback, such as providing codes rather than exhaustive written comments, can force students to actually engage with their work in order to decipher what the problem is for themselves.

This saves the teacher time and supports the development of students' metacognitive skills (such as planning and self-evaluation), as well as removing the problem of them not being able to read our handwriting! Research suggests we could save significant time on marking with no detriment to student outcomes by implementing either code-based marking (Morris et al., 2023) or using a visualiser for group verbal feedback (Kime, 2018).

Of course, we must first **share the rationale** for what we are doing and why, and how students need to respond to make the most of it. When sharing essay feedback for example, we can introduce it by saying:

> You'll see a number of codes or numbers on the essay, which you can look up using the essay feedback sheet. Job number one is to work out why that code is there. Remember, the aim of all of this practice is to give you a detailed understanding of what good writing looks like, and how to avoid common mistakes when doing so. There's no point in me knowing what the problem is if you don't, because then you won't actually be developing your understanding! That's why, as much as possible, you need to work these things out for yourself. If you really can't work out why you have a code or number in a particular place, then discuss it with your partner and see if they can work it out. Ask me as a last resort.

This approach allows the teacher to design feedback responsively to the specifics of the work in front of them (as well as having some things preplanned for those issues we can reliably anticipate).

'Do it again… better'

An easy classroom routine to use with students is 'redrafting' following feedback. This involves simply selecting a section of their work, such as a paragraph in an essay, or perhaps even just a sentence in a shorter answer, and rewriting it to improve it in line with feedback. This ensures that students are immediately able to **secure success**, by demonstrating to themselves that they can produce an improved piece of work than the one submitted. However, improving specific answers in isolation is a limited strategy, as they will likely never see exact questions replicated. After all, the real goal of feedback is to improve the learner, not the work

(Wiliam, 2018). This is why redrafting also needs to be teamed with *targets carried forward*.

Targets carried forward

Out of their review and redrafting process, students can be asked to set themselves one or two targets for a future essay. These targets should be broad and transferable, moving beyond the specifics of the first essay to a more general skill. The targets can then be referred to and incorporated into the next similar piece of work, allowing the students to **feedforward** effectively.

If targets from past work are to be successfully carried forward and acted upon, there is an important role for helping students to keep records of feedback in a way that is simple and accessible. This could be in online journals, bespoke sheets kept in folders or stuck in exercise books, but the important part is that the information and targets they contain are easily implementable into future work. As with any habit, repetition and consistency is then needed to establish it securely, for example, by modelling and explicitly stating that students are expected to refer back to previous targets before any new piece of writing, or by asking students to write previous relevant targets at the top of each new piece of work.

Reviewing tests with students

Reviewing tests can start well in advance of handing back the test papers. It can even start in advance of marking. A very helpful exercise to carry out with students following a test is a revision review, which is a self-assessment of the student's preparation (such as how much time they dedicated to it, what activities they used and how effective they thought it was overall). This helps you to make more accurate inferences from the test performance itself. For example, if a student performs very poorly having rated their preparation as substandard (or non-existent!), we can see that a different path forward is required than for a student who performs similarly but rates their preparation as good. To avoid bias from hindsight, it makes sense to do a revision review in advance of students seeing how they have actually done.

Feedback before the mark?

It's typical in many contexts that students eagerly await the teacher finishing marking the papers, and then a 'feedback lesson' ensues in which, more often than not, the teacher essentially talks the class through the whole paper. While this is undoubtedly thorough and well intentioned, it often fails to lead to any appreciable improvements on the part of the students. Everyone buys into this process (students, parents, teachers and senior leaders) and assumes that this is so obviously beneficial that the practice goes unquestioned.

But an important question we should ask is whether students actually need their marked paper in front of them in order to start receiving useful feedback. Although there may be one or two questions on which everyone did badly, the likelihood is that performance in the paper will be quite varied across the cohort – this can have significant effects on the extent to which the students pay attention to feedback. Students who've scored poorly may be too annoyed (or feel unfairly maligned!) to process the feedback meaningfully while those who got full or high marks on a question may well switch off because they don't feel they need to listen. It may be easy to sympathise more with the latter, but it's likely that those students will still benefit from some well-delivered feedback in order to **secure success** in future, similar questions. Therefore, it may be useful to start giving (depersonalised) feedback as soon as you've started marking, long before the students get their papers back. This approach has several advantages:

- **Managing cognitive load.** You can drip-feed feedback over a number of lessons, focusing on just one or two things at a time rather than giving it all at once.
- Increasing the participation ratio. Students usually can't actually remember what they wrote or how good their answer was. No-one can just switch off because they can see they got high marks; they all need to pay attention because it *could* apply to them. And for those who did do well on something, a bit more practice to reinforce is never a bad thing. Everyone benefits!
- No haggling. Students are only focusing on the knowledge and skills we want them to develop. There's no time wasted on students comparing scores with their peers, arguing over whether someone

should have received an extra mark or having to explain repeatedly to various students why they didn't get a mark.
- Focusing on mastery, not performance. Students are receiving no performance feedback – they don't know their score or grade (and know they're not getting it at the end of the lesson). They aren't being distracted by this because the focus is solely on the knowledge or skill and they haven't got their paper in front of them. This also takes the emotion out of the process.
- **Feedforward**, improving the student, not the work. By talking about the issues in the absence of the paper, we're improving the students' general knowledge and understanding. When they start to do some independent practice, they are developing their ability to answer questions in different contexts, not just improving a specific answer from the paper.

Reduce competition

'What did you get?' This is the classic post-feedback question, often asked within milliseconds of papers landing on desks. Assessment can sometimes feel like a competitive endeavour; it involves all students going through the same process, with their performance often quantified in a way that allows for easy ranking. What could therefore be more natural for a student than to see where they rank against those around them? Competition, however, values performance, whereas feedback is all about learning, and so while competition can have its place in the classroom, this place is not during feedback tasks. How, then, can we minimise competition during feedback?

The first and most obvious method to reduce inter-student competition is to remove the means of making comparative judgements in the first place (marks, percentages or grades). We have already discussed the issues around summative judgements (and we consider this further below), but here the main message is that competition can be reduced by removing numerical marks and grades where possible, or, at the very least, withholding them initially to allow students to process the feedback first. Where this isn't possible, it can be helpful to fall back on rules and routines, such as reviewing test papers in silence, which reduces the ability for students to make comparisons with others and generally focuses their attention on processing their feedback.

Identifying targets for improvement

At an individual level, we have to consider which areas of a test we want to give feedback on, and which things we want students to address. Students often do some form of self-assessment here (for example, the retrieval-augmented generation (RAG-ing) of their answers) but treat their conclusions with caution. For example, students can fixate on questions or topics that are worth the most marks, rather than identifying deeper structural issues such as contextualisation in evaluation. Therefore, it may be more appropriate, for the most part, for us as teachers to explicitly direct them to work on the things that we know are going to be most beneficial.

One method that can encourage students to identify more general areas for improvement can be to keep a tally of marks lost in different categories – in effect, to perform a content analysis, if you want to get some free research methods revision in as well! For example, one of us uses the following three categories:

- Psychology understanding – Where the students don't fully understand the concept or ideas clearly enough to write about them effectively.
- Revision of knowledge – Where they *do* understand the concepts, but simply didn't know them well enough in the exam.
- Exam technique – Where they haven't fulfilled the requirements of the question.

Of course, we still need to treat this information with caution and use it in tandem with our knowledge of the assessment, and of the student; for example, students may be unable, or unwilling, to identify the most appropriate category. Even if they can do this accurately, then identifying the general area may not always be helpful. It could be that lots of marks were lost for exam technique, for example, but all of them for different aspects of technique, in which case identifying 'exam technique' as an area for focus seems too vague to be useful.

Scoring can also be biased by higher tariff questions all being put into one category. The process therefore helps to identify main areas of *potential* focus, and then to see if the marks being lost in these areas can be coherently grouped into more specific ones (for example, 'Writing enough to get all the marks available', or 'Knowing when to apply to a stem' could be exam technique issues that account for a significant proportion of the issues in that category). If we can find such groupings, then students have a clear target for development that is likely to improve the student, not the work.

The final stage is then to get students to commit to targets for development. The more specific the better; it's best to provide students with a clear idea of how these can be implemented and what success would look like. (For the issue of 'Writing enough to get all the marks available', a suitably specific target may be, 'Write a minimum of one sentence of explanation more than you would normally do for each question'.) If issues of revision or knowledge have been identified, then this target setting may involve details of when, where, what and how they are going to study moving forward. This makes it much easier to hold the students to these commitments (or at least to check in to see how they are going).

Section 4D: Interpreting test and exam results

Whether we are analysing a class test or external exam results, we often end up asking ourselves similar questions. 'What have I learned from my students' performance?' 'Why do I think this was?' 'What am I going to do about it?' As discussed in Section 4A, the first of these questions is hard enough to answer with any validity. The second, where we are supposed to draw causal links between performance and some feature of our approach, is even harder. The third, where we have to isolate proposed interventions to rectify this, can be nigh on impossible! At its worst, test and exam analysis in schools (especially the dreaded 'exam report') invites us to make the link between our students' performance and the quality of education that we have provided for them. James Popham likens this to 'trying to measure temperature with a tablespoon':

> Tablespoons have a different measurement mission than indicating how hot or cold something is. Standardised achievement tests have a different measurement mission than indicating how good or bad a school [or a teacher] is. Standardised achievement tests should be used to make the comparative interpretations that they were intended to provide. They should not be used to judge educational quality. (Popham, 1999)

This is not to say, of course, that it's not helpful to be interested in how our students have done or to analyse their performance, nor to claim that the quality of our instruction and curriculum does not play a role in their progress. It is merely to stress that we should be very cautious in drawing overly simplistic links when analysing results (of course, this unfortunately applies to our successes, just as much as it does to our failures!).

When to grade? How to grade?

Regardless of the fact that it will be very hard to grade work of less than a full exam paper (taken under exam conditions) with any degree of validity, we will inevitably have to give out grades at some point!

Grades, far more so than formative feedback, can have unintended consequences for the recipient. Unexpectedly positive results can lead to complacency and reduced future effort or distort their approach through 'metric fixation'. Negative results could dispirit some students or cause them to withdraw entirely – though of course they may also be a powerful motivator for others. This variety of possible outcomes is one reason why Professor Becky Allen emphasises the importance of having a clear 'mental model of responses to grades for your students'; in other words, anticipating very clearly the possible responses of our students, given both their individual characteristics, the social norms and feedback literacy of the class, and also of the school as a whole (Allen, 2019a). For example, we need to consider (or second-guess!) what changes we can make to our students':

- Beliefs about their attainment.
- Beliefs about their ability to learn and get better.
- Desire to keep playing the competition of trying to be the best, maintain their position or avoid the bottom rung.

If we conclude that there are potential positives to providing grades (such as perhaps providing motivational impetus to students who seem to be coasting), and that the student will respond in the desired manner (as best we can anticipate), then there may be value to giving out grades. Allen describes this as 'the ethics of telling un-truths', writing: 'Validity of inference should not be the only concern in working out how you are going to report attainment at school' (Allen, 2019b).

There is therefore a pragmatic case for the (very) judicious use of grading as a part of our feedback. There is also a rather pressing need, in that you are almost certain to be required to do this at intervals by your school's reporting policy. With these in mind, then, we must consider when and how we may do this in a way that (as much as possible) balances accuracy and positive effects on the students.

Grading from anything less than a full, timed exam paper

If you do have to grade a piece of work at a time when you don't really have suitable information for such an inference (anything less than a full, timed exam paper), then there are a number of options available to us. We could create our own bespoke grade boundaries, sacrificing some of the validity of the inference but prioritising the motivational message. This could, for example, involve setting relatively 'high' grade boundaries (the 'kick up the backside' approach) or relatively 'low' ones (the 'warm and fuzzy' approach). Alternatively, we could assess students against a smaller section of an exam paper but use the grade boundaries published for the whole paper. Another option is to 'stratify' the assessment grades against the 'average' distribution of grades for your centre (for example, for the last three or five years, so if you would normally expect 10% of your cohort to get an A* and 20% to get an A, you give the top 10% of students in the assessment an A*, and the next 20% an A and so on).

Both of these latter two approaches aim to prioritise the validity of inference slightly more. Our preference of all of these options is the final 'stratified grading' approach. It is an approach that can be applied across all different assessment types and retain some meaning, both of which are in contrast to the 'whole paper boundaries' approach.

When reporting a grade at any time (but especially when doing so using imperfect evidence), it is useful to **share the rationale** for the distribution and allocation of the grades. Sharing some of the uncertainty around these processes can help to alleviate some of the potential harmful motivational effects of getting a grade, at both ends of the spectrum; successful students will feel less complacent if the grade seems less authoritative, and less successful students will be less disheartened for the same reason. Furthermore, for assessments that are less than a full paper, it's likely that the difference between grade boundaries will be quite narrow, often down to a handful of marks depending on the total available in the assessment. Highlighting this is important to underline to students the caution needed when receiving a grade; it may be that a slightly different answer to just one question on the assessment could make the difference between two grades, or the marks available on one higher-tariff question covers two grade boundaries.

If not a grade, what about a mark?

Perhaps you are suitably convinced by the arguments presented above that regularly grading student work may be unhelpful, but giving marks is ok, right? It's worth examining this further.

Scores on individual questions are not very reliable

It's hard to really trust your own marking. Even trained senior examiners work to a 'tolerance level' of disagreement, which is acceptable when scaled up across the whole qualification but more significant when it's just one piece of work. What if one teacher gives an 9/12 score, but another colleague reads it and suggests 8, or 10, or 7, or 11? There's no objective way to determine who is correct, and we may even change our own mind on a second reading (we've all been in those standardisation meetings, right?) or over time (what may have gained a 7/8 in 2017 may only score 5/8 in 2021 because the way that examiners are trained to interpret and apply marking criteria may change across different examination cycles).

It's also virtually impossible to avoid inherent biases while marking. Even when anonymised, over time we get to know students' handwriting (or sometimes even phrasing), and we are no more able than anyone else to avoid the effects that our knowledge of particular students has on our judgement of their work.

Scores or percentages encourage extrapolation to grades

While it may be true that a student who typically scores, say, 80% on essay questions is then likely gain an A* grade, virtually no student actually performs this way in real exams. But this extrapolation is what our students do all of the time. They either figure out for themselves (based on analysis of some grade boundaries) – or teachers tell them – that 75% is equivalent to, say, an A grade, and then apply that rule to all pieces of work, no matter how many marks it may be worth. The more the content of the test is predictable (the students know what will be on the test to a decent degree in advance), the less valid those inferences become (Wiliam, 2020). Therefore, the kind of smaller assessments that students typically complete throughout the year (such as end of unit tests) are not valid indicators of future performance because the domain sampled is too small, and the content of the assessment is too predictable.

Scores on individual pieces of work don't tell students 'where they are'

'But I need to know how I'm doing' is probably the most common refrain from students when we withhold a mark. This seems like a legitimate argument, but does a score *actually* tell them how they are doing? Whether completed at home or in class, our assessments are often scaffolded to some extent (possibly quite heavily) by teachers first (for example, writing a plan together beforehand, or testing material just covered in lessons), and therefore again makes the work completed unrepresentative of real exams.

Scores or grades on single pieces of work rarely help students improve

What are students actually meant to do with this information? As noted above, if it doesn't really tell them 'where they are' with any real degree of accuracy, then how does this information help them get better? It may, perhaps, provide the motivational prod of realising how below standard their answers are, but we can achieve this in our feedback without giving scores and in far more specific and effective ways. As with grades, the presence of numerical marks decreases the likelihood of students engaging with any feedback comments (Kuepper-Tetzel and Gardner, 2021), which means that number is not going to help students get better.[8]

As we have argued, there are times when giving a mark or grade is appropriate (or, at least, required). When students have completed work under authentic exam conditions, we believe it does truly reflect those students' capabilities, such as when they have been assessed on a significant sample of the domain (such as mocks), or when they are considering their future options and need a rough benchmark of potential attainment to guide their choices. But beyond these specific, and infrequent, situations, there is probably little merit in it.

---

[8] As one teacher commented in a staff survey one of us conducted on marking: 'Most students are not bothered about listening to feedback – once they've got their mark – as they are either chuffed and not bothered or cheesed off and not in the mood to listen!'

Making useful (and generalisable) formative inferences from tests and exams

At class or cohort level, a review of a test needs to help the teacher identify the main *shared* areas of weakness, such as topic areas, exam skills or assessment objectives. Then depending on the extent of the weakness, we may reteach a particular skill or topic area, or otherwise set some work designed to improve student understanding. Often the first step that teachers will take when looking at exam results is to see how their students have done on each question, known as 'question level analysis' (or QLA).

Question level analysis

> Juliet is analysing her students' performance in a test, for which she used questions from the 2019 AQA paper 1 exam. She looks at the average cohort of her students in three questions in the social influence section.
>
> | Question | Cohort average |
> |---|---|
> | Question 1: Outline two explanations of resistance to social influence. (4 marks) | 74% |
> | Question 4: A survey shows that fewer young people are smoking today than in 1987. Using your knowledge of social influence processes in social change, explain possible reasons for this change in behaviour. (6 marks) | 47% |
> | Question 5: Discuss ethical issues in social influence research. (8 marks) | 47% |

Where should Juliet focus her attention moving forward? It seems fairly obvious that there are two areas in which her students have scored significantly worse. Should she therefore devote more class time to social change and ethical issues in the new year? Not necessarily. As Professor Becky Allen points out when writing about QLA:

> There can be a serious issue with using test questions to guide topic selection for re-teaching. Not only do test questions often cover multiple topics, but they also vary by question difficulty (both in question type and content). (Allen, 2021)

In this case, it may simply be that the social change question is harder than the resistance to social influence question (this would hardly be surprising, as it is an AO2 application question compared to simple AO1 recall). In another test with different questions, the performance on these topics may be reversed.

One way around this is to also look at relative performance, compared to national averages from the 2019 exam for example. Juliet does so.

Question	Cohort average	National average
Question 1: Outline two explanations of resistance to social influence. (4 marks)	74%	74%
Question 4: A survey shows that fewer young people are smoking today than in 1987. Using your knowledge of social influence processes in social change, explain possible reasons for this change in behaviour. (6 marks)	47%	44%
Question 5: Discuss ethical issues in social influence research. (8 marks)	47%	53%

This certainly changes the inferences that we can make. We can now see that, comparatively, Juliet's students actually overperformed on question 4, and only performed in line with the national average on question 1. The poorest relative performance was on question 5. So, can we now say that Juliet needs to devote more time to teaching ethics in the new year? Not necessarily.

For starters, exams are not designed to provide formative information about areas for improvement. Question 5 is a mini-essay question requiring both AO1 and AO3 information and will therefore draw on a large range of knowledge and skills. Is the poor performance related to knowledge of ethical issues? The ability to evaluate them? The ability to structure an essay clearly? The ability to write enough in timed conditions? Knowledge of the marks available and how to get them? A combination of all of these? Analysing the low percentage score on this question does not help us to know which area to target moving forward.

It could also be that this is just a low frequency question, of the sort that is unlikely to come up again in anything like the same format. If this is the case, then simply stuffing more into our curricula (known as 'the backwash effect', Prodromou, 1995) may not be the best response. Furthermore, it could be that the difference in performance can be explained by timing. Students tend to do better at questions on topics that have been more recently taught, and so differences in performance could be explained by Juliet's choices in curriculum sequencing rather than anything specific about her content or delivery (such as having chosen to teach social influence early in Year 12).

Of course, if this is the case, then later units in Juliet's sequence should show a relative benefit. As it is not possible to move all units later in the sequence, this relative disadvantage for units taught at the start of the sequence may have to be accepted, on the assumption that sequencing effects will even out over all the exam papers. Finally, it may have been an issue of timing, in that the question on which students performed poorly was towards the end of the paper when they were rushing to finish. Perhaps if it had been the first question on the paper, they would have done much better.

A final major problem when drawing conclusions from performances on exam questions is that there may be *testing-teaching mismatches*. We all teach in slightly different ways, emphasising slightly different aspects of our course in line with our expertise, interests, experiences, curriculum choices and relationships with the students. Sometimes, just by chance, this aligns with the way that particular items on tests are presented… and sometimes it doesn't. The 2023 AQA exams had two great examples of these (great as examples, we mean, not great for the poor teachers on the receiving end of them!). The first was question 6 on paper 1:

> Explain the results of this experiment [results which demonstrated the primacy and recency effect] with reference to the multi-store model of memory. (4 marks)

The primacy and recency effect and the 'serial position effect' study of Glanzer and Cunitz (1966) is not named in the AQA specification, and so this question created a large teaching-testing discrepancy between students who happened to have been taught them as part of their curriculum and those who hadn't. Indeed, the examiners' report mentioned this explicitly: 'Some students completely understood the results of the experiment and could explain them in the context of the multi-store model. Knowledge of the primacy and recency effects was often put to good use.'

Teachers who had made a reasoned decision not to include this research on the primacy recency effect (indeed, one of us had recently removed it from their curriculum on the grounds that there was better and more accessible supporting research available for the multi-store model!) were penalised, unfairly in our opinion, by the research scenario so closely mirroring a study that some students would be familiar with while others would not. It also means, however, that those teachers should not draw too many conclusions should a QLA demonstrate poorer relative performance on that question.

Another teaching-testing mismatch was question 4 of the AQA paper 3 in 2023, in the 'Issues and debates' section. The question was:

> There are different levels of explanation in psychology, ranging from reductionism to holism. Discuss levels of explanation in psychology. Refer to one or more topics in your answer. (16 marks)

The question was generally poorly completed (the national average score was 40%, or 6/16). The relevant specification point is: 'Holism and reductionism: levels of explanation in psychology. Biological reductionism and environmental (stimulus-response) reductionism.'

The phrase 'levels of explanation' does occur in the specification this time, however, in the subsequent (lively) discussion on teacher forums it became clear that many teachers had taken the view that the most important core content for this point was to cover the reductionism-holism debate at various levels, without specifically emphasising the phrase 'levels of explanation' much, if at all. Another cohort of teachers had mentioned the phrase, but not in enough detail for all but the most cognitively flexible of students to be able to base a whole essay around it (this may of course have been the examiners' aim). A final group were lucky enough to have emphasised the idea of levels of explanation throughout the topic, and so were vociferously defending the question as entirely fair and appropriate.

Here we have a testing-teaching mismatch (or match, in the case of the third group of teachers), but in all cases it is hard to conclude that students' performance has not been influenced by chance factors in the choice of emphasis or approach. It would be easy, perhaps, to conclude from this that the third set of teachers were in the right and had done a better job for their students than those who simply prepared their classes for a 'classic' reductionism-holism debate essay; but then again, the question in the AQA 2020 paper 3 was much better suited to exactly this approach:

> 'Psychologists sometimes adopt a reductionist approach to their investigations when they want their research to be objective and empirical.' Discuss reductionism in psychological research. Refer to the statement above in your answer. (16 marks)

In this case, the teachers who had spent their lessons emphasising the concept of 'levels of explanation' may have wished they had simplified things, which is a testing-teaching mismatch in the other direction. We're willing to bet that some poor souls may even have simplified their units following 2020 to reduce references to levels of explanation, and then found that they actually needed them after all in 2023! If this is you, then you have our sympathy.

How could we then use question level analysis usefully? Becky Allen summarises her thoughts as follows:

> Teachers will naturally want to think about how well a class collectively managed to answer particular questions on a particular test because it is a good starting point for a process of enquiry and reflection into what their classes understand and can do. To that end, the QLA reports provided by standardised test providers have some value as a starting point for inference, but only if used with great care. (Allen, 2021)[9]

This warning is really meant for the use of QLA following a public exam (or a test that uses questions taken from a previous exam), when the data available (such as national averages) may inform us more than when we only have our own cohort context. It should therefore be noted that QLA

---

9   Of course, many of these caveats also apply to inferences made from whole exam papers as well.

for other less standardised assessments (such as in-house unit tests) are likely to require even more caution in their interpretation.

Return to the domain, not the sample

So, although QLA *may* give us an idea of the existence of a problem, it is unlikely to be able to tell us exactly what the problem actually is. Therefore, a good rule of thumb when returning to topics is to *return to the domain*, the broader topic area, rather than the specific question (for example, factors affecting eyewitness testimony rather than 'weapon focus'). We then, of course, need to **review regularly**, even more frequently than we may do otherwise given the weakness that we have identified with that domain. A final consideration is whether this weakness may be related to any feature of the lessons or resources that students have received. Often, the best time to update resources for a subsequent year is just after an assessment has taken place.

On the next page is an example as part of the follow-up to an assessment on the topic of obedience.

Follow-up questions to check the domain, not the sample

1. Suggest one strength of using volunteer sampling in Milgram's experiment. (2 marks)
2. Explain one ethical strength of Milgram's research. (3 marks)
3. Describe locus of control as an explanation for obedience. (2 marks)
4. Using Milgram's study as an example, explain what is meant by proximity. (2 marks)

↑

1. Milgram used volunteer sampling to recruit the participants for his study of obedience. Suggest one weakness of using volunteer sampling in this study. (2 marks)
2. Identify one ethical guideline breached in Milgram's study and explain why this may be justified. (3 marks)
3. Describe authoritarian personality as an explanation for obedience. (2 marks)
4. Using Milgram's study as an example, explain what is meant by momentum of compliance. (2 marks)

Students initially identify questions in which they have lost marks and engage with a mark scheme to work out why they lost those marks. Then they are assigned some different questions that target related information or skills (for example, if they struggled writing about a strength of something they now have to give a weakness of the same thing). This is likely to be more beneficial to students (and more indicative to teachers) than simply looking at the mark scheme and rewriting the answer to some specific questions (which often involves students simply copying out mark scheme bullet points anyway!).

Exam paper analysis

Whole exam papers, which sample from a broader section of the specification content and skills, will naturally offer more reliable information about our students' performance. If our students relatively underperform on a whole exam paper, then we can conclude with slightly more confidence that there is *something* going on. The trade-off is that as the amount of material examined and the number of questions included increases, it can become increasingly difficult to identify exactly *what* that something is.

As with QLA (and indeed all assessment inferences), this does not mean that we don't engage with the uncertainty, or that we refuse to make any changes. Instead, in keeping with the **WHAT mindset**, we treat them with the appropriate levels of caution and ensure any hypotheses we have for explaining student performance are also *triangulated* through other sources of information (such as previous years' exam performance, tests, classwork, quizzes and teacher professional judgement), and that any interventions planned as a result of them are initially simple and manageable.

Of course, such a cautious approach to interpreting exam results does not always sit easily with the senior leadership team (SLT), who are sometimes more reassured (or pacified) by overly simple diagnoses of problems and next steps. Paradoxically, however, the more we appreciate the uncertainty inherent in the process of assessment, the more confident and forthright we need to be in resisting such pressure from school leaders. In 2022, one of us found that the AQA paper 3 was comparatively the weakest for that cohort. In 2023, having (thankfully) made no changes to the curriculum, pedagogy or resources, it was comparatively the strongest.

An assessment and feedback calendar

Below is a calendar for assessment and feedback activities that we think, in an ideal world, would provide us with a balance between being able to make high quality formative judgements and sufficient summative judgement points, as well as creating a gradual build-up of skill and challenge and offering the chance for students to **secure success**. It is designed for A-level, although it could be easily adapted for GCSE. Naturally, adaptation to school reporting and assessment schedules may be needed; indeed, neither of us are able to follow exactly this calendar due to such constraints. Importantly, this calendar is only supposed to outline a schedule for larger assessments. It does not include sources of our everyday formative judgements as teachers, such as classwork and homework. Indeed, having a relatively light assessment calendar of major assessments only works if we are taking every other opportunity to learn about what our students can and can't do.

	Assessment activities	Feedback provided
Year 12 – Half term 1	**Key term quizzes** **Core knowledge quizzes**	Purely formative and mastery focused
Half term 2	As above	As above
Half term 3	As above, plus... **Short answer exam Qs AO1 and AO2**	As above
Half term 4	As above, plus... **Short answer exam Qs AO3** **Heavily scaffolded essays**	Purely formative No marks or levels given for essays
Half term 5	As above, plus... **Moderately scaffolded essays**	School-level summative No marks or levels given for essays
Half term 6	As above, plus... **Full exam paper in exam conditions**	End Y12 exams: global-level summative
Year 13 – Half term 1	As above, plus... **Lightly scaffolded essays**	Mostly formative No marks or levels given for essays unless in exam conditions
Half term 2	As above	Mostly formative No marks or levels given for essays unless in exam conditions

	Assessment activities	Feedback provided
Half term 3	As above, plus... **Unscaffolded essays**	Mocks: global-level summative
Half term 4	As above (but **frequent** essay practice)	Mostly formative No marks or levels given for essays unless in exam conditions
Half term 5	As above (but **frequent** essay practice)	Mostly formative No marks or levels given for essays unless in exam conditions

Summary of Section 4

In this section, we've considered the why, what, when and how of assessment, and hopefully one message should be clear: assessment is a tricky business, and all inferences should be made with caution! As we discussed in the introduction, taking an evidence-informed approach means considering what the research tells us but also filtering that through our own experience and professional judgement, alongside taking account of the specific context of our settings. Decisions about things like whether or not to award marks or grades, or whether to use written comments or whole-class feedback, may be partially determined for us by our school systems, but we still have a lot of choice in this regard, particularly in our 'day-to-day' assessment practices.

Perhaps the key principle is that whatever we choose to do is, in fact, a deliberate choice made with consideration of what we think will benefit our students the most in any particular instance, and not just a default approach. We don't have to set endless amounts of practice essays, write comments all over them and award a mark and grade just because that's what we've done in the past and what others seem to do. It may be that in the right context this is genuinely the most appropriate thing for our students, but other approaches deserve some consideration because they could serve students better. As long as this is a reasoned decision, supported by evidence in some form, it remains true to our view of an evidence-informed approach.

While assessment is clearly a key priority for anyone teaching psychology, it's often those leading the subject or department who ultimately need to make some of these decisions. In Section 5, we consider this challenge alongside some of the other key areas that we think contribute to running a successful evidence-informed psychology department.

References

1. Allen, R. (2019a). *Writing the rules of the grading game (part II): The games children play.* https://rebeccaallen.co.uk/2019/04/25/grading-game-part-ii/
2. Allen, R. (2019b). *Writing the rules of the grading game (part III): There is no value-neutral approach to giving feedback.* https://rebeccaallen.co.uk/2019/04/27/grading-game-part-iii/
3. Allen, R. (2021). *The limited uses of question level analysis.* https://rebeccaallen.co.uk/2021/12/29/the-limited-uses-of-question-level-analysis/
4. American Psychological Association, American Educational Research Association, & National Council on Measurement in Education (1999). Standards on educational and psychological testing.
5. Ames, C., & Archer, J. (1988). Achievement goals in the classroom: Students' learning strategies and motivation processes. *Journal of Educational Psychology, 80*(3), 260.
6. Badali, S., & Greve, M. (2023). Can successive relearning enhance performance on application-based exam questions? *Journal of Applied Research in Memory and Cognition.* Advance online publication. https://doi.org/10.1037/mac0000137
7. Bouwer, R., & Dirkx, K. (2023). The eye-mind of processing written feedback: Unraveling how students read and use feedback for revision. *Learning and Instruction, 85,* 101745.
8. Boxer, A. (2019). What to do after a mock? Assessment, sampling, inferences and more. A Chemical Orthodoxy. https://achemicalorthodoxy.co.uk/2019/03/26/what-to-do-after-a-mock-assessment-sampling-inferences-and-more/
9. Boxer, A. (2021, November 7). Golden silence. Achemicalorthodoxy. https://achemicalorthodoxy.co.uk/2021/11/07/golden-silence/
10. Butler, A. C. (2018). Multiple-choice testing in education: Are the best practices for assessment also good for learning?. *Journal of Applied Research in Memory and Cognition, 7*(3), 323-331.
11. Carless, D., & Boud, D. (2018). The development of student feedback literacy: Enabling uptake of feedback. *Assessment & Evaluation in Higher Education, 43*(8), 1315-1325.
12. Carpenter, S. K., Cepeda, N. J., Rohrer, D., Kang, S. H., & Pashler, H. (2012). Using spacing to enhance diverse forms of learning: Review of recent research and implications for instruction. *Educational Psychology Review, 24,* 369-378.
13. Christodoulou, D. (2017). *Making good progress?: The future of assessment for learning.* Oxford University Press-Children.
14. Collin, J., & Quigley, A. (2021). Teacher feedback to improve pupil learning. Guidance Report. *Education Endowment Foundation.*

15. Cottingham, S. (2023). *Ausubel's meaningful learning in action* (T. Sherrington, Ed.). John Catt.
16. Engelmann, S. (1992). *War against the schools' academic child abuse*. Portland: Halcyon House.
17. Falchikov, N. (2007). The place of peers in learning and assessment. In Boud, D., & Falchikov, N. (eds), *Rethinking assessment in higher education* (pp. 138-153). Routledge.
18. Feldman, J. (2023). *Grading for equity: What it is, why it matters, and how it can transform schools and classrooms*. Corwin Press.
19. Glanzer, M., & Cunitz, A. R. (1966). Two storage mechanisms in free recall. *Journal of Verbal Learning and Verbal Behavior, 5*(4), 351-360.
20. Gorin, J. (2014). Assessment as evidential reasoning. *Teachers College Record, 116*(11).
21. Harvard, B. (2020). Confidence weighted multiple-choice questioning. *The Effortful Educator*. https://theeffortfuleducator.com/2020/06/22/confidence-weighted-multiple-choice-questioning/
22. Harvard, B. (2021). Reverse engineering the multiple-choice question. *The Effortful Educator*. https://theeffortfuleducator.com/2021/11/19/reverse-engineering-the-multiple-choice-question/
23. Hayek, A. S., Toma, C., Oberlé, D., & Butera, F. (2014). The effect of grades on the preference effect: Grading reduces consideration of disconfirming evidence. *Basic and Applied Social Psychology, 36*(6), 544-552.
24. Jerrim, J., Sims, S., & Allen, R. (2021). The mental health and wellbeing of teachers in England. *Quantitative Social Science-UCL Social Research Institute, University College London: London, UK*.
25. Khoza, H. C. (2024). Dialogue with students as a valuable tool in teacher inquiry for professional development: A narrative of a novice science teacher educator learning about student interaction in biology classrooms. *Journal of the Scholarship of Teaching and Learning, 24*(1), 44-57.
26. Kime, S. (2018). *Reducing teacher workload: The "re-balancing feedback" trial*. DfE. London.
27. King, P. E., Young, M. J., & Behnke, R. R. (2000). Public speaking performance improvement as a function of information processing in immediate and delayed feedback interventions. *Communication Education, 49*(4), 365-374.
28. Koretz, D. M. (2008). *Measuring up*. Harvard University Press.
29. Kuepper-Tetzel, C. E., & Gardner, P. L. (2021). Effects of temporary mark withholding on academic performance. *Psychology Learning & Teaching, 20*(3), 405-419.
30. Lipnevich, A. A., Panadero, E., & Calistro, T. (2023). Unraveling the effects of rubrics and exemplars on student writing performance. *Journal of Experimental Psychology: Applied, 29*(1), 136-148.
31. Metcalfe, J., Kornell, N., & Finn, B. (2009). Delayed versus immediate feedback in children's and adults' vocabulary learning. *Memory & Cognition, 37*(8), 1077-1087.
32. Morris, R., Gorard, S., See, B. H., & Siddiqui, N. (2023). Can a code-based approach to marking and feedback reduce teachers' workload? An evaluation of the FLASH marking intervention. *Oxford Review of Education, 50*(4), 552-569. https://doi.org/10.1080/03054985.2023.2258779

33. Muller, J. (2018). *The tyranny of metrics*. Princeton University Press.
34. Ofqual (2018). Marking consistency metrics - An update. Available at: https://assets.publishing.service.gov.uk/government/uploads/system/uploads/attachment_data/file/759207/Marking_consistency_metrics_-_an_update_-_FINAL64492.pdf (accessed 23rd December 2023).
35. Popham, W. J. (1999). Why standardized tests don't measure educational quality. *Educational Leadership, 56*(6), 8-16.
36. Prodromou, L. (1995). The backwash effect: From testing to teaching. *ELT Journal, 49*(1), 13-25.
37. Sherrington, T. (2023, June 27). The view from the back: The trouble with 'green-penning' (corrections). Teacherhead. https://teacherhead.com/2023/06/27/the-view-from-the-back-the-trouble-with-green-penning-corrections/
38. Sparck, E. M., Bjork, E. L. & Bjork, R. A. (2016). On the learning benefits of confidence-weighted testing. *Cognitive Research: Principles and Implications, 1*(3) https://doi.org/10.1186/s41235-016-0003-x
39. van den Broek, G. S. E., Gerritsen, S. L., Oomen, I. T. J., Velthoven, E., van Boxtel, F. H. J., Kester, L., & van Gog, T. (2023). Optimizing multiple-choice questions for retrieval practice: Delayed display of answer alternatives enhances vocabulary learning. *Journal of Educational Psychology, 115*(8), 1087-1109. https://doi.org/10.1037/edu0000810
40. Wiliam, D. (2011). *Embedded formative assessment*. Solution Tree Press.
41. Wiliam, D. [@dylanwiliam]. (2018, March 23). This is why I keep on pointing out that the main purpose of feedback is to improve the student and not the work… [Tweet] https://twitter.com/dylanwiliam/status/977265017279033344
42. Wiliam, D. (2020). How to think about assessment. Donarski, S., & Bennett, T. (eds), *The researchED guide to assessment* (pp 21-36). John Catt.
43. Wiliam, D., & Black, P. (1996). Meanings and consequences: A basis for distinguishing formative and summative functions of assessment?. *British Educational Research Journal, 22*(5), 537-548.
44. Wiliam, D., Brookhart, S. M., Guskey, T. R., & McTighe, J. (2020). Grading in a comprehensive and balanced assessment system. *Learning Sciences International Dylan Wiliam Center*. https://www.dylanwiliamcenter.com/whitepapers/gradingpolicy-paper.
45. Xia, M., Poorthuis, A. M., & Thomaes, S. (2023). Why do young children overestimate their task performance? A cross-cultural experiment. *Journal of Experimental Child Psychology, 226*, 105551.
46. Yan, Z., Lao, H., Panadero, E., Fernández-Castilla, B., Yang, L., & Yang, M. (2022). Effects of self-assessment and peer-assessment interventions on academic performance: A meta-analysis. *Educational Research Review, 37*, 100484.
47. Yang, C., Li, J., Zhao, W., Luo, L., & Shanks, D. R. (2023). Do practice tests (quizzes) reduce or provoke test anxiety? A meta-analytic review. *Educational Psychology Review, 35*(3), 87.
48. Yucel, R., Bird, F. L., Young, J., & Blanksby, T. (2014). The road to self-assessment: Exemplar marking before peer review develops first-year students' capacity to judge the quality of a scientific report. *Assessment & Evaluation in Higher Education, 39*(8), 971-986.

Section 5: An evidence-informed psychology department

Lauren

Lauren is planning her first department meeting in her new post at the start of term. Her team includes an experienced member of staff who has been teaching at the school for quite a few years, and an early career teacher (ECT) who is joining the school along with Lauren. Lauren has also noted that all classes are only allocated to a single teacher, and this is different to her previous experience of sharing classes. The numbers of students enrolled on the course is currently looking healthy, although there has been a notable drop-off in students continuing with the second year of the course. A review of new students' GCSE grades highlights a real range in prior attainment, and she has had a flurry of last-minute emails from the Head of Sixth Form about students switching courses. Lauren wants to discuss how psychology is perceived by prospective students and parents, their expectations about psychology, and the experience of students already on the course. She also wants to know more about the range of resources available (textbooks and slides) and how they are used.

Leadership roles can come quickly for psychology teachers. We often work in relatively small (sometimes even single person) departments, and therefore it is not unusual to be taking on managerial responsibilities while still learning the nuts and bolts of how to teach it in the first place. As a result, we offer our thoughts for how we can apply evidence-informed thought processes to middle leadership. Of course, all advice given here needs to be filtered through the restrictions of existing whole school policies, as schools vary enormously in the ways that they do things. A key part of becoming a successful middle leader is to find ways to coordinate your own departmental aims with the ongoing aims and strategies of your school. That's not to say, of course, that these thought processes and principles aren't relevant to any teacher of psychology, as in a well-run department everyone should be making evidence-informed decisions.

WHAT to change (or not)?

The **WHAT mindset** for evidence-informed teaching can be useful when considering any of the areas of department management that are discussed in this section.

- Why – Why do you want to make a particular change (or not)? What issues have you identified? What evidence do you have that these issues are having an impact (or not)? What evidence do you have that your chosen strategy is likely to lead to improvement? What specific benefits can you point to that are likely to result from your suggestions?
- Humble beginnings – How can the strategy be implemented by any or all teachers in the simplest way possible, causing the least disruption to existing routines (accounting for individual differences in pedagogical styles and preferences)?
- Assess – What information will you collect to determine the success or otherwise of the strategy? Initially, this could just be simple qualitative information about adoption and fidelity to the plan you have presented, but later this may also include student-centred data.
- Tweak – How flexible are you prepared to be in order to get any or all members of the department implementing the strategy? What bumps did you discover in the road, and (again) how do you know that these problems are actually problems? If successful, how can the strategy be scaled up, or standardised further? The EEF guidance for implementing change in schools (Sharples et al., 2019), for example, suggests planning well in advance of any change being

implemented how the change will be sustained, including guidance on how to 'continuously acknowledge, support and reward good implementation practices'. This is useful advice for departmental practice, as well as for individual teachers or whole schools.

Section 5A: Managing a psychology department

Alignment versus autonomy

Throughout this book, we have tried to emphasise best *process* over best *practice*. What is best practice for one teacher in their own individual context may not be the same as for another. Using research evidence provides us with both the starting points (such as 'retrieval practice is likely to lead to improved recall and understanding') and the tools (such as the **WHAT mindset**) with which to go through the best process. The outcomes may be different, but the thought processes should be comparable.

In light of this, it would be pretty hypocritical to argue that the only way is our way. When leading a department, the challenge is to create the conditions for all colleagues to be able to follow the best process. This allows enough freedom for colleagues to be able to maximise their own particular strengths to everyone's benefit, while at the same time providing enough cohesion for the department to be able to develop in a coherent direction. Psychology teacher and headteacher Dan Rosen has written about the tension between alignment and autonomy and how this tension inevitably means that some compromises will need to be made (Rosen, 2023), both at a departmental level (perhaps ceding control to individual teachers over some issues) and an individual level (aligning colleagues' practice in other areas).

As we covered in Section 1, autonomy is a key component of motivation. We want colleagues who feel empowered and trusted enough to experiment, and so we need to ensure that departments make at least as many compromises towards protecting colleagues' autonomy as are asked for in the other direction, at least as a starting point. If good evidence can be collected that there is a problem and that more (or less) alignment might help to solve it, then this balance may shift. Equally though, we need to hold our colleagues to the same standards; the further they deviate from a shared plan, the greater the strength of their justification needs to be. We must be happy to push colleagues to reveal their evidence base and their knowledge of why they are using particular strategies. This could, of course, show us that their approach is more justifiable than our own, in which case we may need to align ourselves to them, rather than the other way around!

Alignment, when used well, can provide a shared language and set of aims for a department. It is difficult to discuss the nuances of implementing, for example, checks for understanding, unless there is a relatively consistent understanding of what that means and what sorts of activities may be examples of it. Shared curriculums and resources can save time and workload spent reinventing wheels.

Importantly, this is not an argument for identikit lessons, but merely a suggestion that planning can be made quicker and more effective if it involves 'cognitive preparation' for the lesson rather than resource creation. Alignment can be especially important in areas of teacher life that disproportionately affect their wellbeing, such as time spent marking (Jerrim and Sims, 2021). Less experienced colleagues may benefit more from higher levels of support and alignment than more experienced ones. Ensuring that early career teachers use efficient and effective pedagogical practices may have emotional benefits; for example, first-year teachers who are using evidence-informed pedagogical strategies have been found to report higher levels of school-based wellbeing (Mennes et al, 2023). Alignment may also be especially important for teachers of shared classes, whose students can then transfer habits and routines between different teachers more efficiently.

Alignment of opportunity, autonomy of choice

A compromise is to ensure that colleagues have the *opportunity* to align themselves very closely, but also the freedom to deviate should they so wish as long as they remain true to the overarching aims (and can justify the rationale for the deviation convincingly). For example, in a psychology department this could involve:

- Fully resourcing a curriculum (e.g. with booklets, textbooks or slides), but without mandating how each tool is used.
- Having a scheme of work that describes set points by which time a certain topic should be completed, but without requiring lesson-by-lesson compliance, or providing some freedom over the teaching sequence where appropriate.
- Fully equipping classrooms for alignment (e.g. mini-whiteboards in all psychology classrooms), but accepting that colleagues are in charge of if, and how, they are used.
- Having a shared strategic direction (e.g. 'retrieval practice' as a departmental target) and providing models for what this may look like in your classroom (e.g. a starter quiz of prerequisite knowledge), but allowing colleagues to incorporate retrieval in other forms and at other times of the lesson if they prefer to do so.

Timetable allocation (solo versus shared classes)

Which is better, shared classes or a solo teacher? If you're in a department of more than one teacher, then it's likely this is a decision you'll need to make. There may be constraints that take the choice out of your hands, but given the freedom to choose, which is the best option? As with all things psychology, there's no one right answer here.[1] Let's consider some of the different issues, and the relative advantages of each approach.

	Shared classes	Solo teaching
Accountability for outcomes	Less conducive to a 'blame' culture if one class underperforms relative to another. Increases emphasis on collaboration between teachers.	May be easier to identify successful practice or areas for improvement with only one teacher involved.
Progress through the curriculum	Slower pace (for teachers) as they see classes less frequently. More time for consolidation and eases planning pressures.	Better sense of student progress as you have taught all the material and know exactly how they've encountered it. Supports development of expertise across the curriculum and helps foster synoptic thinking between topics.

---

[1] As if to underline this point, at the time of writing, one of us prefers solo teaching, while the other prefers shared classes!

	Shared classes	Solo teaching
Student-teacher relationships	Can relieve or share the burden of a 'difficult' class. If there is consistency of approach between teachers, then this can also help to depersonalise issues (i.e. it's not just about teacher X).	Get to know students much better, both academically and pastorally.

Resources

As we saw with Lauren, it's not uncommon to arrive in a department that is 'fully resourced'. What this actually means and what one may do with those resources are different questions entirely. Here we consider the relative merits of the most commonly used resources: textbooks, booklets and slides.

Textbooks – worth it or not?

This may be a heretical question to some, but it's worth considering. Textbooks have changed somewhat since we first embarked on our psychology studies. In recent years, two main trends have dominated the market: first, textbooks are now tailored to individual exam board specifications, and second, they tend to contain far less information and more boxes and pictures! Given the considerable outlay they represent, it's worth doing some research and thinking carefully about the pros and cons of adopting them before blowing the department budget.

Advantages	Disadvantages
Time saved in creating other resources (e.g. booklets and worksheets) may be enormous. If they are to be used year-on-year, then the costs are also mitigated to some extent.	They are not written as teaching resources in the same way booklets sometimes are. They may contain some practice questions or other activities, but these are not specific to your setting, curriculum or students.
Quality is usually undoubtedly better than any teacher produced resource, at least from an aesthetic perspective. This makes them seem more reliable (legitimacy of authority!).	Cost relative to booklets is very high, and there are considerations like how to ensure students keep them in good condition and return them at the end of the course (unless the students pay for them themselves, of course).

Advantages	Disadvantages
Students (and parents) like them, and they feel like a reassuring crutch. We shouldn't underestimate the importance of this.	They are not always accurate (Steuer and Ham, 2008), but students may still choose to trust them over what their teachers tell them!
Specification coverage is ensured, and many essentially have the specification written out in various ways, which can be helpful.	Rigidity and coherence. Textbooks usually present material in the default specification order, which may not represent the best curriculum sequencing.
They contain example questions, often with answers.	Some of these are of dubious quality, and do not sequence information or activities in a way that shows any understanding of the science of learning. Many textbook activities prioritise general student activity and busyness over deep engagement and thinking about the material.
For teachers, multiple reference points can be very useful for finding content.	There are multiple versions for each exam board, all with their own strengths and limitations, which can make choosing one to adopt for students difficult.
Some offer digital companions, which provide lots of additional resources and support for both teachers and students.	The range and quality of digital versions is inconsistent across the market, and influenced by market forces.

Using booklets

Many teachers also use booklets to support their teaching, although the variety in what they look like and how they are used is quite significant.[2] However useful they can be, booklets represent a significant investment in time and effort and so you need to be sure they will be worth it. Here are some of the key advantages and disadvantages of using booklets.

Advantages	Disadvantages
Printing and photocopying may involve significant costs, but this will still be far cheaper than buying a set of textbooks for every student.	There is a danger of rigidly trying to stick to the prescribed activities in the booklet and not responding or adapting to the progress students are making.

---

2   Again, case in point, both of us use booklets, but these look considerably different.

Advantages	Disadvantages
Although there is significant front-loading, once booklets are printed you shouldn't need to be regularly spending time printing and copying resources or worksheets on a lesson-by-lesson basis.	Teachers may learn or want to try something new but feel constrained by what's in the booklet, or that they are expected to use the same resources as everyone else.
Teachers can select specific content (e.g. which supporting evidence) and tailor the right level of detail to suit their context.	If students also have access to a textbook, it can be confusing for them if they find different information or studies in there – and some students seem to trust textbooks more than us!
Students have ownership of booklets, as they can highlight and annotate to their heart's content knowing they don't have to give it back at the end of the course for another student to use.	Students can lose them! While they can be easily reprinted, the students also lose all the 'thinking' they have done in the form of notes, practice answers, etc.

If you are going to adopt booklets in your teaching, there are some useful principles to consider in order to make these a more effective tool. Some of these relate specifically to the use of booklets as a shared resource across a department, while some are relevant to the individual teacher.

Decide and agree the teaching sequence before you start writing

If a well-sequenced curriculum is essential to help students **make meaning** of what they are learning, then we may choose to deliver units and topics in an order that does not match up with the specification, and our booklets should be presented in the same way. This allows for smooth progression through the curriculum, rather than jumping around the textbook out of order.

Agree common elements

While course content may vary, there is a high degree of repetition in what students are required to do across the curriculum (learn new information, apply it, evaluate it). This means we may develop certain types of regular activity to facilitate the kinds of thinking we want, such as glossary pages, evaluation tables, essay planning grids, core questions quizzes and sample practice exam questions.

Standardise the format

For common elements, it's helpful to both students and teachers to have each specific element formatted in exactly the same way every time they are used. This helps **manage cognitive load**, because students are not thinking about a new activity structure each time they do it and **positive habits free up processing capacity**, meaning they can focus their thinking on the substantive content instead. This also makes it easier for teachers to check work quickly while circulating in order to **feedforward**, because they are consistently looking in the same place each time.

Agree design principles

If booklets are going to be the place that students spend a lot of time looking, then we ought to spend a reasonable amount of time and effort ensuring they are designed in ways that are conducive to learning. Minimizing the number of different fonts and formatting styles (headings don't need to be in bold, italics and underlined!) and ensuring these are consistent throughout a booklet certainly helps. Reducing the amount of extraneous written information helps **manage cognitive load**, while careful use of paragraphing alignment or tabulation can help draw attention to the most salient pieces of information. Careful use of graphics or pictures that support students learning avoids the plague of extraneous images that distract students from the information they're supposed to be learning.

Finally, remember that a booklet is almost never a finished product.[3] A teacher copy of the booklet is essential so you can annotate as you go along, as well as using it as part of the cognitive preparation for lessons. This may include scripted questions, pre-prepared examples (or non-examples), key ideas or highlighted technical detail. Where possible, it's also useful once you've taught a specific area of content to review the relevant booklet pages immediately to look for any changes (for example, typos, detail to add or cut, restructuring and resequencing, space for questions, etc). Our experience here is that while we often try to use the 'gain-time' in the summer term once Year 13 are on exam leave to complete these kinds of tasks, they are made immeasurably easier if you have an annotated version to work from.

---

3   We have both been teaching the same units for many years and our booklets have been updated every single year.

Slides

We may have in our setting a shared drive populated with resources, including a set of slides for every lesson. While this may be a real boon in some respects, there are also a number of issues with the way in which slides have become the default tool we use to deliver our lessons. There can sometimes seem to be an implicit expectation[4] that every single lesson must be accompanied by a set of slides; these expectations may be shared by senior leaders, students, parents or members of the department. Sharing slides with students may be a useful way to help them consolidate lesson content or support them in catching up on missed work through absence (although a well-designed booklet is likely to be more helpful here). Having pre-prepared slides can help if colleagues need to cover a lesson for you or support their own planning, especially if they are teaching an unfamiliar topic.

However, a crucial principle is that we should never be led into thinking that the slides *are* the lesson. Slides may provide us a way to present information clearly, but it is all too easy – as we have both painfully found out in the past – to allow lessons to descend into 'death by PowerPoint'. It's important to remember that presentation packages such as PowerPoint were never intended as vehicles to deliver content, rather as visual aids to act as prompts during a presentation.

As with booklets, there are some key ideas that need consideration if we are using slides in lessons.[5] Many of these principles may apply to other resources (or lesson planning in general), but given the ubiquity of slides as the mode of delivering lesson content it's worth considering them in this specific context here.

Design slides that are fit for purpose

Sometimes it is far better to work with a blank slide and plan the layout from scratch (perhaps inserting text boxes or shapes manually) than to try to bend content to existing designs. This allows us to take more care

---

4   Although one of us has worked in a school where this was in fact mandated for all teachers, and with all slideshows following a prescribed, standardised format.
5   Of course, it's also worth pointing out that it's perfectly possible to teach effectively without using slides at all.

with the arrangement of information on the slide, considering things like sizing and alignment to support students in making meaning.

Careful use of animation

Done prudently, animation is the perfect way to carefully **manage cognitive** load by introducing information in small chunks and in a sequence that allows students to gradually **make meaning**. However, this does come at a cost, as creating effective slides can take considerable time and effort.

Plan the level of information you want on a slide

We frequently see slides filled with far too much information, which can cause cognitive overload and impair learning. Therefore, we may want to limit our slides to very short points, keywords or diagrams that we then add to with our verbal explanations or annotations during the lesson.

Slideshows are linear; lessons may not be

A danger with slideshows is that they can lead to teachers inflexibly following the slides from start to finish, which can limit our ability to be responsive in the lesson. We need to make sure we have done the requisite cognitive preparation, including having planned the likely examples, extra practice, models or checks for understanding that we can anticipate we may require, and be confident to deviate from our slides should the need arise.

Some pre-planned, fixed elements are helpful

While flexibility and spontaneity are important, there are also times when there are parts of our lesson that would benefit from being carefully planned and scripted in advance. For example, we may include a particular question to check for understanding that will determine whether the class is ready to move on (also known as 'hinge questions'), or a sequence of core questions summarising the learning.

Visuals and diagrams – using slides versus drawing live on the board

If you want to represent information in a way that supports students making meaning, then using some kind of graphic organiser can be really powerful. We may choose to have these pre-prepared on a slide, or we may decide to draw them live on the board (or under a visualiser). Pre-prepared visuals are easier for re-use (especially if you teach the same content to multiple classes) and can help manage teachers' cognitive load (we won't have to draw and talk at the same time). They may also be slightly better quality, depending on your artistic skills! Live drawing, on the other hand, may be better for cueing attention, can allow greater responsivity and allows us to more explicitly model our thinking processes (Zhang et al., 2024).

Developing psychology content knowledge across the department

Regardless of whether you have a psychology degree or are teaching psychology as a 'non-specialist', maintaining and developing strong subject knowledge is an important priority. In fact, even if you have studied psychology at undergraduate and postgraduate levels, you may still find quite significant gaps in your knowledge when faced with an A-level specification for the first time. It was certainly our experience that the early years of our teaching career involved teaching ourselves a significant volume of content that we'd never encountered before – or, at least, had completely forgotten about! But once we get beyond mastering the topics covered on our exam specification, can we stop there?

Why is subject knowledge so important?

Teacher subject knowledge is often split into 'content knowledge' (knowledge about the subject area in general) and 'pedagogical subject knowledge' (knowledge related to the teaching of the subject), both of which may contribute independently to student outcomes (Baumert et al., 2010). The example teaching segments and dialogues throughout this book provide models of pedagogical content knowledge and the thinking behind them, so here we will focus just on the wider aspect of content knowledge, which on its own has still been found to be an important factor in teacher effectiveness and student achievement (Metzler and Woessman, 2012).

Why does a relationship between teacher content knowledge and student achievement exist? First, knowledgeable teachers are more likely to be able to place essential knowledge we must teach students (the core) and the broader context in which this sits (the hinterland), allowing the students to **make meaning** and think flexibly. Second, it can allow us to answer students' questions. While we should have absolutely no problem with saying "I don't know" to students, it is also helpful to be able to answer as many questions as possible! This partly comes down to our own confidence, and partly to credibility and trust; we want the students to have solid faith in us as the experts in the room, and those who trust their teachers report higher academic self-confidence and motivation (Al Nasseri et al., 2014).

For example, while teaching brain scanning techniques, one of us was asked how it is that PET scanners can detect neurotransmitter activity while an fMRI can't, a bit of knowledge that had never seemed necessary to understand previously. Googling proved inaccessibly technical, even to someone with fairly decent starting knowledge, and in the end the author in question had to ask some (probably) quite daft-sounding questions to some very patient biology and chemistry teachers in order to understand this clearly. (In case you're interested, at a very simplistic level the answer is simply that you would use a different kind of radioactive tracer).

Here are some other great student questions. How many could you answer if asked by a student right now?

- How can atypical antipsychotics work to both increase *and* decrease dopamine activity at the same time?
- Where are testosterone receptors?
- What's the latest that you can give someone a hemispherectomy? (As an aside, this led to the discovery of one of our all time favourite paper titles: 'Functional hemispherectomy in adults: all we have to sphere is sphere itself', by Robert Gross in 2020.)
- Was the blind man in the Miles et al. (1977) case study blind from birth?
- Are there gender differences in dreaming?
- Is retroactive interference more common than proactive interference?
- Is operant conditioning embedded in classical conditioning?

- Do people with highly superior autobiographical memory (HSAM) experience false memories?
- Is sound processed in the auditory cortex contralaterally?
- If taxi drivers had larger posterior hippocampi in the Maguire et al. (2000) study, would other parts of their brain be smaller to compensate?
- How does caffeine actually work at the synapse level?
- How do pharmacologists know whether or not to create a reuptake inhibitor (e.g. SSRIs) versus agonist (e.g. Abilify, a partial dopamine agonist) when treating depression?
- Can pain be a conditioned response (i.e. without activation of nociceptors)?

Finally, deepening our knowledge helps us better appreciate the difference between our own expert knowledge and the novice status of our students. Being an expert teacher is about being able to bridge the gap; going through our own change in understanding, developing our schemas to a more sophisticated, connected state reminds us of this process, and better informs us about how to support students to do the same.

How can we maintain and develop our subject knowledge?

In psychology, developing content knowledge will primarily rely on maintaining up-to-date connections with research findings. This can be in fields that are specifically course-related (especially given the importance of 'balancing the classic and the contemporary' when curriculum making, or simply areas of wider interest (and perhaps ideally both). This can be achieved by:

- Signing up for academic journal alerts. Many journals will allow you to subscribe to alerts that provide an overview of new articles published. Open access journals will allow you to access the full article for free.
- Google Scholar alerts for researchers. Google Scholar is a powerful tool, and great for revealing a wealth of previously published material. You can set up alerts to follow particular academics and receive alerts whenever they publish new work or whenever their work is cited by other researchers (broadening your net to include relevant research

that you may never have heard of). You can go even further and ask for the algorithm to alert you to 'related research', which includes anything new that is similar to work previously published by your chosen academics.

- Social media. Social media is, for all its many faults, an amazing source of academic communication. Academics converse, argue and share research findings with each other, and the open nature of many social media platforms means that you can drop in on it! Teacher social media can also be a hugely valuable source of support (and resource sharing; there are active psychology teacher groups supporting each other across X, WhatsApp, Facebook, Threads, Bluesky and many others). Ask around and join them widely.
- Contact academics. If you have a particular question about research that you cannot solve, or if you are struggling to find an open access version of a research paper, then contacting academics is often a very enriching experience. Researchers are almost always delighted to hear from interested teachers and are keen to help (it is a great boost for them to know that their work is being read outside of academic circles). One of us recently emailed David Turk, a researcher at Bristol University, to query a reference that was being used (or misused, as it turned out) in a lot of A-level resources.[6]
- Join a subject organisation. The Association for the Teaching of Psychology (ATP) is a teacher-led organisation supporting psychology teachers. It publishes a magazine, runs CPD courses, offers advice and support via email and social media and organises an annual conference. Similarly, the British Psychological Society (BPS) shares new research on its website, and you can sign up for a weekly email 'digest' that summarises a range of recent studies, often with clear links to curriculum content.

---

[6] Specifically, they were citing Turk et al. (2002) as showing that split-brain patient J.W. learned to talk out of his right hemisphere, and so criticising the idea that speech always has to be lateralised to the left. This is erroneous – the correct citation should be Gazzaniga et al. (1996).

Section 5B: Developing a subject culture

We would probably all agree that it is a desirable thing to create a 'subject identity' in psychology students. Social norms are powerful and relatedness (or a sense of belonging) is a key driver of intrinsic motivation. But beyond the superficial strategies such as referring to 'us' and 'we' as psychologists, we need to know what it is to *be* a psychologist. What is the unique disciplinary knowledge required by psychology, and how should we best embrace and celebrate it? The unique features of psychology we identified in Section 1B as our disciplinary fundamentals provide a good basis for this. We can celebrate and refer to these in our classes, for example, in classroom displays.

We can also encourage a sense of shared identity in a more practical sense, such as:

- Shared communication channels with all students. If you have messages or notices that are relevant to all students, then communicating them through a shared channel can, as well as saving teacher time, help to remind students they are part of a larger unit (especially if you reinforce this through the language choices you make when doing so, as outlined above).
- In-class communication networks. At the same time, you also want each individual class to have their own sense of identity and purpose. This is entirely anecdotal (and may confuse correlation with causation), but some of the most successful classes we have taught have been those who have communicated and worked together best outside of the classroom, often assisted by something like a WhatsApp group.[7]

---

[7] We should be aware of trends in social media, though. One of us recently suggested this to a class and was met with a mix of confusion and horror at the mention of using something as anachronistic as WhatsApp!

- Knowing all the students, if you can. For some larger centres such as FE colleges who have hundreds of students, this is impossible; for single person departments, it's inevitable! For everyone in between, it's something to aim for and prioritise. If (especially as a head of department) you are able to give a smile and a nod and a greeting using their name to *all* psychology students (or as many as possible), then you reinforce a shared identity beyond individual classes.

Student recruitment

Ensuring psychology has a strong profile is important for recruitment. In the introduction, we saw that psychology is typically a very popular choice, but that doesn't mean we should rest on our laurels and assume we will always have packed courses. And, of course, not every student necessarily thrives; this means making our 'pitch' to increase the chances that:

- We get students who are more likely to be successful on our courses, not just those that are choosing it because they weren't good at anything else.
- We get students choosing it as a first option, rather than because they were just looking for something to fill up the third or fourth slot in their timetables.

Ensuring this happens is tricky, especially as we may be beholden to those who hold the purse-strings and just want courses filled. Some suggestions for how we can ensure we have a broad reach with our recruitment messages, and ensure the right messages, are as follows:

- Assemblies for KS3/KS4. If you work in a secondary school (as opposed to an FE setting) then you have a captive audience.
- Taster sessions. These need to be pitched in a way that sells both the interest and challenge of the subject.
- Enrichment opportunities. For example, getting students on the course to run clubs or activities with students in lower years can be beneficial for both parties, and can help raise the profile of the course.

- Displays. As well as simply highlighting what the subject is about (and enrichment opportunities such as clubs or trips), these also offer a way to sell the academic credentials of psychology by, for example, listing potential career pathways or university destinations of former students.
- Open evenings. Our experience is that these are always busy times for the psychology team, so making sure those conversations are honest and informative (while still being enthusiastic and welcoming, of course) is paramount. Student ambassadors are often helpful here, so choose wisely those who are likely to say the right things and coach them on key points if necessary.

An issue to consider here is how the subject is perceived by those without any prior knowledge. Over the years, we've had conversations with, or heard comments from, students, parents, teachers and governors who have all, in their own way, expressed the view that psychology isn't a 'proper' subject. Therefore, we need to make sure we work hard in promoting psychology as an academic subject and highlighting the various pathways it can afford. There are many different ways that psychology students can take their studies further, but it's also worth actively highlighting the various options that psychology also supports.

A further consideration here is how we choose to showcase our subject. For example, our experience has been that taster sessions can somewhat misrepresent what studying psychology is all about. Early in our careers, it seemed fairly common practice that the taster sessions included lots of interactive demonstrations and experiments, and maybe a general overview of the subject, but little introduction to any actual content. These sessions also tended to look somewhat removed from what took place in normal lessons, with a big focus on 'activities'. It's hardly a surprise that many students experienced something of a shock when they actually started the course.

An alternative approach is to prepare a real lesson that represents, to a certain degree, what psychology lessons look like. There will of course be limitations in terms of prior knowledge, but with the right topic this can be a much more meaningful way for students to engage with the subject, grapple with some challenging ideas and set up their expectations for what future lessons might be like.

For example, one of us currently delivers a taster lesson based around the classic Thigpen and Cleckley (1954) study of a patient with multiple personality disorder (MPD, which is now referred to as dissociative identity disorder (DID)). This involves an introduction to the idea of diagnosis of psychological disorders, and a range of different methodologies that can be used to investigate behaviour. Students are tasked with examining a range of evidence from the study to determine the extent to which they think that the subject of the study represented a genuine case of MPD. This includes consideration of the relative quality of different types of evidence (such as the potential reliability of psychometric tests versus EEG recordings), which novice students are able to access, albeit at a relatively simplistic level, with little prior knowledge. It also introduces some key themes of psychological research such as qualitative versus quantitative data, validity, reliability and ethics, and provides a perfect example of a research question to which there is no known correct answer!

Enrichment opportunities

That students can benefit from the opportunity to engage with psychology beyond the routines and content of the classroom is hardly an innovative suggestion. At the same time, anyone who has ever organised a trip (or even written a risk assessment for one) will know that providing the opportunity for such engagement can potentially occupy a good deal of time and energy. Sometimes it can be time and effort that we are very happy to invest, of course; the satisfaction of a well-received trip can make it all worthwhile. At the same time, it's important to acknowledge that not all options are equal in terms of the burden they place on us. The suggestions below are therefore presented in reverse order of the level of commitment required from the teacher!

- Study participation. Keeping an eye open on social media, and occasionally briefly browsing through websites that advertise psychological studies looking for participants (such as https://www.callforparticipants.com, or the pages of local universities), can reveal studies that are appropriate for school-aged students to participate in, and to which you can direct them (you could even set them for homework). As a result of one of us doing this, some students were invited to Cambridge University to take part in a further study, which led to them having an fMRI scan; this is the kind of experience they're unlikely to forget!

- Signpost wider resources. Have a designated area (such as on a school shared drive or similar) in which there is a collection of links, ideas or other recommendations for students who want to explore further (for example, things to watch and read). To further save time, there are a number of these already freely available on social media, some of which are extensive and categorised by different specification areas.
- Essay competitions. These are offered by a number of different universities and represent an excellent opportunity for students to explore areas beyond the curriculum or deepen their knowledge of a particular topic. They also give students a chance to get their teeth into a 'proper' essay free from the constraints of highly prescriptive mark scheme criteria.
- Academic speakers. Local universities are often very keen to satisfy the 'outreach' requirements of their performance metrics by providing free guest speakers for schools. Given the importance of this endeavour to the universities, they are often able to be relatively flexible with dates and times as well.
- Other guest speakers. This requires slightly more effort as the speakers don't come looking for you in the same way (barring some professional speakers who advertise their services). One powerful experience is alumni speakers, who are former students of A-level psychology who have gone on to have a relevant career and come back to talk to students.
- Psychology club. An extracurricular club can be a great tool for engaging students within the subject, or alternatively it can function as a recruitment tool if provided to non-psychology students (such as those at Key Stage 3). This could involve teacher-led sessions, students completing their own independent research project[8] or students running sessions for younger students.

---

8   Depending on the scale of the project and the time students put into it, it's very easy to then submit these projects for a CREST award, the British Science Association's scheme for STEM project work (a project of only 10 hours has qualified for a Bronze award before, for example).

- Conferences, festivals and lectures. A number of universities run relevant events like this, for example, the Cambridge Festival and the Bristol Neuroscience Festival. Other organisations will also often offer conferences such as revision roadshows, which may be appealing for students. Keep an eye out also for regular lecture and seminar series at universities (even ones that are not geographically close will often stream their talks these days). Some schools even take this upon themselves.
- Trips. Trips are undeniably memorable experiences, not necessarily for entirely academic reasons – but then maybe that's partly the point! If you haven't got a lot of experience organising trips already, then it's usually a good idea to start small and choose activities and locations where students can be relatively self-contained. One of us recently ran a trip to London that took in the Freud Museum (which is one house with four or five display rooms in total) and the Science Museum (which is four stories of multiple rooms and what feels like many square miles of floor space). The former venue is rather easier on the blood pressure than the latter! Some other trip suggestions that we have undertaken include:
  - Bethlem Hospital and Museum (London). Students get to view a range of fascinating exhibits charting the history of mental health and participate in workshops examining different mental health issues and the challenges of dealing with psychiatric in-patients.
  - Zoos. Many have their own education department who may be able to put on seminars on things like classical and operant conditioning or animal cognition. It can also be a useful opportunity to get students to design and conduct their own observational studies.
  - Courthouses. If you are delivering a criminal or forensic topic, this gives students a much better insight into some courtroom processes (although the experience of one of us here was that students got to appreciate how mind-numbingly dull it can be watching two barristers arguing over technical points of law, which certainly disabused them of the idea of courtrooms being exciting places!).

Supporting students to take psychology further

Many students who enjoy psychology may decide that they want to study it further but are sometimes a little confused by the options out there. A particularly common trend is for them to want to specialise in line with a particular topic they've enjoyed, most likely either clinical or criminal psychology. Our general advice in this context is that they should be cautious here, and only specialise if they are absolutely sure that this is the path they want to take in terms of a future career.[9] A general psychology degree will give them the opportunity to study a much broader range of areas and research specialisms that they may not encounter on a more specialised course.

A second issue for many students is narrowing down the vast range of institutions and courses out there, which all seem to be offering the same thing. The first year of any psychology degree is likely to be fairly similar wherever you study, and so lists of topics on university webpages are not necessarily a decent guide. An obvious option here is to take advantage of the many open days available to have a proper look around. Another option, which students are rarely aware of, is to spend more time interrogating the psychology department's website, looking more specifically at their research areas. This can be particularly helpful if students do have particular areas of interest but don't want to narrow down their options by specialising at this stage. While students are usually aware that they will complete a research project or dissertation in their final year, most don't realise that what they can do is constrained by the research interests of the faculty staff. As an added bonus, one of us can remember the excitement shown by a student upon discovering that someone they had learned about on the course may be one of their future lecturers!

On a related note, we think it's also important that we help to broaden our students' (and, often, their parents') horizons about just where psychology can take them. Most will have a fairly limited view of the options typically including, again, clinical or criminal psychology, alongside sports psychology. While these are of course legitimate pathways, they

---

9   It may also be the case that some more specific courses will typically have lower entry requirements, which may, of course, be an important factor to consider.

don't represent the full breadth of available avenues. It's often helpful to make a distinction between applied psychology careers and then all of the other career options for which psychology may be particularly useful, such as policing, the law, healthcare, business and management, sales, marketing, human resources and, of course, teaching!

Parental communication

It's hardly groundbreaking to say that parental communication can be a powerful tool, nor that it is a tool that works best when employed *proactively* (before problems arise) and, where possible, *positively* (celebratory phone calls can be as powerful as negative ones and are also far more pleasant experiences!). At a departmental level these truisms remain just as true, but the content changes slightly.

Proactive communication now becomes less about addressing individual student performance (at least initially), and more about clearly communicating departmental expectations and how parents can play a role in helping their children to achieve these. For example, at the start of each academic year, one of us sends a letter to the parents of all new psychology students providing information on:

- The homework schedule for the year ahead (i.e. which sorts of homework will be set on which days each week, and when this will be due).
- An introduction to the key features of the homework (this includes definitions and examples of effective retrieval practice, information about the online platforms used, introduction to STAR tasks.
- Information on how parents can assist in these processes.

If we accept that we may need to help students to understand how learning happens in order to help them do it more effectively, then the same thing applies to parents. Parents are unlikely to know what retrieval practice or generative learning are, for example, nor why they are likely to be more effective than other methods. They are unlikely to know how limited attention capacity is, and therefore how important a home environment conducive to study can be. We therefore need to communicate this information to them, ideally using terminology that then reoccurs in subsequent communication such as report comments.

Positive communication can also be facilitated at a departmental level. A very simple recommendation is to reserve the first five minutes of every departmental meeting for positive communications, through whatever method your school uses. Recognition such as merits, house points, 'student of the week' or positive postcards can also be swept aside in the daily rush. Making it the first agenda item of every meeting means that they are not forgotten, and also starts off your meetings on a lovely, positive note as colleagues share the success stories of their week.

Encouraging a culture of independent learning

Independent work is an essential component of success in school psychology courses. McDaniel et al. (2021) suggest that the development of effective independent learning habits requires four key components:

- Knowledge of the strategies to use.
- Belief that they will work.
- Commitment to their use.
- Planning how they will be used.

Schools are increasingly good at transmitting the knowledge of the science of learning and effective study techniques to students (through assemblies and tutor times, as well as in class), and clearly this is going to be an essential feature of creating a successful independent learning culture. We have talked repeatedly about the importance (and beneficial effects) of sharing the rationale for your actions with students and colleagues, for example, and independent learning is no different. For example: 'Why am I asking you to use some strategies and avoid others?' 'Why do I want you to do it this way?' 'Why at this time?'

However, we are often less successful at encouraging the other three components. Steps to encourage the formation of a shared social norm of effective independent learning, and through doing so go some way to addressing the 'B', 'C' and 'P' components of McDaniel et al.'s framework:

1. Triangulate classwork, homework and independent work so that positive habits and effective work in each can reinforce one another.
2. Reduce the barriers to effective independent work.

Some action research conducted by one of us revealed a key difference between students working below, at or above their target grades. Rather than any difference in knowledge of effective study skills, the 'above-target' students had developed a variety of effective study strategies which allowed them to be productive in a wider range of settings. This, for example, might mean having a revision app on their phone as well as physical flashcards meaning they could revise pretty much anywhere and anytime, rather than being dependent on having their pile of flashcards to hand. This mirrors published research – Wang et al. (2023) found that knowledge of retrieval practice activities predicted students' intention to use them, but that the actual use of the strategies was predicted by their perceived cost (how much time and effort it was perceived to be to implement them). The overperforming students we interviewed had succeeded in reducing the perceived cost of effective study techniques by having a range of well-practised strategies, so that the most appropriate one for the situation could be easily selected.

In order to promote independent work (and make it a habitual activity), we therefore need to make it as easy as possible for students to do the activities that we want them to; reducing barriers makes it far easier to commit to the process. This is especially pertinent given that students' resilience to challenge will be far lower when working independently – we need to create a habit environment. It is incredibly common to speak to struggling students who report wanting to study but *not knowing where, or how, to start*. The knowledge of all the possible strategies and activities that they could be doing can be paralysing, especially when combined with the associated anxieties and guilt. All this creates a huge amount of extraneous cognitive load – no wonder they therefore don't achieve much in the way of academic progress! We can assist in this process by:

- Providing (a variety of) resources, and ideas about when to use them. For example, the STAR task checklist (page 179) provides a variety of useful activities, all of which are resourced by the department should the student so desire. Retaining some degree of student autonomy over the process also makes it easier for students to create a 'plan' for how to use strategies effectively (the final step of the KBCP cycle). Accurate beliefs about how to self-test come from a combination of information about the strategies to use and direct experience of using

them (Rivers, 2023). As we saw in Section 1, a key determinant of motivation is competence and so students who have the belief that they can study successfully will be more motivated to do so.
- Reframing challenge. While we can remove barriers, we can't avoid the truth that learning is difficult, independent learning even more so. Therefore, we also need to acknowledge and celebrate this challenge. Indeed, we need to encourage students to actively seek out this challenge. These are desirable difficulties. People who deliberately seek out discomfort when completing challenging tasks (and who see this discomfort as a signal of self-growth) show higher levels of motivation to engage with difficult tasks and a greater likelihood to achieve their task goals (Woolley and Fishbach, 2022). This is why 'we celebrate mistakes, and forgetting'.
- Creating social norms of effective independent work. Sharing what other students are doing and developing shared habits as a class can be very powerful. Encourage students to share what they have done independently with each other. Encourage them to collaborate (when appropriate), to test one another, or teach one another.

Desirable difficulties

Desirable difficulties are conditions of learning that require effort, but that as a result lead to more secure learning (Bjork and Bjork, 2011). Students need to do things that are hard (such as effortful retrieval from long-term memory and integration with new material), and to find them hard, in order to learn to their maximum potential, but of course this is not something that the vast majority of students intuitively understand. De Bruin et al. (2023) argue that students' perseverance with desirably difficult strategies depends on both the perceived effort and the perceived learning. High effort is acceptable if there is high perceived learning, so students will persevere, but if they have high effort without high perceived learning then they will not.

> Two ways of increasing the likelihood of engagement with the desirably difficult strategies that we advocate for in this book are therefore to either reduce the perceived effort (by reducing the barriers to getting started with the strategies) and to increase the perceived learning (by finding ways to **secure success** through the strategies). De Bruin et al. call this the 'start and stick to desirable difficulties (S2D2) framework', which complements many of the ideas and strategies in this book very nicely.

3. **Secure success.**

As well as reducing the barriers to getting started, we can also increase the likelihood of the students committing to future use of effective learning strategies by giving them a high chance of experiencing success. Some examples include:

- Heavy scaffolding (such as a checklist of success criteria, sentence starters or key vocabulary to include.
- Vaughn and Kornell (2019) found that giving hints to allow initial success increased the likelihood of participants using self-testing (as opposed to restudying) in the future without any detrimental effect on recall, compared to more effortful recall without hints. However, hints that are too easy and are retained for too long lead to less effective learning (Vaughn et al., 2022). Make things easy initially, then slowly withdraw the scaffolding.

4. Monitor and celebrate.

- There is a certain irony in the advice that we need to monitor independent work, but it is undoubtedly true. If we are to create a habit environment for our students, then we need to know whether the target behaviours are taking place and help them to be repeated (for example, monitoring, which STAR tasks have been completed in the past week (with evidence, if you so desire) to make it easier for students to plan for, and commit to independent learning). Simone et al. (2023) found that monitoring participants' use of self-testing significantly increased the likelihood of such strategies being used.

- Hold students accountable for their independent work. Again, this aids commitment and planning.
- Reward and celebrate good independent work and share it with the class. Endres and Eitel (2023) found that the promise of an external reward increased the amount of effort that participants put into their retrieval practice. Rewards can include sweets, merits, postcards and phone calls home, 'psychologist of the week' boards and gold star stickers. All of these rewards can be powerful tools when forming a habit environment,[10] as they increase the students' belief in their chosen strategies and commitment to them.

Summary of Section 5

As we have seen, running a successful evidence-informed psychology department is about more than just being a great psychology teacher; we may consider that *necessary*, but not *sufficient*.[11] Even for those who operate as a one-person department, there are still myriad decisions to be made about how best to support our budding psychology students beyond the delivery of lessons. We think our teaching framework can provide a useful guide to taking an evidence-informed approach to many of these decisions. Furthermore, any changes we may want to implement in our departments can be considered in similar ways to the individual changes we may make in our classrooms. If we adopt the **WHAT mindset** and take care to **share the rationale** with our colleagues, then we hopefully can't go too far wrong.

---

10 In fact, one of us is happy to admit that when we started teaching, to our shame, we initially derided such incentives as being too infantile for the sort of mature and academic classroom we wished to run. This was snobby and foolish, as attested to by the absolute joy that even Year 13s show at getting gold star stickers!

11 It's worth noting that in many schools, those who have demonstrated excellent teaching in their subject often find themselves promoted to middle leadership even if they have little by way of knowledge or experience of the very different skills required (this certainly happened to us!).

References

1. Al Nasseri, Y. S., Renganathan, L., Al Nasseri, F., & Al Balushi, A. (2014). Impact of students-teacher relationship on student's learning: A review of literature. *International Journal of Nursing Education, 6*(1), 167.
2. Baumert, J., Kunter, M., Blum, W., Brunner, M., Voss, T., Jordan, A., ... & Tsai, Y.-M. (2010). Teachers' mathematical knowledge, cognitive activation in the classroom, and student progress. *American Educational Research Journal, 47*(1), 133-180.
3. Bjork, E. L., & Bjork, R. A. (2011). Making things hard on yourself, but in a good way: Creating desirable difficulties to enhance learning. In Gernsbacher, M. A., Pew, R. W., Hough, L. M., & Pomerantz, J. R. (eds), *Psychology and the real world: Essays illustrating fundamental contributions to society* (pp. 56-64). Worth Publishers.
4. de Bruin, A. B., Biwer, F., Hui, L., Onan, E., David, L., & Wiradhany, W. (2023). Worth the effort: The start and stick to desirable difficulties (S2D2) framework. *Educational Psychology Review, 35*(2), 41.
5. Endres, T., & Eitel, A. (2023). Motivation brought to the test: Successful retrieval practice is modulated by mastery goal orientation and external rewards. *Applied Cognitive Psychology.* Advance online publication. https://doi.org/10.1002/acp.4160
6. Gazzaniga, M. S., Eliassen, J. C., Nisenson, L., Wessinger, C. M., Fendrich, R., & Baynes, K. (1996). Collaboration between the hemispheres of a callosotomy patient: Emerging right hemisphere speech and the left hemisphere interpreter. *Brain, 119*(4), 1255-1262.
8. Gross, R. E. (2020). Functional hemispherectomy in adults: All we have to sphere is sphere itself. *Epilepsy Currents, 20*(3), 144-146.
9. Jerrim, J., & Sims, S. (2021). When is high workload bad for teacher wellbeing? Accounting for the non-linear contribution of specific teaching tasks. *Teaching and Teacher Education, 105*, 103395.
10. Maguire, E. A., Gadian, D. G., Johnsrude, I. S., Good, C. D., Ashburner, J., Frackowiak, R. S., & Frith, C. D. (2000). Navigation-related structural change in the hippocampi of taxi drivers. *Proceedings of the National Academy of Sciences, 97*(8), 4398-4403.
11. McDaniel, M. A., Einstein, G. O., & Een, E. (2021). Training college students to use learning strategies: A framework and pilot course. *Psychology Learning & Teaching, 20*(3), 364-382.
12. Mennes, H., von der Embse, N., Kim, E., Sundar, P., Hines, D., & Welliver, M. (2023). Are "well" teachers "better" teachers? A look into the relationship between first-year teacher emotion and use of evidence-based instructional strategies. *School Psychology.* Advance online publication. https://doi.org/10.1037/spq0000593
13. Metzler, J., & Woessman, L. (2012). The impact of teacher subject knowledge on student achievement: Evidence from within-teacher within-student variation. *Journal of Development Economics, 99*(2), 486-496.
14. Miles, L. E. M., Raynal, D. M., & Wilson, M. A. (1977). Blind man living in normal society has circadian rhythms of 24.9 hours. *Science, 198*(4315), 421-423.

15. Rivers, M. L. (2023). Test experience, direct instruction, and their combination promote accurate beliefs about the testing effect. *Journal of Intelligence, 11*(7), 147.
16. Rosen, D. (2023, July 28). The autonomy-cohesion tension. Musings of a DR. https://musingsofadr.wordpress.com/2023/07/28/the-autonomy-cohesion-tension/
17. Sharples, J., Albers, B., Fraser, S., & Kime, S. (2019). Putting evidence to work: A school's guide to implementation. Guidance Report. *Education Endowment Foundation*.
18. Simone, P. M., Whitfield, L. C., Bell, M. C., Kher, P., & Tamashiro, T. (2023). Shifting students toward testing: Impact of instruction and context on self-regulated learning. *Cognitive Research: Principles and Implications, 8*(1), 14. https://doi.org/10.1186/s41235-023-00470-5
19. Steuer, F. B., & Ham, K. W. (2008). Psychology textbooks: Examining their accuracy. *Teaching of Psychology, 35*(3), 160-168.
20. Thigpen, C. H., & Cleckley, H. (1954). A case of multiple personality. *The Journal of Abnormal and Social Psychology, 49*(1), 135-151.
21. Turk, D. J., Heatherton, T. F., Kelley, W. M., Funnell, M. G., Gazzaniga, M. S., & Macrae, C. N. (2002). Mike or me? Self-recognition in a split-brain patient. *Nature Neuroscience, 5*(9), 841-842.
22. Vaughn, K. E., & Kornell, N. (2019). How to activate students' natural desire to test themselves. *Cognitive Research: Principles and Implications, 4*, 1-16.
23. Vaughn, K. E., Fitzgerald, G., Hood, D., Migneault, K., & Krummen, K. (2022). The effect of hint strength on the benefits of retrieval practice. *Applied Cognitive Psychology, 36*(2), 468-476.
24. Wang, L., Muenks, K., & Yan, V. X. (2023). Interventions to promote retrieval practice: Strategy knowledge predicts intent, but perceived cost predicts usage. *Journal of Educational Psychology, 115*(8), 1070-1086.
25. Woolley, K., & Fishbach, A. (2022). Motivating personal growth by seeking discomfort. *Psychological Science, 33*(4), 510-523.
26. Zhang, I., Guo, X. H., Son, J. Y., Blank, I. A., & Stigler, J. W. (2024). Watching videos of a drawing hand improves students' understanding of the normal probability distribution. *Memory and Cognition*. Advance online publication. https://doi.org/10.3758/s13421-024-01526-7

Conclusion

There are a number of things we hope you have been able to take away from this book. First and foremost, we hope that this book has provided a clear window into our classrooms and the thought processes that went into creating those classrooms. This teacher's eye view of the psychology classroom, detailing the nuts and bolts of classroom delivery, was something that we felt was missing from current publications. And second, we sincerely hope that you have found this book to be professionally empowering. A key message that we would want readers to take away is that being evidence informed does not mean surrendering autonomy or professional expertise. Quite the opposite. Indeed, we hope that the framework of the **WHAT mindset** also helps you to feel empowered to disagree with us!

Your classrooms may not resemble ours in many ways, but where they do diverge, we hope we have provided a starting point, and a framework, for deeper thought and conversations about the teaching of psychology in schools. Many of the forums we have cited as being useful for developing subject knowledge are also great places for debating the nuances of subject-specific pedagogy, and increasing the frequency and visibility of such conversations would be of great benefit to the subject. They are also important, and enjoyable, conversations to be a part of, and we look forward to having many more of them with talented and dedicated colleagues in the years to come. After all, being evidence informed also means being willing to change one's mind, and one's practices, if more convincing evidence emerges. The journey will continue...